SAFETY
FIRST

SAFETY FIRST

THE MAKING OF NEW LABOUR

Paul Anderson
and Nyta Mann

Granta Books
London

Granta Publications, 2/3 Hanover Yard, London N1 8BE

First published in Great Britain by Granta Books 1997

A CIP catalogue record for this book is
available from the British Library.

1 3 5 7 9 10 8 6 4 2

ISBN 1 86207 070 9

Typeset by M Rules
Printed in Great Britain by Mackays of Chatham plc

CONTENTS

CONTENTS

ACKNOWLEDGEMENTS

This is a book about the Labour Party and how it came to win its spectacular victory in the general election of 1 May 1997. Although it appears soon after the election, it is not an instant breathless account of the election campaign and Labour's 'first hundred days' – although it covers both – but a serious attempt to explain the politics of Britain's new government, written from a critical libertarian left perspective that is neither 'New Labour' nor 'Old Labour'. We have not attempted to deal with everything: the situation in Northern Ireland was developing too fast in the months after the election, and in some areas of policy, notably health, local government and arts and culture, Labour had little to say of substance when it was in opposition. We have chosen instead to paint a picture of the people and ideas that have played the biggest roles in shaping the new government, concentrating on the most significant events and themes.

We would like to thank the scores of people with whom we have talked over the years whose ideas and stories have fed into this book. There are too many to name them all, and several of our most helpful sources must of necessity remain anonymous. Otherwise, special thanks are due to Alida Campbell, Tim Dawson, Dave Osler and the staff of *Tribune* for help with research and loans of materials; John Booth, Martin Chalmers, Trevor

Fisher, Conor Foley, Jim McCormick, Mike Marqusee, Stephen Marks, Carey Oppenheim, Andrew Roth, Mary Southcott, Simon Taggart, Hilary Wainwright, Fiona Weir and John Williams for providing ideas, expertise and advice; and Kevin Davey, Meghnad Desai, Patrick Fitzgerald, Steve Platt, Marjorie Thompson, Mike Watts and Ben Webb for discussing repeatedly the themes of the book and commenting on its contents. Of course, none of them is responsible for anything that appears in it.

Neil Belton and Becky Hardie at Granta provided just the right mix of superlative advice and menace about what would happen if we missed the deadline; and Jane Robertson's copy editing, in circumstances made chaotic by the production timetable, was brilliant.

We did the typing.

PROLOGUE
THE DEATH AGONY
OF MAJORISM

Rarely has a dying government taken quite so long to expire. Everything started to unravel for John Major within weeks of his surprise victory in the 1992 general election. The Tories had promised that the economic recovery would 'start on Friday', the day after polling day – but instead there was nothing but misery. The government kept interest rates painfully high to maintain the value of the pound in the exchange rate mechanism of the European Monetary System. Exporters pleaded for a change of policy as they were priced out of their markets. Speculators sensed that sterling was riding for a fall, and on 16 September 1992, 'Black Wednesday', they moved in for the kill. In a desperate attempt to shore up the pound, chancellor Norman Lamont put up interest rates by a total of 10 percentage points and the Bank of England spent billions of its reserves buying sterling. But their efforts were swept aside. Lamont eventually admitted defeat and withdrew sterling from the ERM to allow a giant devaluation. The Tories' reputation for economic competence never recovered.

Within weeks, the disaster was compounded when Michael Heseltine, President of the Board of Trade, announced the closure of thirty-one of Britain's remaining fifty coal mines, with the loss of 30,000 mining jobs and as many again in related industries. Middle England and Arthur Scargill united in protest. Facing the threat of revolt from Tory back-benchers, Heseltine ordered a review of the pit-closure plans. Eventually, they went ahead as originally intended: the few collieries that survived were privatized. Norman Lamont's budget of March 1993 completed the job of wrecking the Tories' credibility on the economy with substantial tax increases, including the imposition of VAT on fuel.

Almost as important as its effect on public opinion, 'Black Wednesday' caused the eruption of the festering parliamentary rebellion by the anti-European Tory right over the Maastricht Treaty on European Union. The Europhobes had disproportionate influence because of the government's small majority – twenty-one at the election – and their friends in the cabinet, and they did not shy away from using it. From late 1992 right up to the 1997 election, Major's premiership was an unrelenting struggle to cope with the mayhem they caused. In May 1993, no fewer than forty-one Tory MPs defied their whips to vote against the government on the third reading of the Maastricht bill. A week later, Lamont left the government after being sacked as chancellor and began a bitter anti-European (and anti-Major) campaign from the back benches.

Major tried everything with the Europhobes. He appeased them by vetoing the appointment of Jean-Luc Dehaene as president of the European Commission to succeed Jacques Delors. Then he disciplined them by withdrawing the whip from eight who voted against Britain's contributions to the EU budget. But nothing seemed to work. The rumour-mongering about his future as prime minister was relentless. In June 1995, in a last-ditch attempt to draw a line under the feuding, he resigned the party leadership and stood for re-election, challenging his internal opponents to 'put up or shut up'. It was a serious miscalculation. Against Major's expectations, John Redwood, the secretary of state for Wales, called his bluff and entered the contest. Major won the ensuing ballot, but failed to strengthen his position. More than a third of his own MPs failed to vote for him, and speculation about his likely successor was soon back at fever pitch. Again he tried to appease the Europhobes, backing a referendum on signing Britain up to a single currency and then declaring a policy of non-co-operation with the EU for banning imports of British beef for fear that 'mad cow disease' (BSE) could be passed on to humans. But the Europhobes were not to be appeased. More than 100 Tory candidates disowned the government's 'wait and see' policy on European monetary union in their 1997 election addresses by promising to vote against a single European currency.

Europe was not Major's only problem, however. The government was hoist with its own petard on crime, which rose inexorably in spite of the high priority it accorded to law and order, particularly after the appointment in 1993 of the right-wing populist Michael Howard, as home secretary. The legitimacy of the Tories' pre-1992 privatizations was severely undermined by news of the massive salaries that bosses of the privatized utilities were paying themselves. Death and defections among Major's MPs continued to chip away the Tory majority, until in February 1997 Major presided over a minority government. Even his greatest apparent success, the Northern Ireland peace initiative, foundered after the government reached an accommodation with the Ulster Unionists in parliament in order to ensure the passage of its legislation.

The last nail in Major's coffin was 'sleaze'. The stories started in summer 1992 with a minor sex scandal – David Mellor's extra-marital affair with an out-of-work actress – and there were plenty more of the same kind over the next few years, particularly after the launch of the government's 'back to basics' initiative in 1993, which Major's spin doctors told journalists was about personal morality and responsibility. Much more damaging than sexual peccadilloes, however – except for those directly involved – was a string of revelations that brought into question the integrity of the government and the Conservative Party.

In November 1992 the evidence of former trade and industry minister Alan Clark caused the collapse of the Customs and Excise case against executives of Matrix Churchill, a West Midlands machine tool company, accused of breaking the arms embargo against Iraq in the late-1980s. Clark frankly admitted that the government had known all along that the equipment was not for peaceful purposes, but was instead destined for Iraqi arms factories – just as the defence in the trial had argued. The judge subsequently overruled public interest immunity certificates (in effect, gagging orders) signed by government ministers that would have prevented the disclosure of state documents vital to the defendants' case. Major responded to the uproar that ensued by setting up a public inquiry into the arms-to-Iraq affair, led by Lord Justice Richard Scott. His inquiry provided the government with an excruciating three years of revelations of its complicity in the arming of one of the modern world's most brutal dictators. When Scott's massive report was finally published in 1996, not one minister resigned.

In June 1993, Northern Ireland minister Michael Mates was sacked when it became clear he had once had an improperly close relationship with the businessman Asil Nadir, a substantial donor to Tory Party funds in the 1980s, who had fled to northern Cyprus rather than face fraud charges in Britain. In early 1994, the district auditor found the flagship Tory council of Westminster guilty of gerrymandering on a massive scale under Dame Shirley Porter. Days later, it emerged that the government had given Malaysia aid money in order to build a giant – and environmentally damaging – dam as a 'sweetener' for an arms deal. A couple of months after that, in a sting operation mounted by the *Sunday Times*, two Tory MPs, Graham Riddick and David Treddinick, agreed to table parliamentary questions for £1,000 per question.

This was the start of the 'cash-for-questions' scandal, a saga as long-running as the Scott inquiry but with more deadly effect on the Tories. Three months after the exposure of Riddick and Tredinnick, the *Guardian* revealed that two government ministers, Tim Smith and Neil Hamilton, had as back-benchers received money and other rewards from Mohammed al-Fayed, the owner of Harrods, in return for asking parliamentary questions, with the lobbyist Ian Greer acting as intermediary. Smith resigned as a minister as soon the story appeared. Hamilton hung on until he was sacked – and then instituted libel proceedings against the *Guardian*. In June 1995, chief secretary to the Treasury Jonathan Aitken resigned from the cabinet in order to sue the same newspaper and *World in Action* for libel over allegations about his involvement in the Middle East arms trade and his relationship with the regime in Saudi Arabia.

Aitken's case did not get to court until after the election, in which he lost his seat (he later lost the case too, dropping it when the *Guardian* unearthed evidence showing he had perjured himself). But cash-for-questions reappeared in time to cause maximum damage to the Tories' electoral chances. In autumn 1996, Hamilton dropped his case against the *Guardian* at the last minute, leading the paper to run the memorable and unequivocal front-page banner headline 'A liar and a cheat' above his photograph. Hamilton's spectacular climbdown itself led to further damaging revelations, and to the resignation of David Willetts, a Tory whip close to and favoured by Major, following evidence that he had attempted to interfere with the findings of an earlier Commons committee inquiry into the affair. Despite pressure from Conservative Central Office, at the beginning of the election campaign loyal constituency party members defiantly reselected Hamilton as their parliamentary candidate for his seat of Tatton.

Of all the Conservatives who in their different ways featured in the sleaze revelations that came to light between 1992 and 1997, it is Hamilton – along with his wife Christine – who stuck in the minds of most voters. From beginning to end, he remained completely unabashed by the implications of his activities. He rejected all criticism, refused to acknowledge he had done anything wrong, and appeared genuinely to believe that he deserved to be elected to office once more. To the public, he epitomized all that was wrong with the Conservatives after eighteen years in power: dishonest, shameless, charmless, arrogant and unrepentant. When the journalist Martin Bell, standing as an independent anti-sleaze candidate with Labour and Liberal Democrat backing, beat him in the polls on 1 May, there was rejoicing throughout the land.

1

DOWN TO BUSINESS
TONY BLAIR AND THE
NEW LABOUR 'PROJECT'

Even the spontaneous welcome was minutely choreographed. When Tony Blair arrived in Downing Street for the first time as prime minister – on foot, having left the limousine around the corner in Whitehall – he was met by a flag-waving, cheering crowd that lined the route from the iron gates at the top of the road to the door of Number Ten. With his wife Cherie following close behind, he slowly worked his way past the assembled well-wishers, briefly clasping outstretched hands and waving to those in the crowd he could not reach.

It looked wonderful on television – which is just what had been intended. Tickets for the event were distributed the previous night to selected campaign staff and friends who attended Labour's victory gathering at the Festival Hall on the South Bank of the Thames. Before gathering in Downing Street for the arrival of Blair after his audience with the Queen, they were briefed at Labour's Millbank headquarters about precisely where to stand. Those with children were told to report to 'party stewards' who would indicate the most photogenic spots to place themselves. The Union Jacks that had been stored for the occasion were distributed to all. The biggest cheer had to go up when the Blair family posed on the doorstep of Number Ten. Weeks beforehand, Blair's aides had told broadcasting organizations that he would enter his official residence shortly after 1 p.m., to facilitate live reports for lunchtime news bulletins. As an added treat, Alastair Campbell, the Labour leader's press secretary, had long ago given the cameras permission to accompany the Blairs as they took their first look around their new home. The triumphant photo opportunity was the crowning glory of Labour's long hard slog to power.

The tight control was characteristic of Labour's whole campaign. To the very end, political commentators were unanimous in their complaints of how uninspiring the final stages of the 1997 election battle had turned out to be. The campaign was too long, having begun a full six weeks before polling day; and it was dull, with both main parties' campaigns largely consisting of themes familiar for at least three years. Even those aspects of the campaign that did not go according to plan – the Tories' setbacks on 'sleaze' and their divisions over Europe – were entirely familiar. This was not only the judgement of those professionally obsessed by the minutiae of politics. Voters too appeared unmoved and uninterested. In other words, it was the most boring election campaign that anyone could remember. Yet the result was the most spectacular since at least 1945. The scale of Labour's 1997 victory was extraordinary. The party won 13.5 million votes, 2 million more than in 1992, a total Labour had bettered only once before, in 1951. Its share of votes cast, 43 per cent, up from 35 per cent in 1992, was its highest since 1966. And its haul of seats, 418 (not counting the speaker) in a House of Commons of 659, was better even than the 393 out of 640 it won in 1945. The 1997 election was fought on different constituency boundaries to those of 1992, but the best estimate is that Labour gained 146 seats. The Tories were, quite simply, humiliated. They took only 9.6 million votes, down from 14 million in 1992 and fewer than at any election since 1929. Their share of the vote, 31 per cent, was their lowest since 1832; and their representation in the Commons, 165 seats, was their lowest since 1906, a loss of 178 on the notional 1992 result. The Liberal Democrats won 5.2 million votes, down nearly 800,000 from 1992, but with 46 seats, up 28 on 1992, are more numerous in the Commons than centre-party MPs have been since 1931.

On election night, though, what impressed was not the statistics but the steady stream of Tory disasters. Apart from the defeats of Jonathan Aitken and Neil Hamilton, the highlight was undoubtedly the humiliation of Michael Portillo, the right-wing populist defence secretary, whose expectations of succeeding John Major as party leader were destroyed when he crashed to defeat at the hands of Labour's Stephen Twigg in Enfield Southgate. But there were plenty of other moments to savour. The former cabinet minister David Mellor took a beating from Labour in Putney; Scottish secretary Michael Forsyth, President of the Board of Trade Ian Lang, and foreign secretary Malcolm Rifkind lost their seats as the Tories were swept out of·Scotland. Nicholas Budgen, the right-wing Eurosceptic who had made a play for the racist vote during the election campaign, went the same way in Wolverhampton South West.

All over the country, but particularly in London and the south-east, Labour won victories almost as improbable as that in Enfield Southgate: Hastings and Rye, Finchley and Golders Green, Harrow West, Romford, Wimbledon, Hove, Gillingham. Labour took 99 of the 100 Tory-held seats that were its targets – and the one it did not win, Colchester, fell to the Lib Dems. Of Labour's 418 MPs, no fewer than 178 were elected for the first time. The election transformed the gender and age profiles of the Parliamentary Labour Party: more than 60 of the Labour MPs elected in 1997 were aged forty or under on election day, and 101 of them were women, up from 37 elected in 1992.

All in all, it was a triumph for Tony Blair beyond his wildest dreams. A few days short of his forty-fourth birthday, the youngest prime minister to take office since the notoriously reactionary Earl of Liverpool in 1812, he had led his party into power after eighteen years in opposition, with a majority bigger than any government's since the 1940–5 wartime coalition. Even his most trenchant critics had to admit that he had won an historic victory.

For all his youth, Blair is no political novice. When he became prime minister, he had been a member of the Labour Party for twenty-two years and an MP for fourteen, four more years than John Major had been in parliament when he became Tory leader and prime minister in 1990. He first joined the Labour front bench in 1984 and was elected to the shadow cabinet for the first time as long ago as 1988.

Most politicians who have acquired so much experience of politics at such an early age are either born into it or become obsessed as students. Blair is an exception. His early life offers few clues to the roots of his political beliefs and he did little politically until his mid-twenties.[1] He was born in May 1953 in Edinburgh, and grew up the middle child of three, with an elder brother and a younger sister. His father Leo was the illegitimate son of music hall artistes and had been fostered by a left-wing Glaswegian family. Leo Blair had been a Communist in his youth and had risen to the rank of major in the army during the war. At the time of his second son's birth, he was a tax inspector, although he was studying for a doctorate in law and was soon to become a law lecturer, and his politics were Tory.[2] The mother of the future prime minister, Hazel, was a housewife, the daughter of a Protestant farming family from Northern Ireland, with what one family friend called 'a deep social conscience'.[3] The family moved from Edinburgh to Glasgow and then to Adelaide in Australia as Leo Blair pursued his career, eventually settling in Durham when he got a job as a lecturer at the university there. They were well off – both Tony and his brother William were sent to a private prep school and then as boarders to Fettes, the elite public school in Edinburgh. But they were not quite as secure as they appeared. In 1963, Leo Blair, then forty and ambitious for a career in Tory politics, suffered a stroke that left him unable to speak for three years. The university continued to pay him, and he later made a full recovery. Tony Blair later described his father's illness as 'one of the formative events of my life'.[4] 'My father transferred his ambitions on to his kids. It imposed a certain discipline. I felt I couldn't let him down.'[5]

Blair was at Fettes from 1966 to 1971, a time when, like most British public schools, it was going through a long-drawn-out process of abandoning its more severe techniques for the ritual chastening of young boys – fagging, regular corporal punishment and compulsory rugby. When he started at Fettes, the reform process had barely begun, and he hated the school so much that on one occasion he ran away. But by the sixth form he had settled into the role of tolerated petty rebel. He got into trouble for cheeking masters and for flouting dress and hair rules, and he acquired a taste for the 'progressive' rock music that was all the rage at the time. But he also studied hard for his A-levels and won a place to read law at St John's College in Oxford.[6]

Student militancy was the height of fashion in Oxford when Blair was an undergraduate. Typically, the *cause célèbre* was parochial: the absence, as a result of the university's collegiate structure, of a central students' union. In October 1973, at the beginning of Blair's second year, several hundred students occupied the university's Examination Schools, demanding action from the university authorities. But Blair shunned such adventurism. 'I went through all the bit about reading Trotsky and attempting a Marxist analysis,' he said later. 'But it never went very deep, and there was the self-evident wrongness of what was happening in Eastern Europe.'[7] Nor did he have anything to do with the Oxford University Labour Club, then as ever a magnet for would-be career politicians, including at this time Peter Mandelson. Instead, he sang in a dire student rock band, Ugly Rumours, and had a good time (although he says he did not touch drugs). The nearest Blair came to organized politics was participation in a small discussion group at St John's led by Peter Thomson, an Australian church minister who was studying theology as a mature student. Under Thomson's guidance, Blair became a convinced Christian – he was confirmed in the Church of England during his second year at university – and was introduced to the ideas of John Macmurray, an ethical socialist political philosopher who had been influential in the 1930s and 1940s. 'If you really want to understand what I'm all about, you have to take a look at a guy called John Macmurray,' Blair declared after becoming Labour leader.[8]

Blair left St John's after his finals in 1975, 'clearly left of centre' in his views, as he subsequently put it, but equally clearly set on a legal career.[9] His mother died a fortnight after he left university, which severely shook him, and he joined the Labour Party and the Society of Labour Lawyers soon after moving to London – into a flat in Earl's Court – and starting a one-year course at the Bar. However, it was only after he persuaded Alexander 'Derry' Irvine QC, a friend of a friend of his father, to take him in as a pupil in his chambers that his political ambitions really began to form. Irvine, now Lord Irvine of Lairg and Lord Chancellor in Blair's government, was in the mid-1970s one of the best-connected Labour lawyers. He had studied law at Glasgow University at the same time as John Smith, then a junior minister, and did much of the Labour Party's awkward legal business. It was also through Irvine that Blair met Cherie Booth, his wife to be: both were taken on as pupils at the same time. She had joined the Labour Party as long ago as 1972, and by the mid-1970s was on the general committee of the Marylebone constituency party.

Irvine took Blair on permanently in 1977 after Cherie Booth got a similar position with George Carman QC, the libel specialist, and Blair soon established a reputation as an able commercial lawyer, although his speciality was employment law. In the meantime, he was drawn more and more towards the idea of a political career. In the wake of the Tory victory in the 1979 general election, he made the first tentative steps into the world of public politics by writing a handful of articles for a general readership, contributing first to the *Spectator* and then to the *New Statesman*. After he and Cherie married and moved to Hackney in 1980, the Labour Party became a central part of his life.

Labour was at the time in the depths of the fratricidal bloodletting that had engulfed it after the defeat of Jim Callaghan's government. The activist left in the constituency parties and the trade unions, with support from some left MPs, most notably Tony Benn, was in revolt against what it saw as the failure of the 1974–9 government to put Labour's principles into practice. On policy, it was insistent that Labour adopt unambiguously radical positions, particularly withdrawal from the European Economic Community and unilateral nuclear disarmament – both issues on which it could count on support in parliament not only from Benn and his allies but also from others on the left, such as Michael Foot, who had no intention of denouncing the Callaghan government's record. But the activists' biggest priority was to make the Parliamentary Labour Party accountable to the party as a whole – specifically by making MPs go through a mandatory selection process once every parliament and by expanding the electorate for Labour's leadership elections beyond the PLP. The left coalition was a bizarre mix of radical democrats, Leninists old and new, traditional Labour leftists, feminists, libertarians and decentralists. It was notoriously unstable, not least because it could not agree on the detail of its proposed reforms to the party constitution, and was already beginning to divide into a hard left that wanted to push the revolt to its limit and a soft left that was prepared to compromise. But this barely mattered to the Labour right, which included Callaghan, Denis Healey and most of the ex-ministers that served in his government. The right thought that the left activists of all sorts were an undemocratic rabble and that the structural and policy changes backed by the left were utterly wrong-headed. To cut a long story short, after Labour adopted unilateralism and withdrawal from the EEC as policy, elected Foot as leader, introduced mandatory selection for MPs by constituency party general committees and concocted a union-dominated electoral college for leadership elections, a large segment of the right, led by Roy Jenkins, David Owen, William Rodgers and Shirley Williams, left Labour to create the Social Democratic Party (SDP).[10]

In Hackney, the Blairs allied themselves with a caucus, including local movers and shakers who remain close political friends today, that defined itself as soft left and was rapidly growing apart from the hard left, which was becoming the dominant force in the local party.[11] Tony's articles for the *New Statesman* were solid leftist arguments against the Thatcher government's use of the law against would-be strikers and its plans to outlaw secondary picketing.[12] He also supported the Campaign for Nuclear Disarmament. At the same time, however, he backed one member, one vote for Labour's parliamentary selections rather than the hard left's preference of mandatory selections by general committees; and in 1981 he supported the local Labour MP, Ron Brown, in his battle to avoid deselection by the hard left. Brown survived, only to defect to the SDP. Later the same year, Blair favoured John Silkin as a compromise candidate when Benn challenged Healey unsuccessfully for the Labour deputy leadership. In

1982, when the Labour Party National Executive Committee asked Derry Irvine for legal advice on whether it could expel the Trotskyist organisation Militant by setting up a register of groups in the party, Blair advised the NEC that it could. He then spoke against allowing Militant to remain in the party at the November 1982 conference of the Labour Co-ordinating Committee (LCC), the main internal Labour pressure group involving both hard left and soft left. This was a key meeting: it voted in favour of a ban on Militant and played a major part in making irreversible the hard left–soft left split on the activist left.

Blair gave the clearest statement of his views in this period while on holiday in Australia, in a lecture on the British Labour Party to a university department where a college friend was working as an academic. He attacked the right for its 'tired excuses of pragmatism', argued that the SDP was doomed because 'they have isolated themselves from organized labour, a fatal mistake for any radical party' and argued that 'traditional trade union militancy' was one of 'the necessary strands of radical thought'. But his central point was that the left had to rethink its whole approach. 'It would be absurd if the party descended into populism, merely parroting the views of "the electorate", however those views could be gauged,' he said. 'Equally absurd, though, is the view that there is anything to be gained from capturing control of the Labour Party machine and leaving the voters behind.'[13] Various commentators have managed to detect a distinctive Blair position in this – but in fact it was routine soft left rhetoric of the early 1980s.

Meanwhile, both Blairs had been doing their best to get themselves selected as Labour parliamentary candidates. Cherie was chosen for Thanet North, which she fought and lost in 1983. Tony got nowhere at first but then won the selection for a 1982 by-election in Beaconsfield, one of the safest Tory seats in the country. He lost his deposit but made his mark as an eager and intelligent candidate with mildly independent views. On Europe, for example, he argued a position of 'come out if we must, but not as an article of socialist faith', which was not quite the party policy of withdrawal. Then, a few weeks before the 1983 election, he managed to talk his way, against the odds, into being selected for the safe Labour seat of Sedgefield in Durham. He arrived in the Commons just after his thirtieth birthday, the youngest member of the 1983 Labour intake.

If the 1983 election was a great leap forward for Blair, it was a disaster for Labour. Led by Michael Foot, then nearly seventy and the object of an extraordinary campaign of vilification by the Tory press, it fought a shambolic campaign on a left-wing manifesto and won only 209 seats to the Tories' 397. Worse, it took just 28 per cent of the vote, down 9 percentage points on 1979, only 2 points above the SDP–Liberal Alliance (which took 23 seats) and nearly 15 behind the Tories. Labour did particularly badly among white-collar workers and among blue-collar workers in the south of England, particularly owner-occupiers. The result appeared to be confirmation of the view of many political scientists that the shrinking number of manual workers and the decreasing relevance of class in determining voters' choices at election time condemned Labour to decline unless it radically broadened its appeal.[14]

But how could it do this? The first step was to choose a new, dynamic leader around whom the party could rally – and the obvious choice was Neil Kinnock, who had established himself as the leading figure of the leadership-loyalist soft left under Foot. Just forty-one, but a veteran MP of thirteen years' standing, Kinnock romped home in the leadership contest that followed Foot's resignation, easily defeating the right-wing challenge of Roy Hattersley. (The hard left candidate, Eric Heffer, trailed in a distant third, while Peter Shore, standing on an anti-Europe, anti-unilateralist platform, came in fourth.) Kinnock was keen not to alienate the right, however, and his supporters made great play of the desirability of Hattersley becoming his deputy as the bottom half of a 'dream ticket'. Hattersley won the deputy leadership against Michael Meacher almost as comfortably as Kinnock won the leadership.

Beyond changing leader, it was clear that Labour needed to tighten up its discipline and improve its organization and presentation. The ructions that followed the party's 1979 defeat had subsided after the defection of the SDP in 1981 and Healey's successful defence of the deputy leadership against Benn the same year. But Labour had remained obviously divided right up to the election – over defence, over Europe, over economic policy, over whether it should tolerate organized Trotskyist factions in its ranks – and both left and right had consistently undermined Foot's authority as leader. Just a fortnight before polling day, no less a figure than former prime minister Jim Callaghan had denounced Foot's non-nuclear defence policy in a widely reported speech. As for Labour's organization and presentation, the 1983 campaign had revealed both to be utterly sloppy.

Rebuilding party unity was the overriding theme of Kinnock's leadership campaign. As he put it after winning: 'Unity is the price of victory. Not unity for four weeks before the general election, not unity for four weeks before the European Assembly elections, but unity here and now and from henceforth, not a cosmetic disguise, but a living, working unity of a movement, of a belief and conviction, who want to win in order to save our country and our world.'[15] The Labour right was for the most part prepared to play ball after the victory of the 'dream ticket', and so was a substantial section of the former Bennite left. But the core of the hard left was in no mood for compromise. It saw the 1983 election débâcle as a cue for stepping up extra-parliamentary action against the Thatcher government. To Kinnock's frustration, he was unable to prevent several left-led councils from preparing to defy the law over the Tories' introduction of rate-capping – and then in spring 1984 Arthur Scargill and his allies manoeuvred the National Unions of Mineworkers into striking against pit closures. The rate-capping revolt and the 1984–5 miners' strike persuaded the new Labour leader that he had to take on and defeat the left if he was ever to present a united Labour Party to the electorate. For the rest of his time as leader he spared no effort in his attempts to root out Militant and other Trotskyists and to marginalize the rest of the hard left at every level of the party.[16]

On organization and presentation, the key events in Kinnock's first four years were two appointments made by the National Executive Committee in 1985: the hiring of Larry Whitty as the party's general secretary and Peter Mandelson as its director of communications. Over the next few years, Whitty performed a minor miracle in streamlining the party's creaking bureaucracy and putting its finances on a more-or-less sound footing. Mandelson had a more immediate impact. His first act on being appointed was to commission Philip Gould, a politically friendly advertising executive, to write a report on Labour's communications strategy. Delivered at the end of 1985, its analysis was damning – and entirely in line with the feelings of Kinnock. 'Positive perceptions of the Labour Party tend to be outweighed by negative concerns, particularly of unacceptable "beyond the pale" figures; the party sometimes acts in a way that confirms these concerns by scoring "own goals"; there is some feeling that the Labour Party does not, as it once did, represent the majority, instead it is often associated with minorities; the party has something of an old-fashioned cloth cap image.' Labour's campaigning was too often directed at party activists rather than the public, and the party tended to ignore the tabloid newspapers even though they were read by its target voters. There was little attempt to co-ordinate Labour's message and no control of party political broadcasts, and the party's advertising was poor.[17]

As Gould recommended, Mandelson set up a group of volunteer advisers from the world of advertising, the Shadow Communications Agency, and thus began the revolution in Labour's media management and marketing strategy that reached its apogee in the 1997 election campaign.[18] The SCA was soon playing a central role in Labour's affairs. It transformed the party's corporate image, most noticeably by introducing a red rose logo, and it established the practice of testing out everything about the party, from its leader's perceived strengths and weaknesses to detailed policy, in 'focus groups' of target voters. In the run-up to the 1987 general election, on the advice of Mandelson and the SCA, Labour decided to run a slick presidential-style campaign. Kinnock played the starring role, roaming the country, and the supporting cast were chosen not on the basis of their position in the party's pecking order but on grounds of their focus-group appeal and ability to deal with television, with Bryan Gould as anchorman in London.

On policy, Labour was more cautious. Kinnock inherited a party with a more left-wing programme than it had ever had before. The 1983 manifesto, famously described as 'the longest suicide note in history' by Gerald Kaufman, promised a massive boost in public spending, with the intention of cutting unemployment from 3 million to 1 million in five years, a dramatic extension of public ownership, the repeal of all the Tories' trade union legislation and withdrawal from the EEC. On defence, the manifesto was notoriously ambiguous except in its endorsement of a non-nuclear defence policy. Much of this was deeply unpopular with a large part of the electorate, but Kinnock was at first unwilling to risk massive changes. Between 1983 and 1987, Labour abandoned withdrawal from the EEC and opposition to council house sales, and beat a retreat from the 1983 manifesto's commitments on job-creation and public ownership. The non-nuclear defence policy remained in place, however, and the overall thrust of Labour policy remained unequivocally Keynesian and redistributive.

Blair played a minor supporting role between 1983 and 1987, rising quickly to the front bench and establishing a reputation for himself as a competent junior spokesman and leadership loyalist, but never particularly shining. He got his first break in late 1983 from John Smith, then newly appointed as shadow employment secretary, whom he had met through Derry Irvine and for whom he had written a paper on privatization back in 1981. Smith chose Blair and another 1983 new boy, Gordon Brown, whom he knew from Scotland, as members of the committee examining the Tories' latest trade union legislation. Blair and Brown got on well, sharing an office until Brown was elected to the shadow cabinet in 1987, and Brown became something of a political mentor to Blair. Both were soon noticed as promising youngsters. Blair made it to the front bench first, getting a junior job on the Treasury team in November 1984 (on the recommendation of shadow chancellor Roy Hattersley), a year before Brown was appointed to Smith's trade and industry team. Blair impressed Hattersley with his command of detail and made some well-received interventions in the

House of Commons, but it was Brown who made a name for himself in the media.

Blair's ideas at this time were undoubtedly in favour of 'modernization', as the Kinnock drive to make Labour electable came to be known. 'The image of the Labour Party has got to be more dynamic, more modern. I don't think it's nearly so much a matter of right and left as people make out,' he told *Newsnight* just after arriving in parliament. 'Over 50 per cent of the population are owner-occupiers. That means a change in attitude that we've got to catch up to.'[19] But if he had any particularly original thoughts about what needed to be done beyond what Kinnock was actually doing, he did not make them public. On policy, his every pronouncement followed the party line, right down to arguing against sterling joining the exchange rate mechanism of the European Monetary System. 'The EMS is essentially a Deutschmark bloc,' he declared in the Commons in 1986. 'It could be said that we would be putting Herr Pohl of the Bundesbank in 11 Downing Street.'[20]

In the June 1987 general election, despite the much-praised efforts of Peter Mandelson and Bryan Gould, Labour suffered a third consecutive defeat, winning 31 per cent of the vote and 229 seats to the Tories' 42 per cent and 376 seats. Just about the only solace for Labour was that it saw off the threat of the SDP–Liberal Alliance to supplant it as the main party of opposition: the Alliance won just 23 per cent of the vote and 22 seats. Blair played little part in the campaign, but he was a prominent contributor to the debate on what to do following the defeat, giving strong support to Kinnock's plans for a comprehensive policy review. Labour needed 'profound changes in ideas and organization', he argued in an article in the *New Statesman*: the idea that Labour should turn towards proportional representation was 'just the latest excuse for avoiding decisive choices about the party's future'. Blair was a high-profile defender of the policy review at the 1987 party conference that endorsed Kinnock's plan, and soon afterwards he stood in the shadow cabinet elections for the first time on the soft left Tribune Group slate.[21] Although he was not elected (unlike Brown), his seventeenth place was not a bad showing for a first attempt. Gould chose him as his deputy as City spokesman on the trade and industry team, and Kinnock put him on the policy review group dealing with 'people at work', which had the tricky task of working out Labour's line on industrial relations law and employment policy.

The policy review was sold to the Labour conference as a no-holds-barred re-examination of Labour's programme, but in fact its parameters were strictly defined from the start by the Shadow Communications Agency. The SCA prepared an analysis of the 1987 defeat, *Labour and Britain in the 1990s*, which was delivered to a meeting of the NEC and the shadow cabinet in November 1987. Drawing on several different sources, the SCA argued that Labour had an uphill struggle if it was ever to win again. The party had lost the allegiance of a large segment of the working class, mainly skilled workers living in the south and Midlands, many of them beneficiaries of the Tories' tax cuts and discounted sales of council houses. The party was widely perceived by voters who did not support it as old-fashioned and out-of-touch with their aspirations, a party of minorities and the poor rather than people like them, dominated by the trade unions and vulnerable to extremist takeover. To make matters worse, Labour's policies on tax, public ownership, industrial relations and defence were unpopular, and many voters questioned the party's competence, particularly in economic management. (During the election campaign, one poll showed 56 per cent of voters fearing an economic crisis if Labour won.) Kinnock was also a liability – although the SCA diplomatically excised these findings from the presentation.[22]

The SCA's message to the politicians was simple. Everything they came up with had to reassure voters that Labour was modern, competent, responsible and representative of the aspirations of the upwardly mobile. Anything that focus groups of target voters considered suspect had to go, regardless of its merits. There was sporadic resistance to the new way of doing politics from the left and the trade unions.[23] But by the time of the 1992 general election Labour had ditched a vast swathe of policy: unilateral nuclear disarmament, Keynesian economic expansionism, renationalization of privatized utilities, support for the pre-entry closed shop. Its spending commitments, laid out in John Smith's 1992 shadow budget, were modest: a small emergency employment programme and increases in pensions and child benefit. Publicly at least,

Labour backed sterling's membership of the ERM at the rate at which the Tories had entered in 1990. The party presented itself in 1992 as a proponent of enterprise and free trade, a fan of open government and democratic reform, an enthusiast for high educational standards, a defender of the environment and a believer in strong defence.

Blair played an increasingly important role in all this. He performed impressively as City spokesman, and in 1988 was elected to the shadow cabinet with Kinnock's backing. He was given the job of energy spokesman – which was guaranteed publicity because of impending electricity privatization – and the following spring was chosen by Mandelson for a high-profile position in Labour's European election campaign. (It was around this time that John Prescott, whom Blair had replaced as energy spokesman, started grumbling about the rise of the 'beautiful people' favoured by Mandelson for television appearances.) On the policy review, Blair was, with Brown, one of Kinnock's main allies from the start, but it was from autumn 1989, when Kinnock made him employment spokesman, that he really made his mark. Blair took the job from Michael Meacher, who had resisted Kinnock's attempts to get policy changed to keep the Tories' restrictions on the pre-entry closed shop and secondary industrial action. He did precisely what Kinnock wanted, despite the unions' opposition, and was rewarded with an even higher profile in Labour's media strategy (see chapter 9). By the time of the 1992 general election, he was widely tipped as a future Labour leader.

Still, however, it was difficult to work out what exactly Blair stood for beyond the party line and Kinnock's 'modernization'. His most forthright statement of his position at this time, an article published in *Marxism Today*, was quite extraordinarily opaque. 'We should accept the lessons of our history and build on them, not be intimidated or shackled by them. We must fashion a modern view of society which recognizes the vested interest of both market and state and articulates a new over-arching concept of the public interest standing up for the individual against those vested interests. This requires a new political settlement between individual and society, a bargain between the two which determines rights and obligations on both sides. The notion of a modern view of society

as the driving force behind the freedom of the individual is in truth
the implicit governing philosophy of today's Labour Party. It will
benefit us greatly now, both internally and with the public, if we
spell it out with confidence.'

Labour's 1992 election campaign in the media was just as slick as
that in 1987 – with the exception of the fiasco of the 'Jennifer's
Ear' election broadcast[24] – and the party effectively targeted its
door-knocking and telephone canvassing on 'key seats'. Yet Labour
lost again, taking 34 per cent of the vote and 271 seats to the
Tories' 42 per cent and 336 seats, and Kinnock decided that it was
time to go. The succession was to all intents and purposes determined the weekend after the election defeat, when the leaders of
most of the biggest unions came out publicly in favour of John
Smith as a 'safe pair of hands'. After that, because of the weight of
the union block vote in the electoral college that chose the Labour
leader, any other candidate would risk a humiliating defeat – and
only Bryan Gould was prepared to take the gamble.

The gamble did not work: Gould's campaign, on a radical
Keynesian Eurosceptic platform, never gained momentum, and
Smith won an immensely tedious contest with ease. But the union
leaders' action had one crucial unintended side-effect. By causing
outrage throughout the Labour Party at their presumption that
they had the right to choose its leader, they pushed the issue of
Labour's links with the trade unions right to the top of the party's
agenda. Gould promised that if elected he would ensure that
future leadership elections took place on a one member, one vote
basis, and Smith was forced to follow suit, setting the stage for
more than a year of excruciating wrangling between 'modernizers'
and 'traditionalists' that came perilously close to destroying the
credibility of his leadership.

In the first few days after the general election, Blair toyed
with the idea of going for the deputy leadership. He decided not to
after Smith persuaded Margaret Beckett to stand, and instead gave
vocal support to the Smith–Beckett ticket. He was rewarded with
an important role in Smith's campaign as joint chief ideologue
(alongside Gordon Brown and Robin Cook), with a free hand to

press the case for 'modernization'. The 1992 defeat, he wrote in *Fabian Review*, showed that Labour had 'to continue and intensify the process of change . . . at the level of both ideas and organization'[25] – a point of view that was reinforced for him when pollsters reported depressing evidence that Labour was still seen as old-fashioned, out-of-touch, incompetent on the economy, dominated by the trade unions and vulnerable to extremist takeover. 'Winning the next election for Labour requires not a delicate shift in tactics or strategy, but a project. A project of renewal,' he explained in the *Guardian*. 'It should start with the Labour Party's historic principles, the values that define its identity. It should then apply them, for the modern world, to both its politics and its organization . . . The true reason for our defeat is not complex. It is simple. It has been the same since 1979: Labour has not been trusted to fulfil the aspirations of the majority of people in a modern world.' As for the party's link with the unions, 'Since the election the debate about organizational change has centred almost exclusively round Labour's relations with the unions. No one is suggesting Labour turns its back on the unions. The question is how to make the relationship democratic, how to base it on individual trade unionists or levy-payers. To suggest that those who advocate change are anti-union is a travesty, a form of ideological bullying designed to stop a debate taking place.'[26]

In Smith's July 1992 shadow cabinet reshuffle, Blair landed the plum job of shadow home secretary. He spent some time reading himself into his brief, then got stuck in to the union links row again on the side of OMOV (see chapter 9). But by far the most important event in this period was his visit with Gordon Brown to the United States to study Bill Clinton's presidential victory. Blair was particularly impressed by the way Clinton had managed to overcome the Democrats' long-standing vulnerability to attack from the Republicans – for being 'soft' on crime, welfare dependency and family values – by taking aggressively populist anti-liberal stances. Early in 1993, he made a series of interventions that echoed, in a polite English way, many of the themes of Clinton's campaign.

First, in January, he launched what must rank as the most successful soundbite of the 1990s in British politics, 'tough on crime, tough on the causes of crime', as the cornerstone of his attempt to reclaim law and order from the Tories. A couple of months later, he declared his antipathy to 'rainbow coalition' politics and his belief in the centrality of what Clinton's campaign had called 'the economy, stupid'. 'A mistake that several left-of-centre parties have suffered from is to try and divide society up into a set of different interest groups, give them each a policy, put it together, amalgamate it, and then, hey presto, you've got a majority for government. And life just doesn't work like that, because most people don't look at themselves in that way. I think in particular in relation to the economy you require a unifying economic theme, which I think is based around the notion of community action to provide and enhance individual opportunity, and that is something that will be applied to all groups in society.'[27] Then he talked of the need for 'a new concept of citizenship, in which rights and responsibilities go together and where we cease to posit an entirely false choice between social and personal responsibility. As is so clear the more you examine the rise of crime and social disorder in Britain, the problem has been that the left has tended to undervalue individual responsibility and the right has ignored the influence of social conditions. Indeed to the right, talk of the link between social conditions and crime is to excuse crime. So the obvious common sense – namely that children who are brought up with no chance of a job, poor education, family breakdown, and in bad housing are more likely to drift into crime than those who are not – is denied. A modern notion of citizenship gives rights but demands responsibilities, shows respect but wants it back, grants opportunity but insists on responsibility. The purpose of economic and social policy should be to extend opportunity, to remove the underlying causes of social alienation. But it should also take tough measures to ensure that the chances that are given are taken up.'[28]

Blair's rhetoric of 'responsibilities as well as rights', which was to become a defining characteristic of his approach as leader, soon made him Labour's most controversial politician. Already hated by the party's 'traditionalists' for his antipathy to politics based on class interests, he now earned the mistrust of civil libertarians and feminists for what they saw as his populist

pandering to conservative prejudices. Relations with John Smith
also cooled after OMOV went through at the 1993 party conference and Smith decided not to attempt any further 'modernizing'
changes to Labour's organization. Blair made little secret of his
impatience with what he saw as Smith's complacency, while
Smith made it apparent to friends that he thought Blair's enthusiasm for permanent revolution was dangerously destabilizing.
At the same time, however, Blair won widespread admiration in
the party for his ability to exploit rising crime to Labour's advantage simply by using his common sense – and he was loved by
the media. When John Smith died on 12 May 1994, the overwhelming weight of media support for Blair as his successor
made him unassailable within hours. The two politicians that
might have been expected to give him a real contest had he not
been so widely acclaimed, Gordon Brown and Robin Cook, soon
decided that the risk of humbling defeat was too great and threw
in their lot with Blair's campaign. So too did Peter Mandelson,
who had been out of favour under the Smith regime, although
such was his unpopularity that he was given the code name
'Bobby' by the Blair campaign to keep his central role secret. His
cover was blown only after Blair had won.[29]

Considering Blair's burgeoning reputation, it is remarkable
just how far he still remained an unknown quantity when Smith
died. Despite his outspokenness since 1992 on 'modernization',
the role of the unions in the Labour Party, political strategy, crime,
the family, and rights and responsibilities, there was very little to
go on when it came to his views on economic management, taxation, Europe, education, the future of the welfare state,
constitutional reform, defence policy, the environment or
Northern Ireland. Some of the gaps were filled during the leadership election campaign – but largely through his endorsement of
existing Labour policy. He certainly gave everything his own spin:
his personal manifesto, *Change and National Renewal*, was ringing
in its support for what it described as a 'dynamic market economy': 'In place of the old debates between public or private sector,
market or state, regulation or deregulation, we need to construct
a new agenda. We live in an era of massive economic and industrial change. The issue is how we cope with it. Governments

should not protect industry from change, nor can they guarantee individuals a job for life. We cannot resist change, but neither should we passively allow it to take its course. On the contrary, we should be the advocates of it, helping industry to modernize to meet its challenge, equipping both firms and people with the means to survive and prosper in a new and highly competitive global market.' But this was perfectly in line with the broad thrust of Labour's economic thinking as it had been developed since 1989 by John Smith and Gordon Brown. The only time that Blair dared to express an opinion that differed from the existing party line was when he came out in favour of the publication of league tables of schools' examination results.[30]

Many of his pronouncements during the campaign consisted of banalities carefully crafted to give the idea that his 'ethical socialism' would in practice be wholly unlike anything Labour had done before. He summed up his message with perfect imprecision at a Fabian Society conference early on in the contest: 'The socialism of Marx, of centralized state control of industry and production, is dead . . . By contrast, socialism as defined by certain key values and beliefs is not merely alive, it has an historic opportunity now to give leadership. The basis of such socialism lies in its view that individuals are social, interdependent human beings, that individuals cannot be divorced from the society to which they belong. It is, if you will, social-ism. . . For too long the left has thought it has had a choice: to be radical but unacceptable, or to be cautious but electable. Whilst being radical is defined as the old-styled collectivism of several decades ago, this may be true. Once being radical is defined as having a central vision, based around principle but liberated from particular policy prescriptions that have become confused with principle, then being radical is the route to electability.'[31]

The leadership contest gave Labour acres of free publicity, nearly all of it positive, and Blair easily won the first ever one member, one vote contest, securing the support of 58 per cent of individual members who voted, 61 per cent of MPs and MEPs and 52 per cent of trade unionists.[32] John Prescott, with 24 per cent of individual members, 20 per cent of MPs and MEPs and 28 per cent of trade unionists, came second, and Margaret Beckett trailed in third, with 17 per cent of individual members, 20 per cent of MPs and MEPs and 19 per cent of trade unionists. Prescott won the deputy leadership from Beckett, taking more than half the votes in each section of the electoral college.

Despite the scale of his victory, Blair was not entirely happy. Sixty per cent of Labour's individual members had either abstained or voted for Beckett or Prescott; nearly two out of every five MPs and MEPs had voted against him. He felt that he still needed to do something to stamp his authority on the party. He had been lampooned – with some justification – by the left, the Tories and some sections of the serious press as vacuous and lightweight, a good-looking soundbite merchant with nothing of substance behind the ever-present smile. He wanted to prove his *gravitas*. More important, he believed that he had to show the world that 'change', in particular Labour's embrace of 'a dynamic market economy', was irreversible. Above all, he wanted to prove himself to business. If there is anything that puts Blair's politics in a nutshell, it his comment to the *Guardian* in 1991 that 'You can measure how well you're doing by the number of invitations you get to address businessmen'.[33]

Thus it was that he decided to change Clause Four of the Labour constitution, as the key element of the transformation of the party into 'New Labour'. Before the 1994 party conference in Blackpool, Blair persuaded an initially sceptical Prescott of the sense of the idea and made sure that the conference set and publicity material were emblazoned with the slogan 'New Labour, New Britain'. Hours before he was due to deliver his 'parliamentary report' on 4 October he informed various other key figures of what he planned to do. The actual speech was opaque, despite its injunction to 'say what we mean and mean what we say'. 'It is time we had a clear, up-to-date statement of the objects and objectives of our party,' he said. 'John Prescott and I will propose such a statement to the NEC. Let it then be open to debate in the coming months.'[34] But the party's spin doctors lost no time in making it clear to journalists precisely what he meant: ditching the statement of the party's aims that had changed hardly at all since it was formulated by Arthur Henderson and Sidney Webb and adopted in 1918, Part Four of which read: 'To secure for the workers by hand or by brain the full fruits of their industry and the most equitable distribution thereof that may be possible upon the basis of the common ownership of the means of production, distribution and exchange and the best possible obtainable system of administration of each industry or service.'

Clause Four was originally cobbled together as a deliberately vague form of words acceptable to all the disparate elements that made up the Labour Party as it emerged from the First World War, in the middle of a giant social crisis, as a mass organization for the first time: gradualist Fabian enthusiasts for the centralized controls on the economy introduced during the war, Guild Socialists and radical trade unionists who believed in workers' control, members of the co-operative movement, Marxists who thought that capitalism as a system was doomed to collapse, trade unionists whose main interest was improved wages and conditions, and so on. It was never meant as an endorsement of state ownership of the economy even as a distant goal, let alone as an immediate programme.

By the 1930s, however, Labour had become strongly attached to the idea of socialism as nationalization and planning, largely because of the apparent success of the Soviet Union in securing full employment at a time when the capitalist West was experiencing a slump, but also as a result of the party's own experience in local government running municipally owned utilities and services. This attachment was reinforced by the experience of national planning in the Second World War. As Labour's 1942 'interim report on post-war planning', *The Old World and the New Society*, written by Harold Laski, put it: 'We have learnt in the war that the anarchy of private consumption must give way to ordered planning under national control. That lesson is no less applicable to peace. The Labour Party therefore urges that the nation must own and operate the essential instruments of production; their power over our lives is too great to be left in private hands . . . common ownership will alone secure that priority of national over private need which assures the community the power over its economic future.'[35] Clement Attlee swept to power in 1945 on a manifesto promising extensive nationalization, and put his deputy, Herbert Morrison, in charge of implementing the programme. By 1951 the government had taken a large part of industry into public ownership: coal, civil aviation, electricity and gas, railways and canals, much of road haulage, iron and steel.

Which is where Labour's problems with Clause Four really started. For Morrison and the rest of the Labour right, the post-war nationalizations were pragmatic measures necessary to make a mixed economy work efficiently.[36] After the exertions of war, the right believed, there was a strong case for taking into public ownership those essential industries that were in desperate need of investment only the state could provide. But that was quite enough to be getting on with: Morrison believed that even the iron and steel industry was a step too far, and from 1950 argued strongly for a period of 'consolidation'. For the left, however, further moves towards 'common ownership of the means of production, distribution and exchange' were essential and urgent. The demand for more nationalization was at the heart of the left-wing revolt led by Aneurin Bevan that swept through the Labour Party after it lost power.

At first, the left–right argument was merely one about the speed with which the benefits of nationalization should be spread through the economy. But from the mid-1950s onwards, the right increasingly adopted a different tack. With the arrival of Keynesian techniques of macroeconomic management, the mixed economy, full employment and the welfare state, the argument went, capitalism had been transformed and there was no longer any need to replace it. Instead, socialists should concentrate their efforts on reforms to make the system more efficient and egalitarian. The impact of this 'revisionist' case, most coherently put by Anthony Crosland in his 1956 classic *The Future of Socialism*, was reinforced by opinion polls showing the growing unpopularity of nationalization among the electorate.[37] The left countered that this was the result of the bureaucratic model of state ownership adopted by Morrison and that the solution was the introduction of workers' control – but Hugh Gaitskell, who succeeded Attlee as leader in 1955, was a keen revisionist and would have none of it. In 1959, after Labour lost its third election in a row, Gaitskell called for the party to ditch Clause Four in order to broaden its appeal. The clause, he argued, was not only an inaccurate summary of Labour's plans but a hostage to fortune because it allowed the Tories to scare the voters with claims that Labour would introduce a radical extension of public ownership. To his surprise, the party would not accede to his demand and, faced with a revolt from the left and the unions, he was forced to back down. Clause Four survived. To every subsequent Labour leader until Blair, his humiliation served as a terrible warning about Labour's attachment to its traditional symbols.

As the historian Eric Shaw argues, 'in practical policy terms the retention of Clause Four had a negligible effect'. Labour won the 1964 general election under Harold Wilson with the same minimal commitments on public ownership as when it lost in 1955 and 1959: renationalization of the road haulage and iron and steel industries, which had been denationalized by the Tories in the early 1950s. Then, in opposition after 1970 Labour's National Executive Committee swung sharply to the left, and by 1973 it had adopted a programme of nationalization more extensive than any since 1945. The NEC was particularly receptive to the arguments of Stuart Holland, an economist who had served as an adviser to Wilson, that the growing economic power of giant multinational corporations had undermined the ability of government to control the economy merely through traditional measures of Keynesian demand management. In line with Holland's analysis, the NEC backed the introduction of 'planning agreements' between government and companies to provide the government with the information it needed to intervene effectively and the creation of a National Enterprise Board (NEB) to act as a public sector entrepreneur, taking holdings in leading companies and directing their activities in the national interest. Most important of all, it supported nationalization of a major company in each of the twenty to twenty-five main industrial sectors to give a Labour government the power to influence pricing and investment decisions.[38]

The policy was hated by the right, which succeeded in watering down the promises of nationalization even before Labour's unexpected victory in the February 1974 election. It then

won a string of battles against Tony Benn, industry secretary in
1974–5 and the policy's main supporter in the cabinet, over the
powers of the NEB. To summarize a complex tale, the NEB ended
up acting largely as a 'hospital for sick companies', spending vast
quantities of money on the rescue of British Leyland and Rolls-
Royce, and by 1979 there had been three major nationalizations –
British Shipbuilders, British Aerospace and the British National
Oil Corporation.[39] Although BAe and BNOC were reasonably successful in their short lives in public ownership, and the NEB had
a handful of achievements of which Labour could be proud, the
overwhelming feeling in the party when it lost in 1979 was that
the industrial strategy had proved a failure. The left argued that an
extension of public ownership and planning had to be tried properly next time, and the right responded that it had been
wrong-headed from the start.[40] Much of the left of the party was
convinced that the key was a move away from 'Morrisonian'
nationalization towards workers' control, state-financed co-operatives and municipal ownership. In the early 1980s the left in
local government made experimentation with such ideas one of its
hallmarks.

　　This tussle continued on and off for the next decade, but was
rendered increasingly academic by the Tories' actions. Put simply,
between 1979 and 1997, they reversed every major industrial
nationalization of the post-war years and destroyed the capacity of
local government to intervene economically by curtailing its revenue-raising powers. The privatization process started slowly with
the sale of state holdings in various profitable state-owned firms,
most of which had been rescued by the NEB, then rapidly picked
up momentum. Britoil (as the BNOC was renamed), British
Telecom, British Aerospace, British Gas, British Airways and
British Steel had all gone in whole or in part by 1987; they were
followed by the Rover Group and much of the water and electricity industries by 1992; and by 1997 coal and the railways had
joined them.

　　Labour opposed every single privatization, but as the list of privatized industries grew longer, it started to rethink its whole attitude
to public ownership. The initial spur was the prohibitive cost of
buying back what had been privatized, but as the 1980s progressed,

more and more Labour politicians came to question whether any sort of public ownership was worthwhile. The experiments in municipal enterprise in the early 1980s were not conspicuously successful, and many of the Tory privatizations were very popular. Many believers in 'Morrisonian' nationalization had their faith destroyed as the Soviet bloc command economies entered what turned out to be their death throes. Labour's 1983 manifesto promised a return of everything the Tories had privatized in their first term to public ownership, along with a major expansion of nationalization similar to that promised in 1974 and an extension of the co-operative sector.[41] Between 1983 and 1987, the party dropped its talk of 'public ownership' for the friendlier-sounding idea of 'social ownership', most fully laid out in a document written by David Blunkett and John Smith in 1986, *Social Ownership*, which encompassed co-operatives and municipal ownership as well as 'Morrisonian' nationalized industries. According to the 1987 manifesto, a Labour government would ensure that 'basic utilities like gas or water' were socially owned. It would also create a new state holding company, British Enterprise, to take stakes in high-technology companies and use the state holding in British Telecom (then still 49 per cent) to make it do what it wanted.[42]

By 1992, after the policy review, ideas of social ownership had disappeared from the manifesto: apart from a promise to encourage democratic employee share ownership plans (ESOPs) and co-operatives, there was nothing apart from ambiguous references to the goal of 'public control' of the national electricity grid and water supply.[43] After the 1992 election defeat, several 'modernizers' suggested abandoning Clause Four, among them Giles Radice, Jack Straw and Neil Kinnock,[44] but John Smith resisted the idea as an unnecessarily divisive diversion. Nevertheless, although Labour opposed privatization of coal, the railways and the Post Office – the last of which was eventually scuppered by public opposition, skilfully exploited by the postal unions – the likelihood of its pledging renationalization of any of them once it came to election time had to be slim.

All of which meant that Blair's decision to drop Clause Four represented little or nothing in terms of policy. The gesture was wholly symbolic. It would make it clear to everyone, but particularly

business, that Labour was now a party that believed in capitalism
and that there was no way a Blair government would consider
spending tax-payers' money on taking back what the Tories had
sold, let alone on 1970s-style interventionism. And if Blair could
do what Gaitskell had so famously failed to do and no one else
had dared try, he would at a stroke establish not only his authority but also his audacity.

The idea was not risk-free, as Blair soon discovered. Two
days after his speech, the party conference voted in favour of
retaining Clause Four, and although Blair's supporters dismissed
the vote as the last gasp of Old Labour, within a few weeks it was
clear that he was going to have to work to get his way. In the
absence of any draft alternative for Clause Four from Blair, alarm
about his intentions spread rapidly through the party. The rail
unions made the case that dropping Clause Four would undermine their campaign against privatization of the railways; and an
academic survey of Labour Party members revealed that they were
strongly in favour of public ownership of gas, electricity and water
(even though only around a quarter backed more widespread
nationalization).[45] Blair's reputation with the party then suffered a
severe blow after the *Daily Mail* resurrected an old story about his
decision to send his eldest son to a grant-maintained school. Next,
a survey of constituency Labour parties by *Tribune* found that the
general committees of fifty-eight out of sixty were opposed to
change. Blair managed to get the NEC to agree to hold a special
conference on Clause Four rather than discuss it at the 1995
annual conference – but this in turn encouraged complaints that
the party was being bounced into accepting something it did not
want. Then half of Labour's MEPs were claimed as signatories to
an advertisement opposing the change to Clause Four placed in
the *Guardian* on the very day that Blair was due to address a meeting of the European Parliamentary Labour Party. By the middle of
January 1995, there seemed to be a real chance that Blair was
heading for defeat.

Blair responded by undertaking an unprecedented tour of
the country to put his case to party meetings, in the course of
which, according to his own estimate, he addressed 30,000
people. He persuaded the NEC to pay not only for a propaganda

campaign in his support but also for local parties to ballot their members on Clause Four if they chose (which of course they were urged strongly to do). By early March 1995, when Labour's Scottish conference unexpectedly voted to replace the old clause, it was clear that he was going to get his way. The new Clause Four, launched by Blair and John Prescott the week after the Scottish conference, was circumlocutory and entirely forgettable. According to its first paragraph, Labour 'believes that by the strength of our common endeavour we achieve more than we achieve alone, so as to create for each of us the means to realize our true potential and for all of us a community in which power, wealth and opportunity are in the hands of the many not the few, where the rights we enjoy reflect the duties we owe, and where we live together, freely, in a spirit of solidarity, tolerance and respect'. But it served its purpose. Its endorsement of 'a dynamic economy . . . in which the enterprise of the market and the rigour of competition are joined with the forces of partnership and co-operation to produce the wealth the nation needs' buried for good the idea that Labour was in favour of common ownership, and for the first time made it explicit that Labour was in the business of managing capitalism rather than transcending it. The special conference on 29 April 1995 backed it overwhelmingly. Only three out of more than 500 constituency parties that balloted their members voted against.

The result was exactly what Blair wanted – and it was impossible to miss the tone of triumphalism in his speech to the special conference after the vote was declared. 'Our project is to re-define radical left-of-centre politics for the new millennium,' he said. 'It is to create a new political agenda for the country. It will break new ground and it should. Change and modernization does not stop at four o'clock this afternoon. It goes on.'[46]

Blair's description of Labour as 'left-of-centre', a position he distinguished from the 'old left' and the 'new right', was by now familiar: within a year he would be talking of the need for 'a radical centre in modern politics' and declaring that Labour was 'a party of the centre as well as the centre-left'.[47] He subsequently announced that

he would describe himself as a 'social democrat', which no other
Labour leader had dared do publicly since the defection of the SDP
in 1981.[48] In mid-1995, he hired two former defectors to the SDP
as advisers (see below) and he welcomed a host of others back to
Labour, among them the political thinker and historian David
Marquand. In autumn 1995, he greeted the Tory MP Alan Howarth
with open arms when he decided to switch to New Labour.

His openness to the centre was more than a matter of
rhetoric and making defectors from other parties feel at home,
however. Soon after he was elected Labour leader, he made it clear
that he was prepared to co-operate with the Liberal Democrats in
developing 'left-of-centre' ideas. As he put it in an interview just
before the 1994 Labour conference: 'It is foolish for us to pretend
that the left of centre is solely occupied by the Labour Party, and
it is only Labour that ever has good ideas. It would be absurd of me
to say that my views and [the Liberal Democrat MP] Charles
Kennedy's are a million miles apart. They're not. But this has to
happen through a process of developing ideas, not in pacts or deals
or working out who sits in what position. I try not to be tribal in
my thinking . . . The most important thing is that the left of centre
develops a political philosophy with meaning for the modern
world and the Liberal Democrats clearly have a place in that.'[49]

This was not a shockingly new idea. Labour had governed
with Liberal help in the 1970s, and even in the mid-1980s, when
the Liberals, in alliance with the SDP, were locked in battle with
Labour and hoped to replace it as the dominant party of opposition, the notion that Labour and the Liberals had more in
common than divided them was widespread on the intellectual
left. There was a small but significant campaign for tactical voting
in the 1987 general election, and after that there was a dramatic
growth of interest in co-operation in both parties. On the Labour
side, the election result convinced many people that the party's
hopes of winning power on its own were now slim: for the first
time, internal pressure groups arguing for electoral reform started
to gain significant support, eventually becoming so strong that
Neil Kinnock was forced to set up a commission on electoral systems, chaired by Raymond Plant, to defuse the issue. Among
Liberal Democrats, as the Liberals became after they swallowed

most of the SDP, there was a growing acceptance that the dream of overtaking Labour was unrealizable, and that, particularly after Labour's policy review, the political differences between the two parties were rapidly disappearing. It was non-party forums that provided most of the space for discussion, however, notably the constitutional reform pressure group Charter 88, the Scottish Constitutional Convention set up in 1988 to draw up plans for a Scottish parliament and two magazines: the *New Statesman*, edited by Stuart Weir and then Steve Platt, and *Samizdat*, set up in late 1988 by the historian Ben Pimlott to agitate for a 'popular front of the mind'. The 1992 general election saw a dramatic increase in anti-Tory tactical voting, and over the next year there were plenty of indications of warmer relations between Labour and the Lib Dems. David Marquand, by the early 1990s a key adviser to Liberal Democrat leader Paddy Ashdown, was appointed to the Commission on Social Justice, set up by John Smith to ponder the future of the welfare state; the Labour MP Frank Field was appointed to the Commission on Wealth Creation and Social Cohesion, set up by Ashdown to do much the same thing. In spring 1993, Smith declared for a referendum on electoral reform. Lib–Labbery was in the air long before Blair became Labour leader.

Nevertheless, there can be no doubt that his election and his success in changing Clause Four were what finally opened the door to formal collaboration at Westminster. Relations between the two parties grew steadily warmer from summer 1994 onwards. In May 1995, two influential back-bench Labour MPs, Calum Macdonald and Tony Wright, set up an internal party pressure group to put the case for Lib–Lab co-operation, hinting that it had the support of Blair.[50] Later the same month Ashdown formally abandoned the policy of 'equidistance' from the two major parties. 'The defeat of the Tory government is now the precondition for Britain's future success,' he announced. 'We therefore declare that every vote for the Liberal Democrats is a vote to remove this Conservative government.'[51] The courtship had its setbacks – notably the Littleborough and Saddleworth by-election campaign in summer 1995, which Labour fought viciously against the Lib Dems, and Blair's unilateral decision a year later to hold referendums on devolution to Scotland and Wales. When Blair announced on the eve of the 1995 Liberal Democrat conference that he was in favour of co-operation, he was given the cold shoulder. Labour reciprocated a couple of months later when Ashdown trailed the idea of the two parties working together to ensure a decade of centre-left government. But by October 1996, Blair and Ashdown were confident enough about each other's intentions to set up a joint consultative committee on constitutional reform, chaired by Robin Cook and Robert Maclennan, to agree a common line on devolution, reform of the House of Lords and electoral reform (see chapter 8). In March 1997, in a speech to a conference sponsored by the *Guardian* and Nexus, the Blairite 'ideas network', Roy Jenkins, the Liberal Democrat leader in the Lords, all but called for supporters of his party to vote tactically to secure 'a Labour government on 2 May, with Mr Blair in Downing Street, although I strongly hope with as large as possible a Liberal Democrat element within the anti-Tory majority in the House of Commons'.[52]

Labour was so far ahead in the opinion polls in the months before the May 1997 election that speculation about its forming a coalition with the Liberal Democrats receded as polling day came closer – a big contrast with 1992, when the question of what Neil Kinnock and Paddy Ashdown would do in the event of a hung parliament dominated the last week of the campaign. But it was clear from the point at which Ashdown dropped 'equidistance' that the Liberal Democrats would be there if Labour needed them as coalition partners. What additional horse-trading would have been required to make a coalition arrangement stick, how much resistance would have been put up by anti-coalitionists in both parties and how well it would have worked in practice are now merely matters for speculation. In the event, there was no hard bargaining to be done. Blair's decision in July 1997 to invite the Liberal Democrats on to a new cabinet committee was a unilateral act of generosity: how much influence it will give Ashdown and his colleagues is as yet impossible to judge.

More important than the opening to the centre in politics created by Blair's election and the changing of Clause Four was the opening they provided to business. Labour of course had supporters in the boardrooms of Britain before 1994–5. It was never the party of most business people, but from the 1940s a significant minority backed it out of belief in its approach to economic management, sheer opportunism, sentimental attachment to their humble roots or a mixture of all three. In the early 1980s, however, the party lost many of its business supporters as it swung to the left, opposed the Tories' assault on the trade unions and apparently consigned itself to perpetual opposition. Although some stayed with Labour – notably the tycoon Robert Maxwell, a former Labour MP, who exerted a profound and corrupting influence over the party through his ownership of the *Daily Mirror* and its sister papers – they were small in number.

Even after the post-1987 policy review, despite its best efforts to persuade business that it was on its side, Labour found it difficult to get the endorsement of business people outside a tiny group of loyalists – the most important of whom was Clive Hollick, the multi-millionaire managing director of MAI Group. A close ally of Neil Kinnock, Hollick played a crucial part in the creation of the Institute for Public Policy Research (IPPR), the party-loyalist think-tank, in 1988 and was given a peerage by Kinnock in 1991. Other key business supporters in the early 1990s included Greg Dyke, chief executive of London Weekend Television, Swraj Paul, the Indian-born steel magnate who received a peerage from Blair in 1996, Harsh Kumar, an Indian-born commodities trader, and Chris Haskins, chairman of Northern Foods. Business took a growing interest in Labour the more the party looked likely to win power. But the pre-1992 'prawn cocktail offensive' of City lunches mounted by John Smith and his front-bench economics team at best merely persuaded companies that Labour was not as dangerous as it used to be.

Things began to change after 'Black Wednesday' in September 1992, the subsequent collapse of the Tories' standing in the opinion polls and Smith's confrontation with the unions over OMOV: by 1994, business had its feelers out to Labour both directly and through lobbyists. But it was Blair's election and Clause Four that really made the difference. All of a sudden, senior figures in the business world wanted to be part of the

Labour milieu again, not merely to discover what the party would do to them and to lobby for their firms' particular interests but also to proffer general advice. Labour's embrace of capitalism under Blair might have been unequivocal – but it was by no means clear that the *sort* of capitalism that Labour favoured was the one that the business world wanted.

The issues were brought into sharp focus in early 1995 by Will Hutton, the economics editor of the *Guardian*, in his best-selling book *The State We're In*. It was a passionate critique of the ills of the British model of capitalism, and it is impossible to summarize adequately in a paragraph. The core of its argument was that Britain had declined relative to other economies because of the long-term economic dominance of the City of London, with its obsession with short-term dividends and lack of concern with long-term investment – a process exacerbated by the attempt of the Tory government since 1979 to 'roll back the frontiers of the state' in social and economic policy and allow free rein to market forces. What is more, the Tories' deregulatory drive and social spending cuts had made Britain much more unequal: we were now living in a '30/30/40 society' (the bottom 30 per cent in dire poverty, the middle 30 per cent in insecurity and the top 40 per cent in affluence), which was not only unjust but bad for economic efficiency and social cohesion. The fetishism of the market had also led to an ossification and devaluation of British democracy. What the country needed, Hutton concluded, was nothing less than a 'reconstruction of the state and the economy': a written constitution, reform of the financial system to encourage long-term investment, reassertion of the state's role in managing and regulating the economy, a 'social partnership' model of industrial relations and a revitalization of the welfare state. In other words, 'stakeholder capitalism' on the German social market model, although with a moderately expansionist Keynesian macroeconomics underpinning it.[53]

Hutton's case was embraced wholeheartedly by much of the Labour-supporting intelligentsia, and he had high hopes that it would be taken on by the Labour leadership. But for Tony Blair and Gordon Brown it was anathema. Not only was Hutton a Keynesian, and thus at odds with Labour's thinking as it had been since 1989 (see chapter 2), he was also far too keen on corporatist involvement of trade unions in company affairs and on regulation of the labour market. The 'German model' was not performing well in terms of growth, and its lack of 'labour market flexibility' – in other words, its high social costs, high wages, strong unions and employment protection – was under fire from business and *laissez-faire* economists for making it uncompetitive in the now-globalized economy. From 1995 through to the 1997 election, Blair and Brown did all they could to distance themselves from Hutton's ideas. Blair's message to business, repeated *ad nauseam* in speeches to local chambers of commerce and to business conferences, was that a Labour government would do nothing to undermine the flexible labour market created by the Tories in the 1980s. Although Blair referred to the idea of a 'stakeholder society' in Singapore in January 1996 and the phrase appeared repeatedly in Labour propaganda in the run-up to the 1997 general election, he made it plain that this did not mean that he was emulating Hutton. For Hutton, 'stakeholder capitalism' signified a society in which firms have obligations, codified in law, not just to their shareholders but also to some combination of their suppliers, bankers, consumers and workers, as well as responsibilities to the environment and to local communities. Blair's 'stakeholder society' was one in which companies go about their business as usual but in which every citizen has a stake – which could mean anything, but was usually taken as having something to do with the importance of everyone having a funded second pension (see chapter 6).[54]

More substantially, in April 1995 the IPPR, with Clive Hollick acting as front man, launched a Commission on Public Policy and British Business, along similar lines to the Commission on Social Justice set up by John Smith in 1992, 'to investigate the competitive position of the British economy and the role that public policy should play in it'. The commission, chaired by George Bain, the principal of the London Business School, was heavily weighted towards business: apart from Hollick, it included Bob Bauman, chairman of British Aerospace, Sir Christopher Harding, chairman of Legal and General, David Sainsbury, chairman of the supermarket chain, and George Simpson, the managing director of GEC, along with a selection of management gurus and academics, the most significant of them John Kay, next to Hutton the best known advocate of 'stakeholding'. Only John Monks, the general secretary of the TUC, represented the 'other side' of industry.[55] Although the IPPR went out of its way to insist that the commission was not a Labour Party body, the very involvement of the IPPR was a signal that its findings would be taken seriously by Blair – as indeed they were. The January 1997 launch of the commission's report, *Promoting Prosperity: A Business Agenda For Britain*, was turned into a bizarre spectacle by deputy prime minister Michael Heseltine, who insisted on inviting himself on to the platform, denouncing the IPPR as a front for the Labour Party and defending the Tory government's record of deregulation. Largely as a result, the content of the report and Blair's response to it were eclipsed. But both spoke volumes about New Labour's relationship with business.

The report was moderately critical of the performance of what Hutton had called 'British capitalism'. There were too many unsuccessful companies and too many underachieving people. Investment was in short supply and government policies changed too often. The report backed a host of New Labour policies: a (low) minimum wage, tougher competition policy, improvements in education and training, investment in the transport infrastructure, tax incentives for long-term investment and strict adherence to a tight fiscal and monetary regime. In addition, the Bank of England should be given independence and Britain should join EMU in the first stage if a majority of other EU countries did the same. But the report also made it clear that big changes were not required in the way the system worked. It gave wholehearted endorsement to the Tory market liberalizations of the 1980s and argued for only the lightest of touches to 'foster stakeholding'.[56]

Speaking at the launch, Blair gave this approach strong support. 'Over the past two years, I have addressed over 10,000 individual business people,' he said. 'It has not just been about collecting endorsements and support. It has been about building a genuine new partnership with business for the future. Today I offer business a new deal for the future. The deal is this: we leave intact the main changes of the 1980s in industrial relations and enterprise. And now, together, we address a new agenda for the twenty-first century: education, welfare reform, infrastructure, leadership in Europe. We want to keep more flexible labour markets. Our proposals for change, including the minimum wage, would amount to less labour market regulation than in the USA. Our aim is not to create inflexible labour markets or try merely to regulate for job security but to make people more employable in the labour market by enhancing their skills, talents and mobility . . . In the USA it would never occur to question the commitment of the Democrats to business. It should be the same here with New Labour.'[57]

The participants in the IPPR commission were by no means the only enthusiasts for New Labour in the business world. British Telecom negotiated a deal with the party to cable every school in the country in return for being allowed into the cable entertainment business, which Blair revealed at the 1995 Labour conference. David Simon, chairman of BP, now Lord Simon, the minister for trade and competitiveness in Europe, gave Blair the idea of putting a ten-point 'performance contract' at the centre of his speech to the 1996 Labour conference. Alec Reed, chairman of the employment company Reed, declared that it would be 'a tragedy' if Blair did not become prime minister';[58] Cob Stenham, chairman of Arjo Wiggins Appleton, said that 'serious and forward-looking business people should back New Labour'. Matthew Harding, the insurance broker and vice-chairman of Chelsea football club, gave a £1 million donation to Labour just before he died in a helicopter crash in late 1996; Bob Gavron, the printing magnate, handed over £500,000. In late 1996, Labour announced that its donations from business had topped £6 million. It was subsequently revealed that Trevor Chinn, chairman of Lex Services, Britain's biggest motor dealer, and the industrialist Emmanuel Kaye were among the donors to a 'blind trust' that was funding Blair's private office. Anita Roddick, chief executive of the Body Shop, came out for Labour around the same time, as did Terence Conran, the restaurateur and founder of Habitat: both starred in a Labour party election broadcast.

Most important of all, though, were the media magnates – in particular Rupert Murdoch, boss of the global media empire that included Britain's biggest-selling daily newspaper, the *Sun*, since the mid-1970s one of the Tories' most loyal friends in Fleet Street. When Blair won the Labour leadership, Murdoch was a hate figure for the left because of the *Sun*'s virulent campaign against Labour right through to the 1992 general election.[59] But Blair knew that Murdoch was interested in making money above all else, and that he had never had any qualms about using his papers to support nominally centre-left parties as long as they were business-friendly and orthodox in their foreign policy prescriptions. Equally important, there were some small indications that Murdoch was thinking of switching his allegiance in British politics away from the Tories. In 1992, he had helped to pay for a study of media regulation by the IPPR. More recently, both the *Sun* and *The Times* had become much more critical of John Major's Tory government. Soon after Blair became Labour leader, the media mogul was quoted by the German news magazine *Der Spiegel* as stating: 'I could even imagine myself supporting the British Labour leader, Tony Blair.'

Informal contacts between Murdoch and Blair followed, then dinner, then an invitation to Blair to address the 'leadership conference' of NewsCorp, Murdoch's giant multinational conglomerate, on an Australian island in July 1995. Blair accepted readily and treated his audience to a wide-ranging speech in which he declared his enthusiasm for market forces and the family. 'The old solutions of rigid economic planning and state control won't work,' he intoned. 'What is more, during the sixties and seventies the left developed, almost in substitution for its economic prescriptions, which by then were failing, a type of social individualism that confused, at points at least, liberation from prejudice with a disregard for moral structures. It fought for racial and sexual equality, which was entirely right. It appeared indifferent to the family and individual responsibility, which was wrong . . . My politics are simple, not complex. I believe you can have a country of ambition and aspiration with compassion and a sense of duty to others. The individual prospers best within a strong, decent, cohesive society. These are the real ends of the left of centre. The means of achieving them will, of course, vary from generation to generation and should be pragmatically, not ideologically, driven.'[60]

Blair insisted that he made no Faustian pact with Murdoch to lay off his business interests in government in return for the support of his papers. 'No policy was traded – indeed, the burden of the speech was an attack on the new right,' he wrote in a scathing piece in the *Guardian*.[61] But it was noticeable that after Blair's trip, Labour became much less enthusiastic for strict regulation of the media, particularly on cross-ownership, and that the Murdoch press became much more enthusiastic about Blair. Labour's long-standing promise of a Monopolies and Mergers Commission investigation into Murdoch's media interests was quietly dropped, and Labour opposed the Tory government's proposals for tighter rules on newspaper groups owning television companies, claiming that they would be unfair to the Mirror Group and hinting that it was in favour of complete deregulation. The deal reached by Labour with British Telecom in 1995 to allow it into the cable entertainment industry was very much in Murdoch's interests because of his role as a supplier of television programmes, and Labour was noticeably quiet about the danger of Murdoch establishing monopolies in various aspects of digital television. The *Sun* and its Sunday sister paper, the *News of the World*, came out unequivocally for Labour in the 1997 election, and although the *Sunday Times* stayed Tory while *The Times* took the bizarre position of backing Eurosceptics of left, right and centre, neither gave Labour much trouble. In the middle of the election campaign, Gerry Robinson, the chairman of both Granada and BSkyB, the satellite television company largely owned by Murdoch, was unveiled by Labour as one of its key supporters in the world of business. Another BSkyB director, Dennis Stevenson, now chief executive of Pearson, the media conglomerate that owns *The Economist* and the *Financial Times* (with Greg Dyke as head of its television operation), was appointed by Blair as head of Labour's independent review on increasing the use of information technology in schools.

Blair also put himself out to make his peace with the mid-market Tory tabloids in the *Express* and *Mail* stables, belonging respectively to United News and Media and Associated Newspapers. With the *Daily* and *Sunday Express*, now merged as a seven-day paper, Blair got nowhere until some time after Hollick's

MAI Group took over United News and Media in early 1996. By the time the election campaign started, however, the *Express* was at best lukewarm in its Toryism, while its downmarket tabloid sister paper, the *Daily Star*, backed Labour. With Associated, the story was more colourful. In October 1995, Sir David English, the former editor of the *Daily Mail* who had become editor-in-chief of Associated, wrote a piece in the *Spectator* in which he revealed that Blair had long been a welcome lunch guest at the company – even when Neil Kinnock was Labour leader and the shadow cabinet was boycotting the *Mail* and its sister papers for their vicious coverage of the Labour Party.[62] English had been impressed by Blair's forthright views – and had recently discussed the possibility of the Associated papers coming out for Labour at the next election with his proprietor, Lord Rothermere. '"Could such a thing even be possible?" I wondered. "Well, it certainly would not be impossible, David," he replied, having recently come from a two-hour one-to-one with the Labour leader. So, could Associated Newspapers come out for Labour? It is too early to say. We may or we may not.' Six months later, Rothermere told Sue Lawley on *Desert Island Discs*: 'I think that some of my newspapers might be sympathetic to Tony and others will be sympathetic to John Major.' When it finally came to the crunch, the *Daily Mail* and the *Mail on Sunday* remained Conservative for the 1997 election, but the *Evening Standard* backed Labour – and three weeks after the election Rothermere announced that he would be voting with Labour in the Lords.[63]

In power, New Labour's enthusiasm for business has remained undimmed. As well as the ministerial role for David (now Lord) Simon of BP and the advisory role for Dennis Stevenson of Pearson and BSkyB, the government took on Peter Davies, head of the Prudential insurance empire, to chair an advisory group on tackling youth and long-term unemployment, and Martin Taylor, chief executive of Barclays Bank, to head a taskforce on social security reform. Alan Sugar, the founder of the consumer electronics company Amstrad, was signed up to talk to government business seminars for young entrepreneurs; Bob Ayling, chairman of British Airways, was given a place on the committee organizing the millennium celebrations. Labour's millionaire industrialist MP, Geoffrey Robinson, proprietor of the *New Statesman*, got the number three job in the Treasury, paymaster general; Malcolm Bates, chairman of Pearl Assurance, was drafted in to review the private finance initiative set up by the Tory government to attract private capital to public projects; and Alex Trotman, chairman of Ford in Britain, was recruited to advise on creation of a 'university for industry'.

Despite the relentless repositioning of Labour under Blair, it is remarkable how little policy changed during his three years as leader of the opposition. When he became leader, Labour was following a plan for policy production that had been laid down after the 1992 defeat by John Smith and his supporters, including Blair, and in most respects the new leader stuck to it. The big idea was simple. As in 1992, Labour should at the 1996 or 1997 election put before the electorate a small number of carefully costed, cautious policies for immediate implementation. But unlike in 1992, they should not involve increases in income tax, and they should not be set in stone three years before the election. The plan was that most policies would be in place by 1994 or 1995, ready for an early election, but that Labour would choose its keynote policies and put detailed figures to them where necessary closer to the election.

Smith hived off the most contentious area of policy, reform of the welfare state, to a non-party body, the Commission on Social Justice; everything else was done in house, supposedly according to a new procedure in which policies were drawn up by policy commissions (consisting of members of the shadow cabinet and the NEC) and then went through a National Policy Forum (involving a wider spread of party members) before going to Labour's annual conference.[64] In practice, the process was slow to get off the ground, leaving senior front-benchers with far greater autonomy on policy than had normally been the case in opposition.

By the time Blair became leader, Labour was well on the way to defining its policies for the next election. Most important, shadow chancellor Gordon Brown had firmly established both the broad outline of economic policy and much of its detail – but that was not all. Labour also had more-or-less comprehensive policies on constitutional reform, Europe, education, the environment, transport and defence; and the work of the Commission on Social Justice was almost complete. Many of these policies were not to Blair's liking, but with the exception of education, where he made sure that the party developed a radically different approach, for the most part he stuck with what he inherited. Of course, he tweaked here and there. Europe policy became significantly more populist and sceptical with Robin Cook rather than Jack Cunningham as shadow foreign secretary, particularly with the promise of a referendum on British membership of a European single currency. The constitutional reform programme was changed at the edges by Blair's promise of referendums on devolution and his step back from the promise of an elected second chamber. Blair and Brown made sure that Labour packaged its 'welfare-to-work' measures to give far more emphasis to compulsion than the Commission on Social Justice had done. On the minimum wage, Blair and Brown resisted all pressure to set it before the election, and on employment rights they ensured that Labour's promises were minimal. More generally, everything that the party produced in the way of policy from 1994 onwards was given the New Labour gloss. As *New Labour, New Life for Britain*, the draft manifesto published in July 1996, put it, it was all 'profoundly radical', 'neither old left nor new right', part of a 'different and modern approach' stemming from a 'fundamental reconstruction of the party'. Blair's favourite themes of encouragement for business, 'fairness not favours' for the trade unions, strengthening family life and 'duties matching rights' were all-pervasive.

For all this, the policies summarized in *New Labour, New Life for Britain*, laid out in detail in a policy handbook published shortly afterwards and then repackaged in the 1997 Labour manifesto *New Labour: Because Britain Deserves Better*, were different only in small ways from what Labour would have produced had John Smith not died. On economic policy, the message was that Labour would be hard on inflation and government borrowing, would not 'tax and spend', and would rely on 'supply side' measures to reduce unemployment – in essence what Labour promised in 1992. There were big differences from the party's approach in 1992 on education, social security and law and order, with new emphases on school standards rather than the structure of the education system, 'welfare-to-work' policies rather than increased benefits, and being 'tough on crime' rather than merely tough on its causes. But with the partial exception of education, the biggest changes all pre-dated Blair's arrival as leader. It is perfectly imaginable that a Smith Labour Party would have put to the electorate precisely the same core promises, presented as five 'early pledges', that the Blair Labour Party repeated incessantly: 'cut class sizes to thirty or under for all five-, six- and seven-year-olds, by using money saved from the assisted places scheme; fast-track punishment for persistent young offenders, by halving the time from arrest to sentencing; cut NHS waiting lists by treating an extra 100,000 patients as a first step by releasing £100 million saved from NHS red tape; get 250,000 under-twenty-fives off benefit and into work, by using money from a windfall levy on the privatized utilities; set tough rules for government spending and borrowing, ensure low inflation and strengthen the economy so that interest rates are as low as possible.' For Scotland and Wales, there was an additional pledge to legislate for a Scottish parliament and a Welsh assembly in the first year of a Labour government after referendums.[65]

What was significantly new and indubitably Blair's responsibility, however, was the way *New Labour, New Life for Britain* was adopted as Labour's programme. In March 1996, he sprang on the National Executive Committee the idea that an early version of the Labour manifesto should be put to a vote of all individual party members – and then announced at a press conference that the NEC had agreed to his proposal, an interpretation of events not shared by most of the other people who had been at the NEC meeting. But the grumbling subsided, and eight months later, after *New Labour, New Life for Britain* was endorsed by the 1996 party conference, Labour's members – of whom there were now 350,000, up from 250,000 in 1993 – received ballot slips giving them the chance to endorse the document too.

The plebiscite was intended by Blair as a way of proving the independence of Labour's policy-making process from the trade unions and of depriving the left of the possibility of accusing him of betrayal if it did not like what he did in government. He believed that an enthusiastic vote in favour would show how far New Labour's members agreed with his modernization of the party and tie the whole of the party, in parliament and outside, into support for his minimalist, responsible programme. But as with Clause Four, the exercise came close to going badly wrong. A substantial proportion of members simply ignored their voting slips – and it soon became clear that Blair could suffer the embarrassment of more than half the electorate abstaining. In the end, his face was saved with a 95 per cent yes vote on a 61 per cent turnout, but only after the party splashed out a large sum on mailing and telephoning recalcitrant members and pleading for participation in the ballot.

If the continuities in Labour policy during Blair's period in opposition are remarkable, so too is the continuity in personnel – at least at shadow cabinet and National Executive Committee level. In the three shadow cabinet elections after Blair became leader (in October 1994, October 1995 and July 1996), the Parliamentary Labour Party resolutely stuck to familiar favourites. Sixteen out of the twenty-three members of Blair's first cabinet were members of the shadow cabinet as long ago as 1992–3.

In 1994, only one sitting member, Tom Clarke, was voted off the shadow cabinet, largely because he had committed the cardinal sin for a Scottish politician of playing the religious sectarian card at precisely the wrong moment by defending Catholic-dominated Monklands council against 'jobs-for-the-boys' charges in the middle of the by-election campaign for largely Protestant Monklands West, John Smith's former seat. He was replaced by Gavin Strang, Labour's assiduous agriculture spokesman, who was anything but a Blairite; and the shadow cabinet vacancies created by the elevation of Blair and John Prescott to positions of leadership were filled by Margaret Beckett, whom Prescott had defeated for the deputy leadership, and Harriet Harman, who had dropped off the shadow cabinet in 1993 but had been kept on by John Smith in her post of shadow chief secretary to the Treasury. In

1995, the story was much the same: with an extra member elected to increase women's representation, Jack Cunningham was voted off (but given a job of shadow cabinet rank as national heritage spokesman) with Clare Short winning a place after years of trying and Tom Clarke making a surprise return. In 1996, when the shadow cabinet election was held only to stop MPs moaning about Harriet Harman's decision to send her son to a grammar school and Labour whips pulled out all the stops to ensure the re-election of all sitting members, the beneficiary from Joan Lestor's decision to retire was none other than Cunningham.

Blair was, of course, able to shuffle the pack, but even here he was for the most part cautious. The big question in 1994 was what was going to happen to Prescott, Gordon Brown and Robin Cook. Blair decided to keep Brown as shadow chancellor, give Cook the job of shadow foreign secretary and allow Prescott not to shadow any particular government minister. Each was subsequently allocated a key strategic role, with Brown taking overall charge of the campaign, Cook overseeing policy development and Prescott dealing with campaigning in the regions and key seats. Otherwise, the reshuffle was notable only for the promotions of Jack Straw (from environment spokesman to shadow home secretary), Mo Mowlam (from national heritage to Northern Ireland) and David Blunkett (from health to education), and the demotion of Ann Taylor (from education to shadow leader of the house). Blair promoted Andrew Smith to shadow chief secretary to the Treasury but apart from that his distribution of front-bench posts was conservative, with promotion of the 1992 intake confined to the whips' office.

The 1995 reshuffle was bigger, with Margaret Beckett replacing Cunningham at trade and industry, Donald Dewar moving from social security to chief whip, Short ousting the out-of-favour Michael Meacher at transport, Chris Smith moving to social security from national heritage and Harman taking health. Several of the 1992 intake, among them Stephen Byers, John Denham, Peter Mandelson and Barbara Roche, were given junior front-bench posts for the first time. In 1996, Smith and Harman swapped jobs, Short was demoted from transport to overseas development and Meacher was moved again (from employment to environment), with more junior posts going to young MPs. Mandelson was given a job with shadow cabinet rank because of his role in the election campaign.

On the NEC, where the seven-member constituency section was elected by one member, one vote for the first time in the year Blair became leader, the continuity was almost as remarkable. Robin Cook, David Blunkett, Gordon Brown, Dennis Skinner and Diane Abbott were elected for the constituency section each year between 1994 and 1997, with Jack Straw winning a place in 1994 only to lose it in 1995 to Mo Mowlam because of the introduction of a quota to increase women's representation. There was more turnover in the membership of the twelve-member trade union section, elected by the trade union block vote at the party conference, mainly as a result of retirements (although Tom Sawyer left to become Labour's general secretary). But in the five-member women's section, the only change was that Hilary Armstrong lost her place in 1994 to Margaret Beckett, then regained it in 1996 after Joan Lestor retired. John Evans, representing the socialist societies, retired in 1996, to be replaced by Ian McCartney.

Yet although the people in the shadow cabinet and NEC remained much the same, the roles of the two bodies did not. Blair's period as leader of the opposition saw a massive increase in the power both of the leader's office and of the 'big four' Labour politicians – Blair himself, Brown, Cook and Prescott – at the expense of the shadow cabinet and the NEC.

John Smith had led Labour very much in collegiate fashion. Although he was prepared to fight hard to get his way when necessary, as he showed over OMOV, and was by no means hostile to the idea that Labour should have a professional communications machine both to test public opinion and to advise on strategy, he did not see the need to centralize all power in the party or give a privileged position to outside experts in policy or political marketing. Smith believed that Neil Kinnock had been much too cliquish and confrontational in his attitude to colleagues and that the Shadow Communications Agency had acquired far too much influence before the 1992 general election. On becoming leader, he made a point of running an inclusive operation, tolerating dissent to a far greater extent than Kinnock ever had and working for the most part through the shadow cabinet and the NEC, letting party headquarters at Walworth Road get on with its job unmolested most of the time. The SCA was disbanded, and Peter Mandelson found himself out of the loop.

But Blair had different ideas. Although he had his criticisms of the way the SCA had operated in the 1992 election, he had long been a believer in the central role of marketing in modern politics and was a long-term admirer and personal friend of Mandelson. He was also wary of the shadow cabinet and the NEC, which he considered unreliable and too unwieldy for the rapid decision-making required by campaigning in the television age, and he had nothing but scorn for Walworth Road, not least because the party's general secretary, Larry Whitty, had been on the other side of the argument on OMOV in 1992–3. Soon after becoming leader he removed Whitty from his position, replacing him with the more malleable Tom Sawyer; Whitty was rescued by Prescott and put in charge of liaison with Labour's MEPs and its European sister parties.

Just before becoming leader Blair had declared, 'I don't like cliques. They are dangerous, insular, exclusive and politically unhelpful.'[66] But once he was installed it was a different story. He immediately set about reinforcing his private office and creating an inner circle of advisers. As head of his private office, Blair kept on Anji Hunter, an old friend from his schooldays who had started working for him in the Commons in 1988. He hired David Miliband, a young researcher from the IPPR who had acted as secretary of the Commission on Social Justice, as head of policy, and Alastair Campbell, the former political editor of the *Daily Mirror* who at the time of his appointment was assistant editor of *Today*, as press secretary.[67] They were later joined by Jonathan Powell, who left his job as a career diplomat to become Blair's chief of staff, and Derek Scott, a City economist and a former adviser to the Callaghan government who had defected to the SDP, who was appointed economics adviser.[68] The other key members of the private office were press officers Tim Allan and Hilary Coffman and advisers Geoff Norris, Sally Morgan and Pat McFadden.[69] All were appointed as staffers at Number Ten Downing Street after the 1997 election.

Campbell, Scott and Powell were controversial figures –
Campbell for his bullying manner with journalists and willingness
to act as a public figure after Blair appointed him press secretary,
Scott for his former allegiance to the SDP and his economic conservatism (see chapter 2), and Powell for his orthodoxy on foreign
policy. More controversial by far, however, was Blair's reliance on
Mandelson and various outsiders for advice on policy and strategy.

On policy, the key advisers were Roger Liddle, Geoff Mulgan
and Patricia Hewitt. Liddle was another former adviser to the
Callaghan government who had defected to the SDP; in 1996 he
was co-author with Mandelson of *The Blair Revolution*, the nearest
thing the Blair Labour Party had before the 1997 election to an
intellectual apologia;[70] Mulgan, a former adviser to Gordon
Brown, was director of the think-tank Demos;[71] and Hewitt had
been one of the mainstays of Neil Kinnock's political machine
when he was Labour leader, playing a key role in the Shadow
Communications Agency and in the IPPR, where she was deputy
director from 1989 to 1994 before landing a job as head of
research with Andersen Consulting.[72] Both Liddle and Mulgan
were taken on to the staff at Number Ten after the 1997 election:
Hewitt is now Labour MP for Leicester West and a racing certainty
for fast-track promotion. Unsurprisingly, Brown, Cook and
Prescott were uneasy about their own influence being usurped by
such a high-powered group and did what they could to bolster
their own positions – in Brown's case by building up his own private office, in Cook's by doing everything in his power to raise the
profile of the National Policy Forum, which he chaired.

It was Blair's use of campaign strategy advisers that caused
him most trouble, however. In spring 1995, Blair held an informal
weekend meeting to discuss strategy at the Hampshire home of
Chris Powell, brother of Jonathan, former chair of the SCA and
chief executive of BMP, Labour's advertising agency, with a group
including Mandelson, Gordon Brown and several other veterans of
the SCA, notably Philip Gould. Prescott was not invited – and hit
the roof when he heard about the meeting after the event. Blair
tried to explain it away, but from then on Prescott and Cook
insisted on being kept informed about everything by Brown and
Blair. Their suspicions that Blair's inner circle was over-reaching

itself were confirmed in September 1995, on the second day of the TUC congress, when the *Guardian* published a confidential strategy document, *The Unfinished Revolution*, written by Philip Gould for Blair earlier in the year. The memorandum was severely embarrassing for Labour: it stated baldly that Labour was 'not ready for government', that it did not have 'a campaigning organization that can secure victory', and that it had neither 'a political project that matches the Thatcher agenda of 1979, nor one . . . to sustain Labour in government and transform Britain'. What really angered Prescott and Cook, however, was its argument that Labour should be restructured as a 'genuine one member, one vote party' – hinting at a definitive break with the trade unions – and its call for a 'unitary command structure leading directly to the party leader', involving 'less but better people, a new culture and a new building', with the leader as 'sole ultimate source of authority'.[73] The fall-out from the Gould memorandum forced Blair to institute regular 'big four' meetings with Brown, Prescott and Cook to ensure that everyone knew exactly what was going on. These meetings became the place where key political decisions were made, and remain a key feature of the Labour government.[74]

Nevertheless, with the exception of making sure that Prescott and Cook were included in the 'unitary command structure', the campaign machine that won so many plaudits during the 1997 election was organized very much along the lines suggested by the Gould memorandum, with Mandelson and Brown playing a central role. In December 1995, Labour took a lease on two floors of Millbank Tower in Westminster, where it installed a hi-tech campaign centre modelled on Bill Clinton's 1992 headquarters – essentially, a large open-plan office with masses of telephones and computers, one of which, Excalibur, housed a giant database of press clippings, texts of political speeches and gossip, which was to be the mainstay of Labour's 'attack and rebuttal' unit. Millbank became the hub of Labour's whole campaign operation, dealing with press and television, analysing opinion polls and focus group research and co-ordinating every aspect of propaganda from mail shots in 'key seats' to the pronouncements of the party's most senior figures. Labour's candidates were more thoroughly drilled than ever before to speak with a single voice.

And of course, despite constant private rows involving the main players, it all worked remarkably well, helped along by excellent organization in the 'key seats'. In the year before John Major announced the date of the 1997 general election, Labour maintained a commanding lead in the opinion polls – wobbling briefly in summer 1996 after various semi-public policy disagreements and Clare Short's complaints about being moved from the job of transport spokeswoman – and won two crucial by-elections, in Staffordshire South East and Wirral South. In the six weeks of the campaign proper, there were occasional gaffes and jitters: Blair's comparison of the taxation powers of Labour's proposed Scottish parliament with those of 'any parish council', a mix-up over whether or not Labour would privatize air traffic control, two rogue polls showing Labour's lead collapsing, one of them putting it at just 5 percentage points. But the Tories' campaign was such a disaster that none of them mattered. Labour looked a certain winner throughout. The first fortnight of the campaign was dominated by Tory 'sleaze', in particular the 'cash-for-questions' affair, and for much of the rest of it the Tories spent as much energy arguing among themselves over Europe as they did campaigning against Labour. If few expected a Labour landslide on the scale that eventually transpired, Blair's victory seemed assured from the beginning of the campaign.

Blair acted quickly to form his government after his stunning election victory. Within hours, he had announced the most important of his cabinet appointments: Gordon Brown as chancellor, Robin Cook as foreign secretary, John Prescott as deputy prime minister in charge of a new 'super-ministry' covering transport, the environment and the regions, Jack Straw as home secretary, Margaret Beckett as President of the Board of Trade, David Blunkett as education secretary and Derry Irvine as Lord Chancellor. Apart from Prescott, all got the jobs they had shadowed in opposition. The same was true of most of the other members of the cabinet, named the next day: Mo Mowlam (Northern Ireland), Harriet Harman (social security), Ann Taylor (leader of the House), Ron Davies (Wales) and Clare Short (international development). Of the others, Donald Dewar, who had been chief whip, became Scottish secretary, and George Robertson, previously shadow Scottish secretary, was given defence, leaving David Clark, previously defence spokesman, the job of chancellor of the Duchy of Lancaster. Frank Dobson was shifted from environment to health, Chris Smith from health to national heritage (soon renamed as culture, media and sport), Jack Cunningham from national heritage to agriculture, and Gavin Strang from agriculture to transport. Two members of the shadow cabinet did not get cabinet seats: Michael Meacher, who became environment minister in Prescott's super-ministry, and Tom Clarke, who became minister for film in the Department of National Heritage. Alistair Darling, who had been outside the shadow cabinet, joined the cabinet as chief secretary to the Treasury. Nick Brown was made chief whip. There was no cabinet place for Derek Foster, who had been privately promised one by Blair when he retired as chief whip in 1995.

There was little remarkable in any of this. Meacher and Clarke had long since been tipped as casualties in Blair's choice of cabinet despite the Parliamentary Labour Party rule that all members of a shadow cabinet should automatically be cabinet members after winning an election. The minor surprise was that they were not joined by Strang and Clark. Far more significant were many of the second-string appointments. Brown, Cook, Prescott, Beckett and Straw each ensured that their departmental teams were heavily weighted towards their own close political allies, but Blair made sure that he had his people in key positions everywhere. Peter Mandelson became minister without portfolio in the Cabinet Office with a role of co-ordinating government policy; Frank Field was made deputy to Harman at social security, with a brief to include 'welfare reform'; and Andrew Smith, Stephen Byers, Kim Howells and Alan Howarth became ministers at the Department of Education and Employment under Blunkett. Blair gave peerages to BP chairman Sir David Simon and his old flatmate Charles Falconer and installed them as minister for trade and competitiveness in Europe at the DTI and solicitor-general respectively.

As soon as the new government's ministers were appointed, it was straight down to business. Within a week of taking office,

Brown had unveiled his plans to make the Bank of England independent, Cook had visited Paris and Bonn and declared that Britain would seek a global ban on landmines, Prescott had announced the phased release of receipts from council house sales to fund new building, and Straw had announced that he would take direct control of the prison service. On 7 May, Blair addressed the Parliamentary Labour Party at a meeting in Church House, Westminster, to warn it of complacency: 'We are not the masters. The people are the masters. We are the people's servants. Forget that, and the people will soon show that what the electorate give, the electorate can take away.' The next day, the cabinet met for the first time, and on 14 May the new government laid out an eighteen-month legislative programme in its first Queen's Speech. It promised no fewer than twenty-two bills, the most important of them to fulfil the 'early pledges' that had been at the centre of Labour's campaign since summer 1996 – reduction of class sizes, faster sentencing of young criminals, a windfall tax on the profits of privatized utilities to pay for an assault on youth unemployment, referendums on devolution to Scotland and Wales. Other promises included incorporation of the European Convention on Human Rights into British law, creation of a Low Pay Commission to determine a minimum wage, a referendum on a new authority for London and White Papers on freedom of information legislation, international development and a ban on tobacco advertising.

As if these measures were not enough, the new government continued to announce initiatives that did not require legislation. At the Foreign Office, Cook produced a mission statement giving a high priority to human rights and environmentalism in foreign policy, announced that Britain would rejoin UNESCO, lifted the ban on trade unions at the government's GCHQ communications headquarters and began a review of arms export policy. At the Home Office, Straw unveiled plans to appoint a 'drugs czar' to lead an anti-drugs campaign, announced a clampdown on racial violence, said that fine defaulters would no longer be jailed and relaxed various immigration rules. At the Department for Education and Employment, Blunkett put forward plans for 'hit squads' to be sent in to failing schools, named eighteen schools that were failing and set up a new school standards body. In Northern Ireland, Mo Mowlam made an attempt to revive the peace process and Blair declared his openness to talks with Sinn Fein.

By the last week of May, Blair was confidently striding across the international political stage, visiting his fellow European heads of government in the Netherlands, then attending the summit in France at which Russian president Boris Yeltsin agreed to NATO expansion, then playing host as US president Bill Clinton visited London. After that he returned to domestic politics with a keynote speech on getting single mothers off the dole. Next came a trip to Malmo in Sweden for the congress of the Party of European Socialists, where Blair warned leaders of Labour's sister parties that they must 'modernize or die', then the Amsterdam European Union summit, from which he emerged claiming that he had won an historic victory, then the Denver G8 summit, then the New York Earth Summit, at which he delivered a rousing appeal for action on global warming. The day after he arrived home from the US, he announced a peace plan for Northern Ireland. On 2 July, Brown delivered his first budget, in which, as expected, the central measure was imposition of a windfall tax to pay for Labour's much-vaunted 'welfare-to-work' scheme.

Blair's 'first hundred days' were not all plain sailing. The Tories and constitutional reformers complained that the government was behaving as an elective dictatorship after it forced its devolution referendum legislation through the Commons on a guillotine. The new Labour MP for Govan, Mohammed Sarwar, was alleged to have bribed an opponent during the election campaign and was suspended from the Parliamentary Labour Party pending an inquiry; the same fate befell the veteran MP for Liverpool West Derby, Bob Wareing, after revelations of his links with Serbia during the Bosnian war. At the end of June, the MP for Blaenau Gwent, Llew Smith, caused a minor storm when he claimed that Welsh secretary Ron Davies had threatened him with expulsion if he opposed the government's plans for Welsh devolution. There were reports of divisions in the cabinet over the millennium exhibition and over Scotland; there was controversy over Lord Simon's retention of BP shares after becoming a minister;

and at the end of July Labour lost the first by-election of the new parliament in Uxbridge after parachuting in a Blairite candidate against the wishes of the local party. The MP for Paisley South, Gordon McMaster, committed suicide, leaving a note claiming that colleagues had smeared his reputation; and Robin Cook left his wife for his secretary. In Northern Ireland, the government's standing among the nationalist population was damaged by its handling of the unionist marching season – and then its credibility among unionists slumped because of its response to the IRA ceasefire. But none of this did serious harm to the popularity of the new government with the people who had elected it. As the Tories attempted to recover from the catastrophe of their election defeat and the damage done by their subsequent leadership election, Blair enjoyed an approval rating in the opinion polls never matched by any prime minister before.

How the government will look two years into office is quite a different matter. There can be no doubting Blair's ambitions for his government. He believes that it can conquer unemployment with its active supply-side policies, preside over steady non-inflationary growth, act as a catalyst for reform of the EU and transform the welfare state to make it both more effective and more affordable. In doing all this, he believes, Labour can establish itself as a hegemonic party for a generation. It is just possible that he is right. But Labour will be judged by results – and as we argue in subsequent chapters, in many areas of policy there are serious tensions between the goals that New Labour proclaims and the means it has chosen to achieve them.

2

UNLIMITED SUPPLY
GORDON BROWN AND
THE ECONOMY

All budgets are the subject of speculation, but none in recent memory attracted quite as much as Gordon Brown's at the beginning of July 1997. The main reason was simply that it was the first budget delivered by a Labour chancellor since Denis Healey in April 1979, but expectations were also augmented by Brown's extraordinary first weeks in his post and by the peculiar disjunction between Labour's election promises and the economic circumstances he faced.

No other cabinet minister in the Blair administration had a more immediate impact than the chancellor of the exchequer. Just four days after arriving at the Treasury, he stunned everyone by announcing that he was giving the Bank of England 'operational responsibility' for setting interest rates. A fortnight later, he surprised the City with his plans for shaking up the whole system of financial regulation. He then announced that the Treasury's books would be independently audited – the result of which was the adoption of new assumptions about the state of public finances that were significantly more pessimistic than the ones on which Kenneth Clarke had based his last budget as chancellor in John Major's government in November 1996. By the time that he announced that his budget would be delivered on 2 July, Brown's ambition seemed boundless.

More important, however, he was confronted with a set of problems that were not the ones he had expected between 1993 and 1995 when he first formulated the economic policies on which Labour won the 1997 election. Then, Britain was only just pulling out of a deep recession. Although unemployment was falling, it remained above 2.5 million, however it was counted. Public sector borrowing to cope with the effects of recession was also falling, partly as a result of economic recovery but also because of swingeing tax increases in 1993 and 1994. The housing market was in the doldrums. Memories were fresh of 'Black Wednesday', 16 September 1992, when the pound crashed out of the exchange rate mechanism of the European Monetary System, and of the 1992 general election campaign, in which the Tories had mercilessly attacked Labour for its tax-raising plans. It was in these circumstances that Brown formulated a programme that emphasized Labour's antipathy to devaluation and tax increases. At its centre was a scheme to reduce unemployment, to be paid for by a one-off tax on the 'excess profits' of the privatized utilities. With this one exception, Labour would not 'tax and spend' – a promise firmed up in early 1997 to a guarantee that a Labour government would stick to the Tories' spending plans for its first two years in office and would not increase either the basic or the top rate of income tax.

It all made good political sense right up to election day. In economic terms, however, Labour's programme looked less convincing as time went by. When Labour came to power in 1997, Britain was booming. The level of unemployment as measured by the numbers claiming benefit was down to 1.6 million and falling – not far from its lowest point at the end of the 1980s boom. Consumer spending was on the increase, house prices were rising and inflation appeared to be edging up. The pound, meanwhile, was soaring in value against other European currencies, leading to worries among manufacturers that they would soon be priced out of many of their most important export markets.

Particularly after Brown's decision to give the Bank of England control over interest rate decisions, it seemed to many observers that he would have to put up taxes in the budget to dampen the boom. The only other way of doing it – leaving the

Bank to increase interest rates – would not only make credit more expensive for business but also lead to further appreciation of sterling. What's more, there was growing concern that spending limits inherited from the Tories were impossibly tight if Labour was to have any chance of fulfilling its promises to improve state education and the National Health Service.

In his budget speech, Brown gave plenty of indications that he was fully aware of the dangers of the economy over-heating. 'Britain cannot afford a recurrence of the all-too-familiar pattern of previous recoveries: accelerating consumer spending and borrowing side by side with skills shortages, capacity constraints, increased imports and rising inflation,' he told the Commons. 'Already there are warning signs that the pattern could be repeated. In similar circumstances, some of my predecessors have ignored the signs, while others have deluded themselves that growth, however unbalanced, was evidence of their success. I will not ignore the warning signs and I will not repeat past mistakes.' He also shared the worries of industry about the effects of high interest rates and a high exchange rate. 'My goal,' he said, 'is to ease inflationary pressures without damage to industrial and exporting prospects and to do so in a way that is consistent with our long-term objective of high and stable growth and employment. In this way, we can moderate the upward pressure on interest rates and on the exchange rate as well as further our objective of sustainable public finances. I have therefore decided to tighten fiscal policy.'

But the tightening that he announced was small. The two major sources of new revenue he introduced were the long-anticipated windfall tax, to raise £4.8 billion over two years, and abolition of the tax rebates received by pension funds on dividends on their investments, to raise £6.2 billion in the same period. Both were measures that would primarily hit spending on investment. His only tax increases targeted on consumers were minor – higher petrol taxes, a reduction of mortgage tax relief and higher stamp duties on sales of high-priced property – and he actually cut one element of consumer taxation by reducing VAT on fuel. Otherwise, the budget's main measures consisted of a symbolic pro-business gesture, a small cut in corporation tax, and substantial increases in spending on education and health, paid for by higher-than-expected growth in 1996–7 and a raid on the contingency reserves.

Brown's fiscal measures were enough to keep public sector borrowing on a steady downward course, but it was clear that interest rates would continue to take the strain of containing inflation. Exporters, along with many economists, were unimpressed, as indeed were the utilities and pension funds that would pay most of the extra taxes. But the budget went down wonderfully with the people at whom it was really directed: Labour MPs – apart from the hard left – and voters. Brown had managed to keep all the promises he made before the election. He had not raised income tax, even by the back door, and he had cut VAT on fuel. He had set up the welfare-to-work scheme, paid for by the windfall tax, that was one of Labour's 'five early pledges'. And, best of all, he had found more cash for schools and hospitals. Even if the economics of the budget were questionable, the politics were near to perfect.

Brown has been the consummate politician for a long time. His political career began in the late 1960s as a student at Edinburgh University. Born in 1951, the son of a Church of Scotland minister in the Fife town of Kirkcaldy, he was exceptionally bright. He took his O-levels at fourteen and his Highers (the Scottish equivalent of A-levels) a year later; he went up to university to study history at the age of sixteen, the beneficiary of a 'fast-track' scheme designed to increase Fife's low rate of university admissions. Although he was interested in politics from an early age – he claims to have volunteered at the age of twelve to canvass for Labour after seeing Sir Alec Douglas-Home speaking in the 1963 Kinross and West Perthshire by-election campaign, and has often talked about how his father made him and his two brothers aware of poverty and other social problems – his boyhood passion was sport. He played tennis and football, was a member of his school's rugby team and sprinted in the Scottish schoolboys' athletics championships. But his participation in contact sports was brought to an abrupt end after he was kicked in the head on the school rugby field. He complained of impaired vision, but it was not until some months later, a week into his university course, that he was diagnosed as having seriously damaged both eyes. He came close to losing his sight. After four operations, doctors managed to save his right eye but not his left.

Brown missed much of his first two years at Edinburgh University as a consequence, but once he returned to his studies he threw himself into student politics and journalism. He got involved with the Edinburgh University Student Publications Board, and quickly established himself as the star columnist and feature-writer on its paper, *Student*. In keeping with the spirit of the times, he was very much on the left, a staunch opponent of apartheid and a supporter of greater student involvement in the running of the university. His biggest story – indeed, the scoop that made his name with his peers – was an exposé, in late 1970, of the university's investments in South Africa a matter of weeks after its principal, Michael Swann, had declared that the university did not have 'any interests in companies known to be active in support of apartheid'.[1]

Unlike many of his comrades, who flirted with alternative culture and various brands of revolutionary politics, Brown joined the Labour Party in 1969 and stuck with it. He was a hit with the girls and by no means a prude. But he also worked hard at his studies, gaining a first in 1970 and staying on as a post-graduate; he grew his hair long but never grew a beard, and he habitually wore a tie. Even at the age of twenty he was a hard-headed political realist. In 1971, when most of the student left saw the work-in at Upper Clyde Shipbuilders as the start of the long-awaited British revolution, Brown wrote a feature for *Student* in which he lambasted the 'alternative society seekers, Trotskyist students and liberal documentary makers' who had flocked to Clydeside to visit UCS. 'The trendies,' he argued, 'are looking in vain for their kind of revolution. While they may plan the final end of capitalism, the mass meetings, George Square demos and the fighting talk of the stewards should not belie the real campaign on the Clyde; for this is a work-in not workers' control, an attempt to save jobs not a demand for the abolition of private ownership. The outsiders have been reading too many books and not meeting enough people.'[2]

He was also a pragmatist when it came to student politics. He and his friends on the EUSPB were critical of the gesture politics of the Student Representation Council, the nearest thing Edinburgh had to a student union. They ran the publications board as an autonomous body, eventually turning it into an independent publishing company and, in the wake of the South African investments scandal, used *Student* to campaign for the election of a student candidate, Jonathan Wills, as rector of the university – a position, elected by students, that had become a token post usually filled by a celebrity, but which carried with it the unused constitutional power to chair the University Court, the university's governing body. Wills was elected rector in 1971, beating the humorist Willy Rushton, and duly took the chair of the Court, but decided to serve only one year of his three-year term. Brown, by now a post-graduate, was the obvious candidate to succeed him as the students' champion – which he duly did in November 1972.

Brown's three years as rector were marked by constant battles with the university authorities, including a legal case brought by him after the Court voted not to allow him to chair meetings. He won, then blocked the university authorities' attempt to change the rules to prevent him being chair. (The clinching factor was opposition to the proposed rule-change from the chancellor of the university, the Duke of Edinburgh, who just happened to be the godfather of Brown's then girlfriend, Princess Margarita of Romania.[3]) The experience turned him into a skilled political operator. 'It was quite a revelation to me to see that politics was less about ideals and more about manoeuvres,' he said twenty years later.[4] His exploits developed his reputation far beyond the university. For his last big project as rector, a collection of essays on Scottish politics, *The Red Paper on Scotland*, published by the EUSPB in 1975, he was able to call on the services of an astonishing number of the Scottish left intelligentsia's movers and shakers – among them the MPs Robin Cook and Jim Sillars, the playwright John McGrath and the left-nationalist historian and political theorist Tom Nairn.[5]

The Red Paper was a major *succès d'estime*: Scottish left-wingers of a certain age enthuse about it even now. It is hardly surprising, given the circumstances of its production, that Brown's introduction to the book is not the sort of thing of which New Labour would approve. It is heavily influenced by Marxism, and its proposals for 'the extension of self-management at the workplace', 'a planned economy' and 'public control of banks, insurance and pension companies . . . without compensation' would today cause Labour's National Executive Committee to question the suitability of its author as a by-election candidate. But in the context of its time, Brown's ideas were not outrageously leftist. The Marxism from which he borrowed was not that of the Communist Party's Stalinist old guard – then still a significant force in Scottish left politics – let alone the Trotskyism embraced by so many of his contemporaries on the English student left. Rather, it was a respectably reformist interpretation of the thinking of the Italian Marxist Antonio Gramsci.[6]

For all its fiery rhetoric, Brown's essay explicitly rejected both the belief in impending economic catastrophe and the insurrectionism that characterized the Trotskyist left; and it criticized the old Labour and Stalinist idea that nationalization was a panacea. 'Socialists must neither place their faith in an Armageddon of capitalist collapse nor in nationalization alone,' wrote Brown. 'For if the Jacobin notion of a vanguard making revolution on behalf of working people relates to a backward society (and prefigures an authoritarian and bureaucratic state), then the complexity of modern society requires a far-reaching movement of people and ideas, acting as a stimulus for people to see beyond the immediacy and fragmentation of their existing conditions.'

More important, Brown also gave firm backing to Labour's policy of devolution for Scotland, which at the time was under fire from both nationalists and defenders of the *status quo*, including many in its own ranks. Soon after Labour published its plans for devolution in late 1975, one *Red Paper* contributor, Jim Sillars, left Labour to set up the left-nationalist Scottish Labour Party, which temporarily attracted significant support before collapsing in sectarian feuding.[7] Another *Red Paper* contributor, Robin Cook, became a prominent defender of the *status quo*, second only to Tam Dalyell as a spokesman for Labour's dissident anti-devolutionists. Although, as the historian Christopher Harvie (a close political ally of Brown in the 1970s but now in the SNP) remarks, Brown was in 1975 'an altogether fiercer person' than he is today, even then he was above all a party loyalist and a gradualist suspicious of the supposed benefits of instant solutions.[8]

Brown's stance on devolution was his ticket to respectability with the Labour Party establishment in Scotland. It won him the approval of John Smith, the minister in charge of Labour's devolution legislation between 1976 and 1978 and, like Brown, a Labour Party member in Edinburgh South. It was also a crucial factor in getting him elected in 1977 to Labour's Scottish executive. By now he had a 'real' job – as a lecturer at the Glasgow College of Technology – but nevertheless he applied himself to politics with continued zeal.

In the run-up to the March 1979 devolution referendum, Brown was charged with running Labour's campaign in favour of a 'yes' vote – and he was adjudged by his seniors in the hierarchy to have done a good job in the face of bitter opposition from Labour's anti-devolutionists. In May 1979 he fought Edinburgh South, unsuccessfully, in a first attempt at getting to Westminster, and after that landed a prestigious job as a current affairs journalist with Scottish Television, then, as now, a bastion of Labour's hegemony in Scotland. By 1983, when he was elected as MP for the safe seat of Dunfermline East and took over as chair of Labour in Scotland, Brown was being tipped for great things by many of his colleagues in the Scottish party.

Brown settled in quickly at Westminster, joining the centre-left Tribune Group of MPs and making sure that he got to know all the right people in the Parliamentary Labour Party and the media. (It is a myth that Brown is dour. Despite appearances, he is genuinely charming with a ready sense of humour, although he keeps his private life very much to himself and does not take kindly to anyone who disagrees with him. As a glad-hander in sympathetic crowds, he is second to none.) He rapidly acquired a name for himself by embarrassing the government by publicizing leaks, and he put in some hard work on the Commons select committee on employment. It was little surprise that he was plucked off the back benches after only two years, at the suggestion of John Smith, then trade and industry spokesman (1984–7), and given a post as a junior member of his team, responsible for regional affairs.

He shone in his junior front-bench role and, with a little help from Peter Mandelson, then Labour's director of communications, started appearing regularly on television as a Labour spokesman. It was again no surprise when he was elected to the shadow cabinet in July 1987, at the tender age of thirty-six, or when – again at the suggestion of John Smith, Neil Kinnock's choice as shadow chancellor – he was given the job of shadow chief secretary to the Treasury, second-in-command to Smith on the Labour economic policy team.

Brown first came to widespread public notice when he stood in for Smith after the latter's first heart attack in autumn 1988: after a stunning parliamentary performance against chancellor Nigel Lawson on the autumn financial statement, the quality papers ran admiring profiles of the 'high-flying son of the manse' (*Observer*), a 'good-looking and an accomplished television performer' (*The Times*), who was 'already talked of as Neil Kinnock's successor' (*Guardian*). Two days after his *tour de force* he topped the poll in the shadow cabinet election. But it was in his behind-the-scenes work that Brown made himself really indispensable. Labour had been dogged in the period before the 1987 election by the Tories' relentless assault on its spending plans, which they claimed amounted to £35 billion, and Kinnock had decided that the way to stop it happening again was to make the shadow chief secretary a member of the shadow cabinet, with the power to excise from policy statements and front-benchers' speeches anything that might be interpreted as an uncosted-but-costable spending pledge. He needed someone to do the job who would not be afraid to stand up to colleagues, even under intense pressure, and John Smith thought Brown was the ideal choice. Unlike Smith, who was a stalwart of the old Labour right Solidarity group, Brown was still at this time (and for a couple of years afterwards) strongly identified with the soft left. He was elected to the shadow cabinet on the Tribune Group slate; he was a contributor to the *Tribune* newspaper; and he had just published a sympathetic biography of James Maxton (based on his PhD), the left-wing romantic who led the Independent Labour Party out of the Labour Party in 1931.[9] Even so, Smith believed that Brown could be trusted to do what he was told.

Brown did not let him down. In spring 1989, the policy review set up by Kinnock in late 1987 – which had in its first phase produced a vague statement of values and goals, *Social Justice and Economic Efficiency* – finally came up with detailed draft documents, most of them stuffed with policy ideas that meant increased public spending. The new shadow chief secretary simply removed every proposal from them that could be said to carry a cost, with two exceptions: a pledge to increase pensions and child benefit as soon as Labour was in office, and a promise of a national minimum wage of £2.80 an hour.

The shadow cabinet soft left grumbled, but with local and European elections imminent, did so only in private, and at first the exercise seemed to have worked a treat. In summer 1989, John Major, the conservative chief secretary, asked the Cabinet to get departmental civil servants to cost the policies in the document synthesizing the work of the first two phases of the policy review, *Meet the Challenge, Make the Change*. One of the responses, from the permanent secretary at the Department of the Environment, Sir Terry Heiser, was leaked to Brown by a civil servant annoyed at doing Tory party work. 'The review document has been drafted much more carefully than on some earlier occasions,' wrote Heiser. 'The promises do not readily lend themselves to precise costings. And in most cases the assumptions you have asked us to cost are vulnerable to counter-attack from the opposition.'[10]

Of course, in the end, all Brown's efforts – and those of his successor, Margaret Beckett, whose reiteration of the promise that Labour would spend money over and above the pledges in its minimal programme only 'as resources allow' was dubbed 'Beckett's Law' by the shadow cabinet soft left, a tag taken up by the Tories – failed to protect Labour against Conservative assault. Labour fought the 1992 general election on a carefully costed, modestly redistributive economic policy. Its immediate programme was laid out at the beginning of the campaign by Smith's shadow budget, the main spending promise being £3.5 billion for increases in pensions and child benefit that had been left alone by Brown in the first batch of policy review documents back in 1989. (The national minimum wage did not figure in the shadow budget, but the manifesto promised that it would be set at £3.40 an hour.) To pay for the pension and child benefit increases, along with a modest job-creation and infrastructural investment package, Smith proposed the introduction of a new 50 per cent band of income tax on incomes over £40,000 and the abolition of the ceiling on national insurance contributions.

At the time, the shadow budget was hailed by just about every commentator in the quality press as a model of moderation and responsibility. Yet the Tories still felt able to tar Labour with the brush of profligacy, by pumping out propaganda telling voters that Kinnock's spending plans would mean giant tax increases all round to pay for £35 billion extra public spending. It may have been unfair but, with the help of a massive advertising campaign and the efforts of the Tory tabloids, it had the desired effect. For Brown, the election defeat meant one thing: the clampdown on tax-and-spend had not gone far enough. According to one former adviser, he had long harboured private doubts about the wisdom of going into an election promising income tax increases. Now he resolved that Labour would never get caught the same way again.

In summer 1989, however, the immediate problem faced by Kinnock and Smith was not the Tories' costings of Labour's plans and scares about tax but the general direction being taken by the main policy review group on the economy. Chaired by Bryan Gould, the trade and industry spokesman since the 1987 shadow cabinet reshuffle, the group had Brown and John Eatwell, Kinnock's economic adviser, as members (although Brown was an irregular attender). But it had not delivered what the leadership wanted.

Kinnock and Smith were convinced that Labour needed more than just vigilance against uncosted promises. The policy review, they believed, had to convince voters not only that they would not have to pay more tax but also had to leave behind for good Labour's reputation for incompetence and irresponsibility in economic management. If voters continued to think that Labour was soft on inflation and keen on heavy-handed interventionist industrial policies, particularly nationalization, the party would never win an election again. Equally important, if the electorate was persuaded of Labour's case but the markets were not, a Labour government would be hammered as soon as it took office.

Taking this view, which was backed, by and large, by the academic and City economists that Smith had gathered together in an advisory group,[11] toughness on spending was not just a matter of avoiding electoral hostages to fortune on tax, it was also a demonstration to the markets and the electorate that Labour was serious about price stability – unlike the Tory government, which by early 1988 was struggling to contain the inflationary effects of the mid-1980s boom – and would not countenance a 'dash for growth'. To reinforce the message, Labour also had to show that it had turned its back on devaluation. In other words, Labour had to embrace the macroeconomic orthodoxy of the day, explicitly distancing itself from anything that smacked of Keynesian reflation. Smith, a long-standing pro-European who had defied a three-line Labour whip to vote for entry into the European Community in October 1971, decided that the party's salvation lay in Europe. If it backed sterling's entry into the exchange rate mechanism (ERM) of the European Monetary System (EMS), its credibility as a party of fiscal and monetary rectitude would be unquestionable.

Bryan Gould's ideas were very different. Against the out-and-out pragmatism of Kinnock and Smith, he believed that Labour should engage in an ideological assault on the Tories, based on a critique of British capitalism and a radical alternative programme. Although no enthusiast for 1940s-style nationalization – he outraged Labour traditionalists in 1987 by backing employee share ownership plans (ESOPs), an idea that sounded suspiciously Thatcherite to the old left, and was strongly pro-market – he was prepared to make concessions to the unions that wanted the return of at least some privatized utilities to public ownership. He was a long-standing critic of the role of the City of London in the British economy and a supporter of a strongly interventionist industrial policy. Most important of all, he was a convinced Keynesian reflationist and Eurosceptic, fundamentally opposed to joining the ERM and to European economic and monetary union. Devaluation was the key to his whole approach: he believed that Britain's major economic problem for most of the post-war period had been an uncompetitive exchange rate.[12]

Meet the Challenge, Make the Change, published in May 1989, was dominated by Gould's ideas. It gave strong backing to the market and competition, which it described as 'essential in meeting the demands of the consumer, promoting efficiency and stimulating innovation, and often the best means of securing all the myriad, incremental changes which are needed to take the economy forward', and included several recommendations for 'supply-side' measures to encourage training and investment which were perfectly acceptable to Kinnock and Smith. But it was highly critical of the deflationary implications of ERM membership and, with its talk of 'an uncompetitive currency', at least hinted that Labour would devalue rather than shadow the Deutschmark as chancellor Nigel Lawson was then doing. In its enthusiasm for 'raising demand at a sustainable and predictable rate', it was essentially Keynesian – although 'sustainable and predictable' did suggest that Labour had no intention of engineering a spectacular boom. *Meet the Challenge* also backed a majority state shareholding in British Telecom (much to the annoyance of Kinnock) and the return of other privatized utilities to public ownership; and it proposed an interventionist 'Medium Term Industrial Strategy' (to be run by a massively strengthened Department of Trade and Industry with powers similar to the Japanese Ministry of International Trade and Industry) and two new institutions, British Technology Enterprise and the British Investment Bank, to break the hold of City 'short-termism' on investment.[13]

The document went to the Labour conference in October, where it was passed with minimal dissent. But by then Gould's time was up with Kinnock and Smith. During summer 1989, Smith, Eatwell and Brown had decided privately that the time was ripe for Labour to come out for membership of the ERM – so Gould had to go. Within a month of the conference, Smith had not only declared in principle for the ERM but had also outlined Labour's conditions for joining: 'entry at an effective rate, adequate central bank swap arrangements to tackle speculative attack, and agreement on a strategy for growth'.[14] In the November 1989 shadow cabinet reshuffle, Gould was replaced by Brown as trade and industry spokesman and moved to environment. Brown took over as chair of the policy review group on macroeconomics, and a new sub-committee to oversee every aspect of economic policy was established under Smith's chairmanship.

By May 1990, when Labour produced a new overall policy document, *Looking to the Future*, Brown had erased all traces of Gould's influence on economic policy.[15] Of the privatized utilities, only water was marked out for a return to some form of public ownership. The grand schemes for intervention had been toned down to become small-scale institutional reforms, and Labour was demanding ERM membership 'at the earliest opportunity'. 'There will be no irresponsible dash for growth under Labour,' the document stated, repeating one of Smith's favourite soundbites. 'We will not spend, nor will we promise to spend, more than Britain can afford.'[16] Labour welcomed the government's decision in October 1990 to put sterling into the ERM at a rate of DM2.95 to the pound. By the time of the 1992 manifesto, *It's Time to Get Britain Working Again*, water was earmarked for public control, not public ownership, and Labour's industrial policy – largely written by Brown – was essentially a programme for education and training and tax-breaks for investment. 'To curb inflation,' the manifesto proclaimed, 'Labour will maintain the value of the pound within the European exchange rate mechanism.' As for European economic and monetary union, the timetable and conditions for which had been laid down by the Maastricht Treaty at the end of the previous year, Labour would abandon the Tories' opt-out from Maastricht's Social Chapter and 'play an active part' in negotiations on a single currency.[17]

Inelegantly but accurately, Eatwell summed up the changes he had helped to bring about in a paper published just before the 1992 general election:

> 1. Abandonment of the idea that short-term macroeconomic management is the key to the maintenance of full employment. It is argued that it is no longer possible to have Keynesianism in one country, and hence fine-tuning should be replaced by a search for macroeconomic stability as a framework for long-term investment . . .

2. Replacement of hostility towards the European Community, in which the EC was seen as an inhibition upon Labour's policies, with an enthusiasm for the EC as an arena within which Labour's objectives can best be attained . . .

3. Abandonment of the idea that nationalisation of an industry is necessarily the best way to achieve efficiency, and its replacement by the proposition that regulation may achieve the same results.

4. Replacement of the idea that industrial policy should involve the government in making tactical managerial decisions with the proposition that the state should provide the 'well-springs' of growth – skills, research and development, infrastructure – within a broad strategy of accumulation . . .[18]

The most important point is the first. In ditching Keynesianism in one country, Eatwell, Smith and Brown had abandoned the very core of Labour thinking about political economy since the war. What happened under Tony Blair between 1994 and 1997 was, by comparison, just tinkering.

To grasp the full significance of this, it is necessary here to take a short diversion to look at the influence of John Maynard Keynes – or rather, the ideas associated with his name – on Labour's thinking about the economy.

Keynes (1883–1946) was a Liberal, at best lukewarm about Labour for most of his life as a public intellectual. He hated its class politics – 'The class war will find me on the side of the educated bourgeoisie,' he once famously declared[19] – and was dismissive of its enthusiasm for public ownership. 'The Labour Party has got tied up with all sorts of encumbering and old-fashioned luggage,' he wrote in 1927. 'They respond to anti-Communist rubbish with anti-capitalist rubbish. The consequence of all that is that, whether in or out of office, the business of orderly evolution seems likely to remain with the Liberal Party.'[20]

He was taken seriously by at least part of the Labour intelligentsia from the point at which he resigned from a key Treasury
job in 1919 to write the book that first brought him into the
public eye. *The Economic Consequences of the Peace* was a polemical assault on the Versailles Treaty's insistence that Germany pay
giant sums to the victorious powers from the First World War as
reparations for war damage. But in the mid-1920s, his devalua-
tionist argument against a British return to the gold standard –
most dramatically expressed in *The Economic Consequences of Mr
Churchill* (1925) – found few takers in the Labour Party. The
same fate befell his case for public works programmes, financed
by government borrowing, to alleviate unemployment, elaborated
with the Liberal leader David Lloyd George. The 1928 Liberal
'Yellow Book', *Britain's Industrial Future*, the most comprehensive
account of the Keynes–Lloyd George position, was shunned by
Labour.

Part of the reason for the cool reception was straightforward
political tribalism, but Keynes was also at odds both with the
unstinting *laissez-faire* economic orthodoxy of the Labour leadership and with the Labour left's crude Marxist conviction that
capitalism had entered a final apocalyptic crisis from which it
could not possibly recover. The dominant figure in Labour economic policy-making in the 1920s was Philip Snowden, chancellor
of the exchequer in Ramsay MacDonald's 1924 and 1929–31
Labour governments, a fierce proponent of free trade, low public
spending and maintenance of the value of the currency. On the
left, although the Independent Labour Party at least saw the point
of a radical reformist programme based on increasing the overall
level of demand in the economy, the consensus was that nothing
short of socialism, more and more imagined as a command economy on the Soviet model, had any hope of success.[21]

Even in the 1920s, however, Keynes had his followers in
Labour circles, most notably Ernest Bevin, the right-wing general
secretary of the Transport and General Workers' Union, and Sir
Oswald Mosley, then a maverick left-wing Labour MP with a small
but significant group of supporters in the Parliamentary Labour
Party (one of whom, very briefly, was the young Aneurin Bevan).[22]
And after 1931, when rather than leave the gold standard and

deviate from plans for swingeing spending cuts, MacDonald and Snowden infamously preferred to desert Labour to form a National government with the Tories and the *laissez-faire* wing of the Liberal Party, Keynes and the rump of the Labour Party found friendship in adversity.

Well before his *magnum opus, The General Theory of Employment, Interest and Money*, was published in 1936, Keynes had become a major influence on the 'New Fabian' intellectuals who, under the supervision of G.D.H. Cole, increasingly dominated Labour's thinking on policy, among them Hugh Dalton, Evan Durbin, Douglas Jay and Hugh Gaitskell.[23] After *The General Theory*, Keynes' reputation reached new heights. Cole described it in the *New Statesman* as 'the most important book on economics since Marx's *Capital*' and Jay embraced it enthusiastically in his widely read book of 1937, *The Socialist Case*. By the onset of war in 1939, Keynes' ideas – married to an enthusiasm for nationalization and planning – were the common sense of the Labour intelligentsia.

Not that Keynes' intellectual impact was limited to Labour. Even in the late 1930s, some left-wing Tories had caught on to *The General Theory*'s implications – Harold Macmillan's 1938 book, *The Middle Way*, is a clear statement of the case for a managed capitalism – and after Keynes returned to the Treasury in 1940 his influence became ubiquitous. He played a major role in managing the wartime economy, and in 1944 was chief British negotiator at the Bretton Woods conference that set up the managed post-war international monetary system. William Beveridge, a fellow Liberal and a close friend, consulted him constantly while producing the famous 1942 report that laid down the foundations for the post-war welfare state, and Keynes' followers had a big hand in drafting the 1944 White Paper on employment policy, the opening paragraph of which – 'The government accept as one of their primary aims and responsibilities the maintenance of a high and stable level of employment after the war' – remained an economic policy benchmark for every political party in Britain until the mid-1970s.[24]

Keynes was appointed as an adviser to the Labour government in 1945, and although he died within a year of the Labour victory, shortly after negotiating the US loan that kept Britain afloat after the war ended, for the next thirty years his ideas – or rather, those of his followers and popularizers – were hegemonic in Labour circles. Whatever Labour's quarrels, the idea that the state had the power and the duty to secure full employment by maintaining the overall level of demand in the economy, if necessary by borrowing, was taken for granted by the whole of the Labour Party, just as it was embraced by the Tories and by economic policy-makers and academic economists the world over.

No matter that Keynes himself would almost certainly have distanced himself from the more interventionist growth-at-any-cost variants of this doctrine that emerged in the 1950s and 1960s. No matter either that not one country anywhere repeatedly ran budget deficits to boost demand until the 1960s, when the post-war 'golden age' of full employment was nearing its end.[25] Up to the early 1970s, it appeared to most people at the top of the Labour Party that Keynesianism had solved the biggest problem of hitherto existing capitalism – the recurrent creation of mass unemployment at certain stages in the business cycle. Unemployment in Britain, which never fell below 1 million between the wars, peaking at nearly 3 million in 1932, at no point rose above 900,000 in the 1950s and 1960s, falling to a low of 185,000 in 1955. The big division in Labour's ranks was between those on the right who argued that the success of Keynesianism obviated the need for extensive nationalization, and those on the left who said that it did not.

The right's confidence in the Keynesian revolution was most cogently expressed by Anthony Crosland in his 1956 book *The Future of Socialism*: 'Through fiscal policy, and a variety of physical, legislative and financial controls, the state now regulates (or seeks to regulate) the level of employment, the distribution of income, the rate of accumulation and the balance of payments; and its actions heavily regulate the size of industries, the pattern of output and the direction of investment decisions. The passive state has given way to the active, or at least the ultimately responsible, state; the political authority has emerged as the final arbiter of economic life; the brief, and historically exceptional, era of unfettered market relations is over.' Aneurin Bevan summed up the left's rather more qualified embrace of Keynes in his 1952 book *In Place of Fear*: 'I do not wish it to be thought that I attach no importance to the role of government as an agency for the stimulation of trade when the private sector of industry looks like developing its periodic deflationary crisis. But this must always be looked upon as second best, and not as a substitute for making over society so as to eliminate the possibilities of these crises.'[26]

The Keynesian consensus among economists and politicians started to crumble in the late 1960s with the arrival of 'stagflation', the coincidence of slow growth, rising unemployment and accelerating inflation in Britain as in most developed capitalist countries. Precisely what caused it was much contested at the time and remains so today. But the most credible explanations emphasize two factors: the inflationary financing of the American war in Vietnam; and the willingness of workers to use their bargaining strength in the labour market – at its height under conditions of full or near-to-full employment – to secure above-inflation wage increases and to resist management attempts to increase productivity.[27] The late 1960s and early 1970s saw an explosion of wage militancy throughout the industrial world, much of it outside the control of trade union leaders and thus very difficult to control with incomes policies. In Britain, the phenomenon was magnified by the fact that even trade union leaders were wedded to the idea of 'free collective bargaining'. Long before the 1973–4 quadrupling of oil prices turned inflation from a problem into a crisis, Britain was locked into an inflationary spiral in which above-inflation pay settlements were passed on to consumers through higher prices, which in turn prompted further above-inflation pay settlements, and so on.

Whatever its cause, stagflation was a direct challenge to the assumption of most 1960s Keynesians – although not to Keynes himself – that there was a simple trade-off between unemployment and inflation, so that unemployment could be eliminated by allowing a small but constant amount of inflation. In academic circles, it was seized upon by *laissez-faire* economists, most notably Milton Friedman, who had long argued against government interference in the economy on the grounds that it played havoc with the equilibrium that market forces would create if left to their own devices. The trade-off between unemployment and inflation had fallen apart, they said, because people had started taking inflation for granted and now based their behaviour on their expectations of inflation, particularly in pay bargaining. In such circumstances, boosting demand to combat unemployment simply made inflation accelerate. Instead, governments should concentrate on attacking inflation, letting unemployment rise to its 'natural' level (technically, the 'non-accelerating-inflation rate of unemployment', or NAIRU) to undermine workers' bargaining strength in the labour market. Meanwhile, they should remove the obstacles on the 'supply side' – generous benefits, employment rights – that prevented wages falling to the level at which market forces would provide employment for all.

Some academic Keynesians countered that the key to solving the problem of inflation was stricter wage controls; rather more, recognizing that such policies were unlikely to be successfully applied in most countries, simply integrated into their economic models the idea that creation of unemployment is sometimes necessary to control inflation – and thereby ceased to be Keynesians in any prescriptive sense. By the mid-1970s, the intellectual dominance of Keynesianism among professional economists, at least as Keynesianism had been known since the war, was over.

In Britain, it was the 1974–9 Labour government that had the dubious privilege of finding out what these theoretical arguments meant in practice. Although Labour in the early 1970s was deeply divided on economic policy, it was essentially Keynesian in outlook, just as it had been in the 1950s and 1960s: its disagreements were not about *whether* the state should manipulate demand to secure full employment, but about *what else* was required. The left backed a programme, the Alternative Economic Strategy (AES), that added widespread nationalization, heavyweight economic planning and withdrawal from the European Economic Community to the basic Keynesian package; the right rejected the AES and put its faith in a statutory incomes policy (which was opposed by the left) as the magic extra ingredient that would make demand management work.[28]

Because the right was split over Europe, it was unable to translate its dominance in the party's upper echelons into control of its programme. Labour won power in 1974 on a manifesto that owed much to the AES, promising a referendum on Europe, a radical interventionist industrial strategy and an incomes policy limited to the 'Social Contract' – an agreement with the unions that they would moderate pay demands in return for repeal of the Tories' Industrial Relations Act, strict price controls and big increases in pensions and benefits. The industrial strategy was the subject of some epic battles inside the government, nearly all won by the right (see chapter 1), and there were also ructions in the cabinet from the start over incomes policy and Europe. By contrast, there was only one member of the cabinet, Edmund Dell, the paymaster general, who disagreed with chancellor Denis Healey's decision in mid-1974 – despite having inherited high inflation, a massive trade deficit and a hefty public sector borrowing requirement from the Tories' reckless 1972–3 boom – to reflate the economy to cope with the supposed deflationary effects of the increase in oil prices in the wake of the 1973 Arab–Israeli war.[29]

Within nine months, however, faced with rampant inflation, public spending out of control, soaring unemployment and a runaway trade deficit, Healey had changed his tune. 'I abandoned Keynesianism in 1975,' as he put it in his autobiography.[30] From early in that year, he repeatedly demanded 'real spending cuts on a scale never seen before', against the resistance of Keynesians left and right in the cabinet – and, after a run on the pound in the summer, he began to get his way. It was not enough to satisfy the markets, however. The pound came under pressure again in early 1976, then again, despite more cuts and an emergency loan of $5 million from foreign central banks to shore it up, in the late summer. The government was forced to go cap in hand to the International Monetary Fund for a loan. It got it – on the condition that it introduced an even tougher public spending regime – only after prime minister Jim Callaghan announced to the 1976 Labour conference that the Keynesian era was definitively over.

'We used to think that you could spend your way out of a recession and boost employment by cutting taxes and boosting government spending,' he said, in his most-quoted speech. 'I tell you in all candour that this option no longer exists and insofar as it ever did exist, it injected a higher dose of inflation and a higher level of unemployment. Unemployment is caused by pricing ourselves out of jobs quite simply and unequivocally.'

More than twenty years on, Callaghan's message appears a little crude, but hardly shocking. It is now almost universally accepted by economists that the ability of any medium-sized nation state to manage demand is constrained by the need to keep inflation under control and to avoid balance of payments difficulties. Indeed, in recent years many economists have gone much further, arguing that the liberalization of trade and capital flows – and the consequent globalization of markets and production – has left every state, regardless of size, with next to no room for manoeuvre.

In the late 1970s, however, the Healey–Callaghan U-turn appeared to a large section of the Labour Party as a betrayal of everything the government had been elected to do. After the 1979 election defeat, as the Tories introduced a fiscal and monetary regime of an austerity unprecedented since the war, Labour swung sharply to the left. Amid recriminations about the economic policy of the Callaghan years, it reaffirmed its commitment to the left-Keynesian reflationary approach of the AES despite all the evidence that reflation, in the absence of strict wage controls, would simply result in higher inflation. The 1983 manifesto promised increased public spending, devaluation, widespread nationalization, *dirigiste* planning, withdrawal from the European Community, import controls and exchange controls.[31]

We will never know what would have happened if a Labour government had tried to put the AES into practice. But the chances are that it would not have been any more successful than the expansionist programme of François Mitterrand's French socialist government after 1981, which it was forced to abandon in 1982–3, confronted by rising inflation and a balance of payments crisis.[32] That was certainly the way it appeared to most of Labour's leaders after the party's 1983 defeat. Much of the AES was dropped soon after Neil Kinnock became leader in autumn 1983, beginning with withdrawal from the EC, import controls and exchange controls, and Smith and Healey (by now shadow foreign secretary) pressed hard for an explicitly post-Keynesian framework for economic policy.[33] In 1984, an internal Labour memorandum, almost certainly written by Smith, was leaked to the New Statesman. It declared that 'the Keynesian argument has been tried before and failed', then went on to say, 'We should not promise too much too soon. In particular, the term "full employment" may now appear nebulous and over-ambitious.'[34]

Yet although Roy Hattersley as shadow chancellor made much of the modesty of Labour's public spending plans and his scepticism about devaluation and nationalization, the 1983–7 retreat from the supposed common sense of the AES was ambiguous, lacking in intellectual confidence and largely unnoticed by the electorate. Despite the mounting evidence for scepticism about the feasibility of Keynesianism in one country, Smith and Healey did not really get their way before the 1987 election. Hattersley remained at heart an unrepentant Keynesian. Before the 1984 budget, he argued for 'a planned relaxation of the public sector borrowing requirement', 'the concentration of most of the extra government expenditure on new public capital investment' and 'a reduction in interest rates and a moderate depreciation of sterling'.[35] In spring 1985, he told Tribune: 'There has to be reflation in the sense that there is a shortage of demand in the economy.'[36] The nearest thing the mid-1980s Labour Party had to a statement of its fundamental beliefs, Hattersley's early 1987 book Choose Freedom (for the most part a competent populist reworking of the American liberal philosopher John Rawls' hefty abstract tome, A Theory of Justice) made much of the necessity of a 'socialist supply-side' policy to increase investment and improve training – a theme that was to dominate Labour's economic policy in the 1990s. But Hattersley's most sustained account of his ideas of what to do with the economy, the book Economic Priorities for a Labour Government, was essentially a restatement of the old Croslandite Labour right's case for redistribution under conditions of sustained growth, achieved by traditional Keynesian demand management.[37] Although Labour did abandon the promise of full employment, what replaced it, a pledge to reduce unemployment by one million – eventually cobbled into a more-or-less credible policy by Bryan Gould, then Labour's campaign co-ordinator, in January 1987 – 'relied at least to some extent on a boost to demand', as Gould himself put it.[38]

After the 1987 defeat, Gould, with Peter Mandelson the undoubted star of the election campaign, was disappointed to be passed over by Kinnock as shadow chancellor in favour of the firmly anti-Keynesian Smith. But as trade and industry spokesman and convenor of the main policy review group on the economy, he had high hopes of getting Labour again to embrace wholeheartedly Keynesianism in one country. Gould and his followers were keen backers of the policy review. That they were sidelined with such ease by Kinnock, Smith, Eatwell and Brown left a bitterness among them that still lingers today.

What finally did for them was the government's response to 'Black Monday', the world-wide stock market crash of 19 October 1987. Until then, it was at least plausible to argue that the strong growth of the British economy since 1983 proved that Keynesianism in one country really worked. Since becoming chancellor in 1983, Nigel Lawson had presided over an explosion in demand, the result of a combination of a massive expansion in consumer credit, falling interest rates, increased public spending and, in his 1986 and 1987 budgets, cuts in income tax. Unemployment had been falling steadily since the end of 1985, yet inflation had not become a major problem. If Gould and his supporters were critical of Lawson's chosen means of boosting demand – easy credit and income tax cuts to encourage private consumption, rather than public spending on infrastructure and education – they had no quarrel with his expansionism as such. Indeed, with unemployment still at 3 million in summer 1987, there seemed to be a case for an even more expansionist macroeconomic policy. The idea that, in such conditions, there was any danger that a boost to demand would set off inflation seemed quite ridiculous to them.

Then came the stock market crash – and Lawson, fearing a repeat of 1929, responded just as the Labour Keynesians said he should (as indeed did every other finance minister in the world), cutting interest rates still further. In the 1988 budget came another income tax cut, taking the basic rate down to 25p in the pound. Britain – or at least the large part of it that could get credit – continued the spending spree that had started in 1984–5.

Yet although unemployment fell, it did not do so at anything like the rate the Labour Keynesians thought it would – and it soon became clear that the economy was overheating. Britain was sucking in imports, and house price inflation was out of control. By mid-1988, it was clear that retail price inflation was heading for double figures. So, in the second half of 1988, Lawson slammed on the brakes. Interest rates doubled to 15 per cent between May 1988 and Lawson's resignation in October 1989, and remained there under his successor, John Major, until Britain joined the ERM in October 1990. The housing market collapsed, and from summer 1990 unemployment began to rise sharply.

In the Labour camp, the implosion of the Lawson boom was decisive in the battle over the direction of economic policy. The Labour Keynesians argued for a reversion to expansionism, but for Smith, Brown, Eatwell and the overwhelming majority of the economists advising Labour, the persistence of mass unemployment even when the economy was overheating was definitive proof that increased demand would not on its own cut the dole queues substantially except at an unacceptable cost. It showed, they believed, that without changes on the supply side, namely greater investment in capacity and a better-trained labour force, boosting demand in Britain would always translate rapidly into increased inflation and (unless the rest of Europe reflated simultaneously) balance-of-payments difficulties.

As Brown put it in his book *Where There is Greed . . .*, published in spring 1989, the Tories 'engineered a consumer boom which, since it had not been preceded by an adequate preparation of British industry by investment, was bound to end in rising imports, higher trading deficits and the higher inflation and interest rates that ensued . . . The growth that resulted did not amount to a supply-side miracle: instead it was a demand-side boom, precariously based on speculative credit . . . A consumer boom without prior, adequate and sustained investment effort was bound to be untenable and, tragically, the very weapon chosen to slow it down, that of high interest rates, will itself discourage future investment.'[39] In the absence of co-ordinated European reflation, the only answer to unemployment was 'supply-side socialism', i.e. government action to encourage long-term investment and improve workers' skills.

After John Smith's election as Labour leader in summer 1992, Brown was an easy choice as shadow chancellor. Robin Cook also wanted the job, and had acted as campaign manager for Smith, but he had less front-bench experience in an economic policy brief and, as a Keynesian and mild Eurosceptic, was much less in tune with Smith's views: in the end he had to settle for the position of trade and industry spokesman. Brown had not only proved a loyal and useful ally to Smith since 1985, he had been sensible enough – given the big union leaders' backing for Smith – to resist pressure from supporters to enter the leadership race, leaving Smith to face only a weak challenge from Gould.[40] He was also popular in the Parliamentary Labour Party. In the July 1992 shadow cabinet election, he topped the poll with 165 votes out of a possible 271, 15 clear of Tony Blair in second place.

Within two months, however, the new shadow chancellor's reputation had hit rock bottom because of his handling of the currency crisis that culminated in sterling leaving the ERM on 'Black Wednesday'. Perhaps he should have seen it coming. The policy of maintaining the pound in the ERM at DM2.95 had been accepted only unwillingly even by Labour supporters of economic and monetary union who saw the need for fiscal and monetary discipline. Will Hutton, then the economics editor of the *Guardian*, spoke for many who were holding their tongues in the PLP in a paper published just before the election. 'While it is plainly impossible for Labour openly to advocate devaluation, the commitment to hold today's parities is developing into a major totem of policy,' he wrote. 'At the moment it is doubtful whether the Labour team in office would even dare to press for an exchange rate realignment in case this was interpreted as a fall from the grace of financial orthodoxy; and while credibility is important, Labour has more than once this century hung itself on the cross of defending an indefensible exchange rate. I have a profound sense of foreboding that history may be about to repeat itself.'[41]

History did repeat itself, but not in the way Hutton meant: Labour lost the election, and in the immediate aftermath of defeat, its fragile unity on Europe and economic policy melted away. Although Gould's leadership campaign was a miserable failure, it provided a vent for long-repressed feelings that the policy of maintaining an overvalued pound had left Labour without a credible means of fighting unemployment – and that the Maastricht Treaty's conditions for European economic and monetary union were far too tough. In May, in the second reading of the government's Maastricht Bill in the Commons, fifty-nine Labour MPs voted against, defying the Labour whips' instruction to abstain, among them a group of younger soft-left MPs who said that they opposed Maastricht not as Eurosceptics but as pro-Europeans (the most prominent of whom was Peter Hain, the MP for Neath, newly elected as secretary of the Tribune Group). This in turn sparked Labour's MEPs to set up a campaign to back Maastricht on the grounds that the alternative was worse.[42] Nevertheless, except in the few days after the Danish voted 'no' to Maastricht in a referendum in June, when it looked to some as if the treaty had been killed off, few observers or participants thought that much more would come of all this, not least because the leadership election was expected effectively to close the issue by giving Smith, the author of the pro-ERM policy and a Maastricht enthusiast, a thumping majority.

Instead, the argument exploded into life. As Labour's leadership election campaign ground on relentlessly to its inevitable conclusion, there was growing turbulence in the currency markets as speculators sensed that several ERM currencies, among them sterling, were ripe for devaluation against the Deutschmark, then particularly strong because of the high interest rates incurred by the inflationary side-effects of German unification. As the central banks of Europe intervened more and more desperately to shore up the crumbling edifice of the ERM, Smith came under increasing pressure to declare in favour of a 'realignment' of currencies inside the ERM – based on a revaluation of the Deutschmark if not unilateral devaluation of sterling. By no means all of the pressure came from those back-benchers who had rebelled on Maastricht: just about the last act of Neil Kinnock as Labour leader was to write to the *Financial Times* arguing for a realignment of the ERM and a co-ordinated European reflation across the EC.

With the government insisting that it would never devalue – indeed, that it would match a revaluation of the Deutschmark with a revaluation of sterling – Smith hinted that he might be prepared to back a realignment. As he put it in an interview in *Tribune*: 'The exchange rate mechanism of the European Monetary System is not a fixed-exchange-rate system. It's adjustable. A general realignment could occur. Indeed, I rather anticipate there will be a realignment of some kind before we reach the decision on economic and monetary union.'[43] But his new shadow chancellor took an altogether harder line, refusing to say anything that might be interpreted as Labour going soft on devaluation. By the time of the TUC congress in Brighton in early September, the clamour for him to come out for realignment was deafening. 'The impossibly high exchange rate is pushing up interest rates and turning Britain into a rust-bucket economy,' declared John Edmonds, general secretary of the GMB general union, a long-standing enthusiast for EMU and one of the union leaders whose support for Smith had been decisive after the election defeat. 'Most people in industry know that the pound is overvalued against the Deutschmark. Realignment is now inevitable.'[44]

In the shadow cabinet, Gould, Michael Meacher and David Blunkett pressed strongly, with the support of Cook, for an acknowledgement from Brown that the pound was over-valued. Brown stonewalled. 'Our policy is not one of devaluation, nor is it one of revaluation or realignment,' he told the Parliamentary Labour Party on 10 September. 'One of the things the Germans may wish to propose is whether a realignment of currencies will bring interest rates down. There is no guarantee that that would happen, and it is not our policy.'[45]

Brown's position allowed him plenty of opportunities to crow once sterling was bounced out of the ERM on 16 September. 'The government is left with the economic policy it took to the electorate in April in ruins,' he wrote in *Tribune* the next week. 'Having promised that they would oppose devaluation, stay within the exchange rate mechanism of the European Monetary System and make it the basis of their counter-inflationary policy, the Tories have now abandoned every central economic policy pledge on which they fought the election.'[46]

And of course, he was right. The only small difficulty was that Labour would have faced a similar problem of having promised one thing and done the opposite if it had won. Despite the manifesto promise to 'maintain the value of the pound within the European exchange rate mechanism', a Labour government would actually have attempted to negotiate a realignment of the ERM – essentially a devaluation of sterling and various other weaker currencies against the Deutschmark and the French franc – as soon as it came to power. A majority of the economists advising the Labour leadership (including John Eatwell, Andrew Graham and Meghnad Desai) had long been convinced that the pound was overvalued at DM2.95: Desai joked that they should be known as the 'Ten to Three Club' because they reckoned DM2.50 was a more realistic rate. Immediately after Labour won the election, they believed, the new government should immediately put up interest rates to prevent a run on the pound, then go for realignment. According to Desai, he and John Eatwell met the Monday before election day and confirmed that the plan was an interest-rate hike of 3 percentage points the morning after the election, with realignment negotiations starting at once.[47]

Be that as it may, after 'Black Wednesday' Brown sat tight, blocking all attempts to get Labour to welcome the devaluation or rule out British membership of a European single currency. 'Measures to combat unemployment and for industrial policy are most effectively to be taken through European action,' he insisted.[48] For Gould, it was the final straw. He walked out of the shadow cabinet on the eve of the 1992 Labour conference, complaining to a Eurosceptic fringe meeting: 'We do not yet recognize the futility and damaging consequences of putting the defence of

the exchange rate at the heart of economic policy. There is no sign
that we would not again endorse that policy again in opposition
and pursue it in government. Nor do we seem to recognize that
the ERM as a bridge to economic and monetary union has been
shattered.'[49]

Brown's refusal to enthuse about the 'Black Wednesday' devaluation was sensible long-term politics, even though the economy
benefited greatly from the competitiveness of the exchange rate
once sterling left the ERM. If Brown had welcomed the devaluation, the markets would have concluded that Labour was soft on
inflation, and the Tories would have used it mercilessly in the
run-up to the 1997 election as evidence of Labour's 'unpatriotic'
attitude to the strength of the currency – just as they exploited the
devaluations forced on the Labour governments of the 1940s and
1960s. A declaration in favour of devaluation would also have
been taken by the rest of Europe as a sign that Labour was drifting
dangerously towards Euroscepticism.

In the short term, however, Brown's stance did him no
favours. For the next eighteen months, he was an embattled figure
in his own party, constantly under attack from critics of the ERM
policy demanding a return to Keynesianism in one country and a
commitment to full employment as the cornerstones of Labour
economic policy. The most persistent and vocal were the left
Tribunites around Hain – with whom several soft-left members of
the shadow cabinet, most importantly Cook, were broadly sympathetic[50] – who engaged Brown in an old-fashioned war of
pamphlets and polemical articles in *Tribune* and the *New
Statesman*, the first shot of which was *The Left and Europe*, a
Tribune Group pamphlet by Hain, Roger Berry, Derek Fatchett
and George Howarth, published in November 1992.[51] The GMB's
John Edmonds was almost as insistent, rarely missing an opportunity to proselytise on the necessity of full employment, while
Gould kept up a relentless Eurosceptic assault from the back
benches, throwing his considerable energies into setting up a
think-tank to push for alternative economic policies. (It eventually
emerged as the Full Employment Forum in March 1993, with

backing from the Hain group, the GMB and several economists from Cambridge University, as well as Gould's closest Eurosceptic parliamentary allies, among them Austin Mitchell.) The hard left also harried the shadow chancellor, with Ken Livingstone playing a particularly prominent role. Even the Fabian Society pitched in, with an elegant critique of Labour's ERM policy by a new-comer to the party's arguments, a young *Financial Times* leader writer by the name of Ed Balls, whose discussion paper *Euro-Monetarism: Why Britain Was Ensnared and How It Should Escape* it published in December 1992. Remarkably, given Brown's sensi-tivity to criticism, Balls was hired as the shadow chancellor's chief economic policy adviser a little over a year later.

Brown responded to the onslaught by increasing his already phenomenal work rate. In the year after the Labour conference in 1992, the shadow chancellor made an extraordinary number of television and radio broadcasts and churned out scores of keynote speeches, policy papers and articles for newspapers and maga-zines. Unfortunately, quantity was no guarantee of quality. Although there were some real innovations in Brown's thinking in this period – notably his embrace of the idea that the globalization of production and capital markets had substantially reduced any medium-sized nation state's room for manoeuvre[52] – too much of his output was hackneyed. The shadow chancellor, who had already acquired a reputation for thinking, talking and writing in soundbites, got into the habit of endlessly repeating the same catchphrases. If he liked a formulation – 'the crude Tory dogma of free-market forces', 'Labour offers a new economic approach', 'the role of the community in developing individual opportunity for all', 'a skills revolution through a decade of investment in indus-try and in people' – it would crop up first in a Commons speech, then in a television interview, then in an article in *Tribune*, then slightly modified in an interview in the *Guardian*, then in an offi-cial policy document, then slightly modified again on the Radio Four *Today* programme.

Brown at no point engaged directly with his critics, but – globalization apart – his rhetoric increasingly suggested that he might go some way towards meeting some of their concerns. At the launch of Labour's 'Campaign for Recovery' just before

chancellor Norman Lamont's 1992 autumn statement on public
spending, he talked grandly of 'a British New Deal for the 1990s'
in which 'the public sector must become an engine of growth'[53];
and in early 1993, as unemployment hit 3 million, he referred to
'our aspiration as a Labour movement to full and fulfilling
employment for all'.[54] The major policy document he produced a
couple of months later, *Labour's Economic Approach*, endorsed the
goal of 'a high and stable level of employment' from the 1944
White Paper and accepted that 'the key stimulus to investment
is . . . the prospect of growing demand'.[55] Will Hutton detected
'the first smoke signals that Mr Brown is prepared to concede a
modest if highly qualified Keynesian case' because of the way that
the document distanced Labour 'from the wilder claims of the
current orthodoxy by reducing low inflation to only one of the
policy goals of any chancellor, ranking "sustainable" growth, a
"manageable" balance of payments and the "highest possible level
of employment" as goals of equal rank'.[56]

Hutton's support was important for Brown. Along with
William Keegan of the *Observer*, he was the economics commentator most read in Labour circles, and his moderate Keynesianism
and arguments for reforming the City and corporate governance to
make British capitalism more like its German cousin were widely
influential long before the publication of his surprise bestseller
The State We're In in 1995. For Hain, Gould and the shadow cabinet soft left, however, Brown's pitch was nowhere near good
enough. It was spoilt by his continued insistence on the priority of
supply-side measures over demand management. As he put it in
Tribune, 'There are no quick fixes. Unless we create extra capacity,
expanding demand will in due course bring an even worse balance
of payments and increasing inflation.'[57] Moreover, his concrete
proposals were far too cautious and modest. Only one new idea
stood out: a windfall tax on the excess profits of privatized utilities
to pay for an emergency job-creation scheme, which was to
become a Labour staple for the rest of the 1992–7 parliament.
Otherwise, most of what Brown proposed – an interest rate cut,
tax-breaks for investment, an extension of export credit, relaxation of the ban on local authorities using receipts from council
house sales for house-building – was just what had been expected

from Labour before the 1992 election. Worse, it turned out to be not much different to what Lamont actually did in his 1992 autumn statement and spring 1993 budget.

Soon after the budget, Hain and Berry circulated a draft of a second pamphlet, *Labour and the Economy*, this time co-written by them alone, to the Tribune Group. It argued explicitly for a uni-lateral Labour return to expansionist demand management, and thus implicitly suggested that Brown's economic policy was mis-taken, so they were not expecting him to be pleased. But the worst they were reckoning on from the shadow chancellor was to be dis-owned as a couple of insignificant back-benchers. Instead, Brown was furious, and pulled out all the stops to prevent the pamphlet going ahead. He summonsed Hain to his office and shouted at him for thirty minutes and, when that didn't work, cajoled fifty mem-bers of the Tribune Group into writing identical letters to Hain and Berry urging non-publication. Peter Mandelson, then Brown's closest political ally, warned, apparently seriously, that the pam-phlet could endanger Labour's chances in the then imminent Newbury by-election. Hain and Berry went ahead regardless, with the private backing of Cook and the shadow cabinet soft left.

By now, nothing seemed to be going right for the shadow chancellor. In summer 1993, the ERM – now without sterling – collapsed in another wave of speculation, apparently confirming everything that the Eurosceptics had ever said. And to make mat-ters worse, grumbling about Brown's economic policy and his 'bunker mentality' (as one senior shadow cabinet colleague called it) became entangled with carping about John Smith's plans to introduce one-member, one-vote elections to choose Labour's par-liamentary candidates and leaders. Smith decided to woo Brown's Keynesian critics to win on OMOV. In a speech to the TUC con-gress in September, he declared: 'The goal of full employment remains at the heart of Labour's vision. Labour's economic strategy will ensure that all instruments of macroeconomic management, whether it concerns interest rates, the exchange rate or the levels of borrowing, will be geared to sustained growth and rising employment.'[58]

After that, Brown had to demonstrate agreement with his leader – so at the Labour conference later in the month, he launched a pamphlet, *How We Can Conquer Unemployment* (a title chosen for its similarity to Lloyd George's Keynes-inspired 1929 Liberal election campaign pamphlet, *We Can Conquer Unemployment*), which was more obviously Keynesian than anything produced by a senior member of the Labour economics team since the demotion of Gould in 1989. Full employment, Brown wrote, can only be restored by 'an enhanced Keynesian approach, which treats demand management as an integral part of a structural policy, and which deals with radical institutional reforms'. He referred explicitly to 'a lack of aggregate demand' in the EC as a whole and argued that 'continental European countries can afford to use looser monetary and fiscal policy to kick-start European growth' – although the effect was undermined by his assertion that Britain's own 'persistent and growing trade deficit' and 'low level of educational attainment' would preclude a Labour government joining in with everyone else in using looser monetary and fiscal policy.[59]

The pamphlet came too late to increase its author's vote in the annual elections to the NEC (he scraped back in the constituency section with the lowest vote of anyone elected) – and it played little part in securing Smith's hair's-breadth conference victory on OMOV. But it won Brown handsome praise from Will Hutton. 'Labour is developing a disciplined Keynesianism and a commitment to change radically Britain's institutional structures,' he wrote admiringly.[60] Just as important, the shadow chancellor's radical new language was also enough to persuade some of the erstwhile Tribune Group rebels to change sides. A little more than a month later, Hain, who had issued another pamphlet on economic policy just before Labour conference urging 'an immediate £20 billion programme of public-expenditure driven investment in infrastructure, training and skills',[61] was rewarded for his efforts by being removed from his position as the group's secretary. A phalanx of Brown supporters who had been notable by their absence from the group's weekly meetings for the previous eighteen months – among them Tony Blair, Peter Mandelson and Jack Straw – turned up to its annual general meeting to replace Hain with Janet Anderson.

The coup, although not in itself an earth-shattering event,

marked a watershed. The Tribune Group – the broad mass of the soft left in the Parliamentary Labour Party – was hardly a body of radical insurgents, but with Hain in a key position it had served as a megaphone for advocates of the 'tax, spend and borrow' policies that Brown so detested. Getting it back on side deprived the left Keynesians of their most important platform. It is no accident, as the Marxists used to say, that from autumn 1993, Brown felt able to abandon for good the rhetorical concessions to Keynesianism in one country that had been such a notable feature of his political stance just weeks before, much to the disappointment of Hutton, who found himself increasingly ignored by the shadow chancellor.

The most innovative challenge to Brown in his first two years as shadow chancellor came, however, not from opponents of the ERM or EMU but from a group of MEPs and economists arguing for a counter-cyclical role for the European Community in macro-economic policy. Labour had backed co-ordinated European action against unemployment since the early 1980s, but the policy, if it deserves the description, consisted of little more than a pious hope that a Labour government would be able somehow to persuade all the other EC governments simultaneously to adopt reflationary measures – something the Mitterrand government in France tried unsuccessfully in 1981–3. The idea that the EC as such could be a significant economic factor was given barely a second thought even after the Labour leadership embraced Europe wholeheartedly in the late 1980s: the consensus was that the EC's budget was simply too small (and too skewed towards agricultural subsidies) to have any significant effect, despite a substantial increase in the money allocated to regional development to help poorer areas cope with the effects of the single European market after 1992.

Then, in the negotiations leading up to the Maastricht Treaty in 1991, the Spanish socialist government led the poorer EC states in pressing hard for extra help from the richer countries as they prepared for economic and monetary union – and, with the backing of the president of the European Commission, Jacques Delors, they got their way, at least in principle. The treaty provided for creation of a new 'cohesion fund' to help finance environmental projects and trans-European networks in transport, telecommunications and energy; and in early 1992 Delors proposed a substantial increase in the Community budget to pay for it.[62]

Although the Labour leadership initially took little notice, in part because of the imminence of the general election, there was a direct party connection to Delors' plans – the economist and former Labour MP Stuart Holland. One of the architects of the Alternative Economic Strategy in the 1970s, he had been convinced of the need for the Commission to co-ordinate Community-wide reflation since the early 1980s, and had been working for Delors since 1991.[63] In summer 1992 he produced a plan for expanding the Delors proposals, which were due to go to a European summit in Edinburgh in December, into an ambitious counter-cyclical programme.

Holland's number-crunching was the basis for a 'European Recovery Programme' launched by the Labour MEP Ken Coates, a long-time friend and political ally, on the eve of the Labour conference in 1992. According to the Coates manifesto, joint action for European recovery 'should be led by the European Commission and co-ordinated with member governments. Not only will this be easier than the arrangement of convergent national initiatives outside the framework of the EC, it will provide a necessary catalyst to cross-border flows which can be calculated to maximize development possibilities and the multiplier effect that these can exert.'[64]

There were plenty of doubts in Labour circles about the feasibility of such a 'EuroKeynesian' programme. As Ed Balls put it in his Fabian discussion paper, 'For now the necessary degree of social and political cohesion needed to run a federal tax and transfer system does not exist. The German government has faced enormous difficulties persuading West German citizens to pay more taxes to support the unemployed in East Germany, never mind in Spain or Portugal. Nor are the EC cohesion funds an adequate substitute. They are tiny compared to the US federal budget and act as a means of discretionary redistribution rather than automatic stabilization.'[65] But the idea seemed to offer a way

out for many who had become convinced of the impossibility of
Keynesianism in one country but wanted a policy to compensate
for the deflationary effects of the Maastricht convergence criteria.
A majority of Labour MEPs came out enthusiastically for the
Coates–Holland initiative, as did several pro-European MPs, some
trade unions – notably the GMB and MSF – and both *Tribune* and
the *New Statesman*.

Brown, to his credit, pricked up his ears. In November 1992,
he called for a 'jobs and growth recovery programme for Europe',
which he described as 'new Keynesian', and a couple of months
later *Labour's Budget for Jobs* included the demand for 'new
Europe-wide measures to attack unemployment' that 'must go
beyond the limited measures of the Edinburgh summit', where
Delors had managed to secure agreement to the creation of a new
European Investment Fund.[66] *Labour's Economic Approach* in
spring 1993 backed 'increased use of the European Investment
Bank and its new Investment Fund for employment generation'.[67]

In November 1993, Labour's detailed submission to Delors
was straightforwardly EuroKeynesian. 'The interdependence and
integration of the economy reduces the viability and sustainability
of expansionary initiatives taken at the level of the member state,'
it stated. 'Especially for those member states like Britain whose
competitive capacity is constrained, go-it-alone expansion risks
running rapidly into the buffers of deteriorating trade balances
with consequent pressures on the currency and interest rates. As
each member state's room for manoeuvre is constrained in this
way, there is a net overall reduction in the macroeconomic freedom for the Community as a whole, unless this is compensated
for by joint action and economic initiatives at the Community
level.' It concluded: 'The Community should establish a counter-
cyclical European Recovery Fund to generate jobs by improving
communications, the environment and training. Investment in
Europe-wide infrastructure projects should be accelerated, including progress on a European fibre-optic network.'[68]

But that turned out to be the high water mark of Labour's
EuroKeynesianism. By late 1993, it was becoming obvious from
Labour's private polling that the idea of bigger budgets for
Brussels, even for job creation, would not go down well with an

increasingly Eurosceptical electorate; Labour's 1994 European election campaign, overshadowed by the death of Smith and speculation about his successor, played up domestic rather than European themes. More important, as Delors approached retirement, his plan ran out of steam in the face of a combination of the British Tory government's dogmatic opposition and the budgetary worries of the other three of the 'big four' governments of what was now the European Union: Germany, France, and Italy.

Delors produced a White Paper in November 1993, which moderated his original, already modest, spending proposals and introduced various deregulatory measures. But even that was not enough to secure the support of the relevant governments. Between the December 1993 European summit in Brussels and the June 1994 summit in Corfu, when John Major vetoed the appointment of Jean-Luc Dehaene as Delors' successor from 1995, the Delors plan was effectively killed off. Delors' successor as president of the Commission, Jacques Santer, a Luxembourgeois Christian Democrat, was lukewarm about his predecessor's ideas, and Labour's hopes that the balance of power in the Council of Ministers might shift to the left were dashed by the German Social Democrats' miserable showing in the October 1994 Bundestag election and the defeat of Lionel Jospin, the Socialist Party candidate, in the May 1995 French presidential election. By summer 1995, it seemed likely that, if Labour won a general election before spring 1997, the only other member of the EU 'big four' with a chance of having even a moderately left government when Labour came to power was Italy, where the centre-left – a coalition led by what was once the Italian Communist Party, now the Democratic Party of the Left (PDS) – was unreceptive to Delors' agenda because of its preoccupation with reducing Italy's debt to allow it to take part in the first wave of EMU.

The British Tories crowed; Labour quietly retreated. After Tony Blair's election as leader in summer 1994 and the subsequent appointment of Robin Cook as shadow foreign secretary, Labour increasingly took a populist line on all things European, playing up Labour's worries about EMU rather than emphasizing its backing for EuroKeynesian measures to compensate for its deflationary consequences. Blair made a couple of passing references to the idea of EU action against unemployment[69] and Labour's summer 1995 policy document on economic policy backed Delors-type measures, including 'the creation of a European Recovery Fund that is unashamedly contra-cyclical, permanent and able to draw on the credit-worthiness of European institutions, able to invest not only in infrastructure but in employment projects in a recession.'[70] But Labour was losing interest. In early 1996, Cook pronounced the proposals in the Delors plan beyond resurrection: 'They're now four years old and Europe's economies have moved on since then', although he added, 'We have got to get that kind of reflationary package in place again to tackle unemployment.'[71] There was not even a whiff of EuroKeynesianism in *New Labour, New Life for Britain*, the party's draft manifesto published in summer 1996 and endorsed by its members later that year.[72] By the time that Labour came to power, the whole EuroKeynesian episode appeared to have been entirely forgotten by the party's most senior figures. The unexpected election of the French Socialist Party to government in spring 1997 on a platform with a 'Delors-plus' programme at its heart, was an embarrassment to the new Labour government. Socialist Britain gave only the most half-hearted support to socialist France at the June 1997 Amsterdam summit, arguing that job creation in Europe would come not from the EU injecting demand into the continent's depressed economies but from Europe-wide encouragement of 'labour market flexibility'.

Having seen off the challenge from the Keynesians and developed as much of a EuroKeynesian platform as seemed possible, Brown turned his attentions at the beginning of 1994 to taxation and public spending. In his last budget in March 1993, Norman Lamont had increased taxes massively (most visibly by announcing the introduction of VAT on domestic fuel from 1994 but most importantly by not increasing income tax allowances in line with inflation) and Kenneth Clarke's first budget in November the same year had put them up a little more. With Labour's private polls showing growing popular distrust of the Tories on tax, Brown had already made a start on trying to make tax a Labour issue, declaring in the summer that 'the next Labour government will not tax for its own sake. Labour is not against wealth, nor will we seek to penalize it . . . We only tax if it increases the opportunities for individuals or for the community as a whole. If we cut taxes – and I hope that we will be able to do so – we will ensure that everyone benefits and not just an elite few as has happened under the Tories.'[73]

In the first few weeks of 1994, his Treasury team launched a campaign aimed at exposing the fraudulence of the Conservatives' claim to be a low-tax party. It scored a direct hit almost at once, when Harriet Harman, the shadow chief secretary to the Treasury, managed to get the government to admit that the combined burden of income tax and national insurance on a family on average earnings with two children, 20.9 per cent in 1978–9, would increase to 21.9 per cent in 1994–5.

But then, on the morning of Thursday 12 May, Brown's friend and patron John Smith died after suffering a massive heart attack. Brown was devastated at the loss – and to make matters worse, within hours Tony Blair had emerged as the hot media favourite to take the job of leader, to which Brown had long aspired. Brown dithered, feeling that decency demanded a period of mourning, but the Blair bandwagon became unstoppable long before 31 May, when Brown told Blair over dinner at the Granita restaurant in Islington that he would not contest the leadership.

To add insult to injury, it seemed possible that he might even be demoted if Blair won. Rumours persist that Blair told Robin Cook that Brown's job, which Cook still coveted, was up for grabs, and that Brown was forced to extract from Blair a guarantee that he could keep the shadow chancellorship in return for not running for leader.[74] Whatever the reality, there is no doubt that Brown was desolate at being forced to step aside for Blair as the modernizer candidate for the leadership, or that he felt betrayed by many of his friends (most importantly Peter Mandelson) who backed Blair rather than himself. As if that were not enough, the leadership election campaign deprived him of the limelight while giving John Prescott the chance to attack his economic policy openly by banging on about 'full employment'.[75] Brown made clear his preference that Margaret Beckett should remain Labour's deputy leader.

With Blair installed as leader and Prescott as deputy, Brown and his team returned to taxation and public spending. The trick was simple: repeating *ad nauseam* that Labour had shed its 'tax-and-spend' past. In September, Harman went so far as to produce a document, *Tory Public Spending: Wasting Our Nation*, attacking the government for not cutting expenditure as much as it had promised.

Her big splash was unluckily – or maybe luckily, given the derision it generated in the Westminster lobby – overshadowed the next day by the press-released text of a speech written for Brown to deliver at a conference of economists. It had the shadow chancellor saying that Labour had taken into account 'the importance of macroeconomics, neo-classical endogenous growth theory and the symbiotic relationship between growth and investment in people and infrastructure' – a statement that was mercilessly lampooned for its incomprehensibility by the Tories and the press for the next fortnight.[76] 'It's not Brown's, it's Balls'!,' declared Michael Heseltine to howls of laughter at the Tory Party conference, after the shadow chancellor's chief aide was named as the author of the non-soundbite. What was most unfortunate about the whole episode was that Brown had actually skipped the offending passage in his press-released speech when he delivered his address on the grounds that it was too jargon-laden.

After that, however, Brown's fortunes began to improve. Blair's decision to change Clause Four of the Labour constitution had the welcome side-effect of diverting left-wing grumbling from the shadow chancellor; Kenneth Clarke's November 1994 budget was a damp squib (although it stole several Labour ideas for employment creation, introducing incentives for employers to take on the jobless and changing the benefit system to ease the transition from unemployment to work); and in early December Brown's tax campaign paid off when Labour attracted sufficient support from Tory rebels in the Commons to defeat the government's proposal to increase VAT on fuel to 15 per cent.

In the first few weeks of 1995, Brown again made the running in the media with a campaign – revived from late 1991 – against the inflated pay of privatized utility bosses. For the first time in more than two years, Brown started to appear relaxed and confident in public – and his party once again warmed to him. Economists might praise Kenneth Clarke and even Norman Lamont for laying the foundations of an export-led, non-inflationary recovery; they might argue that the Tories' tax increases were entirely necessary and say that, in macroeconomic terms, the pay of the 'fat cats' was insignificant. But the popular mood was radically different. People did not like the Tories' taxes and were angry at the way that a privileged few in City board-rooms had escaped the seemingly never-ending pain since the end of the mid-1980s boom. In the privatized utility bosses, Brown had found a scapegoat that perfectly fitted the mood of the times.

Behind the scenes, meanwhile, he was busy on policy, draft-ing what eventually became the document passed by the 1995 Labour conference, *A New Economic Future for Britain* – the defin-itive Labour economic policy statement of the 1992–7 parliament. In May, the shadow chancellor made a string of speeches covering everything from competition policy and corporate governance to the principles that would guide Labour on taxation. At least some of the ideas were new, such as tax-breaks for shareholders who hung on to their shares long-term and greater independence for the Bank of England. So too were Brown's specific promises that 'Labour will be committed to meeting the golden rule of borrow-ing – over the economic cycle, government will only borrow to finance public investment and not to fund public consumption' and that 'we will keep the ratio of government debt to GDP stable on average over the economic cycle and at a prudent and sensible level'. But the overall approach was entirely familiar, 'Our empha-sis on strengthening the supply-side foundations of the economy, with a sound financial basis for sustainable increases in demand, is the route to both low inflation and low unemployment in the medium term', as indeed was much of the detail: more and better training, a 'University for Industry', more transparent and accountable regulation of privatized utilities, stricter rules on company mergers, and partnerships between the private and public sectors for infrastructure projects.[77]

Dull it might have been, but with Clause Four out of the way and Labour running so far ahead in the opinion polls that a land-slide election victory seemed likely, it was news for the quality papers, particularly after Brown's message of responsibility on spending and inflation was underlined by Blair, who gave the 1995 Mais Lecture on 22 May. Largely written by his economics adviser, Derek Scott, it described Labour's economics in terms that would have caused a rumpus a decade earlier. 'The control of inflation through a tough macroeconomic framework is even more important than the Tories have said,' Blair declared. 'Low inflation is not simply a goal in itself, it is the essential prerequisite both of ensuring that business can invest and that supply-side measures can work to raise the capacity of the economy to grow.'[78] Will Hutton, by now beginning to get frustrated by the distance between Labour's thinking and his own, discerned a major difference between Brown and Blair in the speech (which he put down to differences between Balls, whom he admired, and Scott, whom he thought pedestrian)[79] and accused Blair of 'more than once' crossing the 'fine line between recognizing the case for fiscal and monetary discipline as an essential adjunct to a left-of-centre programme, and rejecting any macroeconomic policy activism because it might destabilize the basically sound workings of a market economy'.[80] In reality, Blair was simply spelling out the implications of Labour's official thinking as it had been for six years.

Having laid out the principles on which Labour would make policy, Blair, Brown and the Treasury team spent the next six months sorting out missing detail. In June 1995, Harman declared that instead of announcing the level of Labour's promised minimum wage before the election, Labour would have it set by a Low Pay Commission involving employers and unions. At the Labour conference in Brighton, Blair announced an agreement with British Telecom whereby the telecoms giant would be allowed into the lucrative cable entertainment business in return for cabling all Britain's schools for free; and Brown at long last put a figure on the utilities windfall tax, promising to raise £1 billion for an emergency programme to get young people into work. In the next few weeks, the shadow chancellor unveiled plans for tax-breaks for companies investing in new plant and details of the jobs programme, according to which unemployed people aged under twenty-five who refused a place on one of four schemes would have 40 per cent of their income support docked. Just before Kenneth Clarke's budget, which was widely expected to include big tax cuts, Brown declared that on income tax 'our long-term objective is a starting rate of . . . 15 or preferably 10p' and announced 'our desire to cut VAT on fuel to 5 per cent'.[81]

None of these ideas won universal approval. The unions were angry at the party leadership's position on the minimum wage, and an embarrassing defeat for the platform at the 1995 party conference was avoided only by means of vigorous arm-twisting behind the scenes. The putative deal with BT caused ructions with the cable companies, and the utilities squealed at the windfall tax. *The Economist* said that the investment allowance scheme was a 'gimmick' that 'will do nothing in the long term for the level of investment and plenty in the short term to distort its pattern',[82] and the normally sympathetic Andrew Dilnot, director of the Institute for Fiscal Studies, the middle-of-the-road economic policy think-tank, described the 10p income tax plan as 'a con' – a point of view echoed off the record by several members of the shadow cabinet. 'The suggested 10p starting rate would be hugely expensive, as much as £8 billion if it replaced the 20p rate,' he wrote in the *Daily Telegraph*. 'Despite Mr Brown's claims, it is neither the most effective way of reducing income tax for those on low incomes, nor an effective way of improving incentives to work for those who gain little from taking a job.'[83] Even the plan to reduce the rate of VAT on fuel, a massively unpopular tax, drew criticism, this time from environmentalists who argued that VAT on fuel, with compensation for the poor, was a good way of encouraging energy efficiency.

But it was the threat to remove benefit from supposedly work-shy under-twenty-fives that did Brown most damage with his colleagues. Brown first raised the idea in an interview with the *Daily Telegraph* – and the way he did so suggested that Labour was toying with 'workfare', making the unemployed work for their benefits, which was not party policy at all. John Prescott, shadow education secretary David Blunkett and shadow social security secretary Chris Smith (who had just been given his brief by Blair with the injunction 'think the unthinkable') were all furious, and complained to Blair; at the next shadow cabinet meeting, the chorus of disapproval was joined by Robin Cook and others. Brown, with Blair's backing, insisted that all he was doing was repeating Labour's long-standing commitment to the idea that people who refused all work should lose the right to unemployment benefit. But at least one person present at the meeting was not satisfied with his explanation, choosing to leak full details of the row to the *Observer*.[84]

There was more controversy in April 1996, when Brown's staff floated the idea of abolishing child benefit for over-sixteens and using the money saved on means-tested grants for sixteen to eighteen-year-olds who stayed in education – unimportant in terms of the sums involved, but symbolically crucial because it indicated a weakening of Labour's commitment to child benefit. Once again, Smith and Blunkett were incensed, not least because they had just prepared a document reiterating the case for universal child benefit against those who argued for means-testing. But Brown, backed by Blair, got his way. Similarly, when Smith proposed abolition of the Job Seekers' Allowance, the Tories' new plan to reduce the period for which an unemployed person was entitled to non-means-tested benefit from six to twelve months, Brown simply overruled him. (Unfortunately, no one told Michael Meacher, the employment spokesman, whose name subsequently appeared above an article for the left-wing monthly *Red Pepper* promising abolition, causing Brown to hit the roof.)[85] In Blair's July 1996 shadow cabinet reshuffle, Smith was replaced as shadow social security secretary by Harriet Harman and moved to health. On pensions, Brown refused to budge on his refusal to promise increases in the basic state pension and a restitution of the State Earnings Related Pension Scheme (SERPS), despite a concerted campaign led by Barbara Castle that culminated in her impassioned speech at Labour's conference in Blackpool in October.

The same single-mindedness was on show in November 1996, when the Tories unleashed their long-awaited assault on Labour's supposed plans for increased taxes and public spending – which they claimed amounted to £30 billion. Brown simply declared that 'Any previous statements that are not included in the draft manifesto are not election commitments of the Labour Party.'

In January 1997, the document that launched Labour's election campaign, *Leading Britain into the Future*, underlined his point. In Labour's programme, it stated, 'there are no uncosted or unfunded spending increases, no concealed tax increases. Where we plan to spend money we say exactly where it comes from.' As if that were not enough, on 20 January 1997 Brown delivered a speech, portentously entitled 'Responsibility in public finance', in which he committed Labour to the Tories' spending plans for two years and ruled out any increase in either the 40p top rate of income tax or the 23p basic rate for the duration of a Labour government. 'Our first budget will not reopen overall spending allocations for the 1997–8 financial year,' he declared, then went on to promise that in 1998–9 he would stick to 'already announced departmental budgets . . . reordered to meet Labour's priorities'.[86] The speech stunned the commentators and the Tories, who had been expecting Brown to back a 50p top rate of income tax on people earning more than £100,000.[87] But its immediate impact on the voters was small. A poll by ICM for the *Guardian* a fortnight later showed that 55 per cent of voters expected a Labour government to increase income tax – precisely the same percentage as in January 1992.

The 1997 election campaign went much as expected on the economy. With some justification, the Tories talked up their success in securing the highest growth and lowest unemployment of any major European Union economy, at the same time as keeping inflation down. Labour, they claimed, would spoil everything. Labour stuck to its guns, endlessly repeating the message that it would be tough on inflation, tough on tax and tough on spending. The only wobble for the party came at the beginning of April in response to the Tories' persistent claims that there was a '£12 billion black hole' in Labour's spending plans, which they said was accounted for by its rejection of the government's planned privatizations, in particular of the air traffic control service and of student loans. Labour performed a rapid and none-too-convincing U-turn. Brown declared that he would have to 'look' at privatizing air traffic control and his aides hinted that the Tote might be sold off – an idea that was immediately squashed by Robin Cook. A couple of days later, Blair announced that all Whitehall departments would be required by a Labour government to compile inventories of their assets, which might then be sold off – an exercise, his spin doctors said, that could net as much as £122 billion. It was electioneering nonsense, but in its own terms it worked: the '£12 billion black hole' played little further part in the campaign.

Labour's biggest economic policy headache in the period immediately before the 1997 election was not, however, taxation and spending or even privatization but the prospect of European economic and monetary union. Until some time in mid-1996 – it is impossible to put a precise date on it – EMU seemed to most Labour politicians to be a rather distant problem. Of course, the Maastricht Treaty laid down a strict timetable for creation of a single currency, which required the member states of the EU to decide in late 1997 whether or not they wanted to join, with the final decision about who would be admitted being made in early 1998, and EMU itself beginning on 1 January 1999. But after the turmoil in the currency markets in 1992–3, it seemed implausible that this timetable would actually succeed in practice. Italy, Spain and several smaller countries appeared unlikely to qualify for participation under the strict convergence criteria laid down by Maastricht, and it was by no means clear that France, Britain or even Germany would make it either.

With the Tories tearing themselves apart over EMU, it did not look particularly urgent for Labour to come up with a hard-and-fast policy. The formula that the party had adopted in 1991, that it was in favour of EMU in principle but would join only if the conditions were right for Britain, appeared perfectly adequate to take Labour through to the election – particularly as it had been honed by Robin Cook since late 1994. Cook's line, that Labour wanted the proposed European central bank to be 'accountable politically to make sure it pursues policies of growth and full employment' and that it insisted on 'convergence of the real economy – of output, production and growth' before it would recommend British membership of EMU, satisfied all but a handful of the party's MPs and MEPs. Those of a sceptical disposition could take comfort in the qualifications; enthusiasts could point to the backing in principle for the creation of the euro.[88]

This remained Labour's formal position right through to the election, with the addition, in November 1996, of a promise that a Labour government would put British membership of the single currency to a referendum if it decided that it was in Britain's inter- ests to join. Behind the scenes at the very top of the party, however, there was a protracted argument about its adequacy as it became apparent both that EMU was in fact very likely to go ahead on schedule and that most of continental Europe was pre- pared to go through almost any amount of hardship to be part of it. As 1996 wore on, Labour's 'big four', Blair, Brown, Cook and Prescott, were forced into some serious thinking about whether Labour would go for participation in EMU in its first few months in power.

Their problem was that each had a different perception of the issue at stake and different instincts about how to deal with it. Brown was the most enthusiastic about EMU membership in the first wave, Prescott against the single currency on principle. Cook was sceptical about the timetable and worried about the conver- gence criteria, arguing that Britain should not go into the single currency in the first wave but should join later if the conditions were right. Blair took a position somewhere between Brown's and Cook's. Various attempts to reach a consensus had by the end of 1996 resulted merely in agreement that Labour would back a ref- erendum but would not rule out being part of the first wave of EMU – the former a concession by Brown, the latter a concession to him.

The stalemate was broken by Brown conceding the unlikeli- hood of first-wave membership in return for Cook becoming more enthusiastic about the benefits of EMU. Cook announced in a television interview: 'In the short run, you can certainly hold the position of being outside of the single currency. After all, probably half of the countries of the European Union are going to be out- side any first wave – even if that does start in 1999, which is doubtful.' On the other hand, he went on, 'If it goes ahead and it succeeds, then you cannot stay out. It would take a very sober and serious calculation to stay out beyond 2002.'[89] Brown subse- quently argued in another interview that there were 'real obstacles facing Britain and other countries that are increasingly difficult to overcome by 1999'.[90] Almost the same words appeared in the election manifesto.

And so, on 2 May, Brown found himself in the job for which he had been preparing for so long: chancellor of the exchequer in a Labour government.

For four days there were no surprises. He acquired a ministerial team at the Treasury composed entirely of trusted allies – Alistair Darling as chief secretary to the Treasury, Geoffrey Robinson as paymaster general with responsibility for reviving the private finance initiative, Dawn Primarolo as financial secretary and Helen Liddell as economic secretary[91] – while at the Department of Trade and Industry Margaret Beckett, a major player in her own right but also close to Brown, was installed as secretary of state.[92] Brown's allies were also given key jobs in several other important departments: Harriet Harman as social security secretary, Doug Henderson as European affairs minister in the Foreign Office, Alan Milburn as a junior health minister. In his own office, he kept on all the key people who had served him as shadow chancellor: Ed Balls as his special adviser, Charlie Whelan as his press officer and Sue Nye as his political secretary.

But then on the Tuesday after his appointment as chancellor he announced what the *Financial Times* described as 'the most radical shake-up in the operation of Britain's monetary policy since sterling's departure from the European exchange rate mechanism in 1992': he gave the Bank of England 'operational responsibility for setting interest rates'. Instead of interest rates being determined, as they had been under Kenneth Clarke, by a monthly meeting of the chancellor and the governor of the Bank of England, Eddie George, they would be set by a new nine-member Bank of England monetary policy committee consisting of the governor, two deputy governors, two other senior Bank civil servants and four outside experts. As with the 'Ken and Eddie show', the meetings would be minuted and the minutes made public within six weeks of the meetings. The committee would be made accountable through a responsibility to report to the Treasury

select committee of the House of Commons and through a reform
of the Bank's governing body to make it 'representative of the
whole United Kingdom'.[93]

Brown made it clear that the Bank would not be as independent as, say, the German Bundesbank. The chancellor would
continue to set the inflation target, and the Bank would not have
powers to intervene independently in the foreign exchange markets. But his announcement took nearly everyone by surprise.
Labour had been toying with the idea of making the Bank independent for some years – partly because an independent central
bank was a prerequisite of joining a single European currency but
also because it would in itself be an indication to the markets
that Labour was genuinely in favour of low inflation and a stable
currency (and would thus lead to lower long-term interest rates).
Brown's chief adviser, Ed Balls, had backed an independent Bank
of England in his 1992 Fabian discussion paper arguing against
Maastricht, and both Brown and Blair had become increasingly
explicit about the likelihood of increased Bank independence in
their keynote policy speeches from spring 1995 onwards. In early
1997, Brown made it clear that in government Labour would
transfer responsibility for setting interest rates to a new monetary
policy committee. But he also said that 'the Bank must demonstrate a successful track record in its advice and build greater
public credibility' beforehand.[94] Hardly anyone expected that
Brown would act quite as fast as he did. Tony Blair obviously gave
his consent beforehand – but the only other political colleagues
Brown consulted were Robin Cook and John Prescott, who were
telephoned less than forty-eight hours before the announcement.
Eddie George found out about Brown's plans the day before, as did
most of the cabinet.

The business reaction to Brown's move was overwhelmingly
positive, as was that of most commentators. Will Hutton heralded
it as 'part of a process of modernizing the British state and bringing the conduct of monetary policy into line with its conduct
elsewhere. The old City-based Court of Governors, perhaps the
most powerful Conservative quango, is to be sent packing and
replaced with a properly constituted board with representatives of
industry, finance and the unions.' The Bank of England, he went

on, 'will become a central bank for the whole country, not a lobby for City interests'.[95]

However, several members of the cabinet said privately that Brown had bounced the government into making a decision that it would come to regret – and at least some commentators agreed. In the *Observer*, William Keegan described Brown's decision as 'the biggest economic policy mistake of the decade' apart from joining the ERM. 'After an 18-year struggle to regain the levers of economic power, and it immediately throws the most important one away!' he exclaimed. 'I believe, with only modest reservations, that Labour has taken leave of its senses.'[96]

It was easy to see his point. Sterling had been appreciating rapidly since mid-1996 and was now approaching the value against the Deutschmark that it had before Black Wednesday in 1992, with the result that British exports were in danger of becoming uncompetitive. Although there were undoubtedly inflationary pressures in Britain's booming economy that had to be kept under control, it was by no means clear how serious they were. In the circumstances, moreover, increasing taxes to dampen demand made much more sense than increasing interest rates, which would simply lead to further appreciation of sterling. The Bank of England, however, had never been keen on this argument, and with *de facto* independence its view would always prevail. The danger was eloquently summed up by none other than Kenneth Clarke, who wrote in the *Financial Times* the day after Brown's announcement, expressing his concern 'that the Bank will be over-cautious – as its record over the past few years shows – putting up interest rates to make doubly sure of hitting the inflation target, but at the same time squeezing jobs and investment'.[97]

Less than a fortnight later, attention to the Bank's new role in setting interest rates was diverted by another surprise announcement by Brown about its role – that its regulatory powers would be stripped from it and vested in a new 'super-regulator', covering everything from high street banks to City traders, based upon the Securities and Investment Board and incorporating the City's network of self-regulation. The head of the new body would be Howard Davies, the deputy governor of the Bank and former director of the Confederation of British Industry. Brown presented the plan to Eddie George at the Bank as a *fait accompli*, and George subsequently let slip in a press conference that he thought about resigning in protest, leading to widespread press speculation about whether he would last in his job until his term expired in June 1998.

But it was soon back to monetary policy, as the four 'outside expert' positions on the monetary policy committee were announced. The four – Sir Alan Budd, the chief economic adviser at the Treasury since 1991, Charles Goodhart, professor of banking and finance at the London School of Economics, DeAnne Julius, the US-born chief economist at British Airways (bizarrely, a former CIA analyst), and Willem Buiter, the Dutch-born professor of international macroeconomics at Cambridge University – were all anti-inflation hawks, as was to be expected. More important, only one of them, Buiter, had a reputation as a believer in controlling inflation by using taxes to dampen excess demand rather than interest rates. Unsurprisingly, the first meeting of the monetary policy committee agreed to a quarter-point rise in interest rates to add to the quarter-point rise introduced by Brown the day he announced operational independence for the Bank.

Coming almost a month before Brown's first budget, this was hardly conclusive proof that Brown had decided not to use fiscal measures as his main means of keeping inflation under control. In mid-June, moreover, he appeared to indicate that the Bank would be prevented from running an over-tight monetary policy when he announced that his inflation target would be 2.5 per cent, a slight easing of the Tories' '2.5 per cent or less' target, and that the governor of the Bank would have to account publicly for his actions not only if inflation exceeded 3.5 per cent but also if it fell below 1.5 per cent. All eyes were now on the content of the budget to see whether Brown would raise taxes. He did – but not by much, and not in ways that made much difference to consumption.

It is of course possible that Brown's moderate fiscal tightening and the Bank's tweaking of interest rates will prove precisely the right macroeconomic policy, 'strengthening the ability of the British economy to sustain growth with low inflation', as he put it in his June 1997 Mansion House speech. If it does, he will have an easy time as chancellor. Unemployment will continue to fall whether or not 'welfare-to-work' proves successful, and he will have plenty of room to increase public spending without resorting to income tax increases. He will also be able to choose to go into the single European currency whenever seems most favourable politically.

Such a rosy scenario is anything but inevitable, however. The biggest danger is that the reliance on tight monetary policy to keep the lid on inflation will not have the hoped-for effect of dampening consumer demand until high interest rates, by increasing the cost of borrowing and by leading to an appreciation of sterling that makes British exports uncompetitive and sucks in imports, bring on a balance of payments crisis and a recession. (This could be particularly disastrous if sterling becomes a reserve currency as a result of speculators' worries about EMU.) On this turn of events, unemployment will start to rise again, sooner rather than later, perhaps in spectacular fashion. 'Welfare-to-work' will be tested in circumstances in which it has little hope of success – and independence for the Bank of England will look like a major mistake. We will see.

3

CONTINENT ISOLATED
ROBIN COOK AND EUROPE

Robin Cook made it clear that Europe was top of his political agenda as foreign secretary even before he was officially appointed. First thing in the morning after Labour's election victory, he told the BBC Radio Four *Today* programme that Labour was ready to 'hit the ground running' in negotiations on a new European Union treaty to be signed at the Amsterdam EU summit in June. Labour could 'negotiate from a position of strength' he said. 'We have a great asset to offer Britain. In place of a government with a weak leader and a divided party, we have a strong leader – Tony Blair's leadership is overwhelmingly the major reason we have secured this great result – and a large working majority in the Commons. We have sought a mandate to sign the Social Chapter. We got that mandate overwhelmingly, which reflects the fact that the people of Britain want a social chapter because they don't see why Britain should have the worst rights of workers of any country in Europe.'

Within three days, Cook had installed himself in the sumptuous surroundings of the Foreign and Commonwealth Office, ensured that he was given a team of junior ministers that included two close allies, and despatched his new minister for European affairs, Doug Henderson, to Brussels to show the rest of the EU that Labour planned to be friendly.[1] Within a week, the new foreign secretary had visited Paris and Bonn for preliminary talks with his French and German opposite numbers and secured their agreement to a ban on production of landmines. 'It is our commitment that we will draw a line under the sterile, negative and fruitless confrontation which was the policy of the previous British government,' he said in Paris. 'Britain wants to be one of the three major players in Europe.' In Bonn the message was the same. 'I want today to be the start of a new era between Britain and the leading members of Europe,' he declared. 'It is our intention that Britain should now be one of those leading members, not a country on the sidelines seeking to be obstructive.'

Cook then found time to write a mission statement for the FCO, putting human rights and the environment at the centre of its concerns. This was launched with great aplomb on 12 May, along with a video by David Puttnam to be sent to 200 foreign postings; Cook then visited the United States. After that it was back to Europe again, to the detail of treaty negotiations which kept him busy for the next month as the EU prepared for Amsterdam.

Now, however, there was a subtle shift in the tone of Cook's public pronouncements. On European economic and monetary union, although he promised that when Britain took the presidency of the EU in 1998, it would do 'everything in its power' to make it work, he also made it clear that it was highly unlikely that Britain would be a member of the single European currency when it started in 1999. On the Amsterdam negotiations, as well as emphasizing the government's constructive intentions, he made much of its tough conditions for signing a treaty: a British opt-out from any agreement to abolish frontier controls; retention of each member state's power of veto over home affairs and foreign policy in the Council of Ministers; no moves to turn the EU into a military alliance; and a settlement of the dispute over continental fishing boats registering in British ports to dodge EU fishing quotas.

The populist message was reinforced by Tony Blair as he made his first steps on to the European political stage – although hardly as Cook would have chosen. In late May, in the Dutch resort of Noordwijk for his first summit meeting with other EU heads of government, the new prime minister urged his fellow leaders to become less obsessed with the EU's institutions and more concerned with the things that people really cared about – in particular, jobs. 'Europe has to be competitive,' he declared. 'It's got to focus on the basic issues of job creation and employability. The way to do that is not by letting in more and more and more regulations. The way to do that is to make sure people in the labour market have got the skills they require.'[2] That meant that the employment chapter to be agreed at the Amsterdam summit should not be a second Social Chapter but an agreement to encourage flexible labour markets – and it implied a showdown with the European Commission over its plans to extend the scope of the Social Chapter now that Britain had agreed to sign it.

Chancellor Gordon Brown developed this theme at the beginning of June when he announced that the British presidency in 1998 would make a priority of an initiative for a European 'crusade against unemployment' consisting almost entirely of measures to promote labour market flexibility. Blair took it further in a speech the following day to the congress of the Party of European Socialists in Sweden: 'For us and for Europe, jobs must be the priority. To create jobs we must be competitive. And to be competitive in the modern world, knowledge, skills, technology and enterprise are the keys, not rigid regulation or old-style interventionism. We reject the right-wing way of competing on low wages. But we know today that we cannot compete either by stifling enterprise. Instead we must be the enablers of enterprise, equipping our people and business to make the most of their talent and ability.'[3] The deregulationist line went down badly with many of the socialist leaders in his audience – but what really jarred with them all was Blair's presumption in lecturing them about the need for 'modernization', as if they were somehow stuck in the 1960s. The French socialists, just elected to power under Lionel Jospin, were particularly struck by his implicit attack on their proposals for Europe-wide employment creation by expanding EU public spending.

Blair played a slightly more conciliatory role on this at the Amsterdam summit. The Germans were dead set against conceding anything to French demands for a Keynesian economic policy at EU level, but largely thanks to British intervention the summit agreed to expand the lending of the European Investment Bank and strengthen economic policy co-ordination, which was at least a small step in the French direction (although the French were unimpressed). Otherwise, Blair and Cook sided with Germany in opposing a big reduction in the scope of national vetoes in the Council of Ministers and secured an opt-out on the transfer of responsibility for immigration and asylum policy to the EU. On the Franco-German plan for the EU to absorb the Western European Union as its defence arm, Britain allied itself with the neutral countries to fend it off.

The Amsterdam treaty was a damp squib – but that did not prevent Blair and Cook presenting it as a great victory. The pair of them were in triumphalist mood when they appeared before the press at the end of the summit. Everything, it seemed, had gone Britain's way. 'There were two principal objectives that we came to this summit with,' said Blair. 'The first was to ensure that we maintained all the vital British interests in areas like frontiers, asylum and immigration, defence and taxation and so on; and the second was that we also set forward a positive agenda for Europe, dealing with jobs and the environment, the single market and enlargement. We got our frontier controls in the treaty. In all the areas where we said we would retain the national veto, we have retained the national veto. We secured the whole basis of the employment chapter being around how we improve the employ-ability of people in the modern labour market. There were significant steps forward precisely because we were fighting on the ground that we should be fighting, not simply causing a fuss for the sake of it.' Cook agreed wholeheartedly. 'We have made very substantial progress in getting Britain's national interests,' he declared. 'It is quite clear to me from the conversations I have had with my opposite numbers that to a large extent we have made that progress because there is a new negotiating climate.'

Cook has been thinking seriously about Europe for a long time. By his own account, he decided that he was against Britain joining what was then known as the Common Market in 1966, when prime minister Harold Wilson announced his bid to get in where Harold Macmillan had failed.[4] Cook was then twenty, chairman of both the Labour Club at Edinburgh University, where he read English Literature, and the Scottish Association of Labour Students.

Like Gordon Brown, both an Edinburgh student and the Labour Club chairman a few years later, he was acknowledged by his peers as the star of his year. But whereas Brown's reputation was based on his skill at organizing campaigns, his muck-raking journalism and his good looks, Cook's was founded on his forensic intelligence and his ability in the debating chamber, still in the mid-1960s the place to shine in Scottish student politics. The son of a headmaster and grandson of a miner blacklisted for his role in the 1926 General Strike, he first acquired a taste for public speaking while at school, the Royal High in Edinburgh. At the time, he was thinking of becoming a Church of Scotland minister, but university changed all that. On graduating, the young Cook married, worked briefly as a teacher in a comprehensive school and then landed a job as a tutor for the Workers' Educational Association – but his goal was a career in politics.

Along with a group of like-minded young left-wingers (among them Martin O'Neill, now Labour MP for Ochil and Labour's defence spokesman, 1988–92), Cook threw himself into activity in the local Labour Party, which at the time was dominated by a corrupt and ageing right-wing clique. Cook and his friends took it over, and he was selected as Labour candidate in the 1970 general election for the seat of Edinburgh North. He lost, but a year later was elected to Edinburgh City Council, where he rapidly acquired a name for himself as a dynamic left-winger with an eye for detail, rising to the position of convenor of the housing committee.[5] In autumn 1972, he was chosen as parliamentary candidate for Edinburgh Central, which he duly won in February 1974, on his twenty-eighth birthday, by a margin of 961 votes.

Brown, then rector of Edinburgh University, was a close ally at this time: Cook contributed an essay on housing policy to his 1975 collection of radical essays on Scottish politics, *The Red Paper on Scotland*, in which he lambasted Scottish Labour local authorities for building 'vast estates of high-density and frequently

high-rise council housing' where 'the syndrome of social deprivation and a depressed environment has emerged as forcibly as it
ever did among our Victorian slums'.[6] Some time after *The Red
Paper*, they fell out with one another, although why and when are
unclear. A former friend of both believes that the problem started
when Cook and Brown took different sides on Scottish devolution
in the mid-1970s; another says that the cause was a row over a
book on which they collaborated in 1983, *Scotland: The Real
Divide*. Whatever the reason, since the mid-1980s at least, their
relationship has been at best cold and mutually suspicious –
which could well spell trouble for the government, particularly as
Brown and Cook disagree on many of the most important issues
that it faces.

Cook spent the years of the 1974–9 Labour government as a
rebellious back-bencher. He consistently questioned government
policy on defence, nuclear power and civil liberties, and played a
prominent part in the dissident Labour campaign in the March
1979 referendum for a vote against devolution, which he had previously backed. Defence was his particular speciality. His first
political involvement as a teenager in the early 1960s had been in
the first wave of CND, and soon after entering the Commons he
had established himself as an articulate advocate of nuclear disarmament, restrictions on the arms trade and reductions in defence
spending. Anthony Howard, the editor of the *New Statesman*, was
sufficiently impressed to make him defence correspondent, and
Cook wrote regular pieces for the magazine throughout the mid-
and late 1970s. In 1978, he and Dan Smith, former general secretary of CND and a member of the defence study group set up in
1974 by the Labour National Executive Committee, published a
Fabian pamphlet that questioned the wisdom of British membership of NATO.[7]

Among Cook's civil libertarian initiatives were private
member's bills to liberalize Scottish divorce and homosexuality laws,
in 1975 and 1977 respectively: both failed. He publicly opposed the
prosecution of Crispin Aubrey, John Berry and Duncan Campbell
under the Official Secrets Act, and was an advocate of freedom of
information legislation to open up the security state to democratic scrutiny.[8] On devolution, which he favoured in 1974–5, he

became one of the most aggressive opponents from late 1976, describing the government's plans in early 1977 as an 'expensive albatross irrelevant to the real social and economic needs of the Scottish people'.[9] In February 1979, he caused outrage by putting in an appearance at a press conference of the Tory-dominated 'Scotland Says No' campaign. Several years later, after Cook recanted his anti-devolution past (he has been strongly in favour since 1983), the historian Christopher Harvie, an old school friend, attacked Cook for 'a record of deviousness . . . over the issue of devolution that even Lloyd George would be hard-put to beat'.[10] Cook's vacillations earned him the nickname of 'Zebedee' (from the children's television show *The Magic Roundabout*), from Janey Buchan, the chairwoman of the Labour Party in Scotland during the devolution referendum year.

On Europe, Cook swam with the tide of Labour left opinion, campaigning against remaining in the Common Market in the 1975 referendum. He was not, however, as unrelentingly antipathetic as many of his colleagues. In June 1975, after the overwhelming 'yes' vote (65 per cent in the United Kingdom as a whole, 58 per cent in Scotland), he wrote an article for the *Scotsman* in which he adopted a pragmatic democratic reformist position on Europe not unlike the one that is current Labour policy. 'The interests of the people that . . . I represent would have been better served by a vote for withdrawal from the EEC,' he stated, but went on, 'The task before us now is radically to alter the structure of the Community, to democratize the Community so that the European Assembly, representing the peoples of the Community, has more power, and the Council of Ministers, representing its governments, less . . . Major areas of political debate will no longer be settled in a British context . . . The arguments on them have shifted to a wider European forum, and we on the left must now find allies among each of the other member states.'[11] The idea that the EEC might be in any sense reformable was anathema in the late-1970s Labour Party, however, and Cook soon retreated into giving lip-service to the straightforward anti-Common Market position that was a condition of getting anywhere as a Labour left-winger. In June 1977, he was one of 60 MPs who signed an appeal in *Tribune* declaring: 'Membership of the Common Market has been an unmitigated disaster for the British people. The Labour movement should commit itself to taking Britain out of the EEC.'[12]

Cook's ideas were much more in tune with the party leadership after Michael Foot was elected leader in 1980, and shadow chancellor Peter Shore appointed him deputy in his Treasury team, a position he kept until 1983. At this time Shore was Labour's most senior anti-European apart from the Labour leader himself, and if Cook had doubts about his boss's views he kept them to himself. In public, he stuck to the idea – which was party policy from the 1980 conference onwards – that 'the socialist transformation of the economy cannot be carried out unless we first leave the EEC'.[13] Cook was co-author with Shore, Jack Straw and Robert Sheldon of *Labour's Programme for Recovery*, the November 1982 statement that formed the basis of the economic policy on which Labour lost so badly in 1983. Getting out of the EEC was central to this policy.

Cook was widely noticed for his parliamentary performances in his first front-bench post, but it was his interventions on defence policy and his emergence as a spokesman for Labour's soft left that really gave his career a push in the early 1980s. He was a tireless propagandist for the cause of unilateral nuclear disarmament and a nuclear-free Europe, speaking all over the country, contributing articles to a wide range of publications, and serving on the co-ordinating committee of the European Nuclear Disarmament group; and he was one of the key left-wing figures who, in the wake of the defection of the SDP, distanced themselves from Tony Benn's attempt to win Labour's deputy leadership and criticized his Trotskyist supporters.[14] He was a natural choice for Neil Kinnock as his leadership campaign manager after Foot's resignation in 1983 – and few were surprised when he won a seat in the shadow cabinet that autumn.

Kinnock gave him the job of European affairs spokesman, a post that had not existed before in the shadow cabinet. Largely for electoral reasons – but also because he was attracted by the idea of a European recovery programme that had been floated in

early 1983 by the economist and Labour MP Stuart Holland[15] –
the new Labour leader had made changing policy on Europe one
of the planks of his leadership campaign. 'By 1988 Britain will
have been a member of the Common Market for 15 years. That
does not make withdrawal impossible,' he declared in his personal manifesto. 'After that length of time however, withdrawal
should be regarded as a last resort that is considered only if and
when the best interests of the British people cannot be feasibly
safeguarded by other means.' A policy document arguing that
Britain should retain the option of withdrawal but should remain
in the EEC for the duration of the 1984–9 European Parliament
was passed by the 1983 party conference.[16] Even though it was
clear which way the wind would blow under Kinnock, Labour's
anti-Marketeers were stunned by the speed with which he
decided to act – and by the willingness with which Cook took up
the role of accomplice.

Just after Cook's appointment, the pair visited the European
Parliament and spoke to the Socialist Group of MEPs. Kinnock
told them: 'Britain is part of the Community and is going to
remain part of it for the immediate future.' Cook suggested that all
the socialist parties of the EEC contest the next European elections, due in 1984, on a common manifesto: 'We want to fight
those elections with you. We all face common problems in Europe
and we must therefore offer the people of Europe common solutions rooted in our shared socialist values . . . Reflation in one
country is no longer a viable strategy in the modern world. We
will only build a sustainable sustained expansion if we work in co-
operation with each other, not in competition against each
other . . . The Labour Party recognizes that at the moment the
EEC is under profound pressure to change, and we want to be in
there helping to shape what emerges.'[17]

Cook was careful to insist that Labour had serious qualifications to its acceptance of EEC membership. Over the next few
months, he laid them out in detail, most publicly in a column in
the (pre-Wapping) *Times*. The big theme was the need for radical
reform of the EEC. He launched into the Common Agricultural
Policy – the largest single item in the EEC budget and at the time
a target for Margaret Thatcher's ire – as a wasteful protectionist

regime: unless it was reformed, he argued, there would be 'no future for the EEC'.[18] Time and again, he made the case for concerted European action to counter unemployment: 'The real challenge to Europe is how to achieve . . . co-ordinated reflation out of slump.'[19] The means by which Cook thought this might happen is unclear, but it is safe to say that he was not thinking in terms of the EEC itself acting as anything more than a co-ordinating body: he was utterly disdainful of proposals from the SDP that the Community's budget should be increased.[20]

Nevertheless, there is no doubt that Cook and Kinnock in 1983–4 effected a major change in Labour's stance on Europe. For all its qualifications and demands for reform, the party that fought the 1984 European elections was one that wanted to remain in the European Community – at least 'for the term of the next European Parliament', as Cook put it[21] – rather than get out at once. What's more, the change had been pushed through by two politicians who before 1983 had been strongly identified with the Labour left's anti-European consensus. Much of the left was outraged at the way Cook and Kinnock had bounced Labour into acceptance of EC membership. In the European elections, Labour won 37 per cent of the vote and 32 seats to the Tories' 41 per cent and 45 seats, which was hardly a stunning victory but was nevertheless a remarkable recovery from the nadir of 1983, when the party took just 28 per cent of the vote. All the same, once the vote was out of the way a steady stream of bitter left-wing MPs and MEPs denounced the leadership's manoeuvre.

The Labour left was not always overwhelmingly hostile to European integration. Indeed, in the first three years of the 1945–51 Labour government, the goal of a federal Europe was at the core of the idea of a 'third force' socialist foreign policy advanced by non-Communist left-wing critics of foreign secretary Ernest Bevin's pro-American orientation as the Cold War began.

George Orwell put the case with characteristic intellectual pessimism in the New York journal *Partisan Review* in summer 1947. 'Socialism does not exist anywhere' – like many on the libertarian left, he did not accept that Soviet Russia was socialist – 'but even as an idea it is at present valid only in Europe. Of course, socialism cannot properly be said to be established until it is world-wide, but the process must begin somewhere, and I cannot imagine it beginning except through the federation of the western European states, transformed into socialist republics without colonial dependencies. Therefore a Socialist United States of Europe seems to me the only worthwhile political objective today.'[22] A few months before, Richard Crossman, Michael Foot and Ian Mikardo had made the same point in more upbeat fashion in their New Statesman pamphlet, Keep Left, signed by a dozen other MPs and generally considered to be the founding statement of the Bevanite group that rallied left-wing Labour dissent in the early 1950s: 'We British have become Europeans whose prosperity and security depend on that of the rest of Europe . . . A socialist Britain cannot prosper so long as Europe is divided. The goal we should work for is a federation which binds together the nations now under eastern domination with the peoples of western Europe.'[23]

For the rest of 1947, back-bench Labour pressure for a policy of European federalism grew dramatically – largely through the efforts of one of the Keep Left signatories, R.W.G. 'Kim' Mackay, the MP for Hull North West since 1945. Mackay, an Australian by birth, had been convinced of the federalist case since before the war and in 1940 had published a book, Federal Europe, laying out his ideas.[24] In late 1947, Mackay set up a Europe Group of the Parliamentary Labour Party, most of its supporters (including Crossman, Foot and Mikardo) drawn from the left. Within weeks of its launch it boasted at least 80 members – more than one-fifth of the Parliamentary Labour Party – and Mackay's federalism was the talk of the Labour Party, including the bright young right-wingers in Hugh Gaitskell's dinner-party set.[25] He published a widely read book setting out the case for federalism, Britain in Wonderland, and then, against the orders of the Labour National Executive Committee, led a federalist delegation including 27 Labour MPs to the May 1948 Congress of Europe in The Hague, the event that founded the post-war movement for European union.[26] For Mackay, even a federation that excluded eastern Europe, by now Soviet-dominated, was a worthwhile goal: 'the creation of a federation of western Europe would clear away from the influence of the two great powers an area of the world in which conflict is otherwise bound to break out' and 'would create a power which, within a few years, would probably be as prosperous and as stable as either of the other two great powers'. 'We must give up pursuing the shadow of international government and work hard to achieve a real democratic Federation of Western Europe.'[27]

Not long before, this would have been in tune with the ideas of the Labour leadership. The Ramsay MacDonald Labour government had certainly been no friend to the tentative proposals for a political integration of Europe put forward in 1929 by French prime minister Aristide Briand: it had dismissed them peremptorily, claiming that an 'exclusive and independent European Union of the kind proposed might emphasize or create tendencies to intercontinental rivalries and hostilities'. But there had been plenty of dissidents from this line, among them Ernest Bevin who, as leader of the Transport and General Workers Union, moved a successful motion in favour of a federal Europe at the 1927 TUC congress, and in the late 1930s Labour's frame of mind had changed as the post-1918 settlement in Europe collapsed into fascism and war. The idea of a federal Europe was revived by a group of *bien pensant* middle-class intellectuals, who set up a small campaign, Federal Union, in early 1939.[28] It was a remarkably successful initiative: in 1939–40 it won the support not just of a large section of the liberal and non-Communist left intelligentsia (including William Beveridge, Barbara Wooton, J.B. Priestley, G.D.H. Cole and H.N. Brailsford) but also of most of the Labour leadership. Bevin was enthusiastic; Attlee declared in 1939 that 'Europe must federate or perish';[29] Hugh Dalton, the intellectual Labour right's great fixer of the 1930s and 1940s, chancellor of the exchequer between 1945 and 1947 and a key influence on the Attlee government's foreign policy as chair of Labour's international committee, called in 1940 for a post-war federal union. 'It must be a first principle of our action,' he wrote, 'to dilute national sovereignty as much as possible over as wide an area as possible.'[30] More modestly, the young Harold Wilson wrote a paper arguing that 'a federal union should begin as unambitiously as possible in the economic sphere'.[31] By 1944, even Aneurin Bevan had joined the federalists, declaring in *Tribune* for 'an organic confederation of the western European nations', including 'a sane Germany and Austria and a progressive Britain' as 'the only solution likely to lay the foundation for peace and prosperity in Europe'.[32]

The British Euro-federalists of the late 1930s and early 1940s also had a profound influence on many continental Europeans who were later to play crucial roles in the creation of what eventually became the European Community, notably the Italian Euro-federalist Altiero Spinelli.[33] But in the immediate post-war years a federal Europe seemed irrelevant or even dangerous to the Labour leaders most responsible for foreign policy. For Attlee, Bevin and Dalton, the two major challenges facing Europe – post-war reconstruction and containment of the Soviet threat to western European security – required the United States to play an active role in European affairs. A pan-European or west European federation acting as a 'third force' would encourage US isolationism, endangering the prospects for both security and prosperity; conversely, American encouragement of European federalism was merely proof that the US was becoming dangerously isolationist. Just as important for Britain's standing in the world, a European federation would also damage relations with the Commonwealth and the colonies, particularly with what Dalton – a notoriously boorish xenophobe who habitually referred to the Germans as 'the Huns' – called 'our kinsmen in Australia, New Zealand etc'.[34]

Bevin was quite happy to make vague declarations in favour of a united Europe, even for 'a federation of Europe', but he vehemently opposed all suggestions of supranational European bodies. His single overriding goal was to persuade the US to put on to an institutional footing president Harry Truman's March 1947 promise of American support for 'free peoples who are resisting subjugation'— something that he eventually achieved with the creation of the North Atlantic Treaty Organisation (NATO) in April 1949.

Most of the left came round to this point of view rather more quickly than might have been expected, persuaded in part by the American offer of Marshall Aid for reconstruction in July

1947, in part by the realization that democratic socialist parties were unlikely to form governments in most of continental Europe, and in part by the growing evidence of the Soviet Union's hostile intentions – the Communist takeover in Hungary in June 1947, Stalin's rejection of Marshall Aid, the public reassertion of Moscow's control of the international Communist movement with the creation of the Cominform, and the February 1948 Communist coup in Czechoslovakia. Opposition to Russian expansionism did not of course rule out a west European federation allied with the US, but as the Cold War took a grip on the continent it became increasingly obvious that the left would be in a tiny minority in such a body if democratic socialists did not ally themselves with Communists.

The point was made with brutal clarity by the Congress of Europe a few weeks after the Prague *coup*. The Labour delegates found that most of the continental European participants were from anti-socialist centre-right parties; to make matters worse, the undoubted star of the show was Winston Churchill, who had – quite undeservedly – become a darling of continental federalists after backing the idea of a United States of Europe (not including Britain) eighteen months before in a speech in Zurich. In September 1948, the head of Labour's international department, Denis Healey, a protégé of Dalton like so many young Labour men who would rise to prominence on the party's right wing, produced a pamphlet explaining Labour's hostility to European federalism.[35] But by then the Labour left's dalliance with the idea had all but petered out.

Bevin and Dalton thus met little resistance from their party as they obstructed the international committee set up by the Hague conference to look into steps towards European unity, ensuring that all that emerged from its deliberations was a body organized on intergovernmental lines with a purely consultative function – the Council of Europe. Nor was there any great Labour outcry when in 1950 Dalton issued a party document, written by Healey, rejecting French foreign minister Robert Schuman's plan for pooling coal and steel resources under the control of a supra-national authority, the European Coal and Steel Community – the brainchild of the French civil servant Jean Monnet, which

Schuman described as 'the concrete foundation of a European federation'.[36]

The Healey–Dalton line was fierce: 'The Labour Party could never accept any commitments which limited its own, or others' freedom to pursue democratic socialism, and to apply the controls necessary to achieve it . . . Any changes in Britain's relations with western Europe must not impair her position as the nerve centre of the Commonwealth and banker of the sterling area . . . The first immediate aim for British foreign policy must be to construct an organic unity throughout the whole of the non-Communist world . . . No socialist party with the prospect of forming a government could accept a system by which important fields of national policy were surrendered to a supranational European representative authority, since such an authority would have a permanent anti-socialist majority and would arouse the hostility of the workers of Europe.'[37] At the press conference to launch the document – accidentally arranged for the very day that a rather non-committal government statement on the plan was due – Dalton was at his pig-headed worst, behaving, in the words of A.J. Cummings of the liberal *News Chronicle*, 'just like the offensive John Bull depicted by foreign cartoonists in the last century'.[38]

If it was the pragmatist right in government between 1945 and 1951 that defined Labour's antipathy to grand schemes for European federalism, it was the left in opposition in the early 1950s that took the anti-integrationist initiative. The cause was a French proposal – once again the idea of Jean Monnet – for a European Defence Community, first put forward in 1950 in response to American demands that West Germany make a contribution to the west's Cold War rearmament programme. The EDC was supposed to allay fears of a resurgent militarist Germany by ensuring that West German divisions were controlled by a supranational body. The loyally Atlanticist Labour leadership (with the exception of Dalton) backed it on condition that Britain did not join, and the Tories took the same position. But as the EDC negotiations dragged on, Aneurin Bevan and his followers on the Labour left, in insurgent mood after Labour's 1951 election defeat and increasingly critical of American foreign policy, became more and more alarmed at the implications of German rearmament. Particularly after the death of Stalin in 1953, the Bevanites attacked the EDC as a deliberate attempt by the Americans to perpetuate the Cold War by rearming Germany rather than negotiating with the Russians to secure a united, neutral and demilitarized Germany. The EDC had to be stopped before it plunged Europe into crisis.

The point was reasonable enough – but the way the Bevanites made it was not. Aping the Communist Party, they shamelessly fanned anti-German prejudice and fears of a Nazi revival. According to a 1954 *Tribune* pamphlet, *It Need Not Happen*, signed by Bevan, Barbara Castle, Richard Crossman, Tom Driberg, Ian Mikardo and Harold Wilson, 'The 12 divisions will be Nazi-led and Nazi-trained . . . The European Defence Community in fact is not an alternative to a German national army but merely the first step towards its creation.'[39] The EDC was scotched when the French National Assembly voted against it in August 1954 – but the controversy left a lasting mark on Labour politics. It gave some on the right of the party their first glimpse of a technocratic European integrationist politics unsullied by ideas about creating a 'third force' and entirely compatible with Atlanticism; and it gave the left a taste of the efficacy of populist nationalist demagoguery on Europe. The battle lines drawn over German rearmament remain visible today.

In the short term, however, the main effect of the EDC fiasco was to lull Labour into the complacent belief that continental Europe was incapable of agreeing on anything. The party barely noticed the June 1955 Messina meeting of foreign ministers of the six members of the European Coal and Steel Community, which launched 'a fresh advance towards the building of Europe' by agreeing to set up a customs union that would lead to a common market. Nor did it take seriously the subsequent negotiations that culminated in March 1957 in the Treaty of Rome, which established the European Economic Community. Although by 1960 a substantial number of MPs on Labour's Atlanticist right wing – notably Roy Jenkins and George

Brown – had become enthusiasts for British membership of the EEC, in the late 1950s the party leadership was convinced that Europe had nothing to offer it. In Germany, Italy and the Low Countries, reactionary Christian Democrats had established themselves as the dominant parties of government; in France, even before General Charles de Gaulle's constitutional *coup* of 1958, the socialists were weak and ineffectual. Bevan, appointed shadow foreign secretary by Hugh Gaitskell, summed up the mood soon after the Treaty of Rome was signed: 'The conception of a common market for Europe is not the blueprint for European prosperity and stability. It is the result of a political malaise following upon the failure of socialists to use the sovereign powers of their parliaments to plan their economic life . . . Socialists cannot at one and the same time call for economic planning and accept the verdict of free competition, no matter how extensive the area it covers. The jungle is not made more acceptable just because it is almost limitless.'[40]

The Tory government, with implicit Labour support, responded to the founding of the EEC by starting negotiations to create a European Free Trade Area with the Scandinavian countries and Switzerland. But Harold Macmillan had bigger ideas, and in summer 1961 announced his intention of joining the Common Market. Gaitskell dithered, then, to the horror of Jenkins and the rest of the by now quite substantial group of MPs that backed British membership of the EEC, came out unambiguously against joining at Labour's 1962 annual conference. Towards the end of his speech, Gaitskell turned to the question of a federal Europe. 'Now I know it may be said by some: "Why bring up federation?" It is not immediate, it is not imposed on us, it may not happen. But we would be foolish not to recognize . . . the desire of those who created the European Community for political federation . . . What does federation mean? It means that powers are taken away from national governments and handed over to a federal government. It means that if we go into this we are no more than a state, as it were in the United States of Europe, such as Texas or California . . . That is what it means; it does mean the end of Britain as an independent nation state . . . it means the end of a thousand years of history. You may say: "Let it end," but my

goodness, it is a decision that needs a little care and thought. And
it does mean the end of the Commonwealth.'[41]

Gaitskell died in January 1963, four days before de Gaulle vetoed
Macmillan's application to join the Common Market, and was
succeeded as Labour leader by Harold Wilson. The new leader had
long since given up his youthful enthusiasm for a federal Europe,
and appeared to be just as opposed as Gaitskell to British membership of the EEC. Although he did not use his predecessor's
nationalistic rhetoric about 'a thousand years of history', he was as
emphatic in his belief that the Commonwealth, not Europe,
should be at the core of Labour foreign policy. Nevertheless, he
needed to keep the pro-Europe right on board. So Labour went
into the 1964 general election with its position as fudged as it was
possible to be. 'Negotiations? Yes,' Wilson told a campaign meeting. 'Unconditional acceptance of whatever terms are on offer?
No.'[42]

In government, Wilson put the issue to one side for a while,
then in summer 1966 started to drop hints that the government
would be making another application to join the EEC. That
October, he put it to the cabinet, winning approval by a small
margin, then in early 1967 embarked on a tour of Europe with foreign secretary George Brown to test the water, ending with a
meeting with de Gaulle in Paris. Wilson came back completely
convinced of the need for Britain to join, got the approval of cabinet and parliament for a formal application – only thirty-five
Labour MPs voted against – and submitted it in May 1967.

What caused Wilson's conversion to the Common Market
remains a mystery. Some say that he was simply persuaded that
Britain would benefit economically from membership, others that
he needed a 'big idea' to make him look statesmanlike in the wake
of Rhodesian UDI and the economic strains caused by his refusal
to devalue the pound. Some cynics even say that he made the
application in the knowledge that it was bound to fail, because he
knew it would split the cabinet in such a way as to obstruct the
emergence of a widely supported challenge to his leadership.[43]
Whatever, the application came to nothing. De Gaulle vetoed

British membership, telling the world that Britain would be allowed into the EEC only if it disengaged from the United States. Wilson made preparations for another application after Georges Pompidou replaced de Gaulle as French president in 1969, but nothing had come of it by the time Wilson lost the 1970 election to Edward Heath.

In the next two years, Labour was swept by a tide of anti-European hysteria as the Tory government swiftly negotiated the terms on which Britain at long last entered the Common Market. The left, keen to take its vengeance on Wilson for the myriad disappointments of the 1964–70 government, took the lead. Its case had a rational kernel in the familiar arguments that Britain should orient itself towards the Commonwealth and that the Market made impossible the pursuit of a radical left-wing economic policy – but it spiced all this with a populist nationalism that was at best short-sighted and at worst crudely xenophobic.[44] In early 1971 right-wing anti-Marketeers joined in too, among them Jim Callaghan, and by the time the government agreed terms for entry in spring, Labour's mood was firmly anti-Market. At a special conference that summer to determine Labour's attitude to the agreement, Wilson caved in to the pressure and came out against EEC membership on the available terms. Jenkins, by now Labour's deputy leader, was disgusted at what he and his pro-Market allies saw as Wilson's cowardice; in the Commons on 28 October, he led 69 Labour MPs in defying the whip to vote in favour of entry, giving the government a majority of 112.[45] The final straw for Jenkins appeared to come in March the next year when Wilson decided to support a Tory back-bench amendment calling for a referendum on EEC membership – an idea that had been floated by Tony Benn in 1970 and was anathema to the pro-Marketeers. In what Wilson's biographer Ben Pimlott describes as 'a dress rehearsal for the SDP defection nine years later', Jenkins resigned from the shadow cabinet, taking George Thomson and Harold Lever with him, and Bill Rodgers, Dick Taverne, Dickson Mabon and David Owen quit junior front-bench posts.

After that, however, Labour's Common Market row subsided. Wilson patched it up with Jenkins and the party won the February 1974 election with a manifesto promising that 'a Labour government will immediately seek a fundamental renegotiation of the terms of entry'; if the renegotiation was successful, it went on, 'the people should have the right to decide the issue through a general election or a consultative referendum'.[46] It was, again, a fudge. It kept the party superficially united long enough for it to win a working majority in the October 1974 election (the manifesto which promised 'that within 12 months of this election we will give the British people the final say . . . through the ballot box on whether we accept the terms and stay in or reject the terms and come out').[47] But it collapsed as soon as the meagre results of the 'fundamental renegotiation', conducted by Callaghan as foreign secretary, were unveiled. Labour split hopelessly before the June 1975 referendum. A majority of the cabinet, including such recent anti-Marketeers as Callaghan and Healey, now chancellor, joined the Tories and Liberals in the 'yes' camp. But more Labour MPs were against the renegotiated terms than for them, with the left united in opposition. The Labour NEC and the special conference held in April 1975 to decide the party's line in the referendum both strongly opposed the government.[48] Labour left-wingers played the leading role in the 'no' campaign.

The scale of the 'yes' majority stunned Labour's anti-Marketeers, but it silenced them only temporarily. They treated Roy Jenkins with contempt for leaving the government to become president of the European Commission in 1976, then put up spirited resistance in parliament to the bill to legislate for direct elections to the European Parliament.[49] In the last months of the Callaghan administration, the threat of a revolt by the anti-Marketeers was one major reason that the government decided not to participate in the European Monetary System, the managed exchange rate arrangement set up by French president Valéry Giscard d'Estaing and West German chancellor Helmut Schmidt in 1979. (The EMS, the brainchild of Jenkins, was conceived of as an alternative to monetary union, which the Community had adopted as a goal in 1969 but never put into effect. The other major reason Britain did not join was Healey's scepticism about its workability.) By 1979, Labour's mood was once again strongly anti-European. In the left revolt against the leadership that followed the party's electoral defeat, the demand for British withdrawal from the Community played a central role. By the end of 1980, the Labour conference had adopted withdrawal as policy and the Parliamentary Labour Party had elected Michael Foot, an opponent of the Common Market since the 1950s, as leader. (Foot now considers the left's anti-Europeanism 'the biggest mistake we made'.)[50]

Together with the concurrent Labour shift towards unilateral nuclear disarmament, the swing against Europe was the main Labour policy change that prompted Jenkins and a large section of the pro-European right to set up the SDP in early 1981 – and their leaving Labour in turn reinforced its anti-Europeanism. That July, the NEC issued a policy statement explaining that 'Labour will have no choice but to carry through a radical, socialist economic strategy . . . which would inevitably bring us into direct conflict with the EEC . . . our policies are in conflict with either the letter or the practice of the Treaty of Rome.' The 1983 manifesto confidently declared that 'British withdrawal is the right policy for Britain', promising that it would be 'completed well within the lifetime of the parliament'.[51]

The U-turn on withdrawal deftly executed by Cook and Kinnock in late 1983 was as far as Labour went on Europe between 1983 and 1987. Cook was removed from the European portfolio in early 1985 and replaced by George Robertson, a conventional technocratic right-wing Atlanticist pro-European, an appointment that showed there was to be no retreat; and New Socialist, the party magazine edited by Stuart Weir, was allowed to push a left-wing pro-Europe agenda that went far beyond any official party position.[52] But Kinnock did not put the rejection of withdrawal to the party conference, knowing that the major trade unions would be compelled to oppose it because their own conferences remained in favour of leaving; Labour then took a simple oppositionist line on the Single European Act – the amendment to the Community's founding treaties, agreed in 1986, that set up a single European market. The 1987 manifesto mentioned Europe only in passing. 'Labour's aim is to work constructively with our EEC partners to promote economic expansion and combat unemployment,' it stated. 'However, we will stand up for British interests within the European Community and will seek to put an end to the abuses and scandals of the Common Agricultural Policy. We shall, like other member countries, reject EEC interference with our policy for national recovery and renewal.'[53]

After 1987, however, Kinnock pressed ahead rapidly with the transformation of Labour into a pro-European party. The retirement from the front bench of Healey, who as shadow foreign secretary had approached Europe with typical scepticism (in the proper sense of the word), gave him room for manoeuvre. Both Robertson, who kept the European affairs job, and shadow chancellor John Smith were eager for Labour to embrace Europe unambiguously. The same was true of a minority of Labour MEPs, who had become increasingly annoyed at what they saw as the obstinate nationalism of the majority of their colleagues in the British Labour Group and wanted the party leadership in London to sort them out.[54] But what most encouraged Kinnock was the conversion of the party's affiliated trade unions to the idea of a 'social Europe' put forward by Jacques Delors, the former French socialist prime minister, as president of the European Commission. Delors was convinced that the single European market and the planned creation of a single European currency, agreed in principle by the June 1988 European Council meeting in Hanover, necessitated common European standards of employment rights – to join trade unions, to be consulted by management, to be paid a living wage, to work in safety and so on – and in summer 1988 he set out to convince the trade unions and socialist parties of the Community of his cause. His plea for support for the Commission's draft 'social charter' of workers' rights at the TUC congress in Bournemouth in September received a standing ovation.

Delors' reputation with the unions and with Labour was sealed by the vehement reaction of Margaret Thatcher. A few weeks later, she laid into him in a speech in Bruges, in which she famously proclaimed: 'We have not successfully rolled back the frontiers of the state in Britain only to see them reimposed at a European level, with a European superstate exercising a new dominance from Brussels.'[55] Instead of the federal Europe with a substantial regulatory role envisaged by Delors, she argued for a deregulating, intergovernmental Europe, open to trade with the rest of the world, that was much more parsimonious than the Community had become (especially on the Common Agricultural Policy).

The Bruges speech caused consternation on the pro-European wing of the Tory party: in many ways it marked the beginning of the Tories' seemingly never-ending civil war over Europe. But Labour saw Thatcher's antipathy to a social dimension to Europe as an opportunity. The party fought the 1989 Euro-election campaign arguing strongly for a 'social Europe', and won 39 per cent of the vote and 45 seats to the Tories' 34 per cent and 32 seats – the first election covering the whole of the United Kingdom in which Labour had amassed more votes than the Tories since 1974. Support for the 'social chapter' of the Maastricht Treaty, which is based on the principles of the 'social charter' (and from which John Major opted out at Maastricht), remained a Labour theme right up to the 1997 election.

European economic and monetary union, the most far-reaching of Delors' initiatives in the late 1980s, was much more difficult for Labour. The idea of monetary union for the Community had been around since the immediate post-war years, and there had been an attempt in the early 1970s to bring it about through a managed exchange rate system, known as the 'snake'. But this proved a failure, and in the late 1970s Germany and France opted for a less ambitious means of cooperating on currency stability – the exchange rate mechanism of the European Monetary System. What put EMU back at the top of the agenda in the late 1980s was the French government's resentment at the way West German economic strength made the Bundesbank dominant in the ERM, giving it the ability to determine unilaterally the macroeconomic policies of every member country. A single European currency appeared to be a way of giving all participants a say in interest rate and exchange rate policy. The German government agreed in principle, but only on condition that there would be a parallel move towards political integration, that the convergence criteria for joining the single currency would be very tight and that the new central bank would be as tough on inflation as the Bundesbank.

Britain was not in the ERM – and EMU was not a priority even for Labour's most enthusiastic Europhiles until after Delors outlined his three-stage plan for creating a single currency and central bank in summer 1989. But John Smith soon realized that it offered Labour a way out of being seen as 'soft' on inflation. The first of the three stages involved all Community currencies joining the ERM – and if Labour promised to do that, no one could claim that it really wanted to devalue (see chapter 2). Kinnock and the majority of the shadow cabinet took Smith's lead.

But EMU was anathema to many in Labour's ranks who objected to depriving a Labour government of crucial policy-making powers, not all of them out-and-out Eurosceptics. For Bryan Gould and others who believed that Britain's main economic problem was an overvalued currency, even joining the ERM – as sterling did in October 1990 – was a step too far. Many others who agreed with membership of the ERM in principle believed that the pound joined at an overvalued rate. There was also widespread Labour opposition to the German government's insistence on political independence for the planned European central bank and on tough convergence criteria for EMU, both eventually enshrined in the Maastricht Treaty.

Nevertheless, between 1989 and 1992, Labour moved from an explicitly anti-EMU position to one of qualified support as Smith and his supporters, with Kinnock's backing, ousted Gould from his position of influence over economic policy. *Meet the Challenge, Make the Change*, the document produced by the party's policy review in May 1989 when Gould was chair of the group dealing with economic policy, opposed both membership of the ERM and 'moves towards a European monetary union'.[56] Although Smith declared for joining the ERM that autumn, just before Gould was shuffled out of his job as trade and industry spokesman, Labour's next document summarizing its policies, *Looking to the Future*, published in spring 1990, retained a sceptical attitude to 'trying to impose blueprints on the economic and monetary development of Europe'.[57]

A year later, with the pre-Maastricht intergovernmental

conference on EMU in full swing, the shift was complete. *Labour's Better Way for the 1990s* declared in favour of a single currency in principle. Monetary union 'could offer Britain considerable benefits, eliminating currency speculation within the Community and reducing business costs', it argued, although it opposed creation of a single currency on a 'rigid timetable' without 'greater convergence between the different economies of the EC'.[58] Labour also backed the French government's attempts at the intergovernmental conference to get the Germans to accept political control of the proposed European central bank. After the French conceded central bank independence, the party argued for an enhanced role for Ecofin, the Council of Economic and Finance Ministers, which it said should set the external exchange rate of the single currency, with interest rates determined by what Smith described as 'a dialogue between Ecofin and the central bank'.[59]

It was a fudge – as indeed was the party's position on the parallel intergovernmental conference on political union. Here, Labour endorsed the idea of giving the European Parliament greater powers and backed an extension of 'qualified majority voting' in the Council of Ministers to cover social and environmental policies. (This means that on certain subjects the Council operates not on the basis of unanimity among all members but through majority decision-making, with each country's vote weighted to account for differences in population. Where it applies, a measure must have the approval of 75 per cent of these weighted votes to be passed. The Tories backed extensions of qualified majority voting in the Single European Act and the Maastricht Treaty but opposed any extension after that.) At the same time, however, it rejected the idea of a 'European federal super-state', opposed any move towards a military role for the EC, insisted that the Community be expanded as well as deepened, and argued against any reduction in the powers of national parliaments.

Nevertheless, the compromises stitched together in 1991 in the run-up to Maastricht proved remarkably resilient. In essence, they remained the foundation of Labour's approach to Europe right up to the 1997 general election. As with economic policy, the changes to Labour's Europe policy since Tony Blair proclaimed the birth of New Labour have been trivial by comparison with those pushed through by Neil Kinnock between 1987 and 1992.

The party leadership's position on EMU took some sharp criticism immediately after the 1992 general election, particularly after the orgy of speculation that forced sterling out of the exchange rate mechanism on 'Black Wednesday'. But the election of John Smith as leader was tantamount to a guarantee that Labour's general approach would remain the same – and indeed the party's autumn 1992 party conference voted against a Eurosceptic demand for a referendum on Maastricht and reaffirmed Labour's pro-EMU stance. Smith chose Jack Cunningham, a fellow right-wing pro-European, as shadow foreign secretary and kept Robertson on as European affairs spokesman for the duration of the legislative process for ratification of Maastricht. Robertson won plaudits from Labour's pro-Europeans for the skill with which he harried the government without ever putting the treaty in danger. But all that emerged in the way of policy on Europe from Cunningham's first year in the post was an elaboration of Labour's familiar positions laced with some positive remarks about Delors' ideas for increasing Commission spending on infrastructure.[60]

The shadow foreign secretary's dilatory work rate, in combination with his support of the Foreign Office line on Bosnia, led to widespread grumbling among his colleagues, and he scraped on to the shadow cabinet in late October 1993 with the lowest vote of any successful candidate. Even supporters say that he was lucky to keep his job in Smith's subsequent reshuffle, in which Robertson – elected to the shadow cabinet after years of trying – became shadow Scottish secretary. Cunningham's fortunes then took another tumble after the Tories seized upon promises of a 35–hour working week and massively increased powers for the European Parliament in the draft manifesto for the 1994 European election that Labour had drawn up with its fellow socialist parties in the Party of European Socialists.[61] Cunningham should have noticed because he chaired the drafting committee that had produced the document. In the event, the party solved its problem by discarding the PES manifesto, much to the chagrin of its Euro-enthusiasts.

Nevertheless, Labour's performance in the 1994 Euro-elections, which took place just after the death of Smith, was better than anyone in the party had dared hope. It took 44 per cent of the vote and 62 seats to the Tories' 28 per cent and 18 seats and the Lib Dems' 17 per cent and two seats. Labour won even in former Conservative strongholds in the south-east and East Anglia, unseating the Tories' leader in the European Parliament, Sir Christopher Prout, and their chairman, Bill Newton-Dunn. After the election, Labour found itself far and away the dominant force in the PES in Strasbourg, and the leader of the European Parliamentary Labour Party (EPLP), Pauline Green, was easily elected PES leader, a position she still holds today.

MEPs are not public figures in Britain in the way that MPs are. Their constituencies are giant, few of their constituents know what they do, and they are largely ignored by the media except when they embarrass the leaders of their parties in London. Of Labour's 62 MEPs, the only one well known in the world outside the party and the Parliament is Glenys Kinnock, and that is not because of her activities as an MEP.

At one time, Labour MEPs largely deserved their obscurity. Until 1979, the members of the European Parliament were national MPs appointed by their parties, and even the directly elected Parliament was at first no more than a talking shop. Of the 17 Labour MEPs elected in 1979, led by Barbara Castle, the majority were hard-line anti-Marketeers, some of them selected as candidates because no one else could be bothered to run. Although Castle herself made a point of working with other socialists in the Parliament and came round to the view that Labour should ditch the policy of withdrawal from the EC, she caused a furore in 1982 by writing a piece for the *New Statesman* arguing that, instead of getting out of Europe, a Labour government should simply implement its radical economic policies and challenge the other member states to expel Britain if they did not like it.[62] Most of her colleagues adopted an attitude of sullen opposition to all things European and stuck with it.

During the 1980s, however, the powers of the Parliament gradually expanded, in part through its own assertiveness (particularly in using its ability to veto the Commission budget) and in part as a result of the introduction of new rights to amend Council legislation as part of the Single European Act. Meanwhile, the character of Labour's representation was transformed as a result of the 1984 and 1989 European elections. Most of the Labour MEPs elected for the first time in 1984 shared Neil Kinnock's belief in constructive engagement with Europe (among them Christine Crawley, Glyn Ford, Stephen Hughes, David Martin, David Morris, John Tomlinson and Carole Tongue) and the next five years saw a bitter and often farcical battle between them and the anti-Europeans for control of the British Labour Group, with the leadership passing first from Castle to an ultra-Europhobe, Alf Lomas, then to David Martin, then back to another Europhobe, Barry Seal. After the 1989 European election, however, the anti-European faction was swamped by pro-European newcomers, among them Ken Coates, Peter Crampton, Wayne David, Alan Donnelly, Pauline Green and Ian White, and the leadership was won by Glyn Ford, who kept the job for four years until being ousted by Green. Of the 45 Labour MEPs between 1989 and 1994, only 13 voted against the Maastricht Treaty: of the rest, although most were pragmatists who did not want to miss out on anything but did not have a clear idea of where they wanted Europe to go, at least a dozen were federalists in all but name, among them Coates, Crampton, Ford, Martin, Tongue and White.

Maastricht significantly increased the powers of the Parliament, giving it far greater clout in the legislative process and various rights in relation to appointments (including the ability to sack the whole Commission with a vote of no confidence). During Ford's period as leader of what had now been renamed the European Parliamentary Labour Party, Labour's MEPs played an increasingly prominent role in the workings of the Parliament. To take just a handful of examples: David Martin was elected a vice-president of the Parliament and became rapporteur (roughly, committee co-ordinator and spokesperson) on three reports on the Maastricht process; Ken Collins chaired the Parliament's powerful environment committee; Alan Donnelly was successively rapporteur on EMU legislation and German unification; John Tomlinson and Terry Wynn were rapporteurs on the EU budget in 1990 and 1994.[63]

The EPLP was rewarded for its hard work with a much more important position in Labour's structures. The MEPs' leader had long had the right to attend meetings of the party's National Executive Committee – but in 1991 the Labour conference gave members of the EPLP the same voting rights as MPs in party leadership elections, introduced EPLP representation on Labour's new policy forum and set up a regular European conference. The pro-Europe majority in the EPLP was vocal in Labour's Maastricht debate between 1991 and 1993 and was largely responsible for getting the party leadership interested in Jacques Delors' plans for Europe-wide measures to counter unemployment (see chapter 4).

After the 1994 European elections, the pro-European domination of the EPLP was further reinforced (although the number of closet federalists remained the same) as was the EPLP's position in the Parliament. Apart from Green moving up from the EPLP leadership to the PES leadership – to be replaced by Wayne David – Labour added to its haul of committee chairs and rapporteurships, with Stephen Hughes becoming chairman of the social affairs committee, Eddie Newman chairman of the petitions committee, and Ken Coates rapporteur of a new employment committee.

On the face of it, Labour's MEPs had reasonable grounds to expect to be treated with some respect by Smith's successor as Labour leader. Tony Blair, on the contrary, annoyed by a majority of the EPLP voting for Margaret Beckett and John Prescott in the leadership election, was not really interested in them, and the lack of interest soon turned into hostility. In January 1995, as Blair prepared to address a business seminar in Brussels, thirty-two Labour MEPs were named as signatories to an advertisement in the *Guardian* opposing the abandonment of Clause Four. The advertisement, placed by the hard-left Eurosceptic MEP for Scotland Mid and Fife, Alex Falconer, had already been published unnoticed in *Tribune*, but the impact of its second appearance was spectacular. Blair rose to the bait by denouncing the thirty-two for 'infantile incompetence' and his spin doctors described Labour's MEPs as 'nonentities'. That thirty-six MEPs (including some of the signatories) were arm-twisted into signing a letter to the *Guardian* distancing themselves from the provocation did nothing to placate the Labour leader. Ever since, he has given a cold shoulder even to those MEPs who voted for him in the leadership election and had nothing to do with Falconer's little stunt. In opposition, he left John Prescott and former Labour general secretary Larry Whitty to liaise with the EPLP (very effectively, according to most MEPs); in government, despite his hostility to proportional representation, Blair decided to go ahead with a regional list system for European elections to give him the best chance of weeding out critical MEPs before 1999. To their annoyance, Labour MEPs have had little tangible influence on Labour's thinking about policy even where it relates directly to their work.[64]

This, however, is to run away with the story. Before Blair's set-to with the rebel MEPs, he had undertaken his first shadow cabinet reshuffle – and to the surprise of nobody had ditched Cunningham as shadow foreign secretary. Nor was it a surprise that the post went to Robin Cook, who since 1992 had established a formidable reputation as chief trade and industry spokesman by ruthlessly pursuing the government on the arms-to-Iraq affair. For weeks before Blair picked his team in late October 1994, the word on the Westminster grapevine had been that foreign affairs was Cook's most likely destination.

Cook, though, was not pleased with the appointment. He had decided to resist pressure to enter the leadership contest and instead volunteered as Blair's campaign manager[65] – a job he had previously done for Smith in 1992 and Kinnock in 1983 – and had high hopes of becoming shadow chancellor instead of Gordon Brown. Failing the shadow chancellorship, he would much rather have stayed put. 'I think it is perfectly fair to say that I was very, very happy doing trade and industry,' he told the *Scotsman* a year later. 'I had only been doing the job for two years and, yes, I was very keen on what I was doing and there was work I wanted to complete.'[66]

On Europe policy, Cook's task as shadow foreign secretary was less one of determining its broad thrust than one of honing detail and presentation. The detail was necessary because 1996 would mark the start of another intergovernmental conference to tie up Maastricht's loose ends in preparation for expanding the EU to include eastern Europe; by the time Cook was appointed, there had already been a flurry of incompatible proposals from all sides, and Labour needed to decide what it thought of them. In addition, the opinion polls and Labour's focus groups had been showing since 1993 that the British public was becoming increasingly critical of Europe. Voters did not like the Tories' vicious arguments about Europe – but they seemed to be more and more persuaded of the anti-European case, making Labour potentially vulnerable if it did not develop a more populist position.

Cook was the ideal person to do this. Although he played a crucial part in Kinnock's initial abandonment of withdrawal from Europe in 1983–4, he had not subsequently moved as far as Kinnock, Smith and Brown in embracing EMU. He was sharply critical in private of Labour's ERM policy in 1992–3 and was unconvinced of the desirability or practicality of a single currency on Maastricht terms. He still believed, moreover, that the institutions of the EU had to be made much more democratically accountable if they were to win popular approval. If he had little time for hard-core Labour anti-Europeans like Peter Shore and Bryan Gould, he was sympathetic to many of the ideas of (and personally friendly with) those Labour left-wingers, notably Peter Hain and Roger Berry, who opposed Maastricht from a pro-Europe perspective.

In his first year as shadow foreign secretary, Cook subtly repositioned Labour on Europe, producing a new populist overall policy document, A People's Europe, and a detailed position paper on the intergovernmental conference. He summed up his change of emphasis in an early 1996 interview with the New Statesman. On EMU, he said, 'I don't think anyone should underrate the very strong political will behind the creation of a single currency on the part of French president Jacques Chirac and German chancellor Helmut Kohl. But there are undoubtedly problems with the Maastricht timetable for EMU. We can see the benefits of a single

currency, but it can only work if there is real economic convergence among the participating countries – in terms of productivity,
innovation and output as well as public-sector deficits and inflation. Unless we get that, there has to be a question mark over
whether we will be able to give up for all time the right to devalue.
Devaluation has been the way that Britain has compensated for its
failure to compete over the past 30 years. It is not a strategy, but it
does enable you to compensate for the failure of strategy.'

More generally, Cook went on, although 'Britain will never
get the best deal from Europe by remaining isolated', the real challenge 'is how we reconnect with the peoples of Europe. The
problem with Maastricht is that the political elites became uncou-
pled from the concerns and aspirations of their peoples. We have
got to get Europe back to a people's agenda, and the first priority
is jobs.' As for political integration, 'It is simply absurd to describe
us as federalists. Labour's vision of Europe is of independent
member-states voluntarily coming together to co-operate. We do
not want to surrender our independence to some kind of super-
state.' Nevertheless, 'the European Commission should be
accountable to the European Parliament, while the Council of
Ministers should be more accountable to national parliaments'.

The biggest priority, however, was enlargement of the EU to
the east, initially to Poland, Hungary, the Czech Republic, Slovakia
and possibly Slovenia: 'We need to ensure that the countries of
central Europe go down the road of post-war western Europe,
not that of the post-Communist Balkans.' This in turn put a high
premium on reforming the Common Agricultural Policy and on
coming up with a step-by-step approach for east–central European
entry to the EU.[67]

With the addition of the promise of a referendum on Britain joining a single currency, announced in late 1996, and a little
sceptical-sounding tweaking on the need to ensure that the Social
Chapter did not damage British competitiveness and on the possibilities of Britain joining EMU in the first wave,[68] this was the
policy on which Labour won in 1997. According to the manifesto, a Labour Britain 'will be a leader in Europe'. 'Our vision of

Europe,' it went on, 'is of an alliance of independent nations choosing to co-operate to achieve the goals they cannot achieve alone. We oppose a European federal superstate.'[69] Labour's priorities were completing the single market, ending the Social Chapter opt-out, giving a high priority to enlargement and reform of the CAP, working for 'greater openness and democracy in EU institutions with open voting in the Council of Ministers and more effective scrutiny of the Commission by the European Parliament' and backing a limited extension of qualified majority voting in the Council of Ministers.

As for EMU, the manifesto stated that 'any decision about Britain joining the single currency must be determined by a hard-headed assessment of Britain's economic interests . . . But there are formidable obstacles in the way of Britain being in the first wave of membership, if EMU takes place on 1 January 1999. What is essential for the success of EMU is genuine convergence among the economies that take part, without any fudging of the rules.' Early in the campaign, Cook explained that Labour's policy on the single currency meant that 'if you didn't join in 1999, it is unlikely that you'd be joining in the course of the next parliament'[70] – which was widely reported as a statement that Labour would stay out until 2002, although in fact it was nothing of the sort.

Labour's victory was widely welcomed across the political spectrum on the Continent: the sense of relief that the British Tories' histrionic obstructionism was a thing of the past was palpable. But it would be foolish to expect the next few years to be plain sailing for Blair in Europe – particularly if he behaves arrogantly. Many more patronizing lectures like the one he delivered to the Party of European Socialists in Sweden will not go down well with Britain's European partners. Although there is a growing consensus on the continent that Europe does need greater labour market flexibility to compete in a globalized economy, there is little desire in the political mainstream to abandon either the welfare state or the 'social partnership' model of industrial relations and politics. If Britain is seen to be over-zealous in its pursuit of deregulation, it will find itself isolated. Similarly, there is a limit to how far France and

Germany will tolerate Britain's intransigent opposition to the EU acquiring a defence identity and its insistence that NATO should remain responsible for most defence and security collaboration. There is also plenty of scope for friction over the institutional reforms that the EU desperately needs if it is to work effectively and acquire the democratic legitimacy that it currently so obviously lacks. Amsterdam merely postponed the inevitable on qualified majority voting in the Council of Ministers, which will have to be extended if the EU is to function at all efficiently, particularly if it is serious about expanding eastwards. Labour's desire to retain Britain's veto over taxation, defence and security, immigration, European budget decisions and treaty changes is bound to lead to further conflict with other governments – although how serious remains to be seen.

In the same vein, Labour's irrational hostility to 'federalism' – a trait it shares with the Tories but which it has inherited from the worst of its own past – makes it unlikely that the government will sanction the sort of increase in the European Parliament's powers that it needs to hold the Commission to account. This will inevitably lead to tensions with the Parliament, including most Labour MEPs, and with those governments that favour more or less rapid evolution of a federal European polity.

Equally important, although the EU has long since agreed in principle to expand to the east, the Commission's plans for which were published in July 1997, the obstacles to enlargement are even more formidable than those to Britain joining EMU in the first wave. Expansion is impossible without a radical recasting of the EU's spending, particularly on the CAP, which is due to be negotiated in parallel with accession talks with the first batch of five east–central European countries to be considered for membership – Poland, the Czech Republic, Hungary, Slovenia and Estonia. The idea is that agreement will be reached on both budget and enlargement so that the five can join in 2002, but this timetable is a little optimistic given the complexities and vested interests involved and the lag in preparations caused by the stalemate over the 1996 intergovernmental conference and the turmoil over EMU.

Which leaves Labour's biggest Euro-headache, the single currency. The party's pre-election indeterminacy on the subject was a fudge that could accommodate all the players of any weight in the party regardless of their opinion on EMU. But 'wait and see' also made sense on electoral grounds and because of the uncertainty of the whole process of monetary union. Even at the time of writing in summer 1997, although the final decisions about which countries qualify to join the single currency will have to made by May 1998, it is still not clear who will make the grade – and there are a multiplicity of plausible scenarios in which the whole EMU process grinds to a halt.

A British decision on first-wave participation in the single currency cannot, however, be put off for very much longer. If Britain is to join EMU in 1999, the government will have to announce very soon indeed that it intends to do so. Whatever it decides will involve high risks. Opting to stay out means the government having its work cut out if it is to retain its credibility with other EU governments, for which EMU has become the touchstone of commitment to the cause of a united Europe. Opting for first-wave membership means gambling not only on the success of EMU, but also on the willingness of the cabinet and the Parliamentary Labour Party to go along with it, on the ability of the government to counter an overwhelmingly Eurosceptical press, and on the state of public opinion at the time of the referendum.

So it is most likely that Labour will stay out of the first wave but make approving noises about the idea of joining in 2002 or thereabouts, which at least removes the risk of getting caught up in a failing single currency and goes some way to placate the rest of Europe. Such a course of action still leaves the problem of the party, the press and the public, and there is nothing to suggest that it will be any easier to persuade any of them that EMU is a good thing in 2000–2 or 2002–4 than before 1999. It is not what the government wants to hear right now – but it is just possible that the single currency will do to Blair's Labour Party what it did to Major's Tories.

4

GET A MOVE ON
JOHN PRESCOTT'S
SUPER-MINISTRY

It was hardly a complete surprise. The idea that John Prescott might head a 'super-ministry' with responsibility for regional policy and quite a lot else besides had been in the air for at least a couple of years before Labour won the 1997 general election. But there had been plenty of other rumours as well. As little as ten weeks before polling day Tony Blair's spin doctors had poured cold water on a *Sunday Times* report stating that the Labour deputy leader would take over the Department of the Environment, the Department of Transport and the regional development part of Department of Trade and Industry's brief.[1] More important, nobody had given any detailed thought to how the super-ministry would work, where it would have its headquarters or how ministerial responsibilities would be divided within it. When Prescott was appointed secretary of state at the head of a new Department of Environment, Transport and the Regions, his first task was to invent his own ministry.

He set about doing so with characteristic enthusiasm, telling anyone who was prepared to listen that he was in charge and that he would be taking the lead in every area of the new ministry's responsibilities. 'I am delighted that I can bring these parts together in one coherent whole,' he said on his first day. 'It is time to adopt a more coherent approach to regional affairs, to planning development and to providing the environment, transport, infrastructure and other needs of our rural and urban communities. My job is to put these parts together. A significant part will be played by decentralization, enabling the English regions through regional development agencies and regional chambers to set local priorities.'[2]

Prescott moved himself into the spanking new hi-tech offices just off Victoria Street in London that were built by the last government to house the Department of the Environment, and within a couple of days the most important posts in his ministerial team had been finalized: Gavin Strang as minister for transport (with cabinet rank), Michael Meacher as minister for the environment, Hilary Armstrong as minister for local government and housing and Dick Caborn as minister for the regions. Next came four more junior ministerial appointments, and then the job of sorting out priorities for the Queen's Speech. What emerged was much as expected: a bill to allow local authorities to use receipts from council house sales for new building and renovation, another to set up regional development agencies for the ten English regions and a third to hold a referendum on a directly elected strategic authority and mayor for London.

Most politicians would have stopped at this point for a breather – but not Prescott. Immediately after the Queen's Speech, he held an intensive two-day meeting with his ministers and senior civil servants at Chevening, the grand seventeenth-century country house in the North Downs he now shares with foreign secretary Robin Cook. Then he met the rail regulator and announced 'a thorough review of rail regulation in line with our manifesto commitment to introduce a strategic rail authority and to have tougher regulation of the privatised rail industry'. Next, he instructed the managers of Eurotunnel to come up with new ways of improving freight wagons like those involved in the 1996 Channel Tunnel fire. After that, he muscled in on a meeting of water company bosses called by Michael Meacher to discuss water shortages and ordered them to cut down on leakage rates.

He slowed down a little after the first fortnight, but right up to the summer holidays he was making on average a speech a day covering different aspects of his responsibilities: the prospects for inner-city regeneration, the principles of his 'integrated transport policy', the benefits of green taxes and so on. At the same time, he was doing his utmost to absorb as many powers as possible into his new department from other ministries (although he did not manage to wrest control of inward investment subsidies from the DTI) and to stamp his authority both on the Civil Service and on the host of quangos, private companies and regulators that come under his remit. Time will be the judge of the new ministry – but if it fails it will not be for want of effort on Prescott's part.

In many ways, Prescott's position as overlord in the new department fits his experience to a tee – and not just that as a politician. He is the son of a railway signalman, and before becoming an MP in 1970 he was a seaman. He was appointed as a junior front-bench transport spokesman as long ago as 1971, and in opposition from 1979 until becoming Labour's deputy leader in 1994 held a succession of posts in which he had responsibility for transport policy and developed various themes of regional and local government policy.

John Prescott was born in the north Wales town of Prestatyn in 1938. The eldest of five children – three sons and two daughters – he grew up steeped in working-class Labour culture. Both his mother, a former maid from a mining family, and his father were active in the Labour Party, the latter as a local councillor; his maternal grandfather, another committed socialist, was a miner and union official. When Prescott was five the family moved from Wales to Brinsworth, near Rotherham, where he had an early taste of campaigning for Labour, leafleting with his father during the 1945 election campaign. A few years later they moved again, this time to Upton in Chester. It was while at school here that Prescott received notification that he had failed the Eleven-plus – an event that scarred him for life. He has often told the story of the childhood girlfriend who passed the Eleven-plus and ended their relationship by returning a love-letter from him with spelling mistakes corrected. That a brother and sister later passed the exam and went on to grammar school made Prescott's own failure all the more traumatic.

He was already keenly aware of the many ways that class could affect people's lives. He noticed at scout camp that 'the middle-class kids took beautiful things with them, like wrapped-up chocolates. All I had was scones.' When his mother bought him his first pair of football boots, 'I knew she couldn't afford them. I still want to cry about that.' Years after he first entered parliament, he candidly admitted that 'I won't ring a hotel for a room – I prefer someone else to do it for me – and I won't go into a restaurant unless there's a table already booked. I'm afraid of being rejected, of being put down.'³ He grew up an intensely shy boy with an inferiority complex, but with a chip on his shoulder that propelled him on in political life.

Deflated after his Eleven-plus rejection, he left school at fifteen with no O-levels. His headmaster suggested he try his hand in the catering trade. Prescott went to work as a junior porter in a hotel in Bala, Wales, then to another hotel in Warrington as a trainee chef (where he was sometimes too shy to leave the kitchen). In 1955, at the age of seventeen, tempted by better pay and the opportunity of travel, he went to sea as a steward with Cunard liners.

The experience transformed him. He was soon acting as an unofficial shop-steward, in which role he acquired a reputation as a trouble-maker with both employers and the leadership of the National Union of Seamen. He was a key organizer in the unofficial seamen's strike of 1960 and subsequently agitated vociferously for democratic reform of the NUS.

Meanwhile, the young Prescott had discovered an appetite for education. In 1963, after doing a string of Workers Education Association correspondence courses, he won a place at Ruskin College in Oxford to study economics and politics. Ruskin gave him the intellectual self-assurance he had lacked: 'My mind was opened to the pleasures of learning, of shaping the bullets with which to fight. Ruskin gave me self-confidence in mobilizing my arguments. It taught me I had no need to feel inferior to anybody.'⁴ One of his tutors was the historian Raphael Samuel, who later recalled the 'disturbing experience' of teaching Prescott: 'John was one of my very first students at Ruskin, and the remembered pleasures – and travails – of that encounter are not the least of the reasons why, nearly thirty years on, I still find myself teaching at the same institution . . . My student seemed the very incarnation of Jude the Obscure with a tremendous appetite for learning, fiercely independent opinions and a determination, like the tragic hero of Hardy's novel, to crack the secret of knowledge – in his case, economics rather than classics. He loved argument, and tutorials were apt to erupt in fierce disagreement . . . But he usually had something urgent to say.'[5]

Prescott left Ruskin in 1965 hoping to become a full-time NUS official, only to find himself blocked by the union's old guard. So he went to Hull University instead, and three years later the Eleven-plus failure graduated with a BSc in economics. At the same time, he narrowly missed being selected as Labour candidate for a by-election in Hull but instead fought the 1966 general election for Labour in the hopeless Tory seat of Southport, making a name for himself as the author of a pamphlet putting the case for the 1966 seamen's strike, *Not Wanted on Voyage: The Seamen's Reply*.[6] The strike was a major test of the Labour government's incomes policy, and prime minister Harold Wilson famously denounced it in the Commons as a plot by a 'tightly-knit group of politically motivated men, who, as the last general election showed, utterly failed to secure acceptance of their views by the electorate, but who are now determined to exercise backstage pressures . . . endangering the security of the industry and the economic welfare of the nation'. He named many of the supposed plotters on the basis of Special Branch reports of their activities and associations with members of the Communist Party. Prescott escaped mention only because he had been a Labour candidate just weeks before.

After leaving university, Prescott was adopted as parliamentary candidate for Hull East, a safe Labour seat, and the NUS allowed him to become a union official at last, on a strictly temporary basis. In 1970 he became the first NUS-sponsored MP, at the age of thirty-three. The Tory opponent he beat was a twenty-eight-year-old called Norman Lamont. In the Commons, Prescott made a name for himself in no time. He joined the Tribune Group, and came to prominence as an outspoken champion of the merchant navy and opponent of the Conservative government's 1971

Industrial Relations Bill. Within a year of entering parliament he joined the front-bench trade and industry team as a junior spokesman on shipping affairs.[7]

He also made his mark as an opponent of British membership of the Common Market, allying himself with one of Labour's most vocal anti-Europeans, Peter Shore. Prescott was a delegate to the Council of Europe between 1973 and 1975, and when Labour returned to power in 1974 Shore, appointed trade secretary, made him his parliamentary private secretary. He campaigned with Shore for a 'no' vote in the 1975 Common Market referendum, and the same year was appointed a member of the Labour delegation to the European Parliament – which was not then directly elected.

Prescott remained sceptical about Europe, and in early 1976, at the height of the 'cod war' over Iceland's unilateral extension of its fishing limits, provoked a storm by intervening in the dispute with a 'peace plan' conceding the Icelandic case and suggesting that Britain 'do an Iceland' on the EEC.[8] In the end he accepted that the clear 'yes' vote in the referendum meant that Britain would remain a member of the EC. 'The political reality in my view is that the electorate will not be given the chance to vote in another referendum on the issue, nor if they were, would they vote to come out,' he acknowledged in 1977.[9]

His pragmatism earned him the leadership of the British Labour Group in December 1976, a position he kept until the first direct elections in 1979. He proved an effective advocate of Britain's case, winning praise even from such a prominent Euro-enthusiast as David Marquand, who at the end of the decade noted that 'partly because it is . . . extraordinarily difficult for a reasonably gregarious and open-minded human being to belong to any institution for any length of time without absorbing at least some of its values and assumptions, the British Labour anti-Marketeers who entered the European Parliament in 1975 nearly all ceased to be anti-Marketeers in anything but name within a year or two . . . Two former anti-Marketeers – Lord Bruce of Donnington and John Prescott, the leader of the Labour group – played leading parts in the work of the parliament, of a remarkably constructive kind.'[10] However, Marquand over-estimated Prescott's conversion. As late as 1988 Prescott stated: 'I don't believe in the constitution of the Common Market or its economic philosophy,'[11] and he remains opposed to European monetary union in principle. Nevertheless, the contrast between Prescott and most other anti-Europeans on Labour's left at the time was marked.[12]

After Labour's 1979 general election defeat, Prescott became deputy to transport spokesman Albert Booth on the front bench in the Commons. He remained very much on the left: in the 1981 deputy leadership election he voted for Tony Benn (whom he had supported for the leadership in 1976 after Wilson stood down). But again he won admirers on the right for his vigour and enthusiasm, and in 1981, with Michael Foot installed as leader, he moved up the pecking order, becoming front-bench spokesman for regional affairs.

His new job allowed him into the arena of economic and employment policy-making and in the next two years he developed a string of proposals for regional policy. His ideas were most comprehensively laid out in his 1982 paper *Alternative Regional Strategy: A Framework for Discussion*, which backed far-reaching reforms of the machinery for regional planning. Prescott argued for regional planning boards and regional assemblies, initially appointed but ultimately elected, to take over the work of regional offices of government departments. He made the case for a new minister for English local and regional development, with responsibility for local economic policy, including the inner cities, and a new regional planning council, on which would sit the prime minister and representatives of the regional assemblies. The regional planning council would co-ordinate the work of all ministers with economic policy portfolios and act as a forum for making decisions on public expenditure in the regions. After several years, the paper suggested, the regions would control the bulk of industrial policy, the health service and water utilities.

In October 1983, Prescott was elected to the shadow cabinet for the first time, and Neil Kinnock, the newly elected leader, decided to make him chief transport spokesman – not at the time a high-profile position, but an obvious one because Prescott knew the field well. He harried the ultra-free marketeer transport secretary Nicholas Ridley very effectively over his plans to privatize British Airways and Sealink ferries, but was overjoyed to be moved a year later to the post of employment spokesman,[13] a position that had fallen vacant because of the promotion of John Smith to the trade and industry brief.

It was hardly an easy time to represent Labour on employment policy. The miners' strike was at its height, and Kinnock was keen to distance himself from it. Prescott had different ideas. Soon after getting his new job, he told a National Union of Mineworkers' rally: 'I am here to make it absolutely clear that I give my fullest support to the miners' struggle in this particular strike. I give it – how could I [do anything] else? – from a mining family in Wales. But I also give it as a seaman for ten years.' Whereas Kinnock equivocated about supporting a strike that fell outside the law, Prescott did not hesitate, and drew a comparison with his own involvement in the 1966 seamen's strike, 'which was unofficial and illegal. It was illegal because it was illegal for seamen to strike. We broke the law to strike to *change* the laws.'[14]

The tensions between Kinnock and Prescott over the miners' strike were exacerbated by their similar personalities. As Prescott later acknowledged, 'To be fair, you were either with Kinnock or against him. Same with me. So we were against each other.'[15] But it was not until well after the strike had ended that they really fell out. The cause was a scheme developed by Prescott, drawing on his pre-1983 regional policy ideas, for job creation.

The problems started in April 1985, when Kinnock declared that Labour would cut the dole queues by 1 million – without having a clue how it could be done – and Prescott took him at his word. With the help of a large employment policy working group, comprising his front-bench employment team, trade unionists, academics, economists and council leaders, Prescott had by autumn 1985 come up with a highly interventionist – and corporatist – employment-creation package, *Planning for Full Employment*. 'For socialists, there is no alternative to strong and direct involvement by workers and their representatives in partnership with a Labour government. Industrial and public sector planning and a strongly interventionist role in the economy can get Britain back to work,' it argued. 'A radical redistribution of wealth, power and jobs is required if this country is to make real economic progress.'

The paper called for a statutory minimum wage and new ways of extending public ownership, a co-ordinated energy policy to ensure the continued viability of the coal industry, an extension of Wages Councils, reform of trade union law and equal opportunities schemes for women and ethnic minorities. In line with Prescott's previous efforts, it advocated stronger regional planning powers. He also argued for a new government ministry, the Department of Economic and Industrial Planning, which would offset the supremacy (and anti-spending instincts) of the Treasury by taking over 'strategic economic planning functions' as well as 'responsibility for jobs-related public expenditure planning'. Prescott beefed up his 1982 proposal for a regional planning council into a proposal for a national planning council, where unions and employers would meet to plan industrial strategy. In addition, foreign-owned multinational companies operating in Britain would be refused 'access to sell in UK markets' unless they agreed to 'produce, assemble, research and source components in the UK'.[16]

Prescott was immensely proud of his work, but it went way beyond what Kinnock and his deputy, shadow chancellor Roy Hattersley, were after. It was an economic policy, not a jobs policy, and it directly challenged Hattersley's approach, which was to dilute Labour's interventionism and corporatism. To Prescott's annoyance, it was quietly shelved. In spring 1986, however, Kinnock asked him to produce a concrete plan for the creation of one million jobs. Prescott set to work again, and in early 1987 came up with a model based on a job-creation scheme run by Southwark Council. Once again it was a serious piece of work, based on extensive research and consultations. But he made a big tactical mistake in basing it on a London council just at a time when the Labour leadership nationally was trying to distance itself from the activities of some of its inner-city local authorities. To Prescott's fury, Kinnock comprehensively rubbished the plan when it was presented to the shadow cabinet and handed over the task of producing Labour's jobs programme to Bryan Gould, shadow chief secretary to the Treasury.

A humiliated Prescott put his plan out as a discussion paper, with an introductory caveat that 'local authorities are only one – albeit important – part of the picture. The conclusions of these discussions will be considered by the committee established by the shadow cabinet, chaired by Bryan Gould, which is to produce a comprehensive policy for the emergency programme of reducing unemployment by one million in two years.'[17] From now on, there was a complete breakdown of trust between the Labour leader and his employment spokesman. Prescott's resentment at his treatment was compounded by Kinnock's refusal to give him a place on Gould's committee, which included young shadow ministers such as Gordon Brown and Tony Blair.[18] To make matters worse, press reports outlining his failure to deliver the goods began to appear. Prescott blamed Peter Mandelson, appointed as Labour's director of communications on his recommendation eighteen months before.[19]

Over the next few years, Prescott found himself marginalized as Kinnock and his close aides promoted some front-benchers (chief among them Brown and Blair) and unattributably denigrated others. The era of the 'beautiful people', as Prescott would later call them, had arrived. During the 1987 election campaign he was kept far from the television studios of London and consigned to campaigning in the regions; and in the reshuffle that followed Labour's defeat, Kinnock demoted him from employment to energy spokesman. To Prescott, it was an undisguised insult: he had just come second only to Gould in the shadow cabinet elections, and he was after an economic portfolio. Kinnock had not only consigned him to a job entirely removed from his preferred sphere, but to a low-ranking one as well.

That autumn, a resentful Prescott decided to challenge Hattersley for the deputy leadership of the party in 1988. He had toyed with the idea for some time, convinced that Hattersley, like other deputy leaders before him, saw the post as a non-job. To get round the charges of disloyalty to Kinnock and hostility to policy modernization, Prescott took great care to dress up his planned challenge as 'supportive', arguing that the deputy should play a greater campaigning role, working to increase party membership and build up its grassroots organization. 'The deputy leader's role has never been defined properly, either by previous leaders, by the Parliamentary Labour Party, or by conference itself. Organizational matters are as important as policy issues, and I believe that a deputy leader should concentrate on organization and getting our case across to the public, our members and supporters,' he insisted. 'The job has usually gone to someone who has participated in a leadership race. It has always been done by a member of parliament who has also retained a full parliamentary portfolio. In my view, it is impossible to do both jobs properly.'[20] The words were a calculated dig at Hattersley, for whom the deputy leadership was a consolation prize for not winning the leadership itself, and who had been shadow chancellor from 1983 to 1987 and shadow home secretary since then. Prescott intensely disliked Hattersley, regarding him as snobbish, elitist and largely to blame for Labour's failure to produce a convincing tax policy before the 1987 election. After much lobbying from friends and trade union supporters, he was eventually persuaded to drop his bid for the deputy leadership in January 1988, only to resurrect it less than three months later when Tony Benn and Eric Heffer announced their intention of challenging both Hattersley and Kinnock. Prescott wasted no time in throwing his hat back into the ring. But it was to no avail: after a jittery start to their campaign, Kinnock and Hattersley easily saw off the challengers.

Meanwhile, Prescott had also been devoting some of his energies to making the best of a bad job as energy spokesman. Contrary to Kinnock's intentions, it soon became a high-profile position as the government's plans to privatize electricity emerged. In the 1988 shadow cabinet election, which took place shortly after the party conference and leadership contest, Prescott fell to thirteenth place. Kinnock, who had been incensed at the challenge to Hattersley, reshuffled him back to what he thought would be the low-profile post of transport spokesman (Tony Blair, newly elected to the shadow cabinet, was made shadow energy secretary in his place).

Transport was a posting Prescott kept for the next five years. To Kinnock's chagrin, he once again made a success of what had looked to be an unpromising role, as cuts in transport spending, impending rail privatization and, most importantly, a string of road, rail and air accidents forced the subject increasingly into the headlines. By summer 1989, Prescott had a higher media profile than any other Labour front-bencher apart from Neil Kinnock and perhaps John Smith, and had seen off his Tory opposite number, Paul Channon, who was replaced as transport secretary in July 1989 by Cecil Parkinson. In October that year, Prescott won a seat on Labour's National Executive Committee for the first time.

The same year, he produced a transport policy paper, *Moving Britain into the 1990s*, which introduced the idea – a new one for Labour – of marrying public and private finance for investment in British Rail. Treasury rules would be eased to enable BR to borrow money from the private sector. He had fixed on this notion as a way round the tight restrictions on policy pledges by Labour's economic team, who were slapping the inhibiting proviso 'as resources allow' on almost all policy proposals. By stating instead that 'Labour will encourage joint projects using public and private finance', Prescott could promise more spending on transport without drawing on tax revenues.[21] Prescott's plans 'to proceed with a leasing scheme of 188 Networker trains on the North Kent line' as 'the first step in securing private investment to help modernize Britain's railways' took pride of place in the emergency recovery programme promised by Labour's 1992 election manifesto. The next steps included an £800 million upgrade of the West Coast main line from Euston to Glasgow and a high-speed Channel Tunnel rail link, which would be followed by more electrification, a nation-wide high speed train network and an outer circle railway for London.

Prescott's championing of private-sector finance for the rail transport system, then still publicly owned, in no way signalled a softening of his stance against the principle of privatization. The public–private joint finance idea was one he had already considered for other public services. While still energy spokesman, he had argued that the 'public utilities don't have to have their hands tied behind their backs by the Treasury. The public sector can be enterprising and we can encourage innovation and change. But what we must be wary of is appearing to tolerate or even encourage private shareholdings in what should be public utilities. It feeds the idea, which is quite wrong, that owning shares is a way of encouraging accountability of the enterprise and can be seen as compatible with social ownership. I don't think it can.'[22]

Public–private partnerships were not all that Prescott wanted in transport policy. He backed re-regulation of bus services, priority routes for buses, experimentation with road-pricing schemes, reintroduction of trams and a review of the road-building programme. Above all, he argued for a radical shake-up of the Department of Transport. 'The first step is to devolve the roads programme to the regions,' he told *Tribune*. 'The second is to integrate the department so that road and rail and the rest think together what they're trying to achieve. The third is to produce every year a rolling programme of infrastructure planning.'[23]

In spite of his undoubted success as transport spokesman, things did not get better with Kinnock. The Labour leader had initially been pleased to welcome Prescott on to the NEC because he replaced the more left-wing Ken Livingstone. Once on it, Prescott had generally backed the leadership line. But differences over Labour's policy towards the Gulf war in 1991 led him once again to attract Kinnock's fury. Prescott was one of the members of the 'Supper Club' that acted as a forum for soft left MPs critical of Kinnock's support for the government over the war (see chapter 11). In spite of Prescott's eventual falling in line behind Kinnock, the episode sparked another series of anonymous press briefings from the leader's office rubbishing the transport spokesman and labelling him 'treacherous'.[24]

In a re-run of the 1987 election, Prescott found himself deliberately left off Labour's 'key campaigners' list for the 1992 campaign – even though the government's rail privatization plans were increasingly unpopular with the public and the issue was a vote-winner for Labour.[25] After the party's unexpected defeat, he decided to try again for the deputy leadership – and made a point of laying the blame for the unsuccessful campaign on the coterie of unelected advisers around Kinnock. The back-room advisers were 'frankly out of control', he declared. 'It's the fourth election we've lost running under, as I understand it, these people – I call them the "beautiful people" – who have, in fact, run the elections the last two times and we've still lost.'[26] Patricia Hewitt, Charles Clarke, Peter Mandelson, Philip Gould and others involved in the Shadow Communications Agency were chief among his unnamed targets. 'The general feeling is that the campaign was done by a core of people brought in from outside – the ones we had little contact with. I don't think the members of the shadow cabinet had any influence over this . . . I had to peer in on television to see who was on the campaign strategy team and who was making decisions.'[27]

As in 1988, Prescott's 1992 deputy leadership campaign stressed the need for a new kind of deputy with a special organizational and campaigning brief. But it also made clear his dissatisfaction with the policy direction in which Kinnock had taken the party. While the party's modernizers were claiming that Labour had not sufficiently tailored its policies to the middle ground, blaming the pre-election shadow budget that promised to raise taxes on the better-off, he countered their argument with the reminder that 'no disagreements were voiced over our tax and national insurance policies' in the shadow cabinet before the election. Further debate on the reasons for defeat was necessary: 'To appear to rush into rejecting universality of benefits because of ungrateful recipients, or to assume that the pursuit of individual choice favours the privatization of public utilities, is naive and concedes the Tory argument,' he wrote in the *New Statesman*. 'We must learn precisely why so many trade unionists, so many unemployed, and so many of the poor declined to vote Labour.'[28]

The party should remain true to its core values, he said, rather than seek to find drastically new ones. 'There is much talk of the need for a new radicalism and new vision in the Labour Party. But what is wrong with the old vision for full employment, for accountable public services, for good quality health, welfare and education services, for a fairer distribution of wealth, and to provide housing for all? This is our vision – these are our values. It is not new, but it is as relevant in the 1990s as it was in the

1980s. The difference is that we seem to lack the conviction necessary to challenge a society in which the distribution of power and wealth is so unequal and so unjust.'[29]

Prescott was easily beaten for the deputy leadership by Margaret Beckett, who had the backing of John Smith, the comfortable victor in the leadership contest. But Prescott was more than happy to have traded in Kinnock for Smith. He was kept on as transport spokesman rather than demoted – and John Smith's collegiate style of leadership was far more to his liking. The backroom advisers who had prospered under Kinnock were pushed out into the cold. Though Smith was from the old right of the Labour Party, Prescott developed a genuine rapport with him that had been entirely lacking in his relationship with Kinnock. In 1993, when Smith faced the prospect of defeat at the Labour conference over his plans to introduce one member, one vote for Labour's parliamentary selections, it was Prescott who symbolically rescued him with his appeal to delegates to trust the party leader (see chapter 9). His intervention was widely contrasted with Beckett's publicly lukewarm attitude to OMOV. Prescott was soon rewarded with a new job: once the conference was over, Smith made him employment spokesman again – much to the disapproval of shadow chancellor Gordon Brown, who found Prescott's interventionist instincts anathema.

He took to his new position with relish, beavering away on an updated version of the ideas that he had pushed with such conspicuous lack of success in the 1980s. But just as he had finalized a policy document detailing his plans, Smith died. Prescott paid him a glowing tribute. 'I've begun to learn that there's more than left and right,' he told a television interviewer. 'There's about trust, there's about conviction. And that can come sometimes just as much from the right as it does from the left. When you have politicians that are prepared to do that, that means you might disagree with them, but you know where you stand with them, and you know they want to fight for those policies and defend them.'[30]

Now Prescott launched his third bid for the deputy leadership. Although he ran for the leadership as well, he was on record as not considering himself as leadership material – 'I'm out of that league, really,' he had told *Esquire* magazine just before Smith's death[31] – and was under no illusion that he had a chance of winning it against Tony Blair. It was the number two position he was after, and that is what he got, winning comfortably over Beckett, by 56.5 per cent of votes cast in the new electoral college to 43.5. His performance on OMOV had gone down well not just with the party but also with Blair, whose camp made it clear that he preferred him to Beckett as a deputy – despite strong support for Beckett among members of the shadow cabinet, including Gordon Brown – and his campaign had a vigour that Beckett's lacked. Once again, campaigning, building a mass party and tending Labour's grassroots formed the greater part of Prescott's platform. But he also succeeded in setting the policy agenda for a significant part of the contest with his championing of full employment – to be achieved by 'demand management to compensate for cyclical failures of demand and supply-side reforms to remove or reverse structural deficiencies'. Soon after Prescott introduced full employment as his central policy proposal, Blair and Beckett followed suit by picking it up, albeit with qualifications in Blair's case.

At first sight, the pairing of Blair and Prescott as leader and deputy leader appeared as incongruous as that of Jack Lemmon and Walter Matthau in *The Odd Couple*. Blair displayed all the signs of his upbringing in a comfortable professional family, public school and Oxford; he spoke in a posh southern English accent and had a haughty manner when crossed. His wife was a successful barrister who earned vastly more than him, his children were young, he liked rock music and the family home was in a London neighbourhood fashionable with the professional middle class. Prescott, fifteen years his senior, was the archetypal northern working-class bloke-made-good. He was passionate and direct in his speech, if famously ungrammatical. He had a penchant for flashy cars and a big house in his constituency. His wife was a former hairdresser, he liked traditional jazz and his children were grown up. In some respects he was also old-fashioned in some of his attitudes to women: he firmly backed Labour's short-lived policy of all-women shortlists for choosing parliamentary candidates in 50 per cent of the party's vacant and winnable seats, but although he often swore like a trooper himself, he objected to women using the mildest profanity in his presence.

Politically, the two men were also radically different. Blair wanted to loosen Labour's link with the unions: Prescott saw it as essential. 'At heart I am a trade unionist before a politician,' he explained during the leadership election. 'If you question the relationship between trade unions and the Labour Party, then you question the very fundamental being of the Labour Party.'[32] In economic policy, Blair was post-Keynesian in his outlook and believed that public ownership had had its day in Labour's thinking; Prescott saw full employment as the central goal of economic policy and was a champion of public ownership. 'It is essential that the Labour Party has always believed that public ownership is part of our philosophy,' he insisted in early 1993. 'Public ownership is a distinguishing feature between a left-of-centre party and a right-of-centre party.'[33] On Europe, whereas Blair was mildly in favour of further economic and political integration, Prescott was sceptical.

The political tensions between the two men were exacerbated by Blair's preference for making decisions without consulting anyone outside a tight-knit inner circle that did not include his deputy. He had no choice but to secure Prescott's acquiescence in advance of changing Clause Four of the party constitution, but after that Prescott found himself sidelined. He was kept busy enough with the campaigning he had been so keen to make central to the deputy leader's job, addressing meetings up and down the country and playing a key role in by-election campaigns – successfully in Dudley West in December 1994, less so in Littleborough and Saddleworth in July 1995.[34] On big questions, however, he was out of the loop. When in early March 1995 Blair held a summit meeting on economic strategy and campaigning at the home of Christopher Powell, brother of his chief of staff Jonathan, Prescott, unlike Gordon Brown and Peter Mandelson, was not invited.[35] Nor was he shown a copy of the memorandum drawn up at this time by Philip Gould, arguing for Labour to adopt 'a unitary command structure leading directly to the party leader' and to abandon the block vote: he found out about its existence only after it was leaked by one of Blair's allies to Seumas Milne of the *Guardian*, which splashed it across its front page during TUC congress week in 1995. (To make matters worse, Prescott had been informed of Blair's summer 1995 decision to press ahead with reducing the block vote at Labour conference to 50 per cent only after he had insisted in a television interview that Blair had promised that he would do no such thing before the general election.)

Prescott was kept on board with effusive apologies, promises that he would be fully informed in future, and the creation of a regional policy commission, chaired by Bruce Millan, the former Labour MP and European Commissioner, to look into prospects for regional industrial policies. He was also encouraged by the summer 1995 appointment of Michael Heseltine as deputy prime minister. If the Labour deputy leader couldn't secure the economic policy role he craved, at least he might emulate Heseltine by taking the powerful position of head of the cabinet office and chair of several ministerial committees.

Yet Blair's inner circle still conspired to keep him in the dark. Prescott was not consulted about Gordon Brown's plans to remove benefit from work-shy sixteen- to twenty-five-year-olds, announced in autumn 1995; and a few weeks later he found out about Harriet Harman's choice of a selection-based school for her son (and about high-level discussions among senior Labour politicians on how to pre-empt the resulting damaging row) only when he read of it in the newspapers. Matters reached a head in spring 1996 when Brown made a string of policy pronouncements with which Prescott profoundly disagreed. First, with the backing of Blair and (eventually) transport spokeswoman Clare Short, the shadow chancellor proposed abandonment of Labour's promise to renationalize Railtrack, the newly privatized rail infrastructure company.[36] Then his aides let it be known that he wanted to phase out child benefit for sixteen- to eighteen-year-olds and use the savings for a training programme. Then Brown made a speech promising that under Labour the Treasury would be 'both a ministry of finance and a ministry for long-term economic and social renewal'.[37]

Prescott moved deftly to assert his position. He went public with his criticisms of Brown in a speech to a union conference in Bournemouth, in which he lambasted the idea of a 'super-Treasury'. 'It would surely be detrimental to our commitment for a dynamic economy to allow an overbearing role for the Treasury,' he said. 'Too often in the past the dead hand of the Treasury has stifled initiative and motivation, in the public and private sector, with a rigid inflexibility in the interpretation of Treasury rules.'[38] The unspoken implication was that the weight of the Treasury in government should be balanced by another department with a primary interest in job creation – and that this should be led by John Prescott. In the next couple of weeks, with the report of the Millan regional policy commission imminent, his supporters made it clear to journalists that Prescott envisaged a role for himself as 'governor of the English regions', with responsibilities similar to those of the secretaries of state for Scotland and Wales, rolling together the functions of the Department of Trade and Industry (DTI), the Department of the Environment (DoE) and Department of Transport (DoT) with the employment part of the newly created Department for Education and Employment (DfEE).

Blair was unconvinced. With the election looming, it was clear that Prescott was going to have to be offered a job, but Brown was insistent that it should not have the central economic policy role that Prescott wanted. Six months of haggling then began. Several ideas were floated: that Prescott should become home secretary in place of Jack Straw, that he should be put in charge of the DTI, that he should be given a new department comprising the industry part of the DTI and the employment part of the DfEE. But by the end of 1996 it was clear that the compromise most likely to be tolerable to all concerned was to put Prescott in charge of a new department based on a merger of the DoE and some of the regional responsibilities of the DTI. With the addition of the DoT, that is what Prescott now controls.

The part of the new department's brief that Prescott had least experience of handling in opposition was the environmental protection element of the DoE's responsibilities. Of course, as transport spokesman, he argued for reducing pollution and cutting down car use, but his case was based more on the nuisance of traffic jams than on the danger of global warming. Nor was he noticeably concerned with environmental questions when he held the job of energy spokesman in 1987–8.[39] In the short but complicated story of Labour and green politics, Prescott has had only a walk-on role.

This is not altogether surprising. What we now call green politics first sprang to prominence in the late 1960s, but few politicians of Prescott's generation took any notice until the 1980s. If there was one thing that Labour could agree upon, it was that it was in favour of growth and not too worried about the consequences. Anthony Crosland articulated the consensus view in a 1971 pamphlet, denouncing the 'elitist, protectionist and anti-growth view of the environment' held by middle-class enthusiasts who wanted 'to kick the ladder down behind them'.[40] The warnings about the unsustainability of economic expansion raised by the 'Club of Rome' report *The Limits of Growth*, subsequently developed by several writers into a far-reaching critique of industrialism, barely registered with Labour's mainstream.[41] The 1974–9 Labour government passed a Control of Pollution Act, which tidied up existing legislation, and introduced a Countryside and Wildlife Bill on protection of rare species, which was eventually turned into law by the Thatcher Conservative government. But otherwise its record was abysmal. In particular, it failed to take any notice of the growing body of evidence that nuclear power was neither economical nor safe. It pressed ahead with two new nuclear power stations at Heysham and Torness, both of them using unproven advanced gas-cooled reactors, and it responded to public concern about plans to build a new nuclear reprocessing plant at Windscale (now Sellafield) by holding a farcical public inquiry that seemed to most observers to have had its conclusions determined for it in advance. Only a handful of back-bench MPs, among them the young Robin Cook, opposed the government's line.

But the more libertarian parts of the left that grew out of the upsurge of student militancy and workplace and community

activism from the late 1960s onwards were altogether more receptive both to ameliorative environmentalism and to the deeper
critique developed by advocates of what became known as political ecology.[42] Friends of the Earth, launched in Britain in 1970,
drew much of its support from this milieu; so too did several
other pressure groups, among them the Scottish Campaign to
Resist the Atomic Menace (SCRAM), set up in 1975 to campaign
against the nuclear power station at Torness.

As people active in or sympathetic to this political sub-cul-
ture joined Labour – a trickle that became a flood after 1979 – so
the party slowly began to change. In 1973, a handful of activists
set up the Socialist Environmental and Resources Association
(SERA), which by the end of the decade had become an effective
ginger group, particularly in mobilizing Labour opposition to
nuclear power. From the mid-1970s, several local councils, most
notably South Yorkshire, introduced subsidized public transport
schemes that owed at least something to environmentalist arguments. The 1978 Lucas Aerospace shop stewards' plan for
converting their company to socially useful production instead of
arms manufacturing inspired a whole generation of left and trade
union activists to think critically about the uses of technology.[43]
Labour environmentalism was given a further major boost in the
early 1980s by the peace movement – nothing could be a greater
threat to the survival of the planet than nuclear war – and another
by the Greater London Council. Under Ken Livingstone, the GLC
adopted a consciously environmentalist approach to every aspect
of policy. It even objected to the building of the new Sizewell B
nuclear power station in Suffolk (planned as the first of a new generation of pressurized water reactor stations) on the grounds that
an accident there could have disastrous consequences for
London.[44]

It would be wrong, however, to exaggerate the extent of
Labour's embrace of green politics in the early 1980s. Both left and
right of the party remained for the most part hostile to anything
that smacked of a critique of industrialism. As Robin Cook, then as
now SERA's most prominent supporter, argued in the campaign's
magazine *New Ground* in early 1984, the left-wing economic policy
on which the party fought the 1983 election, the Alternative

Economic Strategy, epitomized an 'uncritical commitment to salvation through growth in industrial output'. 'If we are to be frank,
Labour's record on ecological issues is wretched,' he wrote. 'Over
the past couple of years, the party has conducted a lively inquest
into the records of recent Labour governments, but the absence of
ecological perspectives from this review is striking.'[45] Just as
noticeably, Labour lagged behind public opinion even when it
came to the most minimally ameliorative environmentalist measures. It was not until summer 1986 that it published its first
overall statement of environmental policy – including proposals
for a ministry of environmental protection, a new regulatory
framework for air and water pollution and various measures to
make agriculture more environment-friendly[46] – and it was not
until the autumn of the same year that Neil Kinnock created a
shadow cabinet environmental protection portfolio, which he gave
to David Clark. Even then, substantial barriers remained to the
greening of Labour. The unions were understandably unenthusi-
astic about environmentalist measures that threatened their
members' employment, and the same went for MPs with constituents working in industries targeted by environmentalists.

Some of these doubts were assuaged by the promise of jobs
in environmental protection – in early 1987, Clark said that
200,000 jobs could be created at the cost of £10 billion. But
nuclear power was a seemingly intractable problem. Well before
the 1986 Chernobyl disaster, the overwhelming majority of
Labour Party members, along with the TUC and most unions,
had come to the conclusion that nuclear energy was unsafe and
ought to be phased out. But the Sellafield nuclear processing plant
was, and is, situated in the constituency of Jack Cunningham,
the party's environment spokesman from 1983 to 1989, and along
with the nuclear industry unions he put up fierce opposition to
Labour's anti-nuclear lobby. Even the 1986 statement on environmental policy, issued soon after Chernobyl when anti-nuclear
sentiment was at an unprecedented height, refrained from making
any commitment to getting rid of nuclear power. Although the
Labour conference that autumn voted in favour of phasing it out,
the 1987 Labour manifesto referred weakly to 'gradually dimin-
ishing Britain's dependence on nuclear energy'.[47]

Green issues played little part in the 1987 election campaign, and soon afterwards Kinnock decided that environmental protection did not after all deserve a spokesperson of shadow cabinet rank. Clark was given the job of agriculture spokesman. But instead of going away as memories of Chernobyl receded, the environment shot to the top of the British political agenda. The report of the United Nations World Commission on Environment and Development, chaired by the Norwegian Labour prime minister, Gro Harlem Brundtland, *Our Common Future*, published in spring 1987, stimulated a vigorous debate with its argument that 'poverty is a major cause and effect of global environmental problems' and its case for 'sustainable development'.[48] Over the next eighteen months, politicians and the media woke up to concerns, long expressed by academic experts, that deforestation and the burning of fossil fuels could, through the 'greenhouse effect', lead to a catastrophic change in the global climate. In September 1988, to the surprise of just about every commentator, prime minister Margaret Thatcher stole the headlines with a speech to the Royal Society in which she warned of a global environmental crisis.

Afraid of losing the initiative, Labour embraced the rhetoric of Brundtland wholeheartedly in the first report of the policy review, *Meet the Challenge, Make the Change*, published in spring 1989.[49] A few weeks later, the Greens won 15 per cent of the vote in the European elections. Labour's environmentalists pressed hard for a greener approach all round. Chris Smith, who since entering parliament in 1983 had acquired a reputation as one of Labour's most assiduous environmentalists and had risen to become a junior Treasury spokesman, was particularly insistent. 'We need to build into our economic analysis the drive for sustainable growth and the renewability of basic resources and, by so doing, take head on not only the traditional measures of economic success that ignore environmental impact altogether but also the analysis of many greens who believe that all growth is damaging,' he wrote in *Tribune*. 'We need to characterize our approach to energy policy, to transport policy, to the future of local government, to the types of agricultural production we foster, to the protection of the public in relation to food production, to the debt crisis of many developing countries, to the role of tax policy in boosting particular forms of product consumption, and to international relations in Europe and the world, with firm determination that environmental enhancement must be the aim of each.'[50]

In his autumn 1989 shadow cabinet reshuffle, Kinnock replaced Cunningham as environment spokesman, appointing Bryan Gould in his place. The reason was to remove Gould from his position of influence on economic policy, but the effect was a notable greening of Labour's whole approach. Gould's primary responsibility was local government, and most of his time was spent on the fraught process of working out Labour's replacement for the poll tax. He also threw himself with enthusiasm into green issues, however, and in 1990 produced a substantial new policy document, *An Earthly Chance*, which drew heavily on work by David Pearce and others on using the tax system to promote sustainability.[51] 'Labour is prepared to rely not just on the traditional instruments of intervention, through prohibition and regulation, but will also use the market – through the price mechanism and fiscal measures – wherever they can be put to good use,' the document declared. *An Earthly Chance* argued that there were real prospects of creating jobs in environmental protection. But it also stated bluntly that Labour 'must overcome our traditional image as a "producing" party, apparently giving priority to jobs and pay packets rather than to environmental concerns. We need to recognize that some of our decisions will be unwelcome – at least in the short term – to some of our closest supporters.'[52]

After 1990, green politics went off the boil again as Britain went into recession, and the environment did not figure in the 1992 election campaign. But the June 1992 Earth Summit in Rio attracted a welter of publicity, and when John Smith became Labour leader he decided to make environmental protection a post of shadow cabinet rank once more. He gave it to Chris Smith, who had impressed him with his work on the environmental implications of government fiscal measures when he was a junior Treasury spokesman. The new environmental protection spokesman was a long-standing supporter of SERA – 'I've always considered that being green is at the heart of being a socialist,' he told *Tribune* soon after being appointed[53] – and he went to work with an enthusiasm that outstripped even Gould's in 1989–90. In early 1993 he set up an environment policy commission involving every shadow spokesman with a portfolio related to the environment, along with representatives from the unions and local government.[54] By spring 1994 it had produced a policy document, *In Trust for Tomorrow*, that was, in the words of the former Green Party leader Jonathon Porritt, 'genuinely radical stuff' and 'a jewel'.

It proposed radical changes across the board. In the field of economic policy it backed an environmental employment programme (including the creation of 50,000 jobs through promotion of energy efficiency) and new national accounting practices to incorporate indicators of sustainability. In transport, it advocated a moratorium on new road-building pending a review, private-public partnerships for rail, urban light rail and tramway schemes, a doubling of the amount of freight carried by rail, measures to promote use of buses and tax-incentives to encourage fuel-efficient cars. As for energy, it proposed ambitious targets for the introduction of renewable sources of energy, backed combined heat and power schemes and opposed the building of new nuclear power stations. The package was rounded off with proposals for stricter planning controls in rural areas, widespread tree-planting, a drastic reduction in British emissions into the atmosphere of the chemicals that cause acid rain and of carbon dioxide (the main greenhouse gas) and elimination of emissions of the chemicals that damage the ozone layer.[55]

Smith was justifiably proud of the commission's work, but Tony Blair, elected Labour leader soon after it was finished, seemed lukewarm. In his first reshuffle in autumn 1994, he shunted Smith into shadowing the Department of National Heritage, made Frank Dobson environment spokesman and downgraded environmental protection, giving the brief to Joan Ruddock outside the shadow cabinet. Worse, in the eyes of Labour's green lobby, Jack Cunningham was given responsibility for energy policy again as shadow trade and industry secretary, replacing Robin Cook. Soon, an anti-environmentalist backlash seemed to be underway. Before the reshuffle, Martin O'Neill, the party's spokesman on energy, had told a nuclear industry magazine that *In Trust for Tomorrow* was not the final word on energy policy and that he was 'conscious of the environmental advantages of nuclear power'. Now he went further. In a television interview at the beginning of 1995 he said: 'Down the road, nuclear is a possibility for Labour, but it is a fairly remote one. The generating choices we face four or five years from now are of a different order to the ones we had when we fought the last election.'[56]

Labour environmentalists were furious. 'Blair seems to have little interest in the environment,' wrote Stephen Tindale, the secretary of the commission that drew up the environment document, remarking that there was 'a discernible nuclear enthusiasm among some modernizers. If one wants to give a Wilsonian impression of ongoing "technological revolution", it is easier to talk of pressurized water reactors than of windmills and willow trees.'[57] Blair did his best to reassure the leaders of the main environmentalist pressure groups that *In Trust for Tomorrow* remained Labour policy, and the fuss died down for a while. But the lack of priority given by New Labour to green issues continued to cause intermittent yelps of dissent from the environmental lobby until a couple of months before the election. Even Blair's decision in summer 1996 to upgrade the position of environment spokesperson yet again to shadow cabinet rank failed to stop the grumbling, in part because the job was given to Michael Meacher, who was known to be out of favour with Blair and liable for the chop after the election. In early 1997, Charles Secrett, director of Friends of the Earth, wrote an article for the left-wing monthly *Red Pepper* in which he accused Labour of abandoning the policies in *In Trust for Tomorrow* – 'as strong a set of measures as any green could expect from a mainstream political party' – and argued that the Tories and the Liberal Democrats were now much greener.[58] Blair, showing his customary touchiness to criticism, responded by banning Secrett from a meeting with environmentalist leaders.[59]

Nevertheless, Secrett's outburst does seem to have had an effect. The 1997 Labour manifesto *New Labour: Because Britain Deserves Better* was noticeably greener than the 1996 draft for it, *New Labour, New Life for Britain*. It included a plethora of commitments on environmental policy: an 'environmental taskforce' as part of a job-creation programme, a review of road-building, 'a major push to promote energy conservation', 'a new and strong drive to develop renewable energy sources', even 'a target of a 20 per cent reduction in carbon dioxide emissions by the year 2010'. 'All departments must promote policies to sustain the environment,' it proclaimed. Strangely, however, none of this played any part in the election campaign. As in 1987 and 1992, the environment was the dog that didn't bark.

So how will Prescott's super-ministry work out? The scenario that haunts Labour is a repetition of the fiasco of the Department of Economic Affairs in the 1960s. By 1964 the idea of a ministry of economic planning to act as a counter to the 'dead hand' of the Treasury, with at least equal influence, had a long pedigree on the Labour left, but the main reason Harold Wilson decided to go ahead with it when he came to power was to give his deputy, George Brown, a high-status job. It went wrong from the start. As the historian Clive Ponting puts it, Wilson 'never resolved the issue of the exact demarcation of functions between the Treasury and the DEA, nor did he face up to the question of whether the DEA had the necessary powers to carry out its grandiose remit'.[60] Brown produced an ambitious National Plan in 1965 'covering all aspects of the country's economic development in the next five years', with the stated aim of achieving a 25 per cent increase in national output by 1970. But he had no idea how it was going to be put into practice, and within a year the plan had been dumped as the government decided to make its top priority the defence of sterling against pressures for devaluation. The DEA did manage to set up regional economic planning councils covering Scotland, Wales and the English planning regions, but they had few powers of decision-making and no powers to spend money. The department struggled on after Brown was moved to the Foreign Office in 1966, but there were few tears shed when it was wound up in 1969.

John Prescott's new Department of Environment, Transport and the Regions has a regional brief – and it is a way of giving a potentially awkward deputy an important job. Prescott has long been an advocate of a DEA that works, and there can be little doubt that he would like his super-ministry to evolve into just such a body. But the DETR does not have anything like the overarching role that the DEA was supposed to have, and it is difficult to imagine Gordon Brown allowing Prescott to acquire it. Although there are certain to be fierce disagreements between Prescott and Brown, the chances of a precise replication of the DEA–Treasury wrangling in 1964–6 are slim.

Moreover, whereas the DEA was an entirely new creation taking a little of the Treasury's role, a little of the Board of Trade's and a little of the National Economic Development Council's, the new DETR is essentially a merger of two existing large departments with well-established and for the most part complementary functions. Unlike other big departmental mergers, for example the one that created the Department of Health and Social Security in 1968, the creation of the DETR makes a great deal of sense as a measure of bureaucratic rationalization. That hardy perennial of Labour politics, 'an integrated transport policy', is clearly best planned neither at national nor local level but somewhere in between. Similarly, one of the central tasks in environmental protection is the control and reduction of vehicle emissions, which can be most easily done by way of a transport policy encouraging people to use trains, buses and bicycles rather than cars. The environmental impact of road-building is equally obvious, as are the transport infrastructure implications of building everything from out-of-town shopping malls to inner-city regeneration.

The deputy prime minister also has a team that is likely to be competent and fiercely loyal. Of his four most senior colleagues – Gavin Strang, Michael Meacher, Hilary Armstrong and Dick Caborn, responsible respectively for transport, the environment, local government and regional development – all but Strang are already experienced in their fields. None, however, could be described as New Labour, and none, with the exception of Armstrong, could confidently expect to keep a place in a Blair government except under Prescott's wing. Strang, the agriculture spokesman in opposition from 1992 to 1997, is a free-thinking left-winger, pro-European Union, in favour of electoral reform and a committed nuclear disarmer: an elected member of the shadow cabinet, he had been widely expected to miss out on a cabinet seat when Labour won and was surprised when he got one.[61] Meacher, another shadow cabinet left-winger, was demoted when Blair chose the cabinet (as he had expected), although unlike Strang he got the job he had been shadowing.[62] Armstrong, local government spokeswoman before the 1997 election, has less of a left-wing reputation but was much less of a player in the Labour Party between 1994 and 1997 than she had been under John Smith, who appointed her his parliamentary private secretary.[63] Caborn, who was working with Prescott on regional development before the election, is the deputy prime minister's closest political ally.[64] Of the four parliamentary under-secretaries in the department – Nick Raynsford, Glenda Jackson, Angela Eagle and Baroness (Helene) Hayman – Jackson and Eagle are to the left of the centre of gravity in the Blair Labour Party. How well the team works in practice remains to be seen, but it seems unlikely that the DETR will be derailed by in-fighting among its ministers.

Most important of all, Prescott is no George Brown. He might be just as short-tempered and sometimes as petulant, but he is sober and not prone to the histrionic threats of resignation that were Brown's hallmark. There can be no doubt about his commitment to making the new department work, and he has a clear idea of what he wants to do on transport, the regions and housing. Labour did not make a conspicuous success of transport between 1994 and 1997. Riven by divisions over whether or not to renationalize the privatized railway system, the party got through three spokespeople, Michael Meacher (1994–5), Clare Short (1995–6) and Andrew Smith (1996–7), and did little in the way of policy development.[65] But Prescott has a strong grasp of the subject and plenty of ideas. Although there was nothing on transport policy in Labour's first Queen's Speech, a White Paper outlining an integrated transport policy is due in spring 1998. On regional development, Prescott has the blueprint produced in 1996 by Bruce Millan to work with: by April 1999, there should be regional development agencies in operation throughout England, responsible for promoting inward investment, helping small businesses and co-ordinating planning (although how effective they will be is another matter). The referendum on a new London authority and elected mayor is scheduled for May 1998, with elections for both to take place – assuming Londoners want them – two years later. As for housing, the results of putting into practice Labour's long-standing promise to allow councils to use the receipts from council house sales for new building and renovation should soon be visible.

There is, however, one major problem with the new super-ministry, and that is the place of environmental protection in its list of priorities. Labour's manifesto promises are clear enough, but many environmentalists fear that green concerns will be swamped in the new super-ministry and sidelined in other departments with responsibilities that impinge on the environment.

There are good grounds for such fears. The environmental protection part of the DoE's brief always sat uneasily with its responsibilities for local government, and it is now an even smaller element in a much bigger department that includes the DoT, for years one of the bugbears of environmentalists because of its enthusiasm for road-building and the private motor car. The minister of the environment, Michael Meacher, is out of favour with Tony Blair and reliant on Prescott, who is preoccupied by transport and the regions, to push his case in the cabinet. Of the leading environmentalists in Blair's first cabinet – Robin Cook, Chris Smith, Clare Short, Ann Taylor, Mo Mowlam and David Clark – only Cook and Short were given posts with green responsibilities.

Moreover, several government appointments in the key departments with environmental duties do not bode well from an environmentalist point of view. Blair's choice as his first minister of agriculture, food and fisheries, Jack Cunningham, is not only pro-nuclear but acted for more than ten years as a paid parliamentary adviser to two chemical companies, Hays Chemicals and Albright and Wilson, the former a producer of flavourings for animal feeds, the latter a manufacturer of chemicals used in the production of food additives and pesticides.[66] Many environmentalists baulked at his appointment to a department that lost all credibility as a result of its handling of the BSE crisis – and although he started well in his new job, he will be watched carefully for signs of over-friendliness to agribusiness. At the Department of Trade and Industry, which through its responsibility for energy policy will take a leading role in determining government regulation and taxation policies to discourage greenhouse gas emissions, Blair chose – of all people – the chairman of an oil company (albeit the one that has taken most seriously the dangers of climate change), David Simon of BP, as minister for trade and competitiveness, with the specific role of encouraging deregulation in Europe.

Nevertheless, there are also reasons for optimism. Although he is not in the cabinet, Meacher is undoubtedly one of Labour's more environmentalist politicians, and he will fight his corner hard for as long as he survives as a minister.[67] Prescott, despite his lack of a green record and his preoccupation with transport and the regions, is insistent that he is open to environmentalist ideas. On his first day in office, he promised to push hard to ensure that the manifesto promise that all departments 'promote policies to sustain the environment' is kept. 'My appointment to this key role confirms our determination to put the environment at the heart of government policies,' he said. 'This is what sustainable development is all about – getting higher living standards, safeguarding the environment and developing an integrated transport policy to fight congestion and pollution. A key example is climate change and air pollution. We need to do more to tackle the problem at national and international level; and we must make sure that everyone is in a position to play their part locally, too.'[68] Of course, rhetoric is cheap. Prescott failed the first major practical test of his environmentalism by giving the go-ahead in summer 1997 to most of the road-building schemes inherited from the Tories. Nevertheless, he has long seen green transport taxation as a possible means of raising revenue for his regional development agencies, and he has appointed a convinced environmentalist, Joe Irvin, as his special adviser.

Equally important, many key posts in the new administration have gone to politicians who are at least not hostile to environmentalism. Foreign secretary Robin Cook made it clear within hours of taking up his post that he planned to make the achievement of international environmental agreements one of his central goals. Chancellor Gordon Brown might not have seized the chance to introduce green taxes in his first budget – apart from increasing petrol duty – but he is seriously considering them for his next one. At the DTI, trade and industry secretary Margaret Beckett wants to give active support to environmental technologies, which should be good news for the development of renewable energy sources; and energy minister John Battle is an avowed enthusiast for renewable sources and sceptical about nuclear power. At the Department for Education and Employment, employment minister Andrew Smith has thrown himself enthusiastically into setting up Labour's promised environmental taskforce. Last but not least, Tony Blair might not have a reputation as an enthusiastic environmentalist, but his keynote speech at the New York Earth Summit in June 1997 was greener than any statement he had made before. It is too soon to make any firm judgement, but it is just possible that the new government will turn out to be the greenest Britain has ever had.

5

CLASS STRUGGLE
DAVID BLUNKETT AND EDUCATION

David Blunkett's first big public act on becoming secretary of state for education and employment was to humiliate the staff and pupils of eighteen schools.

Less than three weeks into his job, Blunkett unveiled a list of schools from across the country (primary and secondary, grant-maintained and funded by local authorities, comprehensive and secondary modern) that he said had not improved sufficiently more than a year after being failed by the Office for Standards in Education (OFSTED). They would, he announced, now be expected to co-operate with the Department for Education and Employment's 'special measures action recovery team' to draw up recovery plans, and if they did not make sufficient progress by September 1997 would face more drastic measures, such as the replacement of some staff. Any of the schools still failing after the government's promised legislation on school standards took effect might be closed down and reopened on the same site with a new name and new staff.

'The decision to name these schools has not been taken lightly,' said Blunkett. 'But persistent failure will not be tolerated by this government in any one of the 25,000 schools in this country. Our children only get one chance to go to school. If their school is failing it denies them opportunities for which they have a right.' 'There is no easy way of turning round a failing school,' he continued. 'However, I want to see schools and education authorities taking responsibility for raising standards and clearly demonstrating that everything that can be done is being done.'[1]

Blunkett justified the 'name and shame' ploy in an article published in *The Times* the morning of the announcement. 'The government was elected on a manifesto with education at its heart,' he wrote. 'The prime minister has made it clear that our priorities are "education, education and education". Having been given this important brief, my priorities are standards, standards and standards. The aim is to infuse everyone connected with education – teachers, parents, governors and business people – with ambition and purpose.'[2]

But that was hardly the effect on the staff of the schools he named. Most were outraged at being publicly denigrated. Several head teachers in the named schools produced reports from OFSTED congratulating them on their efforts and achievements. 'A government that cannot see the difference between punishment and correction is unlikely to gain the confidence of the half-million teachers that voted for it,' wrote one of them in the *Times Educational Supplement*.[3] Much the same point was made by the teacher unions and by Roy Hattersley in an article in the *Observer*. The schools 'needed quiet help', he wrote, 'not parading through the streets, unjustly branded as wilful failures'. Hattersley went on: 'The damage done to eighteen struggling schools is, in itself, indictment enough . . . But the arbitrary, irrational selection of candidates for ritual sacrifice has deeper and more disturbing significance. The "failing schools" initiative was a carefully contrived signal sent to confirm that the Department of Education aims to "get tough". After years of pointless conflict, a Labour government should have heralded a new era of co-operation and consensus. But the psychology has not changed. Schools are to be frightened into improvement by the threat of exposure. The blame is again heaped on teachers, not the conditions of deprivation in which their pupils live or the inadequate and underfunded buildings in which they are required to teach. Bullying teachers is the cheap as well as the easy option for a secretary of state who genuinely wants improvement but has not been provided with the resources essential to bringing it about.'

Last time Labour came to power after a long spell in opposition its priorities were very different. They were summed up perfectly by Anthony Crosland, education secretary between 1965 and 1967. 'If it's the last thing I do,' he told his wife in a moment of exasperation, 'I'm going to destroy every fucking grammar school in England. And Wales. And Northern Ireland.'[4] He never put it so directly in public, but he was expressing a view that was at the heart of his party's thinking about education from the mid-1950s until 1994. Although Labour could never agree on what to do about private schools – the left wanted to abolish them and the right for the most part did not[5] – there was near unanimity in the party that the top priority in education policy was introduction of comprehensive secondary schools to replace the two-tier system of grammars and secondary moderns implemented by the 1945–51 Labour government after the 1944 Education Act had established universal secondary schooling.

The comprehensive cause was first championed in Labour circles by the left, but it was embraced wholeheartedly by many of the younger right-wingers around Hugh Gaitskell, the Labour leader from 1955 – particularly Crosland, who placed comprehensive education at the core of the egalitarian social democracy expounded in *The Future of Socialism*. The two-tier system, he argued, condemned the majority of pupils to a second-class education, and it did so on the basis of an IQ test, the Eleven-plus, that was wholly inadequate as a measure of potential and discriminated against working-class pupils. The result was that 'the school system in Britain remains the most divisive, unjust and wasteful of all the aspects of social inequality'.[6] As education minister in 1965, Crosland issued a circular requesting local authorities to submit plans for the introduction of comprehensives that gave decisive momentum to comprehensivization. The Tories, with Margaret Thatcher as education minister, were unable to put a stop to the process between 1970 and 1974; and between 1974 and 1979 Labour came close to completing it after legislating to make comprehensives compulsory. Ending the Eleven-plus where it still existed remained a keynote Labour education policy at the 1992 election.

Comprehensives were not, however, all that Labour agreed about between the 1950s and the early 1990s. The overwhelming majority of the party took for granted the 'national system, locally administered' for state primary and secondary education set up by the 1944 Education Act, based on the principles of autonomy for the teaching profession, local authority management of schools and a 'partnership' model of national decision-making. Labour saw the curriculum and teaching methods as rightly the prerogative of head-teachers and their staff, with admissions, budgeting and planning as tasks of local education authorities. Overall policy was a matter of reaching agreement among government, LEAs and the teaching unions (which until the 1980s meant the National Union of Teachers because it was so much bigger than the others).

There was also accord that state education needed to be more generously funded and expanded in scope. Labour consistently supported school modernization, smaller classes, the raising of the school-leaving age from fifteen to sixteen (eventually achieved in 1971), the expansion of higher and further education (one of the great achievements of the 1960s Labour government, not least through its creation of the Open University) and, from the 1970s, universal nursery provision. It was Harold Wilson in 1964 who railed: 'Half of our primary schools, 55 per cent in fact, are still using premises designed in the Victorian era. Sixty per cent of these have no separate dining room for children to have school dinners. Forty-three per cent of primary schools have no inside lavatories . . .' The same points were made again (with different figures and little effect) by the Labour education spokesman before the 1992 general election, Jack Straw.

The Labour education consensus had undoubted strengths. Getting rid of the Eleven-plus was both right and popular, and the emphasis on spending more as the best way of improving the education service, particularly as a response to the swingeing Tory education cuts of the early 1980s, had much to commend it then as indeed it does today, although in office Labour's good intentions were constrained by the limited availability of money.

From the late 1960s, however, Labour's commitment to the settlement embodied in the 1944 Education Act left it vulnerable to attack over standards and parental choice. The problem was a revolution in teaching methods, particularly in primary schools, that had little to do with Labour, at least at a national level. During the 1960s, there was a widespread reaction among teachers and educationalists to the regimentation and rote-learning that had hitherto been the norm in most schools. Throughout the country, teachers set about making their classrooms friendlier places and experimented with new ways of teaching. Some ideas worked but some did not, and soon there was a groundswell of concern among parents and traditional educationalists about the impact of 'progressive education' on standards of discipline and academic achievement. Particularly in urban areas, parents started to demand the right to choose schools for their children instead of having the school determined by the local education authority.

How far this concern about standards was justified was much disputed at the time and remains so today. Some 'progressive' schools of the 1960s and 1970s were undoubtedly educational disasters – most notoriously the William Tyndale junior school in Islington, where parents' complaints about the ultra-permissive teaching led to a protracted dispute between the teachers and the Inner London Education Authority. Nevertheless, there is no incontrovertible evidence of any across-the-board decline in literacy and numeracy in this period as a result of the changing methods and attitudes in primary schools.

What is beyond question, however, is that Labour was extremely wary of the opponents of 'progressive education' and advocates of parental choice. The most vocal of them, the editors and authors of the influential *Black Papers on Education* published between 1969 and 1975, notably Brian Cox, Tony Dyson and Rhodes Boyson, were defenders of the grammar schools, and thus declared enemies of Labour's flagship education policy. Worse, they were inextricably mixed up with the free-market think-tanks of the Tory right. Boyson, a Tory MP from 1974 to 1997, was in favour of increasing parental choice by introducing education vouchers – an idea that in practice would not only make it impossible for a local authority to implement a comprehensive policy but would also give a boost to private education. Labour believed that even a non-voucher system of parental choice would lead to selection by the back door as 'good' schools found they were over-subscribed; and the party's closeness to the NUT and its commitment to the principle of professional autonomy for teachers made it uneasy about getting prescriptive on standards. The Tories had no such inhibitions. Even after they lost office in 1974, they took up the causes of standards and parental choice with enthusiasm.

Prime minister Jim Callaghan tried to outflank the Tories by launching a 'great debate' on education in 1976 with a widely reported speech in which he came out for 'a core curriculum with universal standards' giving priority to 'basic literacy and numer-acy; the understanding of how to live and work together; respect for others; and respect for the individual'. But the great debate produced very little that was tangible: Labour's 1978 Education Bill, which would have increased school governors' autonomy and parental choice, fell with the 1979 general election, and in opposition standards slipped down Labour's agenda. Neil Kinnock, appointed education spokesman by Callaghan in 1979, had two priorities: opposing the Tories' introduction of an assisted places scheme to subsidize bright children from poor families to go to private schools; and resisting their swingeing cuts in the education budget. As he put it in a speech to the Labour confer-ence in 1979: 'We are the party of raising standards, but with cuts of this size you can as well raise the dead as you can raise stan-dards.'[7] Kinnock's successor between 1983 and 1987, Giles Radice, took much the same line.

Apart from the assisted places scheme and spending cuts, the Tories did little of note on education in their first two terms in office after 1979 except to engage the teaching unions in a long drawn-out pay dispute that left morale among teachers at an all-time low. The edu-cation secretary between 1981 and 1986, Sir Keith Joseph, agonized over voucher schemes but nothing came of it: his main legislative achievement was the introduction of GCSEs to replace O-levels and CSEs as the qualifications for sixteen-year-olds. In the run-up to the 1987 election it became clear that the government was planning a major reorganization of the whole education system. Education secretary Kenneth Baker, who took over from Joseph, announced the creation of twenty centrally funded City Technology Colleges outside the control of local education authorities. He then unveiled proposals for a national curriculum, the testing of pupils at seven, eleven and fourteen, and greater autonomy for schools from local authorities in day-to-day management. After Labour lost the election, Baker began a process of structural reform that by the mid-1990s had transformed the workings of the whole education system.

The Tories' 1988 Education Reform Act was massive in scope. As well as imposing a national curriculum and compulsory testing, it introduced a right for parents to opt for the school of their choice. It transferred responsibility for managing school budgets from local authorities to the schools' governing bodies – 'local management of schools' – and allowed schools to apply for grant-maintained status, thus 'opting out' from local authority control, if parents voted for it. (The unstated intention was for all schools to opt out eventually.) As if that were not enough, it abolished the Inner London Education Authority, removed polytechnics from local authority control and ended academic tenure in higher education. By the time of the 1992 election, the government had also introduced student loans, made compulsory the publication of schools' examination results and set in train a massive, and underfunded, expansion of higher education.

The reforms put Labour in a quandary. They were a direct challenge to all its beliefs in how the education system should be run. They were hated by the teachers and so were bound to be difficult to implement. And yet in their emphasis on standards and parental choice they had undoubted popular appeal. Jack Straw, appointed education spokesman in the 1987 shadow cabinet reshuffle, responded by treading a fine line between denouncing the chaos the 'lethal cocktail' of the reforms would (and did) create and applauding the aspirations behind the Tories' legislation.

He later wrote that his main aim had been to 'establish Labour beyond doubt as the party of standards'[8] – and indeed there were plenty of noble aspirations on this score in the various policy documents that emerged from Labour's policy review: expansion of under-fives provision, national monitoring of standards, a target of 80 per cent of sixteen- to eighteen-year-olds getting five GCSEs at grades A to C or equivalent, 'home–school contracts' whereby parents would promise to ensure that children did homework, and better teacher-training. By the time of the 1992 general election, Labour had also decided to retain a version of the national curriculum and a modified compulsory testing system.

For his pains, Straw won the admiration of at least a few of the 'better standards' lobby, among them the conservative columnist Melanie Phillips, then of the *Guardian*.[9] But in truth Labour's emphasis remained fixed on the need for comprehensive secondary education. The main educational focus of the 1992 Labour manifesto was undoing those Tory reforms that undermined the comprehensive system. Grant-maintained schools, it said, would be 'brought together with City Technology Colleges into the mainstream of the local school system';[10] local management of schools would be reformed; selection would be ended; and the assisted places scheme would be phased out.

John Smith's choice for the education portfolio in 1992 was Ann Taylor, a lacklustre right-winger who failed to take advantage of John Patten's bungling arrogance as her opposite number in government. As he provoked the teacher unions into confrontation over the national curriculum and testing, she spent eighteen months consulting everyone under the sun before coming up with a policy document, *Opening Doors to a Learning Society*, published just after Tony Blair became Labour leader in 1994. For the most part this was a résumé of familiar Labour themes: a big expansion of nursery education, smaller classes, an end to selection, 'home–school contracts' and so on. On the Tories' education reforms – which had been augmented since 1992 by the ending of the distinction between polytechnics and universities and legislation to make local authorities publish 'league tables' of schools' performance in tests – it added little to what Labour had been saying in 1992 apart from some criticisms of league tables.[11]

For Blair, the emphasis was all wrong. For him, and for Labour's 'focus groups', the structure of secondary education and the technicalities of testing were boring and largely irrelevant. There were only 1,000 grant-maintained schools out of a total of around 24,000 state schools in Britain, and just 160 grammar schools. Many GM and grammar schools were in Tory-held marginal seats that Labour needed to win. Apart from a handful of left-wing ideologues, he believed, the only people who really cared about their fate were parents who didn't want them closed and were thus likely to vote Tory. On the other hand, everyone was exercised by the failure of much of the state sector to provide the standard of education that was expected of it. If the tests introduced by the Tory government were flawed, that did not mean that the principle of rigorous testing – with the results made public – was mistaken.

In line with this, Blair had made a point during his leadership campaign of arguing in favour of high standards, discipline and parental choice in education. Just before being elected leader, he told a television interviewer: 'For the vast majority of parents, they want to know their kids are brought up in a school where there is proper discipline, where they are given homework and are expected to do it, where the teachers are highly motivated, where you know how well your kid is doing . . . I think it is an absolute scandal that we have a large number of children leaving primary school and they cannot even read or write. These are the things that need tackling.' As for parental choice and league tables, 'parents, of course, must have a choice of school. I would like to see them given the fullest information. I would like to see them know exactly how well their kid is doing and I would like them to be able to demand and expect the high standards of performance throughout our education system . . . Of course you have got to be able to compare schools, but it has to be on a basis that is fair to the school and is accurate.' It would be 'manifestly absurd' for Labour to tell parents that they cannot send their children to grant-maintained schools, although it is 'right for schools to have a relationship with the local education authority'.[12]

Blair insisted on launching Taylor's document himself, using the press conference to make it clear that he was prepared to discuss with the grant-maintained schools Labour's plans for returning them to a 'local democratic framework'; meanwhile his spin doctors told journalists that he was deeply unhappy with the way that Taylor's document almost entirely echoed the views of the National Union of Teachers. It was hardly a shock that, along with Jack Cunningham, she was the main loser in the October 1994 shadow cabinet reshuffle. What was a surprise was that her replacement was David Blunkett, previously the health spokesman, whom few thought close enough to Blair to be entrusted with such a crucial part of the New Labour programme – particularly as he would have to face up in parliament to the redoubtable Gillian Shephard, who replaced Patten in 1994.

In fact, Blair and Blunkett had and still have a lot in common on education, although their own experiences of school and university could not be more different. Whereas Blair grew up in an affluent professional family and enjoyed a privileged education at a leading Scottish public school and then Oxford University, Blunkett's early years were tough.

David Blunkett was born blind in Sheffield in 1947, the only child from the marriage of his elderly parents (though there were half-brothers and sisters, all much older than himself, from their previous marriages). Home was a two-bedroom council house on north Sheffield's massive Parson Cross estate, but Blunkett did not get to spend much time there. When he was four, his parents reluctantly sent him to a boarding school for the blind in Manchester: in the early 1950s there was no integrated education. While the young Blunkett was away at school, his father, a foreman with the East Midlands Gas Board, died a long drawn-out and agonizing death after falling into a vat of boiling water at work. Because he had been working past retirement age, the family received no compensation for several years and fell into severe poverty, unable even to afford a headstone for his grave.[13]

Soon after his father's death Blunkett went on to another specialized boarding school. He had wanted to go to Worcester College, the country's only grammar school for blind boys, but his schoolmasters in Manchester would not let him take the entrance exam. He went instead to the Royal Normal College for the Blind in Shropshire, where grooming pupils to fend for themselves, rather than academic achievement, was the aim. In 1963, when he turned sixteen, he was offered three alternatives: to train as a piano-tuner, as a lathe operator, or in Braille shorthand and typing. He chose the last option.

The same year, he also joined the Labour Party. His family had been Labour voters without being particularly political, but Blunkett was moved to join the party 'because I wanted to change the world; instinctively I wanted to see things improve. All too clearly I recognized what conditions were like where I was brought up, the tragedy of Dad's death, my mother's struggle to survive, how shabbily she had been treated by the Gas Board . . .The lives of our neighbours were not much different.'[14] He was not a left-winger yet, but 'I had already learned sufficient history to appreciate that through the ages there has been a constant struggle not only between right and wrong but also between those with power and wealth and those who have neither . . . At the time, I had no thought of making a career in politics other than the vague belief that getting into parliament must be the way to begin the changes that I wanted to make . . . I came to the instinctive conclusion that, if I were ever going to rise above low income and under-achievement, a sound education with O- and A-level qualifications was crucial.'[15]

On top of training in typing and shorthand, he threw himself into obtaining the education he had been denied so far. While still at the Royal Normal College, he studied for O-levels and one A-level at evening classes, continuing with this even after landing a job as a clerk with his father's old employer (a position he took after a failed attempt to become a journalist). Through a combination of evening classes and day-release courses, he acquired three A-levels, a National Certificate in business studies and a place to read politics and history at Sheffield University. 'I was the first person from our family to go to university and almost certainly the first within a two-mile radius of our home,' he records.[16] After graduating with a 2:1 in 1972, he took a further education teaching course in Huddersfield, and in 1974 became a tutor in

industrial relations and politics at Barnsley College of
Technology – a job he kept until he became an MP in 1987.

It was at university that Blunkett's political career began to
take off. In 1970, by now firmly on the Labour left, he stood for
and won a safe Labour seat on Sheffield city council, and over the
next ten years built up an impressive political base. He got himself
voted on to the important council committees and won a seat on
the new South Yorkshire metropolitan county council – which
soon acquired the nickname of 'Socialist Republic of South
Yorkshire' for its radicalism, in particular its highly subsidized
integrated public transport system. In 1974, he fought his first
general election as Labour's candidate for the then-safe Tory seat
of Sheffield Hallam. Four years later he came within one vote of
being selected as the candidate for the safe Labour seat of
Penistone, by then his home town.[17]

By the end of the 1970s, Blunkett was the leading left-winger
in the city council's ruling Labour group. He was elected leader of
the council after the local elections in May 1980 gave the left a
majority in the group. The new regime set about transforming the
way the council did its business, opening up its decision-making
to the district Labour Party, the unions in the local trades council
and tenants' associations. Sheffield soon became a model for the
municipal new left throughout Britain, although, as Andy
McSmith writes, Blunkett 'was never part of what came to be cari-
catured as the "trendy" left, with its emphasis on "race and
gender" as opposed to "class" issues'.[18] Unlike the Greater London
Council under Ken Livingstone, Sheffield did not dabble in 'rainbow coalition' politics but concentrated its efforts on policy
initiatives for reviving the local economy, then in a state of crisis
because of the collapse of the steel industry in the early-1980s
recession.[19]

Blunkett himself was (and still is) conservative in his attitudes to sexual mores, education and personal behaviour. 'I am
not prejudiced against gays and lesbians but there is no point
trying to delude myself that I feel anything but revulsion at the
idea of touching another male,' he wrote in his column in *Tribune*
in 1986. 'Probably one of the most annoying and patronizing
aspects of trendy left politics today is the way some people simply

trot out the groups which they believe deserve benevolent action . . . we checklist our own sincerity by talking about women (of course not a minority), gays, lesbians, blacks and, if we remember, the disabled.' He went on, 'Perhaps the daftest of all are those politicians or pressure group activists who irritate the bulk of the population beyond measure by suggesting or inferring that, instead of reflecting the variety of lifestyles, cultures and interest in our community, we should go so far as to repress the norm in order to avoid the promotion of one lifestyle above that of another. As someone with a handicap . . . I would no more expect phrases such as "blind as a bat" to be eliminated from usage, than "black-board". I also expect the bulk of entertainment and cultural expression to reflect the fact that the majority of the population is heterosexual.'[20]

In similar vein, in the 1990 Commons debate on the Human Fertilization and Embryology Bill, Blunkett spoke in favour of prohibiting artificial insemination for lesbians because women and children needed men to be 'complete'; neither did he believe that single or widowed women should have access to artificial insemination.[21] In 1994 he was one of thirty-nine Labour MPs who voted against reducing the age of consent for gay men to sixteen.

Blunkett's views on education are similarly traditionalist. 'I believe in discipline, solid mental arithmetic, learning to read and write accurately, increasing expectations and developing potential – all the things which are anathema to many modern children,' he declared in his autobiography.[22] He has also consistently railed against what he described in 1986 as the 'degeneration in standards of attitude and behaviour towards each other that now exists',[23] deploring noisy neighbours and pressing for a much harder Labour stance on law and order long before Tony Blair came up with 'tough on crime, tough on the causes of crime'. At the root of Blunkett's thinking is a strong belief in the importance of community as a source of the common values necessary for social cohesion. He was arguing that 'for young and old alike, the need to identify with neighbourhood and community, to have an affinity with the society they live in, is paramount' as long ago as 1985, nearly a decade before the

American communitarian movement acquired cult status in the Blair Labour Party.[24]

It was Blunkett's record in Sheffield, however, not his political philosophy, that propelled him on to the national political stage. In 1983, he won a seat on Labour's National Executive Committee at his first attempt – quite a remarkable achievement for someone who had never been an MP, especially as he was not on the 'slate' of the Bennite left. (The Bennites dominated the local party delegations at the Labour conference that elected the NEC's constituency section.) He was immediately appointed chair of the NEC's newly created local government committee, and over the next eighteen months was at the forefront of the campaign against the government's legislation to limit council spending through 'rate-capping'. Blunkett saw this as an unacceptable attack on local democracy. 'If this labour movement does not stand up and fight on this issue,' he told the 1983 party conference, 'then I am afraid we will be wiped out as a Labour Party, because local government is the only place where Labour representatives are taking decisions about the well-being and lives of ordinary people.' In June 1984, Sheffield hosted a conference for Labour councillors and activists to work out how to resist the rate-capping measure; Blunkett energetically supported the idea of refusing to set a rate.[25]

To the relief of Neil Kinnock, who was insistent that the councils remain within the law, the planned united rebellion against central government collapsed in spring 1985 as Sheffield, the GLC and every other rate-capped council except Lambeth and Militant-dominated Liverpool lost their nerve. Blunkett was critical of the ferocity of Kinnock's attack on Militant at the Labour conference in Bournemouth that October – 'the grotesque chaos of a Labour council hiring taxis to scuttle round the city handing out redundancy notices to its own workers' – and the next day theatrically offered the possibility of a compromise to Derek Hatton, the deputy leader of Liverpool council and its leading Militant supporter, in the form of an independent inquiry into the city's finances. 'Will you do it, Derek? Derek?' he asked from the platform.

But by early 1986 Blunkett had given up on the hard left and aligned himself with Kinnock. He was elected MP for Sheffield Brightside in 1987 and appointed to the front bench as local government spokesman in 1988, subsequently playing the leading role in Labour's parliamentary assault on the government's legislation for the poll tax. He was one of the first politicians to recognize the potential of the poll tax as a stick with which to beat the government – and although his preferred substitute, a mixed property and income tax, was squashed by shadow chancellor John Smith in 1989, his parliamentary performances were widely praised by his colleagues. He produced figures demonstrating that even with the 'transitional relief' proposed by environment secretary Chris Patten, most households would be worse off under the new tax than under the rates system; and he correctly predicted that the actual bills would be far higher than the government was forecasting.

Meanwhile, on the NEC he formed a soft left triumvirate with Michael Meacher and Tom Sawyer that allied itself with the right to marginalize the hard left and give Kinnock a majority on most key issues. Blunkett did not go along with Kinnock's abandonment of a non-nuclear defence policy in 1987–9 and was uneasy about his enthusiasm for Europe – he remains a unilateralist, and is the most Eurosceptical member of the cabinet apart from Jack Straw.[26] He also remained very much on the left on economic policy.[27] Nevertheless he backed Kinnock against left-wing demands for an anti-poll tax campaign based on non-collection or the encouragement of non-payment, came round to the view that Militant should be expelled from Labour, played a key role in the policy review set up in 1987, and gave Kinnock strong backing when Benn challenged him for the leadership in 1988.[28]

By 1992 Blunkett was well established as a parliamentarian, and it was little surprise when he was elected to the shadow cabinet that July – even though he had backed the wrong horse in the leadership election that followed Kinnock's resignation, acting as campaign manager for Bryan Gould. John Smith gave him the health portfolio. He had a hard act to follow (Robin Cook had held the post before him) but mastered his brief with customary thoroughness and speed, giving the hapless Virginia Bottomley a hard time as health secretary as she presided over the chaos of the first years of trust hospitals and GP fund-holding. By the time John Smith died in May 1994, Blunkett was being tipped for a more demanding role.

Education soon proved as demanding as anyone could wish. Blunkett had been in position little more than a month when a storm broke over Tony Blair's decision to send his ten-year-old son Euan to the London Oratory, a Catholic grant-maintained school. The story had first appeared in the *Daily Express* in June, but it was not until the end of November that Blair confirmed it. 'That's our choice as parents,' he told a television interviewer, 'and I wouldn't want to deny that choice to other parents. Any parent wants the best for their children. I am not going to make a choice for my child on the basis of what is the politically correct thing to do.'[29]

For the Tories, the decision was a godsend: here was a politician who had campaigned for the abolition of grant-maintained schools hypocritically sending his child to one. For many on the Labour side, Blair seemed to be disowning the principle of comprehensive education. Blunkett immediately denied in public that there had been any change of policy, stating in a letter circulated to colleagues, 'We are opposed to schools opting out and remain committed to the pledge to bring such schools back into a "local democratic framework". There is no plan to have a paper on GM schools, nor is there any intention that GM status should continue.'[30]

Blair was not amused: rumours started circulating around Westminster that Blunkett could find himself removed from his new position very soon. Less than a month later, Blunkett was in trouble again after he gave an interview to the *Sunday Times* in which he said that a Labour government would consider putting VAT on private school fees – a measure that had already been ruled out by shadow chancellor Gordon Brown but not passed on to Blunkett. He was forced to eat his words. 'The shadow chancellor and the leader think it is helpful to rule out that possibility in order to avoid confusion,' he told a radio interviewer within hours of his remarks being published.[31]

Anyone expecting him to resist the broad thrust of Blair's ideas about education was soon to be proved wrong, however. He quickly bounced back from his embarrassment over VAT on school fees, regaining his place in his leader's affections by speaking out against the 'culture of complacency' in British schools, calling on teacher unions not to take industrial action over class sizes and then proposing that failing schools be closed down (an idea that so incensed some teachers from the Socialist Workers' Party that they barracked him in front of the television cameras at the Easter 1995 NUT conference).

He also put a great deal of energy into finding a position on grant-maintained status that would keep both Blair and the party happy, eventually producing a document, *Diversity and Excellence*, that attempted to square the circle by proposing that all schools should be funded and regulated locally, but with a great deal more autonomy than under the old regime. Local authorities would become primarily watchdogs on standards; grant-maintained schools would become 'foundation schools', which would employ their own staff but would have two governors appointed by the local authority and would be subject to the local authority's admissions policy. The government's policy of favouring grant-maintained schools in the allocation of funds would be ended. Existing comprehensives would become 'community schools', while voluntary-aided church schools would become 'aided schools'. Selection by examination at age eleven was out, but abolition of the few remaining grammar schools 'would only follow a clear demonstration of support from the parents affected by such decisions'.[32]

Diversity and Excellence was a fudge that was just about acceptable to most education professionals, who were weary of structural change after eight years of upheaval and wanted a quiet life, but for many backers of comprehensives in the Labour Party it was a betrayal of principle. Roy Hattersley, who had first made a name for himself as Labour education spokesman in opposition to the Heath government, laid into it with vigour, arguing that foundation schools were 'grant-maintained by another name' and that the Blunkett–Blair rhetoric of 'parental choice' would reinforce the practice of in-demand schools operating policies of 'social selection'. 'The foundation schools,' he wrote, 'will be assumed to provide the best education. Each spring, applications for admission will exceed the available places. As a result, parents will not choose foundation schools. The heads of foundation schools will choose pupils – usually by interview. There may be, somewhere in England, a headmistress who is anxious to take on boys with learning difficulties and a headmaster who is determined to recruit girls with behavioural problems. But such paragons are rare. Usually, places will be offered to pupils who are judged most likely to enhance a school's esteem. More often than not, they will be the children of the middle classes.' According to Hattersley, Labour should announce that 'all schools in the state sector must give first preference to pupils from the immediate vicinity and the siblings of pupils already on their rolls'.[33]

Blunkett refused to budge. 'The quality of education is what matters,' he wrote. 'We can and must do better if we are to succeed in the new century.' Rather than get bogged down in an argument about grant-maintained schools, Labour needed to work out how to improve the quality of teaching and teacher training. He promised to 'work with LEAs and the profession on schemes of teacher appraisal, and to improve management training for heads. We are examining ways to enable good teachers to continue teaching, as teacher professors, and to improve the ratio of pupils to adults in the classroom to tackle the problem of class sizes . . . We will build on the success of reading recovery and other programmes to tackle illiteracy. We will work with LEAs to develop plans where schools are failing to enable them to improve, and we will intervene to turn schools around where closure seems the only alternative . . . And, finally, we will explore ways to use new technology more effectively so that its benefits are available to every school. We must recognize the social and economic benefits to our nation of well-educated young people and a well-educated workforce.'[34]

The stage seemed to be set for an epic confrontation at the 1995 party conference in Brighton, but it turned out to be an anti-climax. It was not so much that the protagonists' speeches did not live up to expectations: both spoke well, particularly Blunkett. His argument that the focus on grant-maintained status was a 'diversion' and his promise that there would – 'read my lips' – be 'no selection by examination or by interview under a Labour government' won a standing ovation.[35] Rather, the fact was that would-be dissenters from the party leadership line had been carefully lobbied to make sure that they didn't cause any trouble in what might be the last conference before a general election. The vote went Blunkett's and Blair's way by a massive margin.

Blair rewarded Blunkett by promising him publicly that he would be education secretary in a Labour government and by expanding his brief to include employment when the government merged the departments of education and employment. But the conference victory did not put an end to Labour's arguments about education – far from it. Blunkett's next big initiative, *Excellence for Everyone*, a document on improving standards, drew heavily on advice from two controversial educationalists who had been in the Blair–Blunkett orbit for some time: Tim Brighouse, the energetic director of education in Labour-controlled Birmingham, whose initiatives included encouraging schools to set targets for achievement and creating a 'University of the First Age' to make sure no children fell through the education net; and Michael Barber, the professor of education at Keele University, a former Labour chair of education in Hackney who was an evangelist for teaching literacy and numeracy and the pioneer of the idea of closing failing schools and re-opening them with fresh staff on the same site.[36]

Excellence for Everyone promised more and better training for teachers, particularly heads, more rigorous appraisal of their performance at work, smaller classes, more information technology in the classroom, minimum levels of homework for primary and secondary children, secondary school lessons in parenting skills, home–school partnerships, reading recovery schemes to ensure all seven-year-olds were literate – and tough measures to deal with failing schools and incompetent teachers.[37] The last point caused squeals of anguish from the teacher unions when

Blair launched the policy with an article in the *Daily Mail* in early December 1995. Melanie Phillips, now on the *Observer*, was delighted. 'This was Labour's social policy Clause Four,' she crowed. 'It underscores the line Labour is drawing under its past, a message that has to be rammed home to Middle England. Not for nothing did Blair raise the standard of this crusade in last week's *Daily Mail*. If they are not careful, the teachers could become Blair's Militant Tendency, to be used, as Neil Kinnock did in a different context, to demonstrate his toughness in defence of the interests of ordinary people.'[38]

A less welcome controversy erupted early in 1996 with the news that Harriet Harman, Labour's health spokeswoman, and her husband Jack Dromey had decided to send their eleven-year-old son Joe to St Olave's school in Bromley, a grant-maintained grammar school in a Tory-controlled borough ten miles from her home in Southwark. Once again the teacher unions were incensed, and this time they were joined by a large section of the Parliamentary Labour Party, including members of the shadow cabinet, some of whom believed Harman should have resigned from the front bench over the affair. But she hung on, with Blair's support and the grudging acquiescence of Blunkett, and the overall impact on Labour's stance on education was minimal except insofar as it diverted criticism from Blunkett and Blair.

It certainly did nothing to prevent Blunkett from presiding over the production of a mountain of policy documents in the first half of 1996. *Aiming Higher* laid out plans for education for sixteen- to nineteen-year-olds, including higher standards in vocational education, a wider curriculum for A-level students and integration of vocational and academic qualifications. *Target 2000* promised an emergency programme aimed at getting all under-twenty-fives qualified to a level at least equivalent of five GCSEs by the end of the century – something one-third of nineteen-year-olds had not achieved in 1995 – as part of the assault on youth employment paid for by the windfall tax on privatized utility profits. *Lifelong Learning* promised increased access to higher education, reform of the student loan scheme to make loans more easily repayable and development of new research institutes in partnership with business. *Learn As You Earn* set out a programme for individual 'learning accounts' paid for by government and employees which would entitle people to education and training.[39] In May, in a speech to a head-teachers' conference, Blunkett announced what the *Times Educational Supplement* called a 'back-to-basics drive in the classroom', with an assault on illiteracy to be led by a new literacy task force chaired by Michael Barber; the next month Blair made a speech in which he made it clear that he had no enthusiasm for mixed-ability teaching in secondary schools.[40]

Nearly all this found its way into *New Labour, New Life for Britain*, the draft manifesto published in summer 1996, passed by the Labour conference and endorsed by a plebiscite of party members in November.[41] Blair himself made clear just how important he thought it all was in his conference speech: 'Ask me my three main priorities for government and I tell you: education, education, education.' Labour went into the 1997 election with education given pride of place in the manifesto as its 'number one priority' – and the emphasis was almost entirely on standards. 'Standards, more than structures, are the key to success,' it proclaimed. 'Labour will never put dogma before children's education. Our approach will be to intervene where there are problems, not where schools are succeeding. Labour will never force the abolition of good schools whether in the private or state sector.' Among its promises were a year's pre-school education for all (paid for by the scrapping of nursery vouchers schemes); class sizes of fewer than thirty for five, six and seven-year-olds (paid for by the phasing out of the assisted places scheme, which by now involved 34,000 pupils and 355 schools); emphasis on the three Rs in primary school (including new literacy and numeracy targets and summer literacy camps); minimum homework targets for all children over the age of seven; targets of five GCSEs at grades A to C for all students and a stay-on rate for over-sixteens of 80 per cent; and a 'fresh start' closure-and-reopening strategy for failing schools. All that was left of the old commitment to comprehensives was the plan to rename GM schools 'foundation schools' and include local councillors on their governing bodies. On selection, the manifesto said simply that policies would be determined by local authorities; although there would be 'no return to the

Eleven-plus', grammar schools would remain if parents of their pupils wanted them to stay.[42]

The Labour government lost no time in moving on all this when it won the election. Blunkett was confirmed as education secretary in Blair's announcement of his most senior cabinet members, and within a couple of days he had acquired a high-powered team. Two appointments were particularly significant: Stephen Byers, a close ally of Blair, became minister for school standards; and Michael Barber became Blunkett's senior adviser and head of the new 'standards and effectiveness unit'.[43] The other ministers on the education side of the DfEE in the Commons were Estelle Morris and Kim Howells, under-secretaries responsible respectively for various aspects of schools (including the school curriculum and teacher training) and 'lifelong learning'. In the Lords, Baroness (Tessa) Blackstone was given higher and further education.[44]

Two education bills were given pride of place in the first Queen's Speech: a short one, for immediate introduction, abolishing the assisted places scheme and reducing class sizes, and a long one, to be published in the autumn, covering a wide range of issues. The latter would be focused on raising educational standards, including the introduction of new performance targets, improvements in early years provision and vocational training and new powers for the DfEE over failing schools. But it would also legislate for Labour's familiar promises of a new role for local education authorities, a change from grant-maintained to 'foundation' schools, the introduction of a general teaching council and the reform of student loans.

As the DfEE set to work on preparing the White Paper to precede the second bill, which was published in early July 1997, Blunkett kept up the momentum on standards with his 'name and shame' announcement, the appointment of Tim Brighouse and Chris Woodhead to a new standards taskforce (despite a unanimous vote of no confidence in Chris Woodhead by the conference of the National Association of Head Teachers) and the launch of twenty-nine literacy summer schools for children from deprived inner-city areas. Blunkett also announced the end of the nursery vouchers scheme. Towards the end of July, in response to Sir Ron Dearing's massive report on higher education, be promised replacement of all student grants with loans and introduction of a graduate tax to pay for university tuition fees, with the money saved ploughed back into expanding universities and colleges.

The question, of course, is what the results of all this will be. There can be little doubt that Labour has identified some real problems in the British education system. Britain's schools fail too many of their pupils. According to the Basic Skills Agency, perhaps a third of secondary school children and a sixth of adults have trouble mastering the basics in literacy and numeracy – and there has been no increase in the spread of literacy and numeracy since the 1940s. Nearly a fifth of seven-year-olds and two-fifths of eleven-year-olds and fourteen-year-olds fail to reach expected national curriculum standards in English, maths and science. Britain is also lagging behind other countries in educational standards. In the main recent international study of comparative educational attainment, England came twenty-fifth and Scotland twenty-ninth out of forty-one participating countries in tests of the mathematical ability of thirteen-year-olds; in science, England came tenth and Scotland twenty-sixth.[45] With a skilled workforce being a crucial asset in a globalized economy and probably essential for long-term prosperity, the cases for better standards and a bigger and more inclusive higher education sector seem unanswerable on economic grounds.[46]

Class sizes have increased steadily in recent years as a result of spending cuts, teacher shortages and an increase in the number of pupils. Using cash from the assisted places scheme to reduce them should have tangible (if small) effects. As for pre-school education, Britain has the lowest level of state-funded childcare in the European Union – and the Tories' voucher scheme was one of the most ineffective ways of trying to expand it. Again, guaranteeing nursery places for all four-year-olds should make for a modest improvement.

At the same time, however, there are also serious problems with Labour's approach. If it is clear that the education system is failing to deliver what it should, it is not equally clear that

Labour has the solution. Common sense, backed by all the available evidence, suggests that there is much more to improving standards than spending money: the ability of teachers, their teaching methods, the curriculum, the extent and usefulness of parental involvement, the efficiency with which money is spent. It is obviously essential to ensure that teachers are properly trained, that they are teaching effectively, and that schools are well run. But 'naming and shaming' failing schools, increasing the amount of paperwork that teachers are expected to do, and giving the impression that most of them are incompetent are not the best means of achieving this. In the long run, moreover, the problem of failing schools cannot be successfully addressed as long as the school system encourages affluent parents in the inner cities to send their children to socially (if not academically) selective schools miles from where they live. Blunkett's White Paper promised to address this problem, but it is an open question whether the government will actually do so.

More important, spending money is crucial to improving standards even if it is not the only means. Britain spends a lot on state education, nearly £40 billion a year. But this is less than most other industrialized countries in terms of cash per pupil and as a proportion of gross domestic product (5 per cent against an average of nearly 6 per cent). Many of Britain's schools and colleges are housed in crumbling buildings, most are short of computers, books and other essential resources, and many are so strapped for cash that they are shedding staff or not recruiting staff they need. Further education – which is critically important for Labour's welfare-to-work programme – is in a particularly desperate state, with nearly a fifth of colleges in danger of bankruptcy on current spending plans. The university sector is almost as badly off as a result of the under-funded rush for growth of the early 1990s.

Of course, there are ways in which more money can be made available without increasing general taxation. Making university tuition fees payable through a graduate tax is long overdue – although also phasing out student grants, as Blunkett has suggested, would act as a massive disincentive for would-be students from poor families. There is probably still some potential for getting benefits from various partnership arrangements with busi-nesses and the voluntary sector. There is also the option of changing spending priorities within the existing budget, by removing funding from schools in affluent areas and giving it to those in poor ones and so on. In the end, though, there is no avoiding the fact that better standards demand an increase in overall spending beyond that provided by a graduate tax of some description. Labour recognizes this: the party's 1997 manifesto promised to increase the proportion of national income spent on education over the course of a full term, by channelling into the education budget savings from the social security bill as unem-ployment falls – and Gordon Brown's 1997 budget found an extra £2.3 billion over five years for schools, nearly half of it by raiding the contingency reserves.

Whether this will prove anywhere near adequate remains to be seen. But the biggest worry with Labour's current approach to education has little to do with the workability of its drive on stan-dards or with money: it is the single-minded instrumentalism that underlies its thinking. The idea that education is about more than providing Britain with a highly skilled workforce and socially responsible citizenry – that it is a way of helping people to dis-cover and enjoy the infinite richness of human culture, develop their intellectual capacities and their creativity and find personal fulfilment – has been all but forgotten in Labour's enthusiasm for 'investing in human capital in the age of knowledge', as Blunkett put it in the foreword to the 1997 White Paper. For all the government's promises of a 'new approach', its notion of what education is for appears to be as narrow as that of the Tory government that preceded it.

6

THE PARTY'S OVER
NEW LABOUR AND WELFARE

The Aylesbury estate in Southwark, south London, is not the sort of place that politicians usually choose to address the press. A giant system-built 1970s inner-city development housing 12,000 people in 2,400 flats and maisonettes, it has a reputation as a sink estate. Unemployment is running at nearly 20 per cent, and more than half of its households are on housing benefit. More than three-quarters of seventeen-year-olds who live there are not in full-time education. Crime rates have improved since private security patrols and closed-circuit television cameras were introduced in the mid-1990s – but vandalism, muggings and burglaries remain a problem, and drug abuse is rife.

Yet it was not altogether surprising that it was here, or rather at an information technology training centre in the middle of the estate, that Tony Blair made his first keynote speech outside parliament after winning power. His subject was the growth of an underclass and what his government was going to do about it – and of course the setting proved perfect. Although the Aylesbury estate is less than three miles from the Palace of Westminster, for most political journalists it might as well be on another planet. No matter that his audience was composed of men in suits: the exotic location guaranteed Blair maximum media exposure for his 'tough but tender' message.

'For eighteen years the poorest people in our country have been forgotten by government,' he said. 'They have been left out of growing prosperity, told that they were not needed, ignored by the government except for the purpose of blaming them. I want that to change. There will be no forgotten people in the Britain I want to build.' During the 1980s, he said, the choice appeared to be 'vote for yourself or vote for helping the disadvantaged'. Now, however, 'there is a possibility of an alliance between the haves and have-nots. Comfortable Britain now knows not just its own forms of insecurity and difficulty following the recession and industrial restructuring. It also knows the price it pays for economic and social breakdown in the poorest parts of Britain. There is a case not just in moral terms but in enlightened self-interest to act, to tackle what we know exists – an underclass of people cut off from society's mainstream, without any sense of shared purpose . . . We should reject the rootless morality whose symptom is a false choice between bleeding hearts and couldn't care less, when what we need is one grounded in the core of British values, the sense of fairness and a balance between rights and duties. The basis of this modern civil society is an ethic of mutual responsibility or duty. It is something for something. A society where we play by the rules. You only take out if you put in. That's the bargain.'

Blair was particularly direct on what he thought was wrong with the social security system. 'In the absence of a clear philosophy of rights and duties, the welfare system can discourage hard work and honesty,' he said. 'The benefits system penalizes the husband or wife of an unemployed person who takes up a job. It makes couples better off when they live apart. It locks people into dependence on benefits like housing benefit and income support when it should be helping them to get clear of benefits. It offers little incentive to work part-time, or for irregular earnings. Thirty per cent of people live in a household dependent on a means-tested benefit, which discourages work and encourages people to hide any money that is earned.

'The task of reshaping welfare to reward hard work is daunting. But we must make absolutely clear that our challenge is to help all those people who are not working with the jobs, the training and the support that they need. I am asking social security ministers to look at all the key benefits and apply a simple test: do they give people a chance to work, or do they trap them on benefits for the most productive years of their lives?'[1]

Blair did not set out any new policy proposals – he reiterated Labour's long-standing plans for a 'welfare-to-work' package to get 250,000 unemployed young people off the dole and repeated ideas he had previously set out for encouraging single mothers, 1 million of whom live on benefit, to get work once their children were at school – but the speech was as explicit a statement of his attitude to the social security system as any he had previously given. As the journalist Simon Hoggart put it, 'Those of us in work should help those without, providing they agree (a) not to lie in bed all day and (b) not to nick our stuff.'[2] The idea of making Britain a more equal society simply did not figure.

As with education, Labour's thinking on what Blair, following American usage, calls 'welfare', used to be rather different. From the mid-1950s until 1992, the party enjoyed a consensus that the social security system left too many people in poverty and did too little to erase inequality – and that the solution was redistribution. More generous pensions and state benefits should be paid for by taxing the better-off, with the commitment of the better-off to the system secured through a state earnings-related pensions scheme and other earnings-related benefits. Of course, within this consensus there were serious differences of opinion about precisely what needed to be done, and the record of Labour in office in the 1960s and 1970s was much contested at the time and remains so today. But the thinking behind John Smith's 1992 shadow budget plan for increases in the state pension and in child benefit was recognizably in line with Labour's approach as it had been for nearly forty years.

The consensus had its origins in the early 1950s, when it first became clear that the social security system set up by Clement Attlee's 1945–51 Labour government – largely according to the plan laid down by Sir William Beveridge in his famous 1942 report, *Social Insurance and Allied Services* – had by no means eliminated poverty, particularly among the elderly. The core of the Beveridge system was compulsory state-run national insurance for everyone, paid for by employers, employees and the state on the 'flat-rate' principle. Everyone paid the same contributions and received the same payments for old-age pensions and widows' and unemployment benefits. All benefits were set at the level necessary to guarantee subsistence – the 'national minimum' – and people whose contributions were inadequate were provided for by a means-tested 'safety net' of national assistance.[3]

Although the Tories would probably have put some sort of insurance-based social security system in place if they had won in 1945, the implementation of Beveridge's report was seen by Labour as one of the great triumphs of the Attlee government – as indeed it was, considering the economic circumstances of the time. The new system provided an unprecedented security in old age and in unemployment, and had a dramatic effect in reducing poverty, not least because Labour decided to pay pensions at the full rate immediately, rather than phasing them in over twenty years as Beveridge had recommended. It was also massively popular, which was the main reason that the Tories did not dare tamper with it after they returned to power in 1951.

But if the social security system was a great achievement, it also had its faults. Howard Glennerster, the professor of social administration at the London School of Economics, pinpointed some of these: 'The central flaw was the attempt to achieve a national minimum through contributory social insurance. Rights to benefit did not come as a right of citizenship. They came from a contribution record in full-time employment that excluded most women, the disabled and many more. The flat rate benefits that were earned were not to be set at a level sufficient to meet all financial needs, notably rent.'[4]

The first people to pursue this line of criticism to any effect were a group of Fabian social scientists at the LSE, led by the school's first professor of social administration, Richard Titmuss.[5] From the mid-1950s, Titmuss and two young lecturers in his department, Brian Abel-Smith and Peter Townsend, produced a flood of papers, pamphlets and books on the workings of the welfare state, and the ideas on which it was based, that set the agenda on social policy for a generation. Their range of interests was vast and constantly expanding[6] – but in the field of social security their most important early interventions were to criticize the assumption that poverty could be measured without reference to inequality, and to draw attention to the extent to which the social security system was failing pensioners.

They were particularly exercised by the fact that many old people who had no occupational pension were reliant on means-tested benefit to pay the rent because the state pension was so low. The solution, they concluded, was abandonment of Beveridge's 'flat-rate' principle and adoption of a system in which contributions and payments would vary with income. In 1955, Abel-Smith and Townsend published a Fabian pamphlet arguing for a state earnings-related pension scheme in which better-paid workers paid higher national insurance contributions and in return received higher pensions, with payments linked to the overall level of earnings in the economy as a whole – a system similar to that then being developed by many continental countries, notably Germany and Sweden.[7]

Labour, desperate for fresh thinking in the wake of its 1955 election defeat and the election of Hugh Gaitskell as leader to succeed Attlee, seized on the idea with enthusiasm. Richard Crossman, given the task of looking into pensions policy by Gaitskell, co-opted Titmuss, Abel-Smith and Townsend on to a committee, and by 1957 they had produced a blueprint for a state earnings-related superannuation benefit. The Tory minister for pensions and national insurance, John Boyd-Carpenter, dismissed the plan as the work of a 'skiffle group of professors', but it was convincing enough to push the Tories to adopt their own, wholly inadequate, scheme for pensions reform.

The influence of Titmuss and his colleagues on Labour did not stop with pensions, however. Titmuss's late-1950s theorization of the welfare state as the only possible means of maintaining social cohesion in a market society chimed perfectly with the revisionist Labour right's concern with what Anthony Crosland described as the 'significant residue of distress, resentment and injustice' that remained despite the success of Keynesianism in transforming capitalism. For the left, Titmuss's notion of the welfare state as the embodiment of altruism and sol-idarity was not far removed from the idea that it was an oasis of non-market relations in a capitalist world.[8] What had the biggest impact of all was the 'skiffle group's' 'rediscovery of poverty' as its members continued their empirical research through the late 1950s and early 1960s. In particular, *The Poor and the Poorest*, the controversial report by Abel-Smith and Townsend, published in 1965, that showed that the number of families living at or below the level of national assistance had increased in the previous decade, largely as a result of the growing number of large families surviving on one low wage.[9]

Titmuss, Abel-Smith and Townsend continued to advise Labour, and it was largely down to them and Crossman that by 1964 the party had an ambitious plan to make pensions and ben-efits more generous across the board. Harold Wilson was elected to office promising not only a state earnings-related pension but earnings-related unemployment and sickness benefits. There was to be an 'income guarantee' for pensioners, integrating the tax and benefits system and increasing overall spending, which was eventually to be extended to the sick and the unemployed.

Unfortunately the 1964–70 Wilson government failed to deliver most of what Labour had promised in opposition, despite growing public concern at the persistence of poverty. After the election victory, to Crossman's horror, Labour's grand and neces-sarily long-term plans for earnings-related pensions were put on hold in favour of an immediate big increase in the basic state pen-sion. Crossman himself was put in charge of housing.[10] Earnings-related additions to unemployment and sickness benefits were introduced in 1965, but the promised income guarantee for pensioners was abandoned as the government desperately attempted to stave off market pressure for devaluation. What sur-vived was a renaming of national assistance as supplementary benefit and a simplification of the means test for it.

Crossman was eventually made social security minister in 1968, but he failed to get the earnings-related pensions plan through parliament before the 1970 election. By the time Labour left office, the party faced widespread criticism for not having done enough to reduce poverty. Among its most vocal critics was the Child Poverty Action Group, set up in 1965, in response to the findings of Abel-Smith and Townsend, to campaign for a new child benefit. Just before the 1970 election, its new director, a young Christian socialist by the name of Frank Field, issued a document that purported to prove that 'The poor get poorer under Labour'. In fact, its analysis showed nothing of the sort, but it still got massive publicity, not least from Edward Heath, who quoted it repeatedly during the election campaign.[11]

After the brief interregnum of the Heath Tory government, Labour returned to power – and at least at first managed to do rather better than it had in 1964–70. With Barbara Castle as health and social security secretary between 1974 and 1976, it first increased pensions by 25 per cent, then indexed them to whatever was higher of wages and prices. Then it introduced the State Earnings Related Pension Scheme (SERPS), a measure similar to the one Crossman proposed in 1957 and failed to enact in 1970 (Castle's senior policy adviser was Abel-Smith). In 1975, the government legislated for the introduction of child benefit as a replacement for child allowance.

But any hopes that Labour would preside over a measured expansion of pensions and benefits were cruelly dashed by the economic crisis that nearly swept the government away in 1975–6. From spring 1975, chancellor Denis Healey, faced with runaway inflation, public borrowing out of control, a burgeoning balance of payments deficit and a run on the pound, began to insist on tighter controls on public spending – and as the crisis deepened he decided that child benefit would be one of the casualties. His plan to ditch it was scuppered by a guerrilla campaign from April 1976 by Castle, now on the back benches, aided by Field and the CPAG. But the door was firmly slammed shut on any further expenditure that autumn when the government was forced to go to the International Monetary Fund for a loan to save sterling from a catastrophic collapse.

By this point, moreover, the social and political consensus that had sustained the social security system since the late 1940s started to break down. The system was expensive enough at a time of full employment; with the return of mass unemployment in the 1970s – the number out of work reached 1.5 million in 1977, up from 600,000 when Labour took office – its costs spiralled alarmingly. Income tax, paid by only a minority of workers in the 1940s, was by the early 1970s a burden on all but the poorest, and there was growing resentment, particularly among the employed working class, towards money apparently being wasted by the state on benefits for the work-shy. The resentment, fuelled by lurid stories about 'scroungers' in the tabloid press, fitted perfectly with the belief of the free-market Tory right, in the ascendancy since the election of Margaret Thatcher as Tory leader in 1975, that benefits were set at a level that provided a disincentive to work and created an unacceptable burden on the public finances. 'Restoring the will to work' and 'getting value for money in public spending' were two of the key themes in the manifesto on which the Tories won the 1979 general election.

What this meant in practice soon became clear. The Tories introduced tougher rules on eligibility for benefits, increased spending on benefit fraud investigators and implemented drastic cuts in benefit and pension rates. Between 1979 and 1983, as unemployment grew from 1.3 million to 3 million, they froze the level of child benefit, indexed the state pension to price inflation rather than whatever was higher of wage and price inflation, abolished earnings-related unemployment and sickness benefits, and reduced the value of most benefits, making some taxable.

The result was predictable and as the Tories intended: a massive increase in poverty and in reliance on the means-tested 'safety net', with the better off increasingly paying for private provision, particularly for pensions. After the 1983 election, the Tories continued their assault on social security. Following a review of the system, supplementary benefit was renamed income support and reduced in value, housing benefit rates were cut, death and maternity grants were abolished, and the system of one-off payments to needy claimants was replaced with a system of loans, the Social Fund. Most important of all, the government scaled down entitlements to SERPS and offered tax breaks for people to opt out of it into private schemes. After the 1987 election, the Thatcher government rounded off its work by again freezing child benefit, removing entitlement to income support from sixteen and seventeen-year-olds and introducing tougher 'availability for work' rules for claimants.

Coupled with the Tories' income tax cuts, the net effect, as Frank Field, by now Labour MP for Birkenhead, put it in the mid-1980s, was that 'in a country already characterized by marked class differences in income, wealth and power, there has been a significant redistribution to those who are richest'.[12] The process continued unabated right up to the 1997 election. According to the latest government figures, the poorest tenth of the British population is worse off in absolute terms than it was when the Tories came to power. Nearly a quarter of people in Britain live on less than half average income – the European Union poverty line – compared with just under a tenth in 1979. One in six people now claims means-tested income support, up from one in twelve in 1979. Since deregulation of private rented housing in the late 1980s, the number of people claiming housing benefit has doubled. One in three pensioners claims means-tested benefits as well as the state pension.[13]

Until the late 1980s, Labour responded to this extraordinary growth of inequality and reliance on means-tested benefits by denouncing the Tories' policies and promising to reverse them. Labour went into both the 1983 and the 1987 elections pledging big immediate increases in spending to reinstate benefit entitlements that the Tories had abandoned, with the long-term goal of eliminating means-testing as far as possible through a massive expansion of spending and a programme of structural reform. After 1987, the party retained its long-term aims but scaled down its immediate ambitions. What emerged in 1989 from Labour's policy review was a promise of modest increases in child benefit and the state pension – two key benefits symbolic of Labour's commitment to a universal redistributive welfare state because they applied to everyone with children under the age of eighteen and everyone over retirement age.[14] These pledges survived right through to the 1992 general election. A rise of 30p a week in child benefit for the first child and £2.15 for others, and of £5 a week for a single pensioner and £8 a week for a couple, took pride of place in the shadow budget unveiled by shadow chancellor John Smith at the start of the 1992 election campaign. To pay for them, along with a modest job creation programme, there would be increased taxes on those with incomes above £22,000.

The centrality of the shadow budget to Labour's 1992 campaign placed taxation and spending at the centre of the *post mortem* that followed the party's fourth defeat in a row. Bryan Gould made criticism of 'the dominance of our redistributive policies in the election' one of the main themes of his leadership campaign against Smith,[15] and for several weeks after the election defeat an ill-tempered debate about 'selectivity' versus 'universality' in benefits sputtered along in the press, although the only senior Labour figure to contribute to it was Bill Morris, general secretary of the Transport and General Workers' Union, who declared in a *New Statesman* article that he favoured 'a re-examination of the ineffective system of universal benefits'.[16] John Kenneth Galbraith's new book, *The Culture of Contentment*, in which he argued that the US was now divided between a comfortable majority and an excluded minority that the majority was no longer willing to subsidize through a redistributive tax and benefits system, became a minor bestseller.

The stage seemed to be set for a real show-down over the future of the welfare state – but then Smith decided to postpone the row by announcing his intention to set up a Commission on Social Justice, independent of the party apparatus, involving 'specialists and representatives of the majority of the public who want a fairer society' to 'identify a fairer tax and benefits system that will stand the test of time'.[17]

The fuss died down, and in December 1992 the Commission was unveiled to the public. There were obvious limits to its independence from Labour. Although its chair was Sir Gordon Borrie, a lawyer who had been director-general of the Office of Fair Trading and was not known as an apparatchik (even though he had unsuccessfully fought two elections as a Labour candidate), his deputy was Patricia Hewitt, second-in-command at the Institute for Public Policy Research and a key figure in the pre-1992 Labour Party as press secretary to Neil Kinnock and then co-ordinator of the campaign team that lost the election. Its fourteen other members were carefully chosen to represent a broad range of centre-left political opinion from the Liberal Democrats to left-leaning anti-poverty campaigners and economists.[18] The IPPR, set up in 1988 on the initiative of Neil Kinnock, was given responsibility for organizing the whole inquiry, with David Miliband, a young IPPR researcher, as its secretary. The Commission spent nearly two years chewing over research findings and visiting various institutions in different parts of the country, publishing two interim reports in July 1993 and a string of 'issue papers' in late 1993 and early 1994 before producing its final report, *Social Justice: Strategies for National Renewal*, in late October 1994, three months after the election of Tony Blair as Labour leader.[19]

Social Justice was a massive document, densely packed with facts and analysis and with plenty of policy recommendations, but its basic argument was quite simple. It began with the proposition that there are three broad approaches to social policy: those of the deregulators, the levellers and the investors. The deregulators believe in letting the market rip, the levellers simply in redistributing wealth and incomes without thinking about how wealth should be created. The investors, by contrast, 'combine an ethical commitment to equality of opportunity (and all it entails), a vision of the good society, and a compelling analysis of how modern capitalism works – as well as how it can be changed'.[20] From the investors' point of view, Britain had been failing economically for years because its workforce lacked the skills to compete internationally. The result was mass unemployment, in turn the major cause of the poverty endemic in the country. A specific problem, the report argued, was that the growth of unemployment had resulted in an increase in reliance on income support and other means-tested benefits (notably housing benefit), which discouraged participation in the labour market because they are withdrawn as soon as the claimant's income begins to increase – thus leading to the 'poverty trap'.

The conclusion drawn from all this – which of course fitted perfectly with the analysis of the economy developed by Gordon Brown as shadow chancellor – was that the welfare state as a whole needed to be transformed 'from a safety net in times of trouble to a springboard for economic opportunity'. Far from an extension of 'selectivity' being the best way of adapting the welfare state to current conditions, means-testing should be reduced to a minimum and the welfare state returned to the insurance principle that underpinned Beveridge's original plans, bringing the low paid and carers into the social insurance system. A modern welfare state should also intervene far more with what the report called 'welfare-to-work' measures to get people off benefits and into work and to give everyone the skills necessary to prosper.

In the long term, the most important area for change was the education system: *Social Justice* recommended universal pre-school education, literacy targets for seven-year-olds, an end to the academic-vocational divide in sixteen-plus education, an expansion of higher education funded by a graduate tax, the integration of the adult education and training systems, and the establishment of a new funding system, the 'Learning Bank', to allow people access to 'lifetime learning'.

In the short term, however, the priority was action against unemployment and for 'a modern form of full employment'. *Social Justice* was very much a product of the post-Keynesian Labour Party: although it argued for a 'high and sustainable growth rate in overall demand, requiring action at international, European and national level', its emphasis was on supply-side labour-market measures. Here, it rejected as too costly the idea of guaranteeing the long-term unemployed jobs in the public sector and came out strongly against 'workfare' (making the long-term unemployed work for their benefits, an idea imported from the US by the Tory right) on the grounds that it would merely encourage people into criminality. The main positive proposal in the report was for a Jobs, Education and Training (JET) programme, drawing on an Australian model, which would create a proactive 'employment service' to help the unemployed find work, encourage employers to take on the long-term unemployed by offering wage subsidies (conditional on the employer giving training), improve childcare to allow more single parents to work, and attempt to stimulate self-employment among the unemployed. In line with this, the report argued, the benefit and tax systems should be reformed to remove disincentives to work and a string of measures should be introduced to make work more fulfilling – among them a national minimum wage, legislation to improve the employment rights of part-time workers and the rights to consultation embodied in the Social Chapter of the Maastricht Treaty.

As for the two benefits that Labour promised to increase in 1992, *Social Justice* recommended that child benefit be retained, increased and taxed for higher earners – but argued that increasing the state pension was a poor way of reducing pensioner poverty. Instead, it recommended a return to the 'pension guarantee' promised but never introduced by Labour in 1964, with compulsory second pensions for all. Precisely how the second pension scheme would operate was left open, however: one option was to build on SERPS, another to ensure that everyone would contribute to a 'funded' scheme investing contributions. On tax, the report argued that no one should pay more than 50 per cent of their income in tax; it rejected earmarking of taxes for particular purposes and backed green taxes. The report was rounded off with suggestions for a shift in health service priorities towards preventative medicine, various ideas for tackling homelessness and a voluntary service scheme for sixteen to twenty-five-year-olds.

Nevertheless, the report did not have the impact of Beveridge's *Social Insurance and Allied Services*. Its launch in 1994 was overshadowed by Tony Blair's decision a few weeks earlier to embark on rewriting Clause Four of Labour's constitution and by the first revelations that certain Tory MPs had taken cash for asking parliamentary questions. But it was welcomed by a broad swathe of centre-left and centre-right opinion. Although few matched Will Hutton's enthusiasm in the *Guardian* – he described it as 'a landmark effort' and 'a remarkable document' – in the months after its publication, its analysis and many of its prescriptions found widespread support.

Several of its themes were echoed by two other major reports on the future of welfare and work: the Rowntree Foundation's *Inquiry into Income and Wealth*, published in February 1995 by a committee including TUC general secretary

John Monks and CBI director-general Howard Davies; and the Liberal Democrat-sponsored *Wealth Creation and Social Cohesion*, published in July 1995 by a committee chaired by Lord Dahrendorf. Like *Social Justice*, both rejected the free-market right's insistence that inequalities generate wealth, emphasized the primary importance of education and paid work as the key routes out of poverty, rejected means-testing in favour of rebuilding a system of social insurance and advocated an extension of second pensions.[21] Even the government took notice: Kenneth Clarke's November 1994 budget included a modest 'welfare-to-work' programme, with subsidies for employers who took on the long-term unemployed.

Such gestures were token: the government was more interested in 'workfare' than Borrie-type measures and, with Peter Lilley as social security secretary, overall policy remained one of piecemeal spending cuts and expanded means-testing. But even on the centre-left there were limits to the consensus. Many left-leaning welfare policy experts took umbrage – with justification – at the Borrie report's setting up of a straw man in its attack on 'levellers' who wanted to redistribute wealth while giving no consideration to its creation. For Peter Townsend, now an emeritus professor at Bristol University, this was little more than a politically convenient way of dodging a commitment to redistribution from the well-off to those whose poverty could not be alleviated by a move from welfare into work, especially pensioners. Townsend was furious at the way *Social Justice* treated the basic pension. 'The pension is clearly withering on the vine,' he declared to a conference to launch a Transport and General Workers' Union report on the state of welfare the week after the publication of the Borrie report. 'The Commission says, timidly, that improvement of the basic pension would be "expensive". But this view is not properly argued in relation to the movement in earnings levels, insecurity of much present employment, administrative efficiency, public psychology and much else. Above all, it is not argued in relation to economic growth, the aggrandizement of the already rich and the priorities of governments in Europe. To put the matter bluntly: the UK has larger resources than it did in the 1970s to ameliorate the harsh living standards of the poorest pensioners. Yet in the last fifteen years, the disposable income of single pensioners and pensioner couples in the poorest 10 per cent has fallen in real terms compared with 1979.'[22] Townsend was also critical of the report's failure to come out with a ringing endorsement of SERPS as the way to ensure the maximum spread of second pensions.[23]

Frank Field made precisely the opposite point. He had already made it clear that he believed Labour had lost in 1992 because it had not appealed to the self-interest of most voters, declaring in a book published in 1993 that 'no party is going to stand on a programme of universally increasing the state pension to a level adequate enough to free the least privileged pensioners from their poverty'.[24] After the launch of the Borrie report, he lambasted it for not coming out explicitly for compulsory private pensions instead of toying with the idea as a long-term possibility and opting in the short run for a means-tested 'pension guarantee'. 'Pensions are the biggest part of the social security budget,' he declared. 'The universalization of private pension provision offers a true partnership between public and private sector, puts self-improvement at the centre of the drive to reshape welfare, and also provides for the poor.'[25]

Field continued his attack on means-testing in a book published in May 1995, in which he called for a far more fundamental social insurance-based recasting of the pensions and benefits than the Borrie report had dared to contemplate.[26] His scheme was for a new national insurance corporation independent of central government and run by 'stakeholders' – employees, employers and government representatives – to collect contributions from all three parties and provide employees with cover against unemployment and sickness and to fund a subsistence-level basic pension. Contributions from the unemployed and those outside the labour market would be paid by the state, thus eliminating means-tested benefits. Meanwhile, everyone would have to contribute to a private second pension which would be overseen by a new pensions corporation, again run by 'stakeholders'. When Townsend claimed that this system would do nothing to promote equality, Field agreed. 'None of my reforms is about gaining greater equality. The crucial consideration is: how do we rebuild a sense of fraternity and social cohesion, especially in a rapidly changing and flexible labour market?'[27]

A radically different answer to this very question came from another group of critics of the damaging effects of means-testing – the advocates of citizen's income. This was the idea that means-testing should be done away with in favour of a tax-free basic income paid by the state for every man, woman and child, financed by a tax on all other income. Citizen's income was a radical proposal – and it would undoubtedly require tax increases to pay for it if it were to be set at a level sufficient for survival (although how big the increases would have to be has been much contested). But it also has certain undeniable advantages. It would involve the removal of the whole apparatus of means-testing and much of the anti-fraud bureaucracy that currently exists – and it would get rid of the 'poverty trap' whereby many people are better off on means-tested benefits than working. Equally important, it would allow the 'involuntarily employed' – people who currently work because they cannot afford not to but who would rather be in education or looking after their children – to give up their jobs to people who want work but have none.

The Borrie report rejected citizen's income on the grounds of cost and because, by offering 'something for nothing', it could not win popular support – although it did leave the door open to what it called a 'participation income', a citizen's income for all but the lazy, which it said might be worth considering if unemployment proved rather more intractable than it hoped. Meghnad Desai, professor of economics at the LSE and Labour's most prominent supporter of citizen's income, was withering. Borrie, he said, 'ducked the really tough issue', the problem that a system based on social insurance cannot work if a substantial number of people spend long periods unemployed. 'The fundamental problem faced by any welfare state,' he wrote, 'is how to manage a transfer of resources across the life-cycle and also find a feasible and incentive-friendly way of transferring resources within generations, from the working "rich" to the working and non-working "poor". If there is a lifetime employment prospect, with only occasional bouts of unemployment, then the Beveridge principle of social insurance is adequate, at least for working men.

But the task of financing longer or repeated spells of unemployment, as well as claims from those who cannot work, is proving
too burdensome for the Beveridge welfare state.' In the face of permanent mass unemployment, paying a basic income to all
whether or not they are working would secure at least a basic
standard of living for everyone as well as encouraging the flexible
labour market we need in a globally competitive economy.[28]

As for the Labour leadership, it kept its own counsel. The Borrie
report was clearly in tune with the enthusiasm for 'supply-side'
measures to tackle unemployment that had underpinned Labour's
thinking since the late 1980s, and Tony Blair gave it a guarded
welcome. But it was hardly the populist call for reform that could
play the campaigning role of Bill Clinton's 1992 promise to 'end
welfare as we know it', and it was short on detailed recommendations and costings. It left Labour with some difficult decisions to
make, particularly on pensions and benefits and to a lesser extent
on welfare-to-work measures – and the difficulty was compounded by shadow chancellor Gordon Brown's insistence that he
would not be drawn into promising any more spending than could
be funded by the windfall tax on privatized utilities. By autumn
1995, with a spring 1996 election a distinct possibility, it became
a matter of urgency for Labour to sort out what their policies
were. Blair decided that the solution was to give the social security
brief to the brightest of the shadow cabinet's younger members,
Chris Smith, with the injunction to 'think the unthinkable' – if
needs be dropping the ideas of the Borrie report for something
radically different.

    The relatively easy part of Smith's task was welfare-to-work,
in part because the Borrie report's ideas about creating a Jobs,
Education and Training scheme (what Blair called 'a hand-up, not
a hand-out') commanded support throughout the shadow cabinet,
and in part because Brown had already unilaterally decided much
of the detail of Labour policy. A week after Smith was appointed,
the shadow chancellor publicly announced details of his plans
for tackling youth unemployment, paid for by the windfall tax,
whereby anyone under twenty-five who had been unemployed

for more than six months and refused to take up offers of employment, training or education would have their benefit docked: Smith was not consulted. According to Brown's scheme, which was to remain at the centre of Labour's programme until it was implemented in his 1997 budget, there would be four options for the unemployed under-twenty-fives, 'each involving day-release education or training leading to a qualification': 'a job with a private sector employer, who will be offered a £60-a-week rebate paid for six months; a job with a non-profit voluntary sector employer, paying a weekly wage, equivalent to benefit plus a fixed sum for six months; full-time study for young people to achieve educational qualifications on an approved course; or a job on Labour's environment taskforce, as part of our proposed citizen's service . . . There will be no fifth option of remaining permanently on full benefit.'[29]

In June 1996, Smith published a policy document, *Getting Welfare to Work*, based largely on the Borrie proposals. It promised an 'entirely new philosophy' for the Department of Social Security, with 'personalized benefit and employment services' and 'one-stop shops' where the unemployed would claim benefit, look for work and be offered careers and training advice. The unemployed would be encouraged to train and study, and various incentives would be introduced to get spouses of the unemployed to take up paid work.[30]

Pensions and benefits were another matter altogether. Precisely what the 'unthinkable' was that Blair wanted from Smith was by its very nature difficult to grasp. But it seemed to most observers – especially after Blair's speech in Singapore in January 1996 in which he talked of 'a stakeholder welfare system' with the 'aims of promoting security and opportunity across the life-cycle', which 'holds the commitment of the whole population, rich and poor' – that the Labour leader was hoping his new social security spokesman would produce a scheme something like Field's model of a universal social insurance system, part public and part private. Field's idea of compulsory 'funded' private second pensions had the attraction to Blair of not being paid for by non-pensioners' taxes but of being the fruit of pensioners' previous personal saving. Unlike a pay-as-you-go scheme for pensions, such as that

advocated by Peter Townsend and other backers of 'improved
state pension plus SERPS', it would not require tax increases to
pay decent pensions to all – which was the problem with pay-as-
you-go from the 2020s onwards because of the increased
proportion of pensioners in the population.

Singapore was significant as a location for Blair's speech. It
has a social security system based almost entirely on social insurance (although it is state-run rather than part-private,
part-public). All employees have to pay 20 per cent of their earnings (a contribution matched by employers) to a Central
Provident Fund, which lends most of the money raised to the
government, which in turn spends it on infrastructure projects.
The fund uses its contributions income, augmented by the interest it receives from lending to the government, to pay for
unemployment benefit, pensions and emergency health cover.

But if Blair was expecting Smith to come up with a ringing
endorsement of Field or of Singapore, he was disappointed. Smith,
who went to Singapore the same time as Blair, came back convinced that the island did not provide a model that Britain could
follow. The low yields paid by the Central Provident Fund to
savers would not satisfy anyone in Britain who was used to a fast-
growing private pension fund. And although the sense of
ownership that the Singaporean system fostered among savers
was attractive, as was its flexibility – it allowed savers to use some
of their accumulated capital to buy houses – its provision of insurance cover for emergency health care would be unnecessary in
Britain. Worst of all, it did not provide any sort of safety net in the
form of a basic pension or income support.[31] Smith concluded
that the idea of a wholly insurance-based social security system
was simplistic: the best bet was some hybrid model. The document he produced on pensions in June 1996, *Security in
Retirement*, recommended second pensions for all but, apart from
suggesting that SERPS 'could not easily or sustainably be rebuilt in
its original form', made few concrete suggestions about how they
should be paid for.[32]

It satisfied neither Field, who repeated his call for a new
system of social insurance,[33] nor Townsend, who together with
Barbara Castle – who saw SERPS as her outstanding achievement

in office between 1974 and 1976 – set about scotching the fashionable idea that the basic pension and SERPS were too expensive. In July, Townsend and Castle launched a co-authored pamphlet, *We Can Afford the Welfare State*, which argued that it would cost little to increase the basic pension to the level it would have reached if it were still indexed to whatever was higher of earnings and price inflation and made a costed case for returning SERPS to its position as a second pension for everyone.[34]

But it was not Smith that dealt with their assault. In spring, he had clashed with Brown over the abolition of the Job Seeker's Allowance, the Tories' cover for making unemployment benefit payable only for six months rather than a year. Smith argued that entitlement should be restored to twelve months; Brown refused to countenance it. Then, just before Smith published his policy document in June, Brown announced that Labour would withdraw universal child benefit from children over sixteen who were in full-time education. Smith, who was not told of the scheme, was furious and told Blair so. After the shadow cabinet election in late July, Brown insisted that Smith be removed from the social security brief and 'replaced by someone he could push around', as one colleague put it. In the shadow cabinet reshuffle that followed, Smith and Harriet Harman, the health spokeswoman, swapped jobs.[35] Thus it was that she rather than the author of the social security policy had to face the wrath of Barbara Castle at Labour's conference in Blackpool in the autumn – a confrontation that Harman won, but only with the help of behind-the-scenes arm-twisting of a severity unusual even in these days of managed Labour conferences, and only after making the concession to Castle of setting up a committee to work out a compromise acceptable to all sides.

The committee proved, in Castle's words, a 'sham': Harman refused to countenance changing the policy laid out in *Security in Retirement* in order to incorporate restoration of the link between pensions and earnings. Subsequently the 1997 Labour manifesto merely repeated the 1996 document's vague ideas for 'stakeholder pensions' and 'new partnerships between financial service companies, employers and employees', adding only a swipe at the Tories for planning to privatize the basic pension. Needless to say, there was no promise of an increase in the pension.

There was little new after summer 1996 – apart from a harder line on single parents. In January 1997, Tony Blair made a widely reported speech at a conference in Amsterdam in which, drawing on themes popularized by American conservative thinkers, he declared: 'The single biggest threat to social stability in western democracies is the creation of a group of people excluded from society's mainstream – an underclass if you like – who are increasingly set apart, living in a culture that is becoming more and more alienated.' A particular problem, he said, was lone parents on benefit. 'One million lone parents are without work in Britain. They constitute a quarter of all households without work . . . 'The tax bill to pay for them and their children is £10 billion a year – a bill that has risen by 250 per cent under the Conservatives. Lone parents are trapped on benefit because they are left there with no active support from the welfare state, because there is no national childcare strategy, because there is an inflexible benefits system, and because of lack of training and skills. The people who bear the brunt of the resulting hardship are children – one in three children in poverty are in lone parent families.'

Labour did not want to compel lone parents to work or interfere with their arrangements for their children, he went on. But it did want to try to get them into work, by encouraging them to train and by expanding after-school childcare, perhaps using lottery money, to make it easier for them to take jobs. As a first step, Labour would make sure that every unemployed lone parent with children of school age was interviewed by the Department of Social Security and the employment service to discuss job possibilities.[36]

The 1997 manifesto referred obliquely to lone parents being offered advice by a 'proactive employment service', but its centrepiece was Brown's familiar 'welfare-to-work' package to get 250,000 unemployed under-twenty-fives off the dole. On benefits, Labour promised to retain universal child benefit – but everything else would be kept 'under continuous review' to ensure that the tax and benefits systems 'are supportive of families and children'. Brown's scheme for taking away child benefit for sixteen- to eighteen-year-olds, which had come under attack from the Tories, was diplomatically played down to the statement that 'We are reviewing educational finance and maintenance for those older than 16 to ensure higher staying-on rates at school and college, and that resources are used to support those most in need.'[37]

Blair signalled his intentions on social security immediately after his election victory. He made Harman social security secretary and Frank Field her deputy, with responsibility for investigating long-term welfare reform, and he appointed the former Tory Alan Howarth as welfare-to-work minister in the Department for Education and Employment.[38] Opening the Commons debate on the Queen's Speech, Blair promised sweeping changes to the whole social security system. 'We have reached the limits of the public's willingness simply to fund an unreformed welfare system through ever higher taxes and spending,' he said. 'The blunt truth is that the world of 1997 bears little resemblance in work patterns, in industrial production and in social or family life to the world of 1947. Change is inevitable, but that change must be fair. We are therefore undertaking a thorough examination of all aspects of welfare reform.'

Next came news of the creation of a welfare-to-work cabinet committee, chaired by chancellor Gordon Brown, and the appointment of Geoff Mulgan, director of the think-tank Demos, as an adviser to Number Ten on welfare-to-work schemes. To complete the line-up, Brown appointed Martin Taylor, chief executive of Barclays Bank, as head of a 'Whitehall task force' on reforming the tax and benefits systems.[39] After that came Blair's headline-grabbing speech in Southwark.

There were no immediate surprises on policy, however. As expected, Brown's budget had at its centre the measures promised in the manifesto for welfare-to-work: all that was new was the announcement that sixteen- to twenty-five-year-olds who refused a place on one of the schemes would have all their benefit withdrawn rather than some of it.

All this was greeted with enthusiasm by the press. But how effective the welfare-to-work drive will be is uncertain. There is, of course, no excuse for inaction on unemployment, and it might just be that, carried through with energy and enthusiasm, the government's measures are effective. On the other hand, there are also grounds for scepticism. According to the Institute for Fiscal Studies, job subsidy programmes in other countries create little genuine employment: people hired under them tend to be the sort who would find work anyway and are usually taken on instead of unsubsidized employees. The environment taskforce has the potential to be a 1990s version of a Keynesian public works programme, but that would take more money than the government appears to be prepared to spend. Although making after-school childcare more widely available would certainly make it easier for lone parents to go to work, what the *Independent on Sunday* called 'a few mothers' clubs funded by the lottery', even combined with helpful suggestions from job centres, will not remove the most important disincentive to work for lone parents, the withdrawal of means-tested benefits as lone parents start earning wages.

More generally, there is the problem of the quality of the education and training promised as part of the welfare-to-work programme, where again it is difficult to imagine any improvement on previous governments' records without a considerable increase in expenditure, particularly on further education. Most important of all, recession would cancel out the effects of even the most successful welfare-to-work measures.

If welfare-to-work doesn't live up to its promises, the element of compulsion in Labour's programme is bound to come under close scrutiny. Although there have always been regulations on benefit entitlement relating to availability for work – one of the Tories' great obsessions between 1979 and 1997 – Brown's budget package goes one step further. There will be few complaints if unemployed under-twenty-fives really do get a choice of options with high-quality training, and if the participants in the schemes do get proper jobs in the end. The legitimacy of the whole exercise will crumble, however, if they find themselves being forced to accept poorly paid skivvying work, third-rate training or the likelihood of a return to the dole.

What happens on social security after the initial batch of welfare-to-work measures is difficult to predict. Everything suggests that the government is attracted by the idea of replacing benefits paid for by general taxation with benefits paid for by individuals' savings in social insurance schemes. How far and how fast it will go is impossible to tell – but the best guess is that its first priority will be pensions, the promised review of which was set up in summer 1997 by Harriet Harman. They currently account for £43 billion of the £100 billion social security budget; Frank Field has a costed plan for replacing SERPS with compulsory private cover; and Tory social security secretary Peter Lilley came out with what seemed to be a mouth-wateringly money-saving scheme for privatizing the whole of state pensions in the dying days of John Major's government.

The argument is still far from over. Field's calculations are unlikely to sway the Civil Service: one of the reasons that Lilley came out for privatization not just of SERPS but of the whole state pension was that the start-up costs for Field's scheme would be prohibitive. Field liked Lilley's 'Basic Pensions Plus' plan, but it was effectively ruled out by Labour's promise during the 1997 election campaign to retain the basic state pension.

This gives even greater force to the case for reviving SERPS and increasing the basic pension put forward by Peter Townsend and Barbara Castle in 1996 – and indeed to the more general argument against insurance-based social security advanced by Meghnad Desai in the wake of the Borrie report. State pensions work: they cover everyone, regardless of their employment history. In a society in which, despite its affluence, unemployment is endemic and job insecurity the norm, even the best insurance-based system would inevitably leave vast numbers of people with inadequate cover. Unless existing pensioners are condemned to poverty, moreover, any scheme for replacing even a significant part of 'pay-as-you-go' state pension provision means that for up to forty years tax-payers would have to cough up not only the taxes to pay for the state pensions of existing pensioners but also the contributions towards their own funded pensions. Most important of all, any 'funded' scheme is only as good as the performance of the stocks and shares in which it invests. Any attempt to make provision for the distant future involves taking risks on what might happen. For most people it makes less sense to gamble on the markets than on the probability that in 2020 or 2040 there will be a state capable of raising taxes from a reasonably well-off population.

In other words, the only just and efficient way to provide pensioners with an adequate secure income is to pay them pensions as of right, funded by taxing those in work. And if that means that taxes might have to be increased, so be it.

As for other benefits, much the same arguments apply. If Labour is serious about getting rid of the poverty trap created by means-testing, the most sensible and equitable way of doing it is to make benefits all round a matter of entitlement, regardless of contributions – in short, citizen's income. Of course, it would cost money. But the advantages – in eliminating most means-testing, in providing security for all and (whisper it) as an alternative to the minimum wage, with all its negative employment effects, in helping those on low pay – are immense. Any genuinely radical rethink of welfare should have citizen's income at its heart.

7

LOCK UP YOUR DAUGHTERS

JACK STRAW AND HOME AFFAIRS

Home secretary Jack Straw did not have the best of luck with timing when he set out his priorities for government in the Commons. Immediately after he had finished outlining the home affairs provisions of Labour's first Queen's Speech, Ann Widdecombe, a Home Office minister in John Major's Tory government, stunned MPs with a damning attack on her one-time boss, former home secretary Michael Howard, who was standing as a candidate in the Tory leadership election. Howard's account of the sacking of Derek Lewis as head of the prison service in 1995 had, she said, been marked by 'semantic destidigitation'. She made it clear that Howard had made Lewis a scapegoat for his own failings and had misled the House about the extent of his involvement in decisions about prison management when challenged by Straw – notoriously ineffectually – eighteen months earlier.

Her intervention destroyed Howard's credibility and with it his hopes of winning the Tory leadership – and eclipsed Straw's presentation of the new government's Home Office programme. Which was a pity, because his speech, although it contained no surprises about Labour's legislative proposals, was a notably forthright summary of the ambition behind them. 'The better society that we want to build is one that fosters and celebrates strong

British values: decency; reward for hard work; tolerance and respect for others,' Straw declared. 'It is one in which rights for everyone are matched by responsibilities for all.' Labour's legislation, he went on, 'will set a framework for underpinning these British values; for restoring responsibilities and for better protecting rights. That may sound abstract. But the benefits that should flow will be real and concrete for individuals, for families and for communities throughout the United Kingdom. We want to bring about changes in the way in which people relate to one another by changing people's public behaviour and their sense of responsibility towards one another. We want to reclaim our towns, cities and villages so that everyone is free to go about their neighbourhoods in safety and security.'

'Some people would deny that any government can achieve such changes. But the government have at their disposal more effective levers than are available to any private individual or agency. The government also have the responsibility – the moral duty – to use the power that they have for the good of all . . . For the past eighteen years, Britain had a government who preached the value of self-interest above everything else. It should therefore come as no surprise that some people then choose to ignore their responsibilities to other people. When there is "no such thing as society", there can be no shared standards of behaviour. Where there is a steady erosion of community, of shared values, links between individuals collapse and people become fearful and distrustful of others. It's "Get what you can, don't worry about anyone else" – the instincts of those who commit crime. Crime is the ultimate selfish act. It results from the breakdown of rules and from an evasion of responsibility for other people.'

The measures Straw outlined to make a start on instilling responsibility into society were familiar. He gave pride of place in his speech to the government's proposed Crime and Disorder Bill, the main purpose of which was to fulfil Labour's manifesto promise to introduce 'fast-track punishment for persistent young offenders by halving the time from arrest to sentencing'. 'By speeding juvenile justice, we aim to ensure that young offenders are made to see the clear link between crime and punishment, and to face up to the consequences of their offending for their victims and themselves,' he said. The bill would replace repeat cautions of young offenders with a single final police warning, change the law to remove the assumption that children aged between ten and thirteen are not morally responsible, give the courts new sentencing powers, and introduce reforms to the community sentencing system for young offenders. To deal with more general disorder, it would create several new court orders to deal with 'brutish and unacceptable behaviour' as part of 'a strategy of zero tolerance' – community safety orders to restrain named individuals and child protection orders targeting parents who neglect their children – and new offences of racial harassment and racially motivated violence.

In addition, said Straw, the government planned to appoint a 'drugs czar' to lead the 'fight against drugs', legislation to ban possession of handguns, and better services for the victims of crime. There would be an audit of the prison service, and ministers would take proper ministerial responsibility for its workings. The government would ensure at the Amsterdam European Union summit that Britain kept its frontier controls, would make immigration procedures fairer, and would incorporate the main provisions of the European Convention on Human Rights (ECHR) into British law.

Two of the measures Straw outlined, the incorporation of the ECHR and the changes to immigration procedures, were steps that civil libertarians had been urging for years. But Straw's tone and the overall thrust of the plans he outlined were noticeably illiberal – just as Labour had been in opposition. The new government's primary aim was not to increase liberty but to combat license. As he put it at the end of his speech, 'We shall encourage greater responsibility and, in doing so, seek to protect the rights of all.'[1] The 'in doing so' is absolutely crucial.

Things were very different when Harold Wilson came to power in 1964. Labour then had no particularly well worked-out plans for home affairs, but the tone of the party's pronouncements suggested that he would head a modernizing, liberalizing government. Since 1951, when Labour left office, society had changed enormously. Consumerism, greater social mobility, the growth of the youth culture, mass immigration and decolonization, the New Left and the first wave of CND, the rise of a new generation of radical playwrights, novelists and film-makers – all had undermined the deference to authority and social conformism that had characterized Britain in the first half of the century. The Tories had not changed with the times: they remained the party of the intolerant patrician establishment. But Labour had, at least to some extent. If it was not prepared to condone law-breaking – by direct action activists in the peace movement or by dope-smokers – let alone to question the assumptions and practices of the secret state, it was at least willing to consider removing some of Britain's more antiquated restrictions on individual freedom.

The 1945–51 Labour government of Clement Attlee had done much to contribute to Britain becoming a more easy-going society, notably the establishment of the welfare state. But this was not its purpose. The libertarian left of the party – a small group of MPs and intellectuals clustered around Aneurin Bevan, Harold Laski, *Tribune*, the *New Statesman* and what remained of the Independent Labour Party – was anathema to the right-wing trade unionists and stern Fabian planners who dominated the government, and it had no influence on home affairs policy. The home secretary, James Chuter Ede, an austere former schoolmaster who was nearly sixty-three when Attlee appointed him, proved to be 'no innovator', in the words of the historian Kenneth O. Morgan. 'His 1948 Criminal Justice Bill was in many respects a disappointment, especially for his refusal to abolish capital punishment (a view which he later reversed when in opposition in the 1950s). Not only back-bench penal reformers such as Sidney Silverman were disappointed with him; so, too, were government colleagues such as Cripps, Bevan and Griffiths. Nor did Ede radically overhaul the police or their procedures, despite the 1946 Police Act.'[2] The Attlee government did nothing to deal with racial discrimination (despite evidence of it against black immigrants from the West Indies) and was also responsible for the nearest thing Britain had to McCarthyism, the 1948 ban on Communists in the civil service. The lack of non-Communist opposition by the left caused George Orwell to bemoan 'the general breakdown of the democratic outlook'.[3]

During the 1950s, however, Labour's political culture grew slowly more liberal on at least some aspects of home affairs. The right-wing party establishment under Hugh Gaitskell was supremely intolerant of internal party dissent of any kind, and it accepted without question the Cold War security state. But in its attitudes to issues of what was known at the time as 'personal freedom' – homosexuality, abortion, divorce, censorship on grounds of obscenity, the death penalty – it was far closer to its Bevanite arch-enemies than to the Conservative old right of the 1940s.

The two brightest young stars of Gaitskellism, Anthony Crosland and Roy Jenkins, were particularly keen for Labour to take a radically different approach. Crosland pithily expressed their view in *The Future of Socialism* when he declared: 'In the blood of the socialist there should always run a trace of the anarchist and the libertarian, and not too much of the prig and the prude' – a sentiment that would have had Sidney and Beatrice Webb turning in their graves.[4] Jenkins was the leading Labour light in the late-1950s campaign to reform the law on censorship to allow literary merit as a possible defence against the charge of obscenity – an effort that bore fruit in the 1959 Obscene Publications Act, the crucial factor in Penguin Books' successful legal action in 1960 to prevent the banning of D.H. Lawrence's *Lady Chatterley's Lover*. In 1959, he wrote a pre-election Penguin Special, *The Labour Case*, in which he devoted a chapter to an unauthorized programme for Home Office reform. 'There is a need,' he stated baldly, 'for the state to do less to restrict personal freedom.' 'The ghastly apparatus of the gallows', the 'brutal and unfair' law on homosexuality and the 'powers of absolute censorship over all the public theatres of London' exercised by the Lord Chamberlain all had to go; there was also an urgent need to make divorce easier, to liberalize immigration legislation and to get rid of the 'harsh and archaic' abortion laws.[5]

After Labour's victory in the 1964 general election, Harold Wilson's appointment as home secretary was Frank Soskice, a sixty-two-year-old right-winger who between 1945 and 1951 had been solicitor-general and then (briefly) attorney-general. He was

generally considered hopelessly indecisive and lasted only a year
in the job, although in that time he managed to steer through an
act ending capital punishment and the 1965 Race Relations Act,
which introduced the first anti-discrimination laws, so he was
not entirely incapable of making up his mind. Wilson replaced
him in late 1965 with Jenkins, who in two hyperactive years saw
to the decriminalization of homosexuality and abortion (both
back-bench bills that he got the government to help through the
Commons), the abolition of corporal punishment in prisons and
an easing of restrictions on divorce. He also set in train the abolition of censorship in the theatre and the legislative process that
produced the 1968 Race Relations Act, which gave teeth to the
Race Relations Board set up under Soskice.

Although he was not spared criticism by Labour's libertarians on some criminal justice measures – both his abolition of the
need for guilty verdicts to be unanimous in jury trials and his reorganization of the police were judged dangerous by some – the
overwhelming majority of the party's MPs and most of the left
intelligentsia had nothing but respect for Jenkins' reforms. A
handful of Labour traditionalists, most of them Catholics, joined
the Tory right in condemning him as the man most responsible for
the evils of the 'permissive society'. But he weathered the attacks
nonchalantly, even through the epidemics of hysteria that followed the shooting to death of three policemen in Shepherd's
Bush in August 1966 and the escape of the Soviet spy George
Blake from Wormwood Scrubs jail two months later.

Labour's reforming intentions in home affairs in the mid-
1960s never extended to official secrecy or making the security
state accountable. Wilson routinely used briefings from the security services when making appointments and in dealing with
industrial disputes.[6] But the reforming momentum even on 'personal freedom' ran out after Jenkins became chancellor of the
exchequer, swapping jobs with Jim Callaghan after the forced
sterling devaluation of November 1967. Callaghan didn't want to
be home secretary – 'I asked Harold Wilson to let me go to education on resignation from the exchequer,' he records in his
memoirs[7] – and his instincts were conservative. A former parliamentary consultant to the Police Federation, he did not block

those of Jenkins' liberalizing reforms that were still in the pipeline
when he took over. But he resisted all suggestions of anything
more in the same vein (for example, decriminalization of
cannabis, which was recommended by the Wooton report and
discussed in the cabinet in 1969).

Interviewed by Hugo Young in the *Sunday Times* just after
his appointment, he made much of his 'God-given common sense'
and declared: 'Of course, I cannot bear the young men with hair
hanging over their shoulders.' 'I am not ready to take the risks of
permissiveness,' he told a Police Federation conference.[8] On law
and order, Callaghan talked tough and gave the police strong support – on one infamous occasion pre-empting the verdict of the
courts by congratulating the constabulary in the Commons for
having arrested 'one of those responsible for the murder at
Fulham' and 'the man who committed murder in Acton this
morning'. Soon after this incident Wilson remarked to a colleague
that 'Jim isn't as much a minister of justice as a minister of police'.[9]
On immigration, Callaghan was responsible for the restrictive and
implicitly racist Commonwealth Immigrants Act of 1968,
described by *The Times* as 'probably the most shameful measure
that Labour members have ever been asked by their whips to support' – a piece of legislation he subsequently justified on the
grounds that a home secretary had 'to keep a sense of proportion
during waves of public panic.'[10]

Nevertheless, Callaghan also had a keen sense of the limits
of populist law-and-order politics. He pushed the prison service
into accepting the importance of rehabilitation as well as punishment. He coped with the press hysteria surrounding the July 1968
anti-Vietnam war demonstration in London, widely predicted to
bring Paris-style mayhem to British streets, by nonchalantly
defending the right to protest while backing the police plans to
keep the demonstration under control. He banned Dany Cohn-
Bendit, the leader of the students in France in May 1968, from
entering the country – but then turned up in person to take a look
at the demonstrators as they assembled, watched the whole show
live on a police surveillance feed at the Home Office, congratulated the constabulary on their efforts, then went down to the
street again to talk to demonstrators.[11] For all his conservatism

and populism – he even launched a 'war against crime' that had absolutely no effect – 'Uncle Jim' had his charms even for the left.

Jenkins returned to the Home Office for a second time after Labour won the February 1974 general election. But his appointment had less to do with his views on home affairs than with Wilson's need to find something important for him to do once he had decided to make Callaghan foreign secretary and Denis Healey chancellor. Jenkins' heart was not in the job – he had wanted to run the Treasury or the Foreign Office – and his main proposal for reform, a Bill of Rights, soon ran into trouble with large sections of his own party. Part of the problem was that a Bill of Rights would necessarily give powers to the judiciary at the expense of parliament, which many Labour civil libertarians (mostly on the left, but including such right-wingers as Roy Hattersley) opposed on the grounds that the judges could not be trusted. But a bigger obstacle was the growing opposition of the trade unions, who came to see a Bill of Rights as a covert attack on their powers. One of the measures that Labour had promised the unions before the election in return for pay restraint was legislation to let employers with closed-shop agreements refuse to employ non-union labour. The government kept its promise – with Jenkins barely concealing his reservations – and the response was a wave of indignation not just from the right but also from many liberals. To the trade unions and the left, talk of individual rights appeared more and more as code for attacking the collective rights of unions, and they successfully prevented Jenkins' proposed Bill of Rights from ever seeing the light of day.[12]

Not that the political climate would have been conducive to liberal reforms of any description even if Labour and the unions had warmed to the idea of a Bill of Rights. Britain in 1974 was in a state of panic. IRA terrorism, militant trade unionism, the influx of immigrants, the widely publicized antics of the revolutionary left, the country-wide expansion of the youth counter-culture, the seemingly inexorable rise of vandalism, hooliganism and violent crime – all had combined to persuade substantial sections of the middle class and the political establishment that the very foundations of the British way of life were under threat. A vocal part of the right-wing intelligentsia talked of a crisis of ungovernability;

former generals set up private armies; rogue elements in the security services, believing that Soviet subversion was at the root of it all, spread black propaganda about Wilson and his colleagues. Even before Jenkins arrived for the second time at the Home Office, the pressure to clamp down on 'disorder' and 'subversion' was intense.

Then the IRA spread its terrorist campaign to Great Britain, most notably with the Guildford, Woolwich and Birmingham pub bombings. After the Birmingham outrage, faced with near-hysterical demands that something be done to stop the carnage, Jenkins introduced a piece of emergency legislation that ran counter to all his liberal instincts – the Prevention of Terrorism (Temporary Provisions) Act (PTA), which was rushed through parliament. It was, as he admitted, draconian, increasing police powers to arrest and detain suspected terrorists and introducing 'exclusion orders' to ban from Great Britain anyone from Northern Ireland considered to be a terrorist sympathizer. 'I would have been horrified to be told at the time that it would still be law nearly two decades later,' he wrote in his autobiography.[13]

Still, the pressure for action against disorder mounted, particularly after Margaret Thatcher was elected leader of the Conservative Party in early 1975. Although very much influenced by nineteenth-century liberalism in her economics, her thinking about law and order was unambiguously authoritarian. She was strongly influenced by advisers who believed that Britain was descending into chaos and required exceptional measures to reassert the authority of the state and the sanctity of private property.[14] Under her leadership, the Tories adopted an increasingly strident populist rhetoric in which the promotion of freedom from union power, high taxation and state interference in the economy was seamlessly attached to demands for increasing state powers to deal with threats to public order.

Labour simply drifted with the tide. After the PTA, the government became increasingly illiberal, particularly after Callaghan became prime minister in 1976 and Jenkins went off to Brussels to become president of the European Commission, to be replaced as home secretary by the lacklustre Merlyn Rees. Rees, the secretary of state for Northern Ireland between 1974 and

1976, was promoted largely because he had been Callaghan's deputy at the Home Office in the late 1960s and was organizer of his 1976 campaign for the party leadership. The government did nothing to liberalize the obscenity laws, despite the recommendations of a committee it set up under the chairmanship of the philosopher Bernard Williams; and it did not repeal the blasphemy laws after Mary Whitehouse's private prosecution of *Gay News* showed that they were a serious threat to freedom of speech. It did nothing to legislate for freedom of information, and nothing to resist the demands of the police for greater powers, more intrusive technology and wider 'counter-subversive' and 'public order' roles. In Northern Ireland, it maintained the 1970–4 Tory government's abandonment of jury trial.

Worst of all, the 1974–9 Labour government also presided over a string of political trials. In 1975, it prosecuted fourteen pacifists from the tiny British Withdrawal from Northern Ireland Campaign for alleged incitement to disaffection of troops sent to Northern Ireland (they had distributed a handful of leaflets): after a ten-week trial at the Old Bailey, they were acquitted. In 1976, under pressure from the US government, it began deportation proceedings against the journalist Mark Hosenball and the former CIA agent Phil Agee on the grounds that they were dangerous subversives: the pair were duly kicked out. After that, it prosecuted two radical journalists involved in the Agee–Hosenball defence campaign, Crispin Aubrey and Duncan Campbell, and a former Signals Intelligence soldier they had interviewed, John Berry, under the Official Secrets Act; in the course of the trial, which eventually resulted in Aubrey and Campbell being conditionally discharged and Berry receiving a suspended sentence, it emerged that jury vetting was standard practice in 'politically sensitive' trials.[15]

By 1979, the Labour government was beyond redemption as far as most civil libertarians were concerned. As the historian Edward Thompson put it in a celebrated extended essay, 'The State of the Nation', published in *New Society* a few months after the Tories' election victory of that year: 'The injury to liberty, the corruption, and the law-and-order cant has come from an "all-party" consensus.' 'We have had telephones tapped, mail

intercepted and the citizen's privacy invaded by vetters and com-
pilers of files,' he complained. 'We have had official secrets leaked
to right-wing columnists by persons in high public office or the
armed services, and we have seen no trace of even-handedness in
the application of justice. We have had several persons (in
Newcastle, Liverpool, Southall and Glasgow) who appear to have
died at the hands of the police, and others who have been severely
injured and we have neither prosecutions nor public inquiry . . .
The state of the nation is no longer in question. That has already
been decided, although it may never be clear by whom or how.
The nation is to be a property managed by the state. And the state
is to be a station of NATO, a station with a blue light over the door
and sirens moaning in every street.'[16]

Thompson was exaggerating for polemical effect, but his disillusionment and pessimism were widely shared. Civil libertarians
disgusted by the 1974–9 government's relationship with the security state (among them Patricia Hewitt and Harriet Harman, who
were then running the National Council for Civil Liberties, and
Peter Hain) played a significant role in the left-wing revolt in the
Labour Party that followed the 1979 election defeat. The new
Labour left of the late 1970s and early 1980s also exposed the
party for the first time to the 'identity politics' of the women's
and gay movements. The influence of these movements was by no
means unambiguously libertarian – much of the women's movement was strongly in favour of tougher censorship of sexually
explicit material, for example – but they undoubtedly forced
Labour to think seriously about aspects of 'personal freedom' that
had not troubled it before.

It was, however, a right-winger in the Jenkins–Crosland
mould who did most to re-establish Labour's civil libertarian credentials – Roy Hattersley, appointed shadow home secretary after
the election of Michael Foot as Labour leader in late 1980. The big
home affairs issues of the early 1980s were race and immigration,
the powers and accountability of the police, and prisons policy.
Hattersley took strongly liberal positions on them all. Under his
guidance, Labour opposed the legislation that became the 1981

British Nationality Act (the most important provision of which
was to restrict the right to live in Britain to those with British
grandparents) on the grounds that it was racially discriminatory.
In the wake of the 1981 riots in Brixton and Toxteth, Hattersley
emphasized the social context of the disturbances, argued for
making the police more accountable to local communities and
opposed proposals for greater police powers that eventually found
their way into the 1984 Police and Criminal Evidence Act. On
prisons, where the Tories were arguing for more and tougher
incarceration for criminals, he backed a reduction of the number
of people imprisoned for minor offences and better conditions
for prisoners. Hattersley summed up his approach in an essay for
a Penguin Special published just before the 1983 general election: 'The government is half in thrall to the vocal but unthinking
lobby which pretends that harsher laws and less sensitive policing
will cut the crime rate. There is no evidence to support that view.
But whilst the advocates of hanging and flogging are placated,
the attack on individual liberty will continue.'[17]

In the wake of Labour's disastrous performance in the 1983
election, Hattersley was elected deputy leader and took on the
shadow chancellorship; Gerald Kaufman became shadow home
secretary. During his four years in the job, Kaufman stuck to much
the same liberal line as Hattersley, and even showed some willingness to probe the inner recesses of the secret state. He was
sharply critical of the prosecutions of the Ministry of Defence
civil servants Sarah Tisdall and Clive Ponting for leaking official
secrets;[18] and he was an outspoken opponent of the military-style
policing of the miners' strike in 1984–5 (although of course he
always tempered his criticisms with denunciations of violence by
pickets). His opposition to the ban on trade unions at GCHQ and
to the bills that became the 1985 Interception of Communications
Act (which made it illegal to refer in court to the issuing of war-
rants for phone-tapping and mail interception) and the 1986
Public Order Act (which gave the police sweeping new powers
over demonstrations) was notably vigorous. He had little of substance to say on the *Spycatcher* and Zircon affairs, but that was
largely because Neil Kinnock took charge of Labour's response. On
Zircon in particular (where the issue was the government's failed

attempt to prevent revelation of the existence of an expensive spy-satellite programme) the Labour leader made a laughing-stock of himself with his display of ignorance of the politics of official secrecy.

As deputy leader, Hattersley still had a significant input into Labour's thinking on home affairs. But it was in his self-appointed role as chief party ideologue that he had most influence. In early 1987 he published by far the most coherent statement of Labour's case that had been produced since Crosland's death, *Choose Freedom*. In it, he drew on the American liberal political philosopher John Rawls' *A Theory of Justice* to redefine the purpose of socialism as 'the extension of liberty'. 'The true object of socialism is the creation of a genuinely free society in which the protection and extension of individual liberty is the primary duty of the state,' he declared. 'Socialism exists to provide – for the largest possible number of people – the ability to exercise effective liberty.'[19] After Labour lost the 1987 general election, Hattersley's notion of 'socialism as freedom' even became the party's official 'big idea'. Back in the position of shadow home secretary, he was charged by Kinnock with producing a statement of Labour's values which would become the foundation for the policy review set in train by the 1987 party conference. What emerged was *A Statement of Democratic Socialist Aims and Values*, published in early 1988. Its first sentence declared: 'The true purpose of democratic socialism and, therefore, the true aim of the Labour Party, is the creation of a genuinely free society, in which the fundamental objective of government is the protection and extension of individual liberty irrespective of class, sex, race, colour or creed.'[20]

The document sank without trace, but the thinking behind it remained central to Labour's approach right through to the 1992 election – except in its response to the Iranian *fatwa* against Salman Rushdie.[21] The documents produced by the party's policy review took a strongly civil libertarian line, and the party opposed all legislation between 1987 and 1992 that it considered to be threatening to civil liberties, including the bills that became the 1988 Criminal Justice Act (which restricted rights to jury trial), the 1989 Security Service Act (which imposed a duty of lifelong

secrecy on members of the security services) and the 1989
Prevention of Terrorism Act (which required journalists to name
their sources in terrorism cases). The 1992 Labour manifesto
promised a long list of civil libertarian measures, including a
Freedom of Information Act in the first parliamentary session of a
Labour government, 'fair immigration and citizenship laws which
restore the right to British citizenship for every child born in
Britain', anti-discrimination laws covering homosexuals and
people with disabilities, and an end to convictions on uncorrobo-
rated confession evidence. On law and order, the emphasis was on
getting councils to improve crime prevention and getting more
police on the beat. Prison conditions were to be improved and
non-custodial sentences promoted for non-violent crimes.[22]
Perhaps most notably, the party also pledged itself to the introduction of a Bill of Rights. Hattersley had been unconvinced of the
value of such a measure in the 1970s, and was no keener when the
idea was raised again in the late 1980s, largely at the instigation of
the constitutional reform pressure group, Charter 88. His conversion, grudging as it was, was remarkable, as indeed was the
absence of strong resistance to the Bill of Rights from the left.

Hattersley retired from the front bench after Labour lost the 1992
election. When John Smith was elected leader, Tony Blair was
appointed shadow home secretary – a reward for his performance
during the election campaign and for coming second in the
shadow cabinet election. It was the job he wanted, but it was not
clear why. Blair had said next to nothing in public on home affairs,
and there was little in his actions as shadow employment
spokesman between 1989 and 1992 that gave much of a clue as to
how he would behave in his new senior post, although his resistance to union pressures for the return of the legally enforceable
closed shop (outlawed by the Tories' 1990 Employment Act)
brought back memories of the argument over Jenkins' proposed
Bill of Rights in the 1970s.

Anyone who expected Blair to push the liberal agenda he
inherited from Hattersley was soon to be disappointed. The new
shadow home secretary was primarily interested in doing whatever

was necessary to win the next election – and the electoral priority in home affairs was crime. Labour's private opinion-polling showed not only that voters of every class thought that the party was soft on crime but that this belief was the second most common reason (after the party's lack of economic competence) given by wavering Tories for not supporting Labour on polling day. Blair gave some indication of how he was thinking in his speech to the Labour conference in October: 'We do not say that the responsibility of government or society should be substituted for that of the individual. There is no excuse for crime.' But it was not until the beginning of 1993, when he and Gordon Brown took a trip to the United States to meet some of the advisers who had helped Bill Clinton to victory two months before, that he fully formulated his line of argument. The US Democrats had faced a similar problem to Labour's: for years they had been considered soft on crime. But Clinton had overcome this by doing everything in his power to show how tough he was. Some of his actions (in particular his return home to Arkansas at the height of the campaign to sign the death-warrant for a severely brain-damaged murderer) could not be replicated in Britain. But other things, notably his emphases on an ethic of personal responsibility and on the need to rebuild communities, struck a chord with Blair.

Three days after his return from the US, Blair unveiled what became his most famous soundbite: 'Tough on crime, tough on the causes of crime.'[23] This slogan, in fact written by Brown, encapsulated Blair's attempt to claim law and order from the Tories by moving the argument about crime 'beyond the choice between personal and social responsibility, the notion that there are only two sides to the "law and order" debate – those who want to punish the criminal and those who point to the poor social conditions in which crime breeds.'[24] The social causes of crime were no excuse for it; individual duties and responsibilities were as important as rights.

Blair's straddling of both 'sides' of the polarized argument over law and order was aided by the government's long-standing insistence that there was no link between crime and poverty or unemployment – a claim the public was increasingly inclined to greet with scepticism, not least because crime had risen inexorably under the Tories. But it also coincided with a period of government unpopularity among the police caused by home secretary Kenneth Clarke's threats to impose on them performance-related pay and streamlined dismissal procedures (which Blair opposed), and with the deep public anxiety sparked off by the motiveless and brutal killing of two-year-old James Bulger by two ten-year-old children the previous year. Amid the reporting of the trial and the terrible details that emerged, Blair declared that the newspaper headlines had been 'like hammer blows against the sleeping consciousness of the country'. He warned: 'We cannot exist in a moral vacuum. If we do not learn and then teach the value of what is right and wrong, then the result is simply moral chaos which engulfs us all.'[25]

By March, Labour had claimed the prize Blair was after. For the first time, opinion polls showed the party ahead of the Tories when it came to having the best policies on crime.[26] It was a personal triumph for Blair; at last, Labour was soft no more. Political commentators were almost unanimous in applauding him, and the change denoted by his 'tough on crime' approach was hailed as revolutionary.

Emboldened by the polls and the praise, the shadow home secretary went further. In a speech in June 1993, he moved to recapture 'family values' for Labour. 'I have no doubt,' he said, 'that the breakdown in law and order is intimately linked to the break-up of a strong sense of community. And the break-up of the community is to a crucial degree consequent upon the breakdown in family life. If we want anything more than a superficial discussion on crime and its causes, we cannot ignore the importance of the family.' Discipline in the home and at school were crucial, he said, and there should be community-based programmes to help families in difficulty and to 'prevent today's problem children becoming tomorrow's problem families'. All the evidence showed that poor parenting and family disintegration led to crime. 'Common sense should tell us as much. Crime is anti-social behaviour, breaking the rules of good conduct necessary for individuals to live in peace.'[27]

Blair's remarks caused a *frisson* of unease among his colleagues. The problem was not that most of them profoundly disagreed with what he was saying, but that since the rise of 'personal freedom' as a Gaitskellite cause in the late 1950s – and particularly the rise to positions of influence of people who had been young in the permissive 1960s – Labour had been committed to the idea that politicians and the state should steer clear of telling people how to live their private lives as long as they were not breaking the law. Whereas 'tough on crime, tough on the causes of crime' in itself was a common-sense slogan that could have been used quite credibly by any Labour politician since the party was founded, Blair now seemed to be breaking an unwritten rule of Labour politics.

The ideas behind his questioning of liberalism on 'personal freedom' came from the United States. Just as Hattersley in *Choose Freedom* used John Rawls' *Theory of Justice* to provide intellectual credibility for his idea of 'socialism as freedom', so Blair's thinking about the dynamics of crime, family and community drew heavily on the ideas of the American communitarian movement, especially as expressed by the sociologist-turned-polemicist Amitai Etzioni. It was Etzioni and his colleagues who had provided Bill Clinton with the intellectual underpinning for his tough-on-crime rhetoric in the 1992 election campaign, and the new President had appointed several communitarians to his White House staff.

Communitarianism is not a difficult intellectual position to understand. Put simply, it is a school of thought that believes that we need to create what Etzioni calls 'a new moral, social and public order based on restored communities'. It is, first of all, decentralist and opposed to big government: a good society is one in which people live freely, take responsibility for themselves, their families and the communities, and solve most problems at the level of the neighbourhood or household. 'Only if a solution cannot be found by the individual does responsibility devolve to the family,' wrote Etzioni in the most comprehensive account of his ideas, *The Spirit of Community*, published in the US in 1993 and a runaway bestseller. 'Only if the family cannot cope should the local community become involved. Only if the problem is too big for it should the state become involved.'[28]

Secondly, and most importantly, it emphasizes that citizens have not only political and economic rights to make demands on their fellow citizens, but also duties to others. And in most modern western societies, the argument goes, the emphasis is too much on rights. The prime task in such societies is to redress the balance with measures – at family, community and state levels – that encourage people to recognize their duties and to act on them.

What is most distinctive about the measures that communitarians propose is their intrusiveness into spheres generally marked out as private by liberal politics. Because of the crucial role of the family in socializing children, parents should be actively discouraged from separating and single women dissuaded from having children: the state should provide generous maternity and paternity leave, better child allowances and improved childcare, while making divorce more difficult and introducing economic incentives to make it easier for one parent to stay at home rather than work. At the same time, the education and criminal justice systems should be reformed to make their main purpose the encouragement of a sense of civic responsibility, particularly among the young – with the public shaming of miscreants playing a major role. Communitarians in the US have backed compulsory community service for teenagers, curfews on teenagers to prevent them roaming public areas at night, censorship of anti-social and violent television, films and music, and random drug-testing of train-drivers and other public employees.

None of this was new even in 1993. The communitarian movement had been around and much-discussed for the best part of a decade in the US, and the ideas behind it were a lot older. Arguments about liberty and duty go all the way back to Ancient Greek political thought, and the debate about the actual and desirable relationships of individual, family, community, civil society and state has been at the core of western political and social thinking since the late nineteenth century. To assert the primacy of community over all the other categories, either as description or prescription, is hardly novel. Even in the small arid world of Anglo-American academic political philosophy, broadly communitarian critics of the abstract individualism that afflicts most liberal political theory have been vocal since the 1970s, largely in response to Rawls' *Theory of Justice*. Such thinkers as Michael

Sandel, Alastair MacIntyre and Charles Taylor (the latter two were veterans of the first New Left in Britain) were arguing long before Etzioni that any useful theory of politics has to be based not on considerations of what individuals would do in impossible hypothetical circumstances but on the needs of real people in the real world, rooted in families and communities.

The emergence of American communitarianism in the late 1980s as a potent current of ideas outside the academy was nevertheless significant. Regardless of their lack of originality, Etzioni and his colleagues addressed directly the widespread sense among Americans (not just intellectuals) that the ideologies dominant in the previous quarter century of politics had failed in practice. Neither the welfare-state liberalism hegemonic in the 1960s nor the free-market conservatism of the 1980s had been able to reverse the social fragmentation that many felt was likely to engulf America in a wave of crime, drug abuse and moral irresponsibility. Indeed, it seemed that both had made matters worse by failing to place the encouragement of social responsibility and the common good at the centre of their concerns.

On the one hand, the 1960s-style liberals, dominant in US politics until the end of the Carter administration, attacked the family as oppressive, pressed for a never-ending expansion of individual rights, and put their faith in ever-greater state provision to cope with the social fragmentation that their permissive ideology encouraged. But they failed to recognize that the welfare state actually reinforced fragmentation and irresponsibility, effectively legitimizing family breakdown and creating an underclass of passive clients. On the other hand, 1980s-style free-market conservatives recognized some of the problems of the 'dependency culture' and the abnegation of personal responsibility that went with it. But their favoured solution, simply reducing the scope of the welfare state, did nothing to help matters, and their fetish of individual material wealth made a religion of selfishness and irresponsibility – and further encouraged family breakdown.

The first response to this American disillusionment with mainstream liberalism and conservatism was the ultra-conservative Moral Majority movement, arguing for a straightforward reversal of liberal permissiveness, punitive sanctions against criminals and single mothers and a return to traditional Christian values in schools. Communitarianism was a response to this response. According to Etzioni, 'I believe that although they raised the right questions, they provided the wrong, largely authoritarian and dogmatic, answers.'[29]

The resonance of this line of thinking with Blair is hardly surprising. It not only squared with Labour's electoral needs, it also squared with common-sense perceptions. Britain like America had gone through successive periods of hegemonic social-democratic liberalism and free-market conservatism, and neither appeared to have worked. In 1990s Britain, as in the US, there was a widespread sense, particularly in the middle class, that the balance between rights and responsibilities needed to be restored by giving greater weight to responsibilities. The instability of families, the rise in youth crime, the dependency culture and the decline of community had been recurrent themes in British debates since the late 1970s – and the left, burdened with liberal assumptions, had proved incapable of addressing them in a language attractive to the middle class. Blair believed that he had discovered an important and useful 'big idea'.

It was soon put to the test. In May 1993, John Major reshuffled his cabinet, making Michael Howard home secretary. Howard, a right-wing populist whose enthusiasm for tough law-and-order policies knew no bounds, was charged with coming up with something to put Labour back on the defensive on home affairs. At the Tory party conference in October he announced a package of twenty-seven measures to clamp down on crime, and two months later unveiled the Criminal Justice and Public Order Bill.

The bill, given pride of place in the legislative agenda for the 1993–4 session of parliament, was the most illiberal and coercive law-and-order package for decades, undermining and removing swathes of fundamental rights. It proposed effective abolition of the right to silence, an end to freedom of assembly, increased police stop-and-search powers, severe restrictions on freedom of movement, and further limits on the right to jury trial. It also brought the police for the first time under direct political control. Its public order provisions were designed to criminalize specific behaviour and lifestyles deemed anti-social by giving police sub-stantial new powers against New Age travellers, ravers, hunt saboteurs, squatters and protesters.

Howard fully expected Labour to oppose it, revealing itself once again to be unwilling to take the necessary steps to stamp out crime. Blair had different ideas. It took some persuading, but he convinced John Smith and the rest of the shadow cabinet that Labour should not oppose the bill. Instead, it would table 'rea-soned amendments' to particularly objectionable clauses, but abstain on its second reading. Blair later triumphantly recalled that on announcing this position in the Commons, he caused Michael Howard's jaw to 'drop about six inches'.[30]

To critics on his own side, Blair defended the decision to abstain on the grounds that the bill contained some measures worth supporting, such as reducing the age of consent for gay men and ending judges' warnings to juries in rape trials that they should not convict solely on the evidence of the victim. In answer to those who complained that, by refusing to oppose the bill as a whole, Labour was effectively accepting all that was worst about it, Blair argued that many of its more unpalatable measures had been 'vigorously opposed'. 'To have opposed everything would have been wrong in principle and tactically inept. What we have done and will do is to set out clearly what parts we do oppose.'[31] It was false, he insisted, to claim that by abstaining Labour had acquiesced in the sweeping away of rights that had been part of the British way of justice for centuries.[32]

Targeting as it did the new movements of green activists, New Age travellers and ravers, the bill mobilized young people in their thousands against it: Labour's decision to abstain probably did more to alienate young people from the party than anything else it had done for years.[33] But Blair's position did him surpris-ingly little harm in his own party. After John Smith died suddenly in May 1994, Blair easily won the subsequent election for the Labour leadership.

Blair's choice as shadow home secretary in October 1994 was Jack Straw, the MP for Blackburn, Labour's environment spokesman since 1992 and before that in charge of the education portfolio. Straw had no reputation for being interested in home affairs and was not considered to be a high flier. He had certainly been on the front bench a long time (since 1980, in fact), but he had performed at best competently in his two most senior posts. When he got his new job, there were several sharp intakes of breath among his colleagues.

For Straw, though, it was no more than he deserved for his years of dogged political work. Born John Whitaker Straw in 1946, he was the son of politically active parents – his father, an insurance clerk, had been a conscientious objector; his mother was a teacher and Labour councillor – and grew up one of five children in a council maisonette in Loughton, Essex. In 1957 he won a scholarship to the local public school, Brentwood. While some of his council-tenant neighbours remember him as a snob, 'a little toffee-nosed boy nobody wanted to play with',[34] to his fellow pupils he was, at least at first, an oik from an estate. There was some bullying (Straw later confessed he was sometimes the guilty party, as well as the victim) but he eventually rose to become head of house and deputy head boy of the school.

He was politically ambitious from an early age. His parents had taken him on the first Aldermaston march in 1958. A year later, at the age of thirteen, he made his first political speech, at a Labour candidate's adoption meeting, and decided he wanted to become an MP. He joined the party in 1961, at the age of fifteen. When he left school he went to study law at Leeds, a subject he chose 'because of its inter-relationship with politics'.[35] He soon showed himself adept at working his way up the political machine, becoming president of the college's student union, and after graduating (with a disappointing 2.2), stood successfully for the presidency of the National Union of Students.

It was 1969, a time when the student movement in Britain was at the height of its militancy and its more excitable left-wingers, grouped together in the Revolutionary Socialist Students Federation, dreamt that 'Red Bases' in the universities would be the vanguard of the proletarian revolution. But Straw was not one of them. He was the 'Broad Left' candidate to lead the NUS, which in the jargon of the day meant that he had Labour left and

Communist Party backing: the revolutionaries considered him a contemptible reformist. Nevertheless, his victory did mark a change at the top: for several years before, the NUS had drifted along under a succession of lacklustre right-wing Labour leaders who seemed primarily interested in proving their anti-left credentials to would-be employers in the Labour and trade union bureaucracies. Straw promised to turn the union over to its members: 'Make the union respected, not respectable,' was his campaign slogan. Under his stewardship, the NUS came to be seen as a legitimate representative of students' interests.

While others in the NUS called for the legalization of cannabis and support for overseas guerrilla groups, Straw stuck to campaigning for higher grants and student electoral registration. It was at the NUS that he learned the political value of good organization and a firm hand on bureaucratic procedures. He admired the dedication of his Communist Party allies, and was for many years afterwards fond of quoting Stalin: 'Once the political line has been settled, organization counts for all.' The ever-present infighting, caucusing and factional battles of student politics also provided useful training for his political ambitions in the outside world.

He left the NUS in 1971, having first got himself elected as an Islington councillor. He kept his seat for seven years, and is most remembered for the local uproar caused when, as vice-chairman of the housing committee, he proposed and pushed through a ban on council tenants keeping pets. In 1972 he took his bar finals and came third in all England – a result of hard application to his previously neglected studies. Still, his mind was on politics. In 1972, after trying for and failing to get the Labour parliamentary nomination in Hampstead, he was selected as candidate for safe Tory Tonbridge. The next year, he became deputy leader (at twenty-six, the youngest ever) of the Inner London Education Authority. In February 1974, after losing Tonbridge, he gave up the bar to become special adviser to social services secretary Barbara Castle in the new Labour government – an appointment that came about through his friendship with her husband, Ted, a fellow Islington councillor.[36]

After Castle was sacked from the cabinet by Jim Callaghan

two years later, Straw moved on to work for Peter Shore – a colleague of Castle's in the 'no' campaign in the 1975 referendum on Europe – at the Department of the Environment. He remained on friendly terms with his old boss, and in 1977 duly won the Labour nomination in her Blackburn seat after she announced her retirement. Civil Service rules forced his resignation from the job with Shore, so he went to work as a researcher at Granada TV for *World in Action*. By the time he arrived in the House of Commons in 1979 at the age of thirty-two, Straw was already a Westminster veteran, familiar with many senior Labour politicians and with an impressive network of contacts throughout the party and in the media. Politically, he was very much on the left. On entering parliament, he immediately joined the Tribune Group (at that time still the single left-wing caucus in the Parliamentary Labour Party) and within six months he had established his civil libertarian credentials by introducing a private members' bill which, if successful, would have given local council committees more power to control local police operations. In May 1980, he defied the whips' instructions to vote against the defence estimates.

But by far the most important cause to which he attached himself was opposition to British membership of the EEC. A founder of the Labour Common Market Safeguards Committee, the main anti-European pressure group in the party, he agitated tirelessly for withdrawal from Europe and for a reflationary Keynesian economic policy with import controls at its centre.[37] 'If we want to see our socialist policies implemented by the next Labour government,' he told Labour's May 1980 special policy conference, 'then a prerequisite for that and a central part of our manifesto must be a pledge to withdraw from the Common Market immediately.'[38] During the 1980 leadership contest that followed Jim Callaghan's resignation, he joined Shore's campaign team, and was rewarded with a junior post on the front-bench Treasury team after Michael Foot won the election and made Shore shadow chancellor. Straw had been in parliament for just eighteen months.

Straw was at first sympathetic to the Bennite left. But like many others on the soft left, he opposed the electoral college for Labour leadership and deputy leadership elections introduced at the January 1981 Wembley special conference. Afterwards, he urged Tony Benn not to stand against Denis Healey for the Labour deputy leadership. For his pains, he was named by the Bennite Rank and File Mobilizing Committee (listed as one of a 'Gang of 150' MPs) as a target for deselection. Although he voted for Benn in the second round of the deputy leadership contest after backing John Silkin in the first,[39] by early 1982 he had put himself beyond the Bennite pale by backing expulsion of members of the Trotskyist Militant Tendency who were trying to unseat him. From now on he was to be above all a leadership loyalist.

As a member of the Treasury team, Straw played a part in formulating the economic policy on which Labour fought the 1983 general election, and just before the campaign started published a pamphlet, *Putting Blackburn Back to Work,* explaining what the party's mixture of reflation, protectionism, nationalization and devaluation would mean for his constituents. 'The private enterprise, free market does not work. It's anarchy,' he wrote. 'No one can believe any longer that private enterprise can deliver the goods . . . so socialism will have to step into the breach. That does not mean that we shall be nationalizing corner shops or the small, or medium-sized firms. Indeed, if only they could realize it, the owners of the small corner shop, or the small firm, are just as tyrannized by the big boys, the multi-nationals and the City, as are workpeople. But it does mean that alongside our planning system we shall extend public ownership in key areas of industry, and extend control of the financial institutions.' This sort of thing would not be tolerated by today's Labour Party. But in 1983 it was party policy.

Straw campaigned for Shore again for the party leadership after the 1983 election defeat. But Shore lost badly, coming a distant last in the electoral college behind Neil Kinnock, Roy Hattersley and Eric Heffer, and was demoted from the shadow chancellorship. Straw was given a junior front-bench post under environment spokesman Jack Cunningham, in which he played an important role in the Labour leadership's balancing act on local government. He was vocal in his opposition to the government's legislation introducing rate-capping and abolishing the Greater London Council and the other metropolitan boroughs, but he also disowned those left-wing councils that decided to defy the law on rate-capping and he did his best to distance Labour nationally from the excesses of the 'loony left' in Labour-run town halls and the inefficiency and incompetence of much Labour local government. He was hardly a star performer, and his stance won him no friends on the left, but he did exactly what Kinnock wanted him to do. In 1987, after he was at long last elected to the shadow cabinet on his fifth attempt – with the lowest vote of any successful candidate – he was rewarded with the job of shadow education spokesman. Once again, he proved diligent, reliable and utterly unsparkling. But his efforts to make Labour the party of educational standards (see chapter 5), together with his strong support for the policy review set up by Kinnock in 1987 and his backing for changing Labour's internal organization, was enough to establish him as a 'modernizer' along with Tony Blair and Gordon Brown. Even so, he was never personally close to Brown and Blair, and was not a member of Kinnock's own inner circle.

After Kinnock's resignation in 1992, John Smith appointed Straw shadow environment secretary. He yet again showed himself to be rather pedestrian but hard-working. He made a splash when he suggested in a self-published pamphlet in 1993 that Clause Four of the Labour constitution should be abandoned – a point of view that had hitherto been considered taboo for senior Labour politicians and was seen by Smith as unnecessary boat-rocking in the run-up to the vote on introducing a one member, one vote system for party elections. Later the same year, Straw argued for a change in the composition of the party's union-dominated National Executive Committee. But none of this suggested that he was a candidate for one of the 'big four' shadow portfolios.

That Tony Blair made him shadow home secretary in 1994 was in part a reward for having jointly managed his leadership campaign. But it was more to do with Straw's extreme distrust of anything smacking of metropolitan trendiness. For more than a decade as a front-bencher, he had taken what both of them saw as common-sense positions against fashionable idiocies in local government and teaching. On home affairs, his views were similarly populist. He believed that law and order was a far more important element of the Home Office brief than the constitution, and he agreed wholeheartedly with Blair's 'tough on crime' approach to it (and had told him so). Insofar as he could be bothered with the constitutional aspect of the job, he was in favour of changing the Lords, lukewarm about the efforts of Charter 88 and, like Blair, an implacable opponent of proportional representation. Unlike Blair, he was also viscerally antipathetic towards the Liberal Democrats, largely because he saw them as Labour's enemy in local government. But the pair shared an opposition to 'defeatist' talk that Labour could not win a parliamentary majority on its own.

When Straw took up his position in late 1994, both Labour and the government suspected that the party was still vulnerable on law and order. The Tories spent much of the summer immediately after Blair's election as Labour leader trying to come up with a way to win back 'their' issue. The consensus was that the solution was to get ever tougher on law and order. As Tory deputy chairman John Maples, the former MP for Lewisham West, put it in a memorandum that was leaked during the autumn, hard-line policies, such as the introduction of identity cards, should be used to test to destruction the new Labour leader's supposed toughness: 'Either Blair will support our proposals and divide his party, or oppose us and show he does not really mean what he says about . . . crime.'[40]

A battle to see which party could outdo the other ensued – with predictably dire consequences for the level of public debate on crime. With Labour determined not to be outflanked by the Tories on law and order, and the Tories in turn determined to outflank it, the room for discussion was increasingly restricted to whatever played well with the tabloids. Both parties locked themselves into an escalating bidding war of ever-tougher proposals. Straw took up the reins with gusto. With Blair's full backing, he came up with a host of policy proposals which indicated that once Labour got into office he would be, as one modernizing member of the shadow cabinet predicted, 'the most illiberal Labour home secretary in history'.

Among the first of these were Labour's plans to crack down on 'noisy neighbours' and 'families from hell' who indulge in persistent criminal or anti-social behaviour.[41] The idea was that police or local councillors should be able to apply for community safety orders to restrain 'criminal' families. Breaches of the order (which would be based on civil evidence, and thus require a lower level of proof than criminal evidence) could lead to prison sentences of up to seven years. It was certainly tough, but magistrates believed the plan to be ineffective in dealing with the problem. Prison governors criticized it as 'draconian and dangerous'.[42] Liberty, as the National Council for Civil Liberties was now known, was of the opinion that the policy 'could amount to a breach of the European Convention of Human Rights'.[43]

Straw's next big outing was a bizarre call to 'reclaim the streets for the law-abiding citizen' from the 'aggressive begging of winos and addicts' and 'the "squeegee merchants" who wait at large road junctions to force on reticent motorists their windscreen cleaning service', all of whom were 'obstacles faced by pedestrians and motorists in going about their daily business'. 'Graffiti, a much-neglected crime in my book, "adorns" much street furniture,' he declared. 'Even where graffiti is not comprehensible or racialist in message, it is often violent and uncontrolled in its violent image, and correctly gives the impression of a lack of law and order on the streets.' All this seriously interfered with 'walking down a street [which] should be the most straightforward of pleasures, for a chance conversation, some window shopping, or simple amble to establish one's stake in the local area'.[44]

Before delivering it, Straw had nursed great hopes for his speech. Its content was inspired by the 'zero-tolerance' strategy developed by William J. Bratton, the police commissioner for New York, and Rudolf Guiliani, the city's new Republican mayor. Straw had visited America a month earlier, and he felt that the new approach would both upstage Howard and give a boost to his campaign for re-election to Labour's National Executive Committee (to which he had been elected for the first time the previous year). Instead, Straw was showered with ridicule from all corners – charities for the homeless, agencies dealing with alcohol-related problems, MPs on his own side, opportunistic and gleeful Tories and political commentators.

Taken aback by this reaction, Straw backtracked twenty-four hours after making the speech and talked rather belatedly of the need to address the social causes of the 'disorder' he had so vividly identified. His researchers pleaded with journalists requesting full copies of the speech from his office to hold off running any follow-up pieces until they had 'talked through the wider context' with his staff. But after consulting Blair and receiving his backing, Straw unrepentantly insisted that his non-Tory critics were 'falling for the sedulous Tory trap that safety and security on the streets is an intrinsically right-wing issue'.[45] A month later, he lost his place on the NEC.

The same feet-first approach was on display in summer 1996 when Straw blundered into a row over curfews for young people. Again, he had been inspired by practice in America. Again, he badly miscalculated how far he should go for a headline when he suggested the introduction of blanket curfew powers on children and teenagers.[46] This sparked another round of ridicule, with even his shadow cabinet colleagues publicly dismissing the proposed new powers. Donald Dewar, Labour's chief whip, was moved to distance the party from Straw's remarks within hours of their being made.[47] Straw responded by insisting – too late – that he proposed the measure more in the spirit of child protection for the under-tens than the policing and criminalization of young people.[48]

In fact Straw had precisely tailored the plan towards older children, and the only reason he had come up with the curfew idea in the first place – a complete surprise for his colleagues in the shadow home affairs team as it was for everyone else – was that a journalist had asked him if Labour was considering American-style curfews to clear young people off the streets. Taken with the notion and eager to pre-empt the Tories, Straw hurriedly cobbled together the impromptu 'policy initiative' in order to ensure it was covered in the Sunday newspapers.[49] By such accidents is policy made, and later that year Blair upgraded the *ad hoc* proposal to one of his 'family values' measures towards a 'decent society'.[50]

Straw remained defiant in the face of objections that his ideas for noisy neighbours, squeegee merchants and curfews were not only illiberal but would have little effect on crime. He was contemptuous of his critics, especially those who worked in the criminal justice field: 'In social services and the probation service, and among those who provide the intellectual framework for our sentencing system, namely academic researchers, there is too much distance in public understanding,' he declared.[51] He railed against the 'moral relativist brigade who argue that there is little point doing anything much about young offenders from deprived areas . . . until the underlying cause of their deprivation has been tackled'. The way Straw saw it, his critics tended to come from comfortable middle-class backgrounds, while he had grown up on a council estate and knew what life was really like at the sharp end. He saw no reason to make any concessions to them.[52] Along with proposals to introduce more rapid sentencing for young offenders, 'zero tolerance' measures took pride of place in the section of Labour's 1997 manifesto on crime.

Straw's ideas for action on crime were only part of his grand strategy for consolidating the reputation Labour had gained under Blair for being tough. He also made it the norm to respond to government legislation on law and order by abstaining or supporting it – just as Blair had done on the Criminal Justice Bill – as it passed through parliament. Opposition was avoided wherever possible. When it was unavoidable – and the litmus test for this was whether any likely internal rebellion could be contained – it was pursued on the basis of the pragmatic effectiveness of any proposed new laws, rather than points of principle.

In April 1995 the prime minister used his speech to the annual Conservative Central Council to confirm that an identity-card scheme – a measure massively popular with the Tory grassroots – was on the way, and subsequent briefings stressed that the only question was whether the cards would be compulsory for all adults or would be voluntary and confined to social security claimants.[53] Officially, Labour adopted a 'wait-and-see' stance on the proposals, insisting that no comment was warranted until detailed plans emerged from the Home Office. Behind the scenes, however, Straw immediately began to cajole members of his home affairs team to accept ID cards in principle, and set about drawing up a separate proposal with which he hoped to trump Howard: Labour would announce its own ID card scheme. It would go by the friendlier title of 'access card', and initially act as a guarantor of entry to premises such as local authority leisure centres.

Labour was on the verge of unveiling its new card to the public when a cabinet split and Tory opposition to compulsory cards put the issue on the back-burner. Straw ditched the 'access card' plan and instead lambasted this latest example of Tory disarray. By the time the government got round to publishing much watered-down plans for an optional card based on the driving licence, Labour could safely hail it as a climb-down and at the same time support the scheme without causing a fuss internally. (The government's proposal to introduce some form of ID card fell by the wayside altogether in autumn 1996, when the legislative decks were cleared of all but the most important proposals in anticipation of the 1996–7 session of parliament being curtailed to hold the general election.)

By the time the annual renewal of the Prevention of Terrorism Act was due, in March 1996, no one was surprised when Blair and Straw decided that the party would abstain instead of opposing it as it had done since 1983. As recently as 1993, Blair himself had led that opposition from the party's front bench, eloquently arguing for 'judicial intervention' before a PTA detainee was held for more than four days. Together with the exclusion orders that amounted to internal exile, the act contained what Blair described then as 'serious and fundamental departures from the normal processes of British law . . . contrary to the principles of British justice . . . virtually unique in the western world'.[54] Nothing had changed by 1996 apart from Labour's new determination to eradicate by any means necessary the 'soft on crime' tag.

To make matters worse, less than a month later Straw was suckered into accepting a strengthening of the PTA. Howard summoned Straw to a snap 'security briefing' at which he justified his proposals by referring to 'intelligence' regarding expected terrorist activity in the coming weeks. The home secretary wanted to 'top up' the PTA by granting the police additional powers, the most contentious of which was that, on the authority of a senior officer, they could stop and search any pedestrian in a given area, including their clothing and belongings, even where there was no previous suspicion about that person. Howard wanted to push this through at once, with the bill to be subject to a guillotine motion to cram its passage into one day. He was informing Straw as a courtesy not only to explain the unseemly haste, but to allow Labour to express its own support for this speedy action in the name of national security. Of course, if Labour couldn't bring itself to support the bill – well, the government would have to proceed with the fight against terrorism without the support of Her Majesty's Opposition. Straw fell for Howard's ploy, and agreed not to oppose the bill. Thirty-three Labour MPs voted against the guillotine motion for the bill – though this number dwindled to just twelve against the bill itself by the time it came to its third reading. Plenty of the abstainers did so shamefacedly, or toed the line only after several drinks as the sitting wore on into the small hours. One Labour whip, seen in a Westminster bar downing pints at an unusually rapid rate, explained: 'Well, you don't think I could whip this vote sober, do you?'

Once the new powers became law, Labour received a deserved dressing-down not just from civil libertarians but also from those commentators in the quality press who were usually most sympathetic to New Labour.[55] The hostile reaction from normally reliable supporters pushed Straw into making an unambiguously civil libertarian policy promise in public for the first time since he became shadow home secretary. The following weekend, he sheepishly made it known that a Labour government would abandon the PTA's provisions for 'exclusion orders' to prevent 'suspected terrorists' from travelling from northern Ireland to the rest of the United Kingdom.[56]

After the summer break, MPs returned to Westminster for the Tories' final session of parliament before the election. The first piece of law and order legislation with which they had to contend was the Crime (Sentences) Bill 1996, introducing mandatory life sentences for repeat violent and sexual offenders, and minimum terms for repeat burglars and hard-drug dealers. It largely removed the discretion of judges when it came to imposing sentences on individual cases – and was fiercely criticized for doing so even by two former home secretaries, Kenneth Baker and Douglas Hurd, who weighed in against it.[57] A former Master of the Rolls, Lord Donaldson, led senior judges in opposing the bill in the Lords, warning that it would lead to an 'explosion in the prison population'. Labour abstained.

The next item on the pre-election law and order menu was the Police Bill. While much of it dealt with policing structures, taking into account the evolving National Crime Squad and increased cross-border co-operation with other nations, Clause 89 gave police the power to authorize themselves to enter private premises, plant listening devices, inspect, copy and remove files, correspondence or any other matter 'likely to be of substantial value' to their investigations. The powers covered not only the private property or workplace of those suspected of crimes – specified rather vaguely as 'serious' – but also premises used by non-suspects. No longer would a court warrant have to be sought. The belief of a chief constable or assistant chief constable that surveillance might be of use would be sufficient. All material seized and information derived from such searches would be admissible as evidence in a trial.

The bill trampled over the principle established in the eighteenth century that no officer of the state may enter a citizen's premises without a warrant from a judge: it amounted to a licence for the police to bug and burgle whomsoever they saw fit – not just suspects, but their lawyers, their friends and acquaintances, journalists, campaigners and anyone else. Once again, there was outrage at its implications, with a large body of opinion arguing that the bill had to be amended to ensure that a judge authorized any use of the new powers.[58] But the government's insistence that the bill was needed to combat organized crime, drug-trafficking and serious financial fraud was sufficient to ensure Labour's acquiescence. Straw supported the government's line that to allow a judge, rather than a chief police officer, to supervise and act as the authorizing agent for searches and so on would result in the judiciary's 'impartiality being called into question'.[59] To those who criticized the bill for destroying the freedom of the citizen from arbitrary intrusion, he argued that the police had been carrying out such searches for years under Home Office guidance following the 1984 Police and Criminal Evidence Act, but without statutory authority. In other words, the police had been acting outside the law for more than a decade, and the solution was to make their unlawful behaviour legal.[60]

As the bill started its progress through parliament in November, Straw stood firm as the clamour against it mounted, beginning with a one-man campaign by Hugo Young in the *Guardian*, focusing on the plans to give police unfettered powers to bug, trespass and purloin at will in pursuit of their enquiries. The Bar Council then came out against both the bill and Labour's failure to even promote debate on it. By early 1997, opposition had spread to include the *Daily Telegraph*, *The Times*, *Daily Mail*, and *The Economist*. More senior serving judges joined in, as did Lord Callaghan, the former Labour prime minister.

It was not until the afternoon of the day before it was due to be debated in parliament that Straw announced a climb-down: Labour would, after all, table an amendment seeking prior authorization from an independent agent. This was not a U-turn, he insisted: it was part of 'the continual process of evolution'.[61] The abrupt backtrack was in reality the result of a meeting with the party's House of Lords whips that afternoon, who told Straw that unless he changed tack, Labour peers – including lawyer peers on the front bench – would rebel against the joint Labour government line and support the Liberal Democrats instead.

It was the prospect of humiliation, not any point of principle, that had forced Straw's hand. He later made clear privately his frustration at the government for having paved the way for the bill's amendment by his own party. Due to pressure of legislative timetabling, it had been introduced into the House of Lords rather than the Commons. Straw knew that if it had made its first appearance in the lower chamber, Labour MPs – more fearful of party discipline than the Lords and accustomed by now to toeing the party line while holding their noses – would have accepted the bill. Once the party's position had been thus set down in the Commons, Labour's peers would not have dared contradict it in significant numbers. To Straw's chagrin, the government's tactical ineptitude prevented Labour from supporting it in an attempt to overturn one of the most fundamental principles of the common law: that an Englishman's home is his castle.

Straw's energetic efforts to keep pace with the Tories on crime and punishment were reinforced by Blair's increasingly explicit moral fervour and defence of 'family values'. At first, it was all done with some restraint, not least because Blair had been badly burnt by the television interviewer Brian Walden just after being elected Labour leader. Asked whether, as prime minister, he would tell women who choose to have children 'before they have formed a stable relationship' that they were wrong, Blair replied: 'Look, if someone's making the choice to bring up a child as a single parent, I'm very surprised at that. The vast majority of single parents do not choose to be single parents . . . But if what you are saying to me is do I believe that it is best that kids are brought up in a normal, stable family, the answer is yes, I do believe that.'[62] (He also made it clear that he disagreed with the 1960s 'tendency for certain people on the left to say, well, you did your own thing'.) The response from feminists was one of horror: here was a Labour Party leader 'contributing to the restriction of a freedom to choose how to live and care for other human beings', as Sheila Rowbotham put it.[63] Blair reacted by toning down the rhetoric and emphasizing his commitment to equal opportunities, stressing that he did not want to punish single parents or to make women stay at home with their children.

But he was not prepared to drop the communitarian theme of family, responsibility and discipline. He gave a string of speeches and interviews in which he reiterated the message that 'strong families' are the basis for a 'strong community'. In line with this, to the intense discomfort of many Labour secularists, he also increasingly displayed his religious convictions to the public – an odd thing to do for someone who 'can't stand politicians who go on about religion'.[64] Having passionately declared at the 1995 Labour conference: 'I am my brother's keeper, I will not walk by on the other side,' for Easter 1996, he granted a lengthy interview to the *Sunday Telegraph* on how Christianity informed his politics. At that year's Labour conference his speech was consciously modelled on a sermon, with ten 'vows' for the first term of a Labour government, and a 'covenant with the British people'. He even cited the 'ancient prophets of the Old Testament'.[65]

Towards the end of the year Blair felt confident enough about his critics' powerlessness to launch the nearest thing he could to a moral crusade. In a speech in South Africa that the parliamentary press corps was told was a ground-breaking initiative, the Labour leader declared that the central objective of a Labour government would be to strengthen and nurture family life to create 'the Decent Society' through 'a new social morality'.

The family unit, the fount of that morality, was 'under threat', he said. He assured his listeners that his 'tough on crime' stance was developed 'not simply with the burglar-alarm classes in mind, but the families on housing estates up and down the country whose lives are made hell by teenage tearaways, vandals, drug-dealers, muggers, graffiti artists and the culture of despair that has been spawned by a breakdown in the decent values on which Britain was built'. 'It is in the family that we are taught basic good manners,' he went on. 'But do we witness the basic courtesies as much as we did? Families have the right to live in secure communities that are orderly and safe for their children to live, learn and play in. But parents have a responsibility to know where they are and what they are doing.' A visit to a juvenile court would prove to anyone that there was a direct link between the break-up of family and community bonds and the breakdown in law and order. It was in the family that 'we learn that there is such a thing as society. And it is upon the values of the extended family that the Decent Society will be built.' Blair steered clear of the subject of sex, saying that he did not seek a return to 'the ill-fated "back-to-basics" campaign of the Conservatives'.[66] But he subsequently side-stepped questions about whether his vision of the family included homosexuals and mothers who chose to be single[67] – and the speech was aggressively spun by Blair's media staff to highlight the message that Labour was issuing a clarion call for a return to traditional family values.

A few days later, Straw and his deputy Alun Michael

reinforced the message by publishing a document that identified bad parenting as a major cause of crime. Then Straw and Janet Anderson, Labour's women's affairs spokeswoman, went further with another paper that argued that 'the roots of criminal and delinquent behaviour are planted in childhood' and made the case for 'confronting parents with their responsibilities when young people are inadequately supervised or out of control'. It included a proposal for a new 'parental responsibility order' requiring the parents of persistent young offenders to attend guidance sessions to help them cope. At the launch, Straw raised the possibility of local authority approved bedtimes for children.[68]

Straw's off-the-cuff remarks on official bedtimes were widely lampooned, but otherwise what Labour was saying fitted perfectly with the mood of the times. Just as in the aftermath of the killing of James Bulger, Britain was in the grip of a wave of anxiety about crime, morality and social breakdown. The inquiry into the massacre by Thomas Hamilton of sixteen children at Dunblane primary school in Scotland the previous spring had just published its final report, recommending a ban on handguns as advocated by the Snowdrop campaign set up by Dunblane families – something Labour had backed but which the government appeared to be procrastinating over. Within days of the report's publication, a sixteen-year-old boy was found guilty of the murder in December 1995 of the west London headmaster Philip Lawrence. Frances Lawrence, his widow, caught the imagination of the media when she launched a personal campaign for 'healing our fractured society' by changing the moral climate 'for the better', protecting and encouraging family life and introducing 'good citizenship' lessons at school.[69] Among her prescriptions was a ban on combat knives (her husband had died of stab-wounds): Labour took up the call for a ban, while Howard again appeared to procrastinate by citing the difficulty of defining such weapons in law.[70] Worries about irresponsible parenting and uncontrollable children were further fuelled when a Nottinghamshire school had to be closed as a result of a strike by teachers who claimed that a disruptive ten-year-old boy had made it impossible to teach the other pupils; at another school, in Halifax, teachers threatened to walk out after demanding the expulsion of sixty-one (10 per cent) of its pupils whose behaviour, they claimed, made them unteachable.

Many in the Labour Party were uneasy with the leadership's populist response to the moral panic. In private, many MPs felt the appeal to 'family values' was at best vacuous and at worst a means of legitimizing unacceptable intrusion by the state into personal decision-making. But with a general election imminent, they did nothing and said nothing to rock the boat.

But that was opposition. What about government? The great hope of civil libertarians is that now he is in office, Straw's 'tough-on-crime' populism will be tempered by a liberalism that was kept under wraps before the election. Such an outcome is not impossible. Home Office ministers privately admit that, having won power, Labour is inclined to be more liberal than its pre-election stance suggested. Straw's overly tough and sometimes crass rhetoric was employed in opposition to neutralize the Tories' attacks – and it worked, apparently. During the election campaign, the polls showed that Labour's approach to law and order was preferred to that of the Tories, who as a result devoted only a single press conference to the subject. With the election safely out of the way, the pressures have eased. Ministers draw particular attention to the government's commitments to the incorporation of the European Convention on Human Rights into British law and to a White Paper on a Freedom of Information Act, both of which appeared in the government's first Queen's Speech.

Incorporation of the ECHR will not give British citizens any added rights, because the United Kingdom is already bound to observe the convention and to abide by and implement rulings of the European Court of Human Rights. Until the convention is put on the statute books here, however, cases can be heard only in Europe, and so are costly to bring and extremely slow to process. Under Labour's plans, British citizens will instead be able to access the rights contained in the ECHR directly; the judiciary will be expected to interpret existing law in a way that is consistent with the convention.

Allowing the courts to apply its provisions may serve as a

safe way of 'smuggling in' changes to domestic law that Labour is wary of initiating itself. Prime candidates are several laws passed by the last Conservative administration that Labour at the time could either not bring itself to oppose or to pledge overturning through fear of appearing soft on crime, for example, the effective abolition of the right to silence contained in the 1994 Criminal Justice Act and the far-reaching snooping powers for the police in the 1997 Police Act. But it would be foolish to exaggerate the impact of the ECHR. According to Straw's plans, if there is a conflict between domestic law and the convention, it will be the domestic law that prevails. Parliament will be expected to change the law, but if it does not do so the courts will be powerless. Given Labour's record in opposition, it is by no means inconceivable that, in some circumstances, it will find it useful simply to ignore the courts.

The promise of a Freedom of Information Act is a survivor from 1992, when it was going to be the first piece of legislation passed by a Kinnock government. At that point the measure was based on a wide-ranging draft bill drawn up by the Campaign for Freedom of Information – and it is possible that Labour will introduce something similar after the White Paper promised in the first Queen's Speech. If so, it will have a dramatic effect on the culture of secrecy that afflicts British government.

Apart from incorporation of the ECHR and the Freedom of Information Act, Labour is promising to strengthen anti-discrimination legislation and replace the Prevention of Terrorism Act. It is also likely to be a little more liberal than the Tories in the way it runs the asylum and immigration system, which it says it will overhaul. Early indications of this were the promise in the Queen's Speech of a bill to allow people liable to deportation on grounds of national security to appeal against the decision.

But the biggest broadly liberal changes in the law-and-order functions of the Home Office are likely to come in the prison system. Since the 1993 Tory conference, when Michael Howard declared that 'prison works', Britain's prison population has grown by a third. By summer 1997 it stood at 62,000, a record high, and included a substantial number of petty, non-violent offenders (such as fine defaulters and TV licence non-payers). Britain sends a higher proportion of its population to jail than any other European country, and as a result of the 1997 Crime (Sentences) Act, the length of sentences given to convicted offenders has increased.

The policy has been a disaster in every respect. The increase in the prison population has taken place without a proportionate increase in funding, and most extra spending has been earmarked for new jails (which of course take time to build). The result is a prison system in which overcrowding is the norm and rehabilitation, treatment and education programmes have been cut in many places to the bare minimum. Meanwhile, vast resources have been committed to a prison-building programme to accommodate the new, and longer-staying, inmates. Originally costed by the Home Office at £1.2 billion, the real cost is expected to be much higher. If it was obvious in 1991 even to the then home secretary David Waddington – a right-wing Conservative who came into the job believing in the restoration of the death penalty – that prison is 'an expensive way of making people worse' and ought to be reserved as a last resort, mainly for sexual and violent criminals, it is even more apparent today. The Labour government has inherited a prison system that is ludicrously expensive, overburdened to the point of collapse and in desperate need of reform.[71]

Early indications of Labour's intentions were ambiguous. Straw made it clear that the government intended to implement the mandatory sentencing provisions of the 1997 Crime (Sentencing) Act for serious violent and sexual offenders, gave the go-ahead for the opening of a controversial prison ship based in Portland and repeated his pre-election promise to honour existing contracts for private prisons. But he also insisted that 'any government must take account of the public spending implications of a rising prison population'.[72] Unless the government is prepared to meet the ever-increasing cost of maintaining a rising prison population, a move towards alternatives to incarceration seems inevitable.

On the other hand, there are plenty of areas where Labour in government is unlikely to be markedly different from the Tories. It is stuck with hard-line criminal justice measures introduced by its predecessor: having pinned its electoral credibility on supporting them (as Straw himself proudly put it at the beginning of 1997, 'We haven't opposed a criminal justice measure since 1988'[73]) it dares not suddenly move to reverse them. On decriminalizing use of soft drugs, repeal of the blasphemy laws, making the secret state more accountable, relaxing the licensing laws and reforming the libel laws to prevent them being used to suppress freedom of expression – all live issues in the past five years – Labour is either against change to the *status quo* or silent.

The biggest difficulties that civil libertarians are likely to have with the government, however, are to do with its efforts to protect society from the 'anti-social behaviour' that Straw identifies as a key precursor to crime. It is undoubtedly the case that 'families from hell', noisy neighbours and uncontrollable children exist – and it's true, as both Blair and Straw said repeatedly in opposition, that victims of crime are more likely to be poor than rich. The danger is that Labour's measures will mean a massive increase in the powers of the state at the expense of the basic freedoms of some of the most vulnerable people in our society. There is a strong element of playing up to middle-class fears and prejudices about the poor in Labour's whole approach. In describing 'winos, squeegee merchants and aggressive beggars' as a menace, in the talk of 'disorder' on the streets and unruly council tenants, in the equivocations about single parents, Labour has come perilously close to identifying the central problem of society as the need to contain and control the underclass.

It is not difficult to imagine Labour's enthusiasm for curfews on teenagers and 'zero tolerance' of aggressive drunks and beggars transmuting into the police being empowered to whisk off the streets the poor, young, shabby or deranged in any area where they don't fit in. The measures to clamp down on anti-social behaviour by council tenants could all too easily become a licence for pursuit of vendettas by intolerant neighbours and meddling bureaucrats that adds to the ranks of the homeless. In combination with a 'tough' approach to 'scroungers' and squatters – particularly if Labour's plans for getting the long-term unemployed into work prove unsuccessful – there is a real danger that the government's encouragement of 'responsibility' will have the unintended consequence of further marginalizing those people already living on the edge of society. The attack on crime and its causes, in other words, might just mean 'sirens moaning in every street' and an increase in crime.

Such a nightmare is certainly not inevitable. But the government will have problems with crime even if its polices merely fail to reduce it. Labour has carefully – and wisely – refrained from claiming that under its rule crime will fall. But at the same time the force of its rhetoric has strongly implied that things will most definitely improve. It would not take much for this to come back to haunt the party, in the same way it did the original 'party of law and order'.

8

VOTE EARLY, VOTE OFTEN
NEW LABOUR AND THE CONSTITUTION

There was a huge smile on the face of Donald Dewar, the secretary of state for Scotland, when he unveiled the Referendums (Scotland and Wales) Bill at a press conference in Glasgow the day after the Blair government's first Queen's Speech. 'The show is well and truly on the road,' he affirmed. 'It is a measure of the importance the government attaches to devolution that the referendum bill is the first to be introduced in the new parliament.'

The bill laid out the wording of a two-question referendum in Scotland, where voters would decide whether there should be a Scottish parliament and whether it should have tax-raising powers, and a single-question referendum in Wales, where voters would decide whether there should be a Welsh assembly. The plan, said Dewar, was to get the bill through parliament as quickly as possible. He gave an 'absolute undertaking' that White Papers detailing the government's substantive plans for devolution would be published before the summer recess, and he promised that the referendums would work on the basis of simple majorities of those voting. 'There will be no fancy franchises,' he said. 'We firmly believe we will get that mandate.'[1]

And with that, it was down to business. That afternoon, the bill was given its first reading in the Commons, and within three weeks – thanks to the use of the guillotine to cut short debate – it had passed through its third reading. It got more difficult after that as Welsh secretary Ron Davies became embroiled in an unseemly row with the anti-devolutionist back-bencher Llew Smith. A couple of weeks later, the cabinet split over the precise powers that the Scottish parliament should have, with several English ministers, among them Jack Straw, Frank Dobson and Jack Cunningham, arguing for a more limited devolution than Dewar and most of the Scots in the cabinet wanted. But even this was small beer compared with what many had expected before Labour took power. On 22 July, Davies launched a White Paper setting out proposals for a 50-seat Welsh assembly elected using the additional member system of proportional representation. Two days later, Dewar triumphantly unveiled the equivalent document detailing plans for a 129-seat Scottish parliament, to be elected using the same system but with tax-raising and legislative powers denied to the Welsh assembly.

Although he did not shadow his current post immediately before the 1997 election, Dewar did not come to it unprepared. He was shadow Scottish secretary for nine years from 1983 to 1992, and before that served for three years as deputy to Bruce Millan on Labour's front-bench Scottish team. Few were surprised when he was appointed Scottish secretary by Blair: George Robertson had not performed well as shadow Scottish secretary, and the job needed someone of stature. Dewar was the obvious choice. Leaving aside his years as shadow Scottish secretary, he was due a reward for his work as chief whip since 1995.[2]

Dewar has been involved in politics for a long time, and has been a convinced devolutionist since his early thirties. He was born in Glasgow in 1937 to a professional middle-class family: his father was a consultant dermatologist, 'a gentle old-fashioned liberal nationalist'. By his own account, 'it wasn't a background which conditioned a Labour response and I find it very difficult to pin down when and why I became a Labour supporter.'[3] He was an only child, and both his parents suffered from serious illnesses when he was very young, leading him to be looked after by family friends who ran a preparatory school in Perthshire. His parents were well enough for him to return home by the time he was eight, and he went to Moss Park primary school before becoming a day-boy at the fee-paying Glasgow Academy, 'which is where the doctors' sons went in Glasgow'.

He felt like a fish out of water at both establishments. At Moss Park 'there was a certain amount of tension. I stood out like a sore thumb. I was a quiet child with spectacles and not much confidence and I also had a rather odd accent because almost all the children at my first school were English'.[4] At the all-boy Academy, a bastion of conservative respectability, he was a 'total misfit': 'I was a slightly disorganized rebel, the only person to be two years in the sixth form without being made a prefect and for years the longest-serving unpromoted cadet in the Combined Cadet Force'.[5] While there he did his first bit of campaigning for the Labour Party, during the 1955 general election: he pinned Labour posters under his jacket and flashed them at passers-by. He joined the party the following year aged eighteen.

But while Dewar's school-days appear to have been a study in playground pathos (by his own account he was bad at games, 'very lonely' and introspective, and left the Academy 'with no social experience at all', particularly with girls)[6] he came into his own at Glasgow University. He went there at the age of twenty – it took him four attempts to pass the requisite Higher Latin – and straight away joined the Labour Club, where he soon discovered that he had a talent for debate. He was, with John Smith and Alexander Irvine (now, as Lord Irvine of Lairg, the Lord Chancellor), one of the main figures on the Gaitskellite right of the club, and according to a left-wing contemporary, the journalist Hugh MacPherson, now *Tribune's* parliamentary columnist, by far the most fervent factionalist. Dewar became chairman of the Labour Club in 1960, the year after Smith held the post, and went on to become president of the university union a year later. Together the pair won a *Scotsman* debating trophy, and the prized *Observer* Mace award in 1963.

The Glasgow University Labour Club was a much more serious affair than student politics south of the border. It enjoyed direct encouragement from the Labour Party in Scotland, which organized student canvassing and recruitment 'expeditions' across the city during election times, and offered direct entry into adult politics. In 1962, while still a student (he followed his history degree with a law degree), Dewar got himself selected to fight South Aberdeen, a Tory seat since 1918. He failed to win it in 1964, but got in on his second attempt two years later. He was soon parliamentary private secretary to the President of the Board of Trade, Anthony Crosland. In this role he developed a considerable public profile in the Scottish media, regularly making headlines with his speeches. From the time of the Scottish National Party's Hamilton by-election victory in 1969, he was a vigorous opponent of 'the crazy logic of separatism',[7] and he was one of Labour's earliest supporters of devolution. He backed Harold Wilson's attempt to join the Common Market and attacked the Tories relentlessly for trying to make political capital out of law and order. A glittering political career seemed to beckon.

But in 1970 he lost his seat to the Tories, and it was to be eight more years before he returned to the Commons. He spent five years as a social work reporter (an administrative post with Lanarkshire's children's panel) before becoming a partner in a firm of solicitors, fitting in some journalism for Radio Clyde at the same time. In the meantime, his marriage collapsed and his wife Alison subsequently remarried his old university chum Alexander Irvine. Dewar remained politically active – he was one of the pro-devolution minority on Labour's Scottish executive in the mid-1970s – and put himself forward for nomination as a Labour candidate in various safe seats. But it was not until 1978 that he was selected, to fight a by-election in the inner-city Glasgow seat of Garscadden, where the sitting Labour MP, Willie Small, had announced his retirement and then died.

Garscadden had always been a safe Labour seat – but Labour believed that it faced a serious challenge from the SNP, which over the previous year had enjoyed a surge in support. Dewar took the nationalists head on. 'I think it is a whining, selfish, intolerant and mean society they propose,' he told Labour's Scottish conference in a widely reported speech during the by-election campaign in March 1978. 'It's up with the drawbridge, and I'm all right, Jack.' The SNP, he went on, was nothing more than a 'rag, tag and bobtail army of malcontents'.[8] The SNP was equally uncompromising. Garscadden was home to a significant Catholic vote, and the SNP candidate came out against abortion early on. In 1967 Dewar had voted in favour of David Steel's groundbreaking Abortion Act. During the by-election campaign he told the anti-abortionist Society for the Protection of Unborn Children – which distributed leaflets making it clear that Dewar was the least 'sound' candidate on the issue – that he now believed 'it should be amended, improved, to stop abuses'.[9] He promised to support the organization's campaign to make it more restrictive.

Throughout the contest, Labour nerves jangled at the prospect of losing the seat. But in the end Dewar was elected by a comfortable margin, and his victory was widely regarded as the turning point in Labour's battle to see off the nationalists. Back in the Commons, he took up where he had left off in 1970 as a technocratic, pro-European right-winger.[10] He played a major role in Labour's campaign for a 'yes' vote in the 1 March 1979 referendum on devolution. 'Devolution is about a greater say for Scotland within the framework of the United Kingdom,' he wrote in the *Glasgow Herald* a fortnight before the vote. 'It is a way of standing up against nationalism and forging stronger links with the rest of Britain. I believe that an assembly working and contributing to better government is the right way to answer a nationalism which will become increasingly irrelevant . . . The assembly is a long overdue extension of democracy. It is not the creation of a new tier of government but an opportunity to control and scrutinize in the public interest an administrative tier which is already in existence.' Replace 'assembly' with 'parliament', and this could be the text of a Dewar speech delivered in summer 1997.

The story of Labour and devolution goes back a lot further than the 1970s. 'Home rule all round' – rather than just for Ireland as William Gladstone wanted – was one of the main demands of Keir Hardie's Scottish Labour Party in the 1880s, and was one of Labour's top priorities as the party emerged as a major electoral force throughout Great Britain in the first two decades of this century. The party's 1918 conference resolved that 'there should be constituted separate legislative assemblies for Scotland, Wales and

even England'. But the party leadership was much more interested in the prize of power of Westminster. Neither of Ramsay
MacDonald's minority governments did anything to bring about
home rule, and the main source of pressure for it disappeared
with the disaffiliation of the Independent Labour Party in 1932.
From the early 1930s, home rule was dismissed by most of the
Labour right as an irrelevance and by the majority of the Labour
left as a threat to the unity of the working class. Labour oppor-
tunistically embraced home rule for Scotland again after the
Scottish National Party won its first-ever parliamentary seat in
the April 1945 Motherwell by-election, but the Attlee government did nothing to implement the promise after it won its
landslide election victory three months later (in which the SNP's
gain was wiped out). A cross-party campaign for home rule for
Scotland, the Scottish Convention, led by John MacCormick, who
had left his position as a leader of the SNP after it had rejected his
ideas for co-operation with other parties, subsequently won substantial support: its 1949 Scottish Covenant, calling for a new
constitutional settlement, was signed by more than 2 million
people. But by then MacCormick had won the enmity of Labour
by standing against it in a 1947 by-election. In Wales, support for
home rule had little resonance within the Labour Party.[11]

Labour gave barely a second thought to devolution during
the 1950s. But the 1960s saw an unexpected revival of nationalism
in both Scotland and Wales. In 1962, the SNP came second to
Labour's Tam Dalyell in the West Lothian by-election, then
enjoyed an explosive growth of membership. In 1966, Plaid
Cymru won its first-ever by-election, in Carmarthen; and in 1967,
the SNP's Winnie Ewing won a stunning by-election victory in the
safe Labour seat of Hamilton. In the words of Tam Dalyell, 'the
election of Mrs Ewing went off like an electoral atom bomb in the
Labour establishment'.[12] Labour spent months squabbling over
what should be done. The party in Wales was largely sympathetic
to some form of devolution, but that in Scotland was largely hostile. Prime minister Harold Wilson eventually set up a Royal
Commission on the Constitution in 1969. In its evidence to the
Royal Commission, the Scottish Council of the Labour Party (generally known as the Scottish executive) proclaimed: 'Any form of

assembly with substantial legislative devolution would be a slippery slope towards total separation, or at least a form of separation which would set up divisions within the United Kingdom.'

In the 1970 general election, both nationalist parties lost their by-election gains (although the SNP won Western Isles) and the national question went off the boil – but not for long. Both in Scotland and in Wales, resentment at the actions of Edward Heath's government, elected without majorities in either country, grew rapidly. In Wales, Labour moved tentatively towards embracing devolution, but in Scotland the anti-devolutionists remained dominant in the party apparatus if not among MPs. The day before the Royal Commission, by now chaired by Lord Kilbrandon, published its pro-devolution report in October 1973, Labour's Scottish executive issued a policy document that rejected a 'new-fangled assembly'.

By now, however, the SNP had discovered the political utility of claiming for Scotland the substantial deposits of oil that had been found in the North Sea. Hot on the heels of the publication of the Kilbrandon report, the SNP's Margo Macdonald won a by-election in the hitherto safe Labour seat of Govan; and in the February 1974 general election the SNP, campaigning on the slogan 'It's Scotland's oil!', made the breakthrough that it had always wanted, taking seven seats in the Commons. Within weeks, the Labour leadership in London decided that the Scottish party executive's anti-devolution position was an electoral liability and that Labour needed to embrace devolution. But the Scottish executive would not budge. In June 1974, at a meeting missed by many of its members who were watching the Scotland football team playing Yugoslavia in the World Cup, it rejected an elected legislative assembly, declaring that 'constitutional tinkering does not make a meaningful contribution towards achieving socialist objectives'. The NEC responded by demanding that the Scots call a special conference, which duly took place in August at the Co-operative Hall in Dalintober Street, Glasgow. The Scottish executive's position was swept away by trade union heavies doing the NEC's dirty work. Labour went into the October 1974 general election promising elected assemblies in Scotland and Wales. A Scottish assembly would have limited legislative powers – a point inserted into a government White Paper in September 1974 without any consultation with the party – while a Welsh assembly would be little more than a talking shop.[13]

It is not too cynical to suggest that Labour would have quietly ditched its promise if Harold Wilson had won a massive Commons majority. But he had an overall majority of just three. The SNP did even better than nine months before, taking 30 per cent of the vote in Scotland and eleven Commons seats, while Plaid Cymru won 11 per cent of the vote in Wales and three seats, one more than in the previous election. Dropping devolution was politically impossible.

The problem was that Labour was hopelessly divided on the issue. There was by now strong support among Scottish MPs for devolution. But many members of the cabinet, including the Scottish secretary, Willie Ross, and the leader of the House of Commons, Ted Short, were at heart hostile, and there were several back-benchers who were publicly opposed to the party's policy. None was more vocal than Tam Dalyell, who in early 1975 – when he realized that the promise of legislative powers for the Scottish assembly had been slipped into the September 1974 White Paper – began an obsessive campaign against devolution, arguing that it was costly, unwanted and a constitutional minefield. Dalyell's main constitutional point, repeated incessantly, was that a legislative assembly in Scotland would create the anomaly of English MPs being unable to vote in the Commons on those aspects of Scottish affairs that had been devolved, while Scottish MPs could vote on everything relating to England. Enoch Powell dubbed it the 'West Lothian question', after Dalyell's constituency. It had particular resonance for Labour because the two most widely touted solutions short of federalism, a reduction of Scottish representation at Westminster and a ban on Scottish MPs voting on English and Welsh affairs, were obviously not in the party's interests. The former would make it less likely that Labour would win a Commons majority, while the latter would tend to give Labour's opponents a majority on English and Welsh affairs even when the party had a Commons majority. (Federalism, the neatest solution, was, and is, simply too radical for Labour. The party in England has never questioned English domination of the

United Kingdom. As a result, it has never seriously considered how England could rule itself and has consistently come up with excuses for not thinking about it. One is the claim that a federation of nations could not work because England is much bigger than Scotland and Wales – a wholly irrelevant consideration in a truly federal polity. Another is the argument that a federation of Scotland, Wales and the English regions would be impossible because of the absence of English regional identities – again wholly irrelevant to the creation of a workable federation.)

In an attempt to placate both opponents and supporters of devolution, the government developed a blueprint for devolved assemblies with no economic policy role or tax-raising powers, which was eventually published in September 1975. It satisfied no one. The devolutionists in Scotland were particularly angry: the most radical of them, the young MP Jim Sillars, seceded from Labour and set up the short-lived Scottish Labour Party with one other defecting Labour MP and a group of activists. The government made a few concessions to keep other devolutionists on board, but did not accept the taxation powers they wanted, and eventually published its Scotland and Wales Bill in late 1976. By now, Jim Callaghan had succeeded Harold Wilson as prime minister and replaced Scottish secretary Willie Ross with Bruce Millan and leader of the House of Commons Ted Short with Michael Foot, both devolutionists. Another devolutionist, John Smith, was given the task of steering the bill through the Commons.

But Labour's Commons majority had disappeared. Indeed, the bill's primary purpose was to provide Plaid Cymru, the SNP and the Liberals with an incentive not to bring the government down – and Labour's anti-devolutionists saw a chance to create mayhem. Leo Abse, together with Neil Kinnock, the most prominent anti-devolutionist Welsh Labour MP, got Michael Foot to concede post-legislative referendums on devolution.[14] Then, in early 1977, Labour anti-devolutionists, led by Dalyell, allied with the Tories and the Liberals to defeat the government's attempt to push the legislation through on a guillotine motion. The Scotland and Wales Bill fell, although nine months later, with Liberal support, much the same measures were reintroduced as two bills, one on Scotland, one on Wales.

Again, Dalyell and Abse led a series of back-bench revolts in parliament, in which Labour MPs from the north-east of England predominated. The most important was in support of an amendment moved by George Cunningham, the right-wing MP for Islington South, and passed in February 1978, which made it necessary in the referendums for more than 40 per cent of the electorate to vote 'yes' (as well as a majority of those voting). In the run-up to the referendums on 1 March 1979, much of the Labour Party campaigned against devolution both in Scotland and Wales, and the results were disastrous for the pro-devolution camp. In Scotland, 33 per cent of the electorate voted 'yes' and 31 per cent 'no', meaning that devolution fell because of Cunningham's amendment. In Wales, where a majority of constituency Labour parties declared against devolution, the vote was 11 per cent 'yes' and 47 per cent 'no'. The SNP moved a successful motion of no confidence in the Callaghan administration, bringing it down, and Margaret Thatcher won the subsequent general election.

The referendum dished Labour's commitment to a Welsh assembly, but the 1979 election had the effect of reinforcing Labour support for devolution to Scotland. The Tories' victory was a triumph only in England: Labour took exactly twice as many seats as the Tories in both Scotland and Wales, and in Scotland there was a small swing to Labour. While the SNP responded to the loss of nine of the eleven seats it had won in October 1974 by engaging in a bout of internal feuding, Labour in Scotland, little affected by Bennism or by SDP defections, soon became the beneficiary of a widespread popular opposition to English Tory *diktat*. Bruce Millan shadowed his former position of Scottish secretary, and devolutionists took a firm hold on the party's Scottish executive. Labour went into the 1983 election promising a Scottish assembly with legislative and revenue-raising powers – but its manifesto contained no coherent policy for Wales and the English regions.

Nineteen eighty-three was a much better year for Labour in Scotland than it was elsewhere: it lost just three seats, and the forty-one Scottish Labour MPs returned constituted nearly one fifth of Labour's total parliamentary strength. Under Neil Kinnock, who had quietly abandoned his 1970s opposition to devolution, the party's policy on Scotland remained much the same as under Michael Foot. Donald Dewar, appointed shadow Scottish secretary to replace Millan in 1983 and elected to the shadow cabinet the next year, proved a safe pair of hands. He kept his distance from the cross-party Campaign for a Scottish Assembly and successfully resisted Scottish left-wingers' demands that Labour adopt the argument that the Tories had no mandate to govern Scotland. Just about his only policy innovation was to promise legislation for a Scottish assembly in the first parliamentary session of a Labour government.

The 1987 election, held under the shadow of the Tories' introduction of the poll tax to Scotland a year earlier than in England and Wales, reinforced Labour's dominance north of the border. It won fifty seats, its best-ever performance, while the Tories were reduced to ten, their worst ever. Dewar again initially rebuffed the Campaign for a Scottish Assembly, which now wanted to involve Labour in a Constitutional Convention to establish a consensus on the form of home rule among all political parties and the institutions of civil society. But the campaign won widespread backing for its 1988 declaration *A Claim of Right for Scotland*, putting the case for Scottish self-government, and then Jim Sillars won the 1988 Govan by-election for the SNP. Dewar did a nimble about-turn and entered negotiations with the SNP and the Social and Liberal Democrats (as they were then) on getting the Constitutional Convention under way. The SNP dropped out of the process early on, but Labour and the Liberal Democrats (as the SLD soon became) played a full part in the deliberations of the Convention, along with representatives of the trade unions, churches, local authorities and ethnic minorities. The Convention proved a remarkable experiment in co-operative politics. By 1990, it had agreed on the principle that a Scottish parliament should be elected by some more proportional system of representation (the first time Labour had signed up for any sort of change to the electoral system since the 1930s), that it should have economic planning powers, and that it should be the first step towards a new federal constitution for the United Kingdom. The Convention's recommendations were the basis for both Labour and Liberal Democrat manifestos in 1992. It produced a final detailed report in 1995.

Labour performed worse in Scotland in the 1992 election than in 1987, losing votes both to the Tories and the SNP, and the Liberal Democrats fared badly by comparison with the Liberal–SDP Alliance; Labour lost one seat to the Tories. For the fourth election in a row, Scotland ended up with a Tory government in London after voting decisively against the Tories, and frustration among Labour's most radical home-rulers boiled over. Straight after the election, three Labour MPs, George Galloway, John McAllion and Dennis Canavan, set up a cross-party pressure group, Scotland United, to campaign for a referendum on Scotland's constitutional arrangements. It won support from the leaders of the Scottish TUC and from several celebrities, but it fizzled out in the face of opposition from Dewar and the rest of the Labour establishment, to whom the idea of working with the SNP had once again become anathema. John Smith, a firm but moderate devolutionist, made his old friend Dewar social security spokesman in his first shadow cabinet reshuffle in summer 1992, appointing Tom Clarke as shadow Scottish secretary, a surprise addition to the shadow cabinet, in his stead. But the change made no difference to Labour policy. Nor did Smith's replacement of the affable but lacklustre Clarke with George Robertson in 1993.

Labour's policy for Wales and the English regions made few headlines in the late 1980s and early 1990s, but in some respects it changed more radically between 1983 and 1992 than its policy on Scotland. The impetus for change came initially from John Prescott and other northern English MPs who were convinced that interventionist policies at regional level should be a key element of Labour's economic approach – an idea inspired in part by the experience of Labour local government in the early 1980s and in part by continental European examples. The notion that these regional bodies should be democratically accountable was something of an afterthought – by the late 1980s Labour had more or less come round to supporting elected assemblies for Wales and the English regions with a wide range of functions devolved from central government and unelected quangos but no legislative powers. There was no consensus on the urgency of setting up these assemblies, however: in 1992, Labour promised a Welsh assembly in the lifetime of a parliament but left the timetable for elected English regional bodies deliberately vague, much to the consternation of many northern Labour MPs.

Devolution was one of the policies inherited from John Smith that Tony Blair was least happy about when he became leader in 1994. Of course, he made all the right noises about devolution to Scotland during the leadership campaign, echoing Smith's description of a Scottish parliament as 'unfinished business' and promising one in the first year of Labour government.[15] But somehow he didn't seem to be very keen on it, let alone on the other parts of Labour's devolution policy. Several Labour MPs complained that it was largely resentment at the imminent election of a middle-class Englishman as Labour leader – albeit one born and educated in Edinburgh – that almost deprived Helen Liddell of victory in the Monklands East by-election after Smith's death. The grumbling continued even after Blair's reiteration at the party conference in autumn 1994 of his pledge of legislation for Scottish and Welsh devolution in Labour's first year in office. Soon rumours started doing the rounds that the new Labour leader wanted to deprive the promised Scottish parliament of its revenue-raising powers, prompting George Robertson, kept on as shadow Scottish secretary, to reaffirm that it 'would have assigned to it all income tax and value added tax raised in Scotland' and 'the discretion to raise or reduce the standard rate of income tax by 3p'.[16]

The Tories responded by going on the offensive – but at first the effect was minimal. Both Scottish secretary Ian Lang, with his warnings of a 19p tax increase as a result of the creation of a Scottish parliament, and John Major, with his denunciations of 'one of the most dangerous propositions ever put before the British nation', seemed mildly hysterical; and Labour appeared supremely confident of the popularity of its case.[17] Gordon Brown gave a speech in early January arguing that the solution to the West Lothian question was devolution to the English regions: 'A Scottish parliament and an assembly for Wales go hand in hand with the offer of greater regional democracy throughout Britain.'[18] A month later, George Robertson won over a largely nationalist audience in a televised 'great debate' with SNP leader Alex Salmond in the old Royal High School in Edinburgh, the building that was supposed to become the chamber of the Scottish assembly in the 1970s, when he announced, 'I would be proud to be a member of this parliament. When it comes to the day, I want to be here.'

At this point, unnerved by polling evidence that there was little support for regional assemblies in England except in the north, the Labour leadership started to wobble. First John Prescott refused to confirm to journalists that Labour's plans for the revenue-raising powers of the Scottish parliament were set in stone, starting a flurry of speculation in the press and prompting an unconvincing damage-limitation exercise by Robertson. Then in early March 1995 Blair and Prescott disagreed in public about English regional assemblies. Confronted by Blair's statement in an interview with *Scotland on Sunday* that 'We are not committed to regional assemblies but there is a desire for decentralization', Prescott told a television interviewer: 'No, I don't say that's the position, that we're not committed to it.'[19] A couple of days later Blair more or less disowned the solution to the West Lothian question laid out by Brown two months before, telling the *Scotsman*: 'I do not see Scottish devolution in any way, shape or form dependent on what happens in the English regions.' The West Lothian question, he went on, was 'not really a basis for legislating for the English regions' and Labour had no plans for reducing the number of Scottish MPs in Westminster as the Liberal Democrats were now demanding.[20] In summer 1995, shadow home secretary Jack Straw confirmed the cooling of Labour's enthusiasm for elected English regional assemblies with a consultation paper arguing for 'indirectly elected regional chambers' as a first step, with directly elected assemblies to follow only where and when voters expressed their desire for them in referendums.[21]

Labour's vacillations on the West Lothian question did not stop the Tories being routed in the spring 1995 Scottish local elections – but they were enough to give them heart. After he had seen off John Redwood's leadership challenge in June, John Major decided to replace Ian Lang as Scottish secretary with Michael Forsyth, an aggressive right-winger with a populist touch. From the moment of his appointment he subjected Labour to a ceaseless barrage of invective against the 'tartan tax' and the West Lothian question while making small symbolic concessions to the Scottish sense of nationhood such as repatriating the 'stone of destiny' and wearing a kilt as often as possible.

It was hardly sophisticated, but it was enough to put the frighteners on Labour. Worried by the effects of the 'tartan tax' campaign, Blair and a small group of trusted confidants, including Straw and Lord Irvine as well as Brown and Robertson, started meeting to decide what to do. They could not ditch devolution, but they could tone it down. Soon leaks began to appear in the press to the effect that Labour was planning to announce a referendum on devolution or drop the parliament's tax-raising powers. Robertson dutifully rebutted each one. 'There is no question of the Labour Party supporting calls for a referendum,' he told the Glasgow *Herald* on 20 February 1996. 'The will of the people is behind the scheme and they will vote that way in the general election.' Two months later, he wrote a letter to the *Scotsman* declaring that there was 'not a single scrap of evidence' to support a story it had run suggesting that Labour was about to dump the tax-raising powers.[22]

Five weeks later, however, to Robertson's apparent surprise, the *Independent* reported that Blair had decided on a pre-legislative referendum on devolution – it subsequently emerged that he had been persuaded of the idea by Straw – and on 27 June the shadow Scottish secretary found himself announcing plans for a two-part referendum, with one question on the principle of a Scottish parliament and one on whether it should have tax-raising powers. (At least Robertson had been a member of the group that was meeting to discuss Labour's devolution plans: his Welsh counterpart, Ron Davies, had not even known that referendums were under consideration. Davies nevertheless argued confidently for the change as if he'd known about it all along. In return he secured Blair's agreement to proportional representation for the Welsh assembly, which the Welsh Labour executive had until then resisted, and the promise of a cabinet seat.)[23]

The Scottish party and its Liberal Democrat partners in the Constitutional Convention were aghast.[24] John McAllion, Labour's spokesman on the Constitutional Convention, resigned his post after hearing about the referendum plan not from Blair but from a Lib Dem colleague; Lord Ewing, who as Harry Ewing had been a junior minister in the Scottish Office between 1974 and 1979, quit his position as vice-chair of the Constitutional Convention and denounced Blair's scheme. Elizabeth Smith, John Smith's widow, was persuaded not to come out publicly against what she saw as Blair's assault on everything her husband had held dear only after several hours talking with Donald Dewar. Blair rushed up to Edinburgh to deliver a speech to reassure the Scottish executive that the purpose of the referendum was to determine 'not if, whether, but how . . . to make devolution a reality and destroy the scurrilous and dishonest campaign against it' and the executive reluctantly agreed to the principle of a referendum.[25]

Agreeing to the question on tax-raising powers was another matter. It took two months of concerted arm-twisting to get the Scottish executive to accept it – and then it did so only on the condition that a post-legislative referendum on whether the parliament would actually use its powers of taxation should be added to Blair's pre-legislative two-question referendum. This ludicrous position, put forward as a pragmatic sop to both sides in the argument by Mohammed Sarwar, the Glaswegian Asian millionaire who became Labour MP for Glasgow Govan in 1997, was aptly described by the journalist Neal Ascherson as 'the sort of Sellotape compromise which is just about bearable on a sub-committee split on the colour of traffic signs, but totally out of order on a matter of national policy'.[26] Blair welcomed it as 'a mature and sensible decision', then five days later reverted to his original position after a well-deserved pasting from the Scottish media.

Blair's problems with Scotland did not stop there. The clumsy attempts by Blair supporters to organize a caucus in Scotland – known as 'The Network' – created more bad blood, particularly after they forced the resignation of Tommy Sheppard, the popular devolutionist deputy general-secretary of the Scottish party, in early 1997. In late 1996, the Labour leader described the Scottish media as 'unreconstructed wankers' for their obsession with devolution, after they leapt on leaked Labour focus group reports showing that some Scottish voters found him 'smarmy'.

Finally, Blair's launch of Labour's Scottish manifesto in early April was overshadowed by an interview with the *Scotsman* in which he tactlessly compared a Scottish parliament's tax-raising powers with those of 'the smallest English parish council' and proclaimed, apropos of the West Lothian question, that 'sovereignty rests with me as an English MP and that's the way that it will stay'.

Even in the fortnight before polling day in 1997, Labour was widely expected to lose substantial support as devolutionist Scots plumped for the SNP – but nothing of the sort happened. Labour's result in Scotland as everywhere else was better than anyone in the party dared hope.

Labour took fifty-six seats in Scotland, with the Liberal Democrats winning nine and the SNP six: the Tories were wiped out. Labour's share of the Scottish vote was 46 per cent, up 7 points on 1992, and the SNP failed to make inroads in Labour's heartlands in the central belt. Although the SNP won three more seats to take its total to six, all were gains at the Tories' expense. Its overall share of the Scottish vote increased by less than a single point, to 22 per cent, and in all but six Labour-held constituencies where the SNP was the main challenger there were swings from the nationalists to Labour. Among Labour's seven gains were Stirling, where Anne McGuire beat Michael Forsyth by 6,411 votes, and Edinburgh Pentlands, where Linda Clark beat foreign secretary Malcolm Rifkind by 4,862. In Wales, the result was just as good for Labour. The party took thirty-four of the forty Welsh constituencies, with the Lib Dems winning two and Plaid Cymru four: as in Scotland, the Tories were wiped out. Labour's share of the vote in Wales was 55 per cent, up 5 points on 1992.

'The size of Labour's victory gives us a vote of confidence unprecedented in my political life,' said Dewar, and it was impossible to disagree with him or to miss the implications for Labour's plans for devolution. Even during the campaign, it had seemed that pushing through the Scottish parliament and the Welsh assembly would be one of the most problematic elements of Labour's programme. Although few predicted a replay of the farce of 1976–9, the party faced a string of hurdles that looked likely to take considerable effort and skill to surmount. If getting the promised referendums through parliament appeared likely to be difficult only if Labour had a small majority or was in a minority, getting a 'yes' vote in Wales and a 'yes-yes' in Scotland appeared to be a real challenge. After that, there was the even bigger potential headache of getting the legislation for creating the parliament and the assembly through the Commons and the Lords. Even with a comfortable majority, Labour faced the prospect of prolonged debilitating wrangling – about the Scottish parliament's powers, about the over-representation of Scottish MPs at Westminster and about Labour's failure to resolve the West Lothian question.

But the landslide means that, as long as the government gets the referendum results it wants, it is hard to imagine anything other than the smooth introduction of a Scottish parliament and a Welsh assembly. Although the government's substantive legislation on devolution will undoubtedly be given a searching examination in both the Commons and the Lords, the sheer scale of Labour's majority means that any attempt to filibuster or wreck it should be easily defeated. (The House of Lords is also constrained by the fact that devolution is a Labour manifesto pledge, and historically it does not oppose such measures.) The government's decision to reduce the number of Scottish MPs should silence critics of Scottish over-representation at Westminister; and although the West Lothian question still applies in theory, the most compelling reasons for Labour MPs to invoke it have disappeared. In practice the 'problem' of Scottish MPs voting on English and Welsh legislation is irrelevant because Labour has 329 seats in England, not just an overwhelming majority of the 529 English seats but precisely half the seats in the Commons, not counting the Speaker. The prospect of a Labour government relying, post-devolution, on Scottish Labour MPs' votes to force through legislation that applies only to England and Wales is no longer a pressing problem. By the time Labour has lost its English majority, it could be well on the way to solving the West Lothian question by introducing elected regional assemblies in England. Ironically, Labour's current dominance in England means that Tony Blair is well placed not only to exorcize for good the ghost of 1979 but also to end forever England's position of supremacy in the United Kingdom. One positive side effect might be the development of an English sense of nationhood that goes beyond sport and the assumption of the right to speak for the Scots, Welsh and Irish.

If New Labour's plans for devolution date back to the 1970s, its programme for reforming the Lords is even older. What the party is promising today (although not in the first session of parliament) is a slightly souped-up version of Richard Crossman's 1960s scheme for abolishing the voting rights of hereditary peers, wrecked in 1969 when Enoch Powell and Michael Foot – respectively demanding no change and outright abolition – combined in the Commons to talk it out.[27]

As with devolution, this time round should be different. Labour looks set to add to its sole previous successful attempt at changing the Lords, the Parliament Act of 1949 – a minor piece of legislation reducing the Lords' delaying powers from two years to one, pushed through by Clement Attlee only because Aneurin Bevan and the left wanted reassurance that the Lords would not block steel nationalization – with an act that radically changes the composition of the upper house. Labour not only has a mandate for its policy, it is also united behind it.

All of which makes it particularly galling that the party toned down its reform policy in opposition between 1992 and 1997 for fear of parliamentary obstruction. In 1992, Labour's policy on the Lords was unequivocally democratic. The party manifesto promised 'replacement of the House of Lords with a new elected second chamber' with limited powers to delay certain sorts of legislation dealing with individual or constitutional rights.[28] Labour believed that, as an unelected legislative body, the Lords was an affront to the basic principles of democracy – and it was not afraid to say so. Whereas in the early 1980s it had argued for simple abolition of the Lords, which would have left Britain with a unicameral legislature, the experience of rampant Thatcherism had by the late 1980s persuaded the party of the benefits of an upper house acting as a revising chamber and as a check on 'elective dictatorship'.[29] Replacing the Lords with an elected second chamber was the only solution compatible with democratic principle.

By the time of the 1997 election, however, Labour was promising not to replace the Lords with an elected second chamber but merely to end 'the right of hereditary peers to sit and vote in the Lords'. This, its manifesto stated, would be 'an initial, self-contained reform, not dependent on further reform in the future', although it would also be the 'first stage in a process of reform to make the House of Lords more democratic and representative'. The next stage would be a review of the system of appointments of life peers 'to ensure that over time party appointees more accurately reflect the proportion of votes cast at the previous general election'. After that, a committee of MPs and peers would consider further reforms. Nowhere in the manifesto was an elected second chamber mentioned.[30]

Why the change? In 1993, when Tony Blair as shadow home secretary first recommended abolition of hereditary peers' voting rights, it was very much as the first stage in a process leading to an elected second chamber. As the document on constitutional reform passed by the 1993 Labour conference put it: 'As a first step, hereditary peers should not be able to sit and vote in the House of Lords. We should then begin the process of introducing proper democratic elections.'[31]

The reason given for going for a two-stage process was that it would make a real start on Lords reform that would be less vulnerable to Tory wrecking tactics in the Commons than simple legislation for an elected second chamber. There was undoubtedly some sense in this – and indeed there still is. Getting rid of the hereditaries would be good news in itself. The hereditary peers – 755 of the 1,024 members of the House of Lords eligible to vote in March 1997, 333 of them taking the Tory whip – 'wield power on the basis of their birth, not merit or election', as Blair once put it.[32] Together with the incorporation of the European Convention on Human Rights into British law, abolishing the powers of the hereditary peers would be a massive step towards establishing citizenship – 'equal rights for all' – as a defining principle of British political life. What is more, it is the simplest way of reducing the Tories' giant majority among party-political peers. In March 1997, the Tories had 480 peers to Labour's 116 and the Liberal Democrats' 57; among the life peers 147 were Tory, 101 Labour and 33 Lib Dem. Without the hereditaries, a relatively small number of new life peers – say, 60 or 70 – would be enough to ensure that the Lords cannot obstruct the Labour government's legislative programme, including, of course, a bill to introduce an elected second chamber.

But none of this means that Labour should stop with abolishing the hereditary peers. The argument that legislation for an elected second chamber would be vulnerable to Tory opposition in the Commons is incredible since Labour won its massive majority. More important, there is a real danger that Labour will stop the process of Lords reform after getting rid of the hereditaries. However much of an improvement it would be, creating a second chamber consisting solely of life peers would not address the fundamental problem with the Lords – its lack of democratic legitimacy: life peers are political appointees, not elected representatives. If it were anything other than a stop-gap, it would be proof that Labour's commitment to a comprehensive programme of citizenship-based democratic reform was a sham. Yet the temptation for Blair to go no further than the creation of an appointed second chamber is massive. A wholly appointed House of Lords would enhance the powers of patronage he enjoys as prime minister, and it would remain the weak check on the government's powers that the Lords is today – 'a seraglio of eunuchs', as Michael Foot memorably described Crossman's 1960s scheme.[33]

That the government is aware of the convenience of an appointed second chamber there can be no doubt. Peter Mandelson alluded to it obliquely in the book he co-authored with Roger Liddle in 1996, *The Blair Revolution*, which stated that an elected upper house 'would have more power to block what the government of the day wants to do – and this area will inevitably generate a lot of opposition to change'.[34] Blair himself hinted on several occasions that a wholly elected second chamber might not be the way Labour decides to 'incorporate democratic accountability' into the Lords.[35] Most important of all, the wording of the manifesto was left deliberately ambiguous about Labour's long-term plans.

To no one's great surprise, Lords reform was not in the May 1997 Queen's Speech, which means that a wholly appointed Lords is probably not going to be in place until late 1998 at the very earliest. Add the time for the committee of Lords and Commons to come up with recommendations for further reform, and it begins to look very unlikely that Britain will have an elected second chamber by the time of the next general election.

But it would be an unforgivable mistake for Blair to yield to the temptation of dropping the goal of an elected second chamber. The case for a second chamber strengthened by democratic legitimacy to act as a check on 'elective dictatorship' is by now unanswerable – and that case applies regardless of the colour of the government.[36] There are, of course, important arguments to be had about the precise powers of such a chamber and about the system used to elect it. There are also grounds for having its members elected by members of regional assemblies rather than directly by voters, although this would obviously require assemblies to exist throughout Britain. But Labour will not be credible as a party of democratic renewal unless it sets up an elected second chamber. If it is not at least in Labour's next election manifesto as an 'early pledge', nothing else it says about making Britain a more accountable society will be worth taking seriously.

The third major element of Labour's programme for the constitution is a referendum on changing the electoral system for the Commons. As with the reform of the Lords, it is not for the first session of parliament, and as with an elected second chamber, it might not happen before the next election, or indeed at all. Labour has just won a famous victory under the existing set-up – first past the post (FPTP) – and many Labour MPs are not keen on change. Even if the referendum does take place, it might not make any difference to the electoral system. Labour's plan is to offer voters a choice between the status quo and a proportional alternative recommended by an independent commission, and a strong campaign against change is inevitable.

Nevertheless, the electoral reform referendum could turn out to be the Blair government's most radical constitutional measure. A vote in favour of proportional representation for the Commons would transform British democracy in a manner that Labour would have found unthinkable for most of its life.

It is true that in its earliest years Labour was largely in favour of the single transferable vote system of PR in multi-member constituencies (STV).[37] For Keir Hardie and many other founders of the party, it was the obvious way for Labour to overcome its reliance on an electoral pact with the Liberals – the secret deal that gave Labour thirty MPs in 1906 and forty in January 1910.

But as Labour's parliamentary strength grew, so its enthusiasm for proportional representation waned. Ramsay MacDonald was a strong opponent from early on, believing that the best system for Labour was the alternative vote (AV), a non-proportional system in which the single-member constituency is retained but voters choose their candidates in order of preference rather than by a simple 'X'. He believed that AV would favour Labour where it came second to the Tories on first preferences with a Liberal behind.[38] During the 1910s, the party wavered on electoral reform, first backing AV then shifting to STV after Lloyd George's failure to push through any kind of change in 1918.[39]

At the 1923 election, however, Labour won a larger percentage of seats than of votes and formed a minority government for the first time – and suddenly electoral reform of any kind vanished from its agenda as the party saw the possibility of marginalizing the Liberals for good under first past the post. In 1924, a majority of Labour MPs voted against a private members' bill that would have introduced PR, and the 1926 party conference ditched its nominal commitment to STV – just as the Liberals came round to the view that STV was essential to their survival.

In 1929, the second MacDonald government, desperate for Lloyd George's support, set up a speaker's conference under Lord Ullswater to look into the electoral system, which eventually produced an entirely opportunist agreement between Labour and the Liberals to back AV – a system that neither side really wanted but both could live with.[40] There were few complaints when the government gave up its attempt to legislate for the change after the Lords passed a wrecking amendment in 1931 which would have exempted all but urban areas from the new electoral system. As the historians Barry Jones and Michael Keating put it, 'It is difficult to interpret the moves to reform the electoral system between 1929 and 1931 as other than a rather cynical attempt to keep the Labour government in office.'[41]

After the defection of MacDonald in 1931, electoral reform became a symbol of collaboration with the enemy for Labour. Although there were renewed Labour calls for proportional representation during the time of the Communists' Popular Front campaign in the late 1930s and then again during the war, it remained for the most part a Liberal cause, and Clement Attlee's 1945 landslide banished all Labour thoughts that the electoral system was unfair.[42] The result showed not only that Labour could win decisively under first past the post but that FPTP was a prerequisite of so doing: Labour took less than 50 per cent of the vote even in its finest (pre-1997) hour. Even the party's 1951 election defeat, when it won fewer seats than the Tories despite winning more votes, failed to shake the conviction that it was in Labour's interest to maintain the *status quo*. It was not until the 1970s when the Liberals' recovery became impossible to ignore that even the slightest criticism of the electoral system was heard again from Labour. After Labour took less than 40 per cent of the vote in October 1974, the lowest proportion since before 1945, a handful of concerned Labour activists set up a study group which in 1979 became the Labour Campaign for Electoral Reform (LCER).[43]

In the early 1980s, proportional representation was too closely associated in most Labour members' minds with the hated SDP defectors and their Liberal allies to make any headway in the party. But after the 1987 general election, the mood changed rapidly. For the third time in a row, the Tories won a thumping parliamentary majority with less than 45 per cent of the vote and Labour failed to win representation in large swathes of southern England. As Labour started its policy review and the Liberals swallowed most of the SDP, leaving David Owen out in the cold, proportional representation and the prospect of centre–left coalition became fashionable with the left-leaning intelligentsia – if not with the Labour leadership. In autumn 1988, the historian Ben Pimlott started a magazine to promote the idea of a 'popular front of the mind', *Samizdat*, which had an influence far broader than its tiny circulation would suggest; proportional representation was one of the central demands of Charter 88, the cross-party campaign for constitutional reform set up by Anthony Barnett and *New Statesman* editor Stuart Weir a few weeks later.[44] Further impetus was given to pro-PR feeling when the Green Party won 15 per cent of the vote but no seats in the 1989 European elections. By 1990, a rash of books, pamphlets and magazine articles had appeared putting a left-wing case for changing the electoral system.[45]

Inside Labour, the LCER enjoyed a spell of rapid growth. Some of its new members were backers of AV or STV, the rival systems over which Labour and the Liberals had wrangled in the 1910s and 1920s. But the overwhelming majority tended towards a third system that had not figured in Labour's debates in the early years of the century – the additional member system (AMS) used in Germany, in which most MPs are elected from single-member constituencies but some are chosen from regional party lists to make the result proportional.[46] The core of support for AMS came from people who took a keen interest in the politics of the German Greens, who had played a major role in European left politics since their electoral breakthrough in 1983, particularly in the peace movement. The most vocal advocate of AMS in the Labour Party before the 1992 election was also the most prominent environmentalist and nuclear disarmer, Robin Cook.

The new enthusiasm for electoral reform soon made an impact. In 1990 the Labour Party in Scotland decided that it could not endorse first past the post for elections to a Scottish parliament. Then the National Executive Committee agreed to set up a working party to look into electoral systems for everything except the Commons – Labour was at the time planning an elected second chamber and English regional assemblies as well as a Scottish parliament and Welsh assembly – and the party conference that year voted to expand its brief to cover the Commons too. It held its first meeting in December 1990 under the chairmanship of Raymond (now Lord) Plant, professor of politics at

Southampton University, and in July 1991 produced an interim report, *Democracy, Representation and Elections*, laying out the options for electoral systems.[47]

The Plant report was an exhaustive technical work. But the working party was deeply divided among proponents of the different systems, as indeed was the Labour leadership, and it did not reach any conclusions on the desirable electoral system for the Commons. In the absence of consensus, the party adopted a policy of wait-and-see, although it accepted AMS for the Scottish parliament in early 1992.

Neil Kinnock, in the meantime, had become privately convinced of the case for AMS all round, and could not conceal the fact that he had changed his mind about the wonders of first past the post, much to the annoyance of Roy Hattersley, who refused to countenance change for the Commons. In early 1992, Kinnock told a radio interviewer that 'people who are entirely defensive about the possibility of change are simply not in touch with the fact that people's opinions in this country are much more dynamic and forward-looking than some politicians give them credit for'.[48] A week before the 1992 general election, he dropped another big hint that Labour might change the electoral system, talking about 'enhancing' the role of the Plant committee – then stepped back by refusing to reveal his own opinion of proportional representation in a television discussion. The Tories responded by making a stir about the dangers of a hung parliament that many Labour opponents of PR, among them Peter Mandelson, blamed for Labour's subsequent electoral defeat. Immediately after the election, the party's two leading 'modernizers', Tony Blair and Gordon Brown, both made speeches attacking proportional representation as a defeatist option that deserved no credibility.

For all this, 1992 gave added vigour to the campaign in the Labour Party for PR. John Smith as leader was unconvinced by the case for changing the electoral system for the Commons, but he agreed to let the Plant committee continue its deliberations. In summer 1992, it produced a second interim report, which ruled out STV for the Commons, then in early 1993 published a final report recommending a version of AV – although Plant himself made it clear that he had favoured AMS.[49] For Labour's proposed elected second chamber and for European Parliament elections, the committee proposed a regional list system.[50]

The report pleased neither Labour's supporters of the *status quo*, by now organized into a small First Past the Post Group led by the MP Derek Fatchett, nor its advocates of proportional representation, and its publication generated a heated debate – which was the last thing that Smith wanted in the middle of his stand-off with the trade unions over the introduction of one member, one vote for Labour's internal elections. At the May 1993 NEC, Smith kicked for touch, announcing that although he was personally unconvinced of the need for changing the electoral system, he believed that there should be a referendum on the issue 'during the first term of the next Labour government'.

And that, with a couple of wobbles and the addition of some important detail (notably agreement to use AMS for the Welsh assembly and a regional list system for the European elections), was where Labour rested until the 1997 election. Tony Blair made no secret of his opposition to proportional representation during the leadership campaign that followed Smith's death – 'I have not been persuaded that under PR you do not end up with disproportionate power being wielded by small parties,' he told the *New Statesman*[51] – and after becoming leader he chose a hard-line opponent of PR, Jack Straw, as shadow home secretary. Over the next year, supporters of first past the post pushed hard to get the referendum promise reversed, and they nearly succeeded. In summer 1995, after successfully lobbying several trade union conferences for support, FPTP campaigners were privately jubilant that Blair had as good as promised them that the commitment to a referendum was to be axed. It was only after protests from the PR lobby that Straw reaffirmed the pledge.

With the referendum confirmed as Labour policy, discussion turned to the form it would take. One problem was that proponents of change could not agree on what the change should be. Although most Labour reformers were in favour of AMS, there was substantial Labour backing for AV; and the Liberal Democrats, on whom many Labour politicians expected a Labour government to rely for a Commons majority, were committed to STV. A straightforward multi-choice referendum would obviously

split the pro-reform vote – even if it were limited to these three
options plus FPTP – so at first the reform lobby argued for a two-
stage referendum, with a first vote on the principle of change and
a second one (assuming the first went its way) offering voters a
choice of several alternative systems. This idea was rejected by
supporters of FPTP, who argued with reason that it was unfair to
them. A lot of arcane wrangling ensued, until eventually a solution emerged from the Labour–Lib Dem joint consultative
committee on constitutional reform set up by Blair and Paddy
Ashdown in October 1996 and convened by Robin Cook and
Robert Maclennan, the Lib Dems' home affairs spokesman. It
agreed that 'the referendum should be a single question offering a
straight choice between first past the post and one specific proportional alternative', with the alternative to be recommended by
a commission on voting systems to be appointed 'early in the
next parliament', which would report within twelve months.[52]
What was most significant about this agreement was its use of the
word 'proportional': as Blair made explicit in an interview with
the *New Statesman* just before the election, AV would be ruled out
because 'it's not proportional'.[53]

Electoral reform played little part in the 1997 election campaign,
and the promise of a referendum did not figure in the May 1997
Queen's Speech. It is not popular among the heaviest hitters in the
new government, most of whom – including Blair, John Prescott,
Gordon Brown, Peter Mandelson, Jack Straw, Margaret Beckett
and David Blunkett – are opposed to changing the electoral system
for the Commons, although some have indicated that they might
accept AV. Indeed, of the government's most senior figures, only
Robin Cook is a champion of proportional representation,
although there are a few of like mind a little way down the pecking order, notably Mo Mowlam and Clare Short. Among junior
ministers, however, there is much more support for PR, and
among Labour back-benchers, particularly younger ones, it is one
of the most popular causes. (On the left, there are several former
supporters of the *status quo* who are now toying privately with PR
in the expectation of eventually leaving Labour for a new left

socialist party.) Roughly a quarter of Labour MPs before the 1997 election were in favour; the proportion is now close to a third of a much larger number and, according to the Labour Campaign for Electoral Reform, growing fast.

What happens next depends crucially on the deliberations of the commission on voting systems. It has a delicate task. It needs to come up with a system that is both easy to understand and accepted by most reformers. Its most likely choice is some form of AMS, simply because it is the only system that can combine much greater proportionality with retention of single-member constituencies. But many Liberal Democrat supporters of STV are suspicious of AMS because of the role most versions give to party machines in drawing up the lists from which the 'top-up' MPs are drawn to make the system proportional – and many Labour backers of AV are worried by the way AMS creates two classes of MP and by the likelihood that its adoption would give parliamentary representation to the far right and far left. (AV would give greater, though not proportional, representation to the centre, but would make it as difficult for small parties to win Commons seats as first past the post.) It would be possible to invent a form of AMS that made it very difficult for small parties to win seats, for example by electing all the single-member constituency MPs by AV and denying regional top-up seats to any party that has not won seats on this basis – but such a system would be opposed by everyone who backs PR as a means of ensuring representation in parliament for minority opinion.

Labour's PR lobby hopes that the commission will negotiate this minefield and produce a recommendation that is endorsed by Blair, who will then lead a successful campaign for a vote for change in 1999. They will be lucky to get what they want because of Blair's antipathy to PR, but they deserve to. First past the post, of course, has one advantage over most other systems. It usually produces a clear result in which a single party wins a comfortable overall majority of seats, which means that incoming governments rarely have to engage in the messy business of coalition building. Labour is currently enjoying this in-built tendency of the system to the full.

Against this, however, there are several reasons why Labour

should be wary of sticking with the *status quo*. For a start, on grounds of pure *Realpolitik*, the system has not on the whole been beneficial to Labour: the 1997 election is only the third time, since emerging as a major parliamentary party, that Labour has won a comfortable majority in the Commons. Of its nine election victories, four have produced minority governments (1924, 1929, 1964 and February 1974) and two have given it majorities too small for comfort (1950, October 1974). By contrast, since 1922 – when the First World War coalition broke down and Labour first became the second-largest party – the Tories have won eleven elections with comfortable majorities and one, 1992, with a small one that was nevertheless enough to sustain the government through a full five-year term. In the seventy-five years from 1922 to 1997, the Tories were in office for fifty-four and Labour for just over twenty-five, including the Second World War coalition.

More important, first past the post has lost any claim to fairness in the past thirty years. Between 1945 and the early 1970s, when Britain effectively had a two-party system, FPTP could reasonably be said to yield results in most general elections that reflected the spread of opinion in the country, although on two occasions, 1951 and 1974, the party that won a majority of the popular vote did not win a majority of seats. Since the mid-1970s, though, with the emergence of three-party politics in England and four-party politics in Scotland and Wales, the system has consistently produced results that have been patently unrepresentative of the level of parties' support. The Tories took between 43 and 45 per cent of the vote in every general election from 1979 to 1992, yet won handsome parliamentary majorities in every one except 1992; Labour's 1997 landslide was achieved on just over 43 per cent of the vote. Except in the south-west and in Scotland, the Liberal Democrats and their predecessors have consistently piled up votes without winning seats. The same has happened to the SNP in central Scotland, and – except in 1997 – to Labour in the south-east of England. In 1997, the Tories were wiped out in Scotland despite winning more than a sixth of the vote. The case for a system in which a party's strength in the Commons is proportionate to its support in the country is overwhelming – and if that means that parties have to negotiate compromises in order to form coalitions, so be it. Everyone else in Europe has been doing it one way or another for years without coming to grief, and the disadvantages pale beside those of being ruled by a government that cannot claim the legitimacy of majority backing.

But this is not all. First past the post means that the voters that matter most are those in marginal seats. This has always been the case, and has generally tended to pull the major parties towards the safe centre ground of politics, leaving voters who find the centre ground disagreeable with the choice of plumping unwillingly for the least bad candidate, abstaining or wasting their vote on a no-hoper. In recent years, however, as the ever-increasing dominance of the political process by television and market research has given the parties' central media machines unprecedented power, this tendency has become stultifying. Everything and everyone in politics is now market-tested for conformity with the prejudices of swing voters in target marginals – and whatever and whoever does not go down well with the focus groups is sidelined, regardless of merit.

Of course, there can be no going back to the world as it was before television and focus groups, and no one can blame the major parties for operating in the most effective way they can under first past the post. But at least in most PR systems every vote counts, which means that parties take core supporters for granted at their peril. Even with a high threshold for representation, there is always the possibility that small parties can attract sufficient voters to force the major parties at the very least to take notice of concerns about which they have become complacent. Granted, there is the danger that anti-democratic parties gain representation or credibility that they would be denied under first past the post, but as with the supposed problem of inevitable coalition, this is much exaggerated in Britain by defenders of the *status quo*. There is little evidence that such parties would win any seats in the Commons even with a low threshold for representation. The Green Party, the UK Independence Party, a black rights party, a Muslim party, a left socialist party or a radical civil libertarian party based on the direct action groups in the anti-roads protest groups – all of which could play an immensely reinvigorating role in parliamentary life – are much better placed to do well under PR than the British National Party or any of the Stalinist or Trotskyist sects. Eternal vigilance is all very well, but the best guarantor of liberty is a vibrant pluralist democratic polity, not one in which the only voices that count are those of 'floaters' and 'switchers'.

Although devolution and an elected second chamber would be a real tonic to Britain's creaking democracy – as indeed would Labour's other promised measures of constitutional change, from incorporation of the European Convention on Human Rights into British law to reform of parliamentary procedure – the biggest test of the government's commitment to democratic renewal will be its willingness to embrace proportional representation.

9

IN PLACE OF BEER AND SANDWICHES
NEW LABOUR AND THE UNIONS

The reaction of Britain's trade union leaders to Labour's 1997 election victory was overwhelmingly positive. After eighteen years out in the cold, shunned by a Tory government that saw trade unions as at best a barrier to labour market flexibility and at worst as 'the enemy within', they at last had a government that was prepared to talk.

Even better, the new government's choice of ministers to deal most directly with the unions' immediate concerns was, at least at first sight, not bad. The union-friendly Ian McCartney was given responsibility for implementation of the European Social Chapter in the Department of Trade and Industry, and the senior minister in the employment team under David Blunkett at the Department of Education and Employment was not Stephen Byers, who had been disliked by the unions as opposition employment spokesman, but Andrew Smith.[1]

A fortnight after polling day, the ban on trade unions at the government's GCHQ intelligence-gathering centre was lifted. The next week, the general secretary of the Trades Union Congress, John Monks, visited Number Ten Downing Street for informal talks with Tony Blair on the government's plans for introducing a minimum wage, signing the European Social Chapter and legislating for a statutory right to union recognition. At the beginning of June, the unions claimed a small victory over the appointment of the chair of the Low Pay Commission set up by the government to set the minimum wage – George Bain, head of the London Business School. Blair's original choice, Whitbread chief executive Peter Jarvis, was, the unions claimed, too unsympathetic to their cause. Then, in the first major speech by a cabinet minister to a union conference, David Blunkett told the annual congress of the GMB general union in Brighton that the government would pro- duce a White Paper in the autumn on employment rights, including statutory union recognition. 'The mood music is fan- tastic,' said one union leader.

There was, however, a discordant note amid all the har- mony – and typically it was sounded by John Edmonds, the forthright general secretary of the GMB. The theme of his speech to his union's conference was the enormous debt Labour owed the unions for their support in winning the election. 'It was the best- organized campaign that I have ever known,' he said. 'And the trade unions contributed mightily to it. We set up the general election fund which paid the bills. We funded the bright new Labour Party campaign centre. We paid agents in the key seats so that a sustained campaign was fought over three years and not just over three weeks . . . The GMB did even more. I visited 33 con- stituencies during the election campaign and everywhere I went I found GMB members providing the backbone of the campaign organization. In the GMB we will remember the effectiveness of Tony Blair's leadership during that long campaign. And we trust that the Labour politicians will also remember how our members worked and how our members voted. The GMB seeks no favours. But let us trust that, in the years ahead, every time a Labour MP walks through the House of Commons, they remember the help they received from the GMB and so many other trade unions.'[2]

The message was clear to everyone who was listening. The unions had not spent so much money and effort getting Labour elected just so they could be ignored. And they would not be pleased if Blair turned round and told them that their role in the Labour Party was finished – even if the government and the unions might at times find themselves at loggerheads with each other over the next five years. 'Life will not always be as good as these first triumphant weeks,' Edmonds declared bluntly. 'Our first instinct will always be to support the Labour government. We did not vote Labour to see Labour fail. But our loyalty cannot be unthinking. We will be a friend, but from time to time we will also be candid. We have our own priorities set by this congress, and they will not always be the priorities of the government.'

Labour's link with the trade union movement goes right back to its very origins.[3] The party grew out of the Labour Representation Committee set up in 1900 after the 1899 TUC congress had voted to explore ways of increasing union representation in parliament. One crucial factor behind the creation of the LRC was a legal decision by the House of Lords that effectively outlawed picketing; what gave the new organization decisive momentum was the Lords' Taff Vale judgement of 1901, which made unions liable for costs incurred by industrial action. From the start, the unions provided nearly all the money for the party – and from the start they defined the parameters of Labour politics by holding the overwhelming majority of votes in the fledgling party's conference and National Executive Committee (which until 1937 was elected by the conference as a whole). Their formal dominance was taken as read in Sidney Webb's and Arthur Henderson's 1918 Labour Party constitution which added individual membership to the existing federal structure.[4]

But the unions' power was never unqualified. They were joined in setting up the LRC by various small socialist organizations, notably the Fabian Society and the Independent Labour Party, and from the beginning nearly everyone involved accepted the idea that the two 'wings' of the labour movement, the industrial and the political, had largely separate spheres of activity.[5] Although at first most Labour MPs were union-sponsored, even in the early years some were not, and the proportion increased with the growth of Labour representation in the Commons: only 87 of the 122 Labour MPs elected in 1922, the year that Labour for the first time became the second-largest party in the Commons, were sponsored. From the start, the parliamentary party had the leading role in drawing up the election manifesto, and in 1907 it was given discretion over how and when it implemented conference and NEC decisions. After the 1922 election the Parliamentary Labour Party further enhanced its independence from the conference and the NEC by electing its own 'chairman and leader' and executive committee.[6]

Labour's brief spell in government in 1924 firmly established the autonomy of the PLP, and for the most part the unions, overwhelmingly right-wing, accepted the *fait accompli*. They had enough to do in the industrial sphere – 1926 was the year of the General Strike – and were content to let the politicians get on with the politics, although they supported the PLP leadership at the party conference against its left-wing critics in the ILP and played a major part in ensuring that Labour shut the door on the newly emergent Communist Party. By 1928, Ramsay MacDonald could confidently declare: 'As long as I hold any position in the Parliamentary Labour Party – and I know I can speak for my colleagues also – we are not going to take our instructions from any outside body unless we agree with them.'[7]

But after the débâcle of 1931, when MacDonald, prime minister since 1929 in the second Labour government, abandoned the party to form a national government with the Tories, the unions took a much more dominant role. Ernest Bevin and Walter Citrine, respectively the general secretaries of the Transport and General Workers' Union (TGWU) and the TUC, effectively took control of the party when MacDonald left. Their position was formalized by the reconstitution of the consultative National Joint Council of representatives of the TUC general council, the Labour NEC and the PLP as a powerful policy-making National Council of Labour, dominated by the TUC. The PLP soon reasserted itself, however. Although Bevin and Citrine were able to secure the downfall of the left-wing pacifist George Lansbury as Labour leader in 1935, their favoured candidate to succeed him, Arthur Greenwood, lost the leadership election to Clement Attlee.

Attlee took a considerably more humble line on the autonomy of the PLP leadership than MacDonald. 'I am not prepared to abrogate to myself a superiority to the rest of the movement,' he wrote in 1937. 'I am prepared to submit to their will even if I disagree.'[8] But by the end of the 1930s, the union leaders and the

PLP leadership had found a *modus vivendi* only a little less accommodating than that of the 1920s. The deal was simple: the unions used their block votes at the party conference and their majority on the NEC to back the leadership against the left, in return for guarantees of detailed consultation on policy and freedom in the industrial sphere. (The unions were confident enough about the arrangement to accept changes in the party constitution in 1937 that slightly expanded constituency party representation on the NEC and introduced a new system for electing the NEC whereby only constituency party delegates elected the constituency section.)[9]

The *modus vivendi* survived intact through the war, the 1945–51 Labour government and most of the 1950s. But it was dependent on two things: the dominance of the right in the unions, and the party leadership's acceptance of the unions' role. Both began to break down in the late 1950s at the first signs of militancy over pay as workers realized their bargaining strength at a time of full employment. On the one hand, the left's influence grew in several unions, a development symbolized by the election of the left-wing Frank Cousins as general secretary of the TGWU in 1956. On the other, Hugh Gaitskell as Labour leader from 1955 became increasingly convinced that there were electoral gains to be had from being seen to stand up to the unions. He launched the 1959 election campaign at the TUC congress by declaring: 'We are comrades together, but we have different jobs to do. You have your industrial job and we have our political job. We do not dictate to one another. And believe me, any leader of the Labour Party would not be worth his salt if he allowed himself to be dictated to by the trade unions.'[10] After his speech, delegates sang 'For he's a jolly good fellow!' but in private the union leaders were furious.

Gaitskell was forced to eat humble pie twice in the next eighteen months when union votes, on the NEC and at the party conference respectively, blocked his attempts to ditch Clause Four of the party constitution and backed unilateral nuclear disarmament. He fought back successfully on unilateralism, then won the support of Cousins and the other left-wing union leaders for his vehement opposition to joining the Common Market. For a while the party's difficulties with the unions melted away. Labour won the 1964 election under Harold Wilson, promising a new deal on industrial relations, the central element of which was a policy of voluntary pay restraint – as Wilson put it, 'planned growth of incomes' – agreed with the union leaders as part of a package incorporating limits on dividends, profits and prices, an expansion of production and social policy reforms. The unions were also promised a bigger role in economic planning through the tripartite National Economic Development Council, set up by the Tory government in 1961. Cousins was given the job of technology minister.

Instead of a flowering of corporatist co-operation between the government and the unions, however, the relationship soured rapidly. The reason was simple: it soon became clear that neither Wilson and his colleagues nor the union leaders were in a position to deliver their side of the bargain on pay. From the start, the government proved incapable of keeping inflation down or securing the rapid economic expansion it had promised, while the union leaders found themselves unable to control the growth of militancy on the shop floor. The government responded by turning the voluntary incomes policy into a statutory one; most union leaders did their best to keep pay demands in check. But it didn't work. Unofficial strikes multiplied, and the left – with the Communist Party playing a major organizing role – won key elections in several major unions. The most important was the Amalgamated Engineering Union (AEU), which in 1967 elected Hugh Scanlon as president. In alliance with the TGWU, where Jack Jones succeeded Cousins as general secretary in 1969, the engineers formed an unprecedentedly powerful left-wing bloc in the TUC and in the Labour Party.[11]

By late 1968, the wave of unofficial strikes was causing the government serious concern. Barbara Castle, the employment secretary, came to the conclusion that the only way to stop the spiral of unofficial strikes was to introduce legal sanctions into the framework for industrial relations – and in January 1969 she produced a White Paper, *In Place of Strife*, outlining her plans. In return for giving workers a statutory right to join a trade union and to strike, she proposed the introduction of a compulsory month-long 'conciliation period' before a strike could proceed and compulsory pre-strike secret ballots.

For most union leaders, already smarting because of their members' dislike of Labour's incomes policy, Castle's proposal was an outrageous attempt by the political wing of the movement to impinge on the right of the industrial wing to engage in collective bargaining. A special TUC congress rejected the government's proposals, as did Labour's most union-friendly MPs, including home secretary Jim Callaghan. To Castle's disgust, *In Place of Strife* fell by the wayside.

The Heath government introduced compulsory conciliation and compulsory pre-strike ballots in its 1971 Industrial Relations Act, along with bans on the pre-entry closed shop and sympathy strikes and a new National Industrial Relations Court to deal with recalcitrant trade unions. But there was no chance that the Labour leadership would acquiesce in it. The act, despite its many similarities with *In Place of Strife*, was anathema to the unions and to the left, which now found itself for the first time with majorities both at the party conference and on the NEC. Labour's 1971 conference came out for a repeal of the act 'in the first session of a new Labour government' and instructed the NEC to consult with the TUC general council on an acceptable voluntary alternative.

The result was a union-led collaboration on policy unlike anything since the 1930s. A TUC–Labour Party Liaison Committee was set up in January 1972, composed of the NEC, the parliamentary leadership and the TUC general council, and within six months it had come up with plans for legislation giving new rights to workers and trade unions: the right to join a union, protection against unfair dismissal, and a statutory procedure for unions seeking recognition from an employer. After that, the Liaison Committee reached agreement that a new Labour government would introduce strict price controls, improve public transport and housing, increase pensions, expand public ownership in industry and extend industrial democracy. In return, the assumption – of the PLP leadership if not of the union leaders – was that the unions would exercise restraint in pay demands. This

deal, the 'social contract', was at the centre of the Labour manifesto in the February 1974 election, with its ringing declaration in
favour of 'a fundamental and irreversible shift in the balance of
power and wealth in favour of working people and their families'.

The 1974–9 Labour government was not treated kindly by
events – in particular, the impact of the oil price shock – and for
much of its life had to struggle along with either no parliamentary
majority or a minuscule one. It was criticized for its spending
cuts and much else by the left; and it was lambasted for giving the
unions too much power by the Tories – led from 1975 by Margaret
Thatcher – by the press and by much of the Labour right. (The
Labour right was particularly critical when the unions blocked
Roy Jenkins' plans for a Bill of Rights on the grounds that it would
involve judges in industrial relations.) With the benefit of hind-
sight, however, its record appears rather more creditable
considering the circumstances in which it operated. Its legislation
on workers' rights and its social security measures – particularly
the inflation-proofing of the state pension and the introduction of
SERPS and child benefit – were substantial achievements, and the
voluntary pay restraint of 1974–7, painfully negotiated with the
union leaders, was largely successful in dampening down inflation
and creating the conditions for economic recovery. Had it not
been for the public sector strikes of the 1978–9 'Winter of
Discontent', Labour's close relationship with the unions in the
1970s would have been judged by posterity as a moderate success.

As it was, however, prime minister Jim Callaghan decided
not to go for an autumn 1978 general election but to hang on until
spring 1979 – and was roundly beaten by Margaret Thatcher.
Within weeks, Labour erupted into a civil war in which the party's
structures and its relations with the unions became the major battlefield. The left in the constituency parties felt betrayed by the
actions of the 1974–9 government – especially over Europe, the
abandonment of the interventionist industrial policy and the austerity programme imposed in 1975–6. It believed that the solution
was to bring the parliamentary party under the control of the
membership, by making MPs stand for reselection once every parliament, by expanding the franchise for Labour leadership
elections to include the whole party and not just MPs, and by

giving the NEC, rather than the party leader, prime responsibility for the election manifesto. The right, concentrated in the PLP, believed just as strongly that the unions had sabotaged the government – and that the far left was trying to make scapegoats of hard-working moderate MPs.

By dint of single-minded determination and effective organization, it was the left that won all the first battles. Mandatory reselection was passed at the 1979 party conference; the 1980 party conference agreed in principle to extending the mandate for leadership elections; and a special conference in January 1981 voted – after manoeuvring of Byzantine complexity – for an electoral college for leadership and deputy leadership elections in which the unions had 40 per cent of the vote, the PLP 30 per cent and the constituency parties 30 per cent.[12]

The momentum for change ran out soon afterwards, with the defection of the SDP, the defeat of Tony Benn's attempt later the same year to win the deputy leadership of the party from Denis Healey and, most important, the unions' decision to call a halt to the feuding. NEC control of the manifesto proved a step too far for the left. Nevertheless, the implications of mandatory selection and the electoral college for Labour's links with the unions were profound enough in themselves. Mandatory selection made no difference to who chose Labour parliamentary candidates. They had always been selected by general committees of constituency parties, which meant that trade unions affiliated to local parties had a role, often a dominant one, in the process through their representation on the committee. Before mandatory reselection, however, once a candidate had become an MP he or she was not answerable to anyone apart from the voters except in extraordinary circumstances. Making reselection by general committees mandatory gave them a great deal of extra power. It inevitably raised questions about how representative general committees were of Labour's members. Most media attention focused on the disproportionate role played in some by the far left, but it was just as striking how many constituency parties were fiefdoms of right-wing, usually trade union, political machines.

The electoral college for leadership elections was an even bigger innovation – and far more problematic. The wider franchise raised the spectre of a Labour leader backed by the party in the country but not by the PLP, and the 40:30:30 formula gave the unions a predominance that was difficult to justify. Most important, the use of block voting by unions and constituency parties, and the absence of any compulsion to ballot members meant that the electoral college was open to the charge that it lacked democratic legitimacy. As the Benn–Healey deputy leadership contest immediately showed, if big unions left decisions up to their executive committees, a vast number of votes could be cast on the say-so of a handful of backroom fixers. Just about the best that could be said about the operation of the block vote in the electoral college was that it was not as transparently undemocratic as its use in the normal run of events at the Labour conference, where it counted for 90 per cent of the total vote and the four biggest unions – in 1980, the TGWU, the AUEW, the GMWU and NUPE – could effectively command a conference majority.

For all these reasons, Labour's 1979–81 constitutional settlement did not deserve to last. Getting agreement on changing it, however, proved immensely difficult because of the different vested interests involved, as Neil Kinnock found to his cost soon after becoming the first leader elected using the electoral college.

In 1984, Kinnock proposed a change in the system for parliamentary selections to 'one member, one vote' (OMOV), with all local party members as the electorate. His plan was rejected not only by much of the left in the constituencies but also by the TGWU, which was insistent on retaining a union role in selections. After the 1987 election Kinnock had another attempt, eventually settling on a local electoral college for selections in which unions were given up to 40 per cent of the total vote, with the rest going to individual members. The electoral college proved nightmarishly complicated, and in 1990 the conference voted to replace it (and to hold full selection procedures only when party members had voted for one). The alternative the NEC came up with in 1991 – according to which constituency parties could adopt OMOV if they wanted but could also use a 'weighted wider franchise' to include members of affiliated organizations living in the constituency – might just have worked, but it was never tried in practice.[13]

Kinnock had more luck with OMOV for elections to the constituency section of the National Executive Committee (introduced in 1990) and for European Parliament selections (introduced in 1991). But there was little at stake for the unions here. With the system for leadership and deputy leadership elections it was a different story, and there was no change during Kinnock's leadership, although the NEC encouraged constituency parties to hold ballots when Kinnock and Roy Hattersley were challenged by Tony Benn and Eric Heffer in 1988. As for the block vote at Labour conference, there was general agreement in the party's upper echelons – including among union representatives on the NEC – that it needed at the very least to be reduced in weight. The 1990 Labour conference voted for a reduction in union voting strength from 90 per cent to around 70 per cent, although the change was not put into practice. Nothing was done under Kinnock about altering the composition of the NEC to make the unions less dominant, although here there was far less pressure for change apart from demands from the left that the women's section of the NEC be elected by the left-dominated women's conference rather than by block votes at the annual conference. Union NEC representatives played a crucial part in Labour's policy review groups and were promised a major role in the new National Policy Forum created (at least on paper) by the 1990 Labour conference.

The upshot was that, when Kinnock announced his resignation after losing in 1992, the unions had much the same role in Labour's internal organization as they had a decade earlier – except in parliamentary selections and the policy forum. It is true that they had rather less influence over policy: the TUC–Labour Party Liaison Committee still existed but had long since ceased to play an initiating role, and since 1987 had been usurped as the main means of party–union liaison on policy by a secretive 'Contact Group' of the party leadership and the half-dozen or so most important trade union leaders. Nevertheless, the unions controlled 90 per cent of the votes at the party conference and 40 per cent of votes in leadership and deputy leadership elections. Of the twenty-five NEC members elected by the party conference, twelve were union representatives; another six (the treasurer and the five from the women's section) were elected by the block vote. Unions were represented on the general committees of constituency Labour parties and at regional level.

Just as important, the unions also had much the same role as a decade earlier in paying Labour's bills. In 1992, the unions affiliated some four million members to the party at £1.60 each, contributing £5 million of the party's £6 million national income from affiliations and membership subscriptions. The unions contributed at least £9 million of the £12 million the party raised between 1988 and 1992 for its general election fund and paid the costs of the party's telephone and direct mail fund-raising.[14] On top of this, the unions subsidized Labour's London headquarters, let the party use union premises for free during the election campaign, provided the party with 'free' drivers and helpers and contributed to constituency Labour parties. Overall, between 80 and 90 per cent of Labour's income in 1992 came from the trade unions. It is hardly surprising that they were less than pleased when, soon after the 1992 election defeat, unidentified Labour 'modernizers' were reported in the press as blaming the party's links with the unions for losing the election.

If, after the upheaval of 1979–81, the unions' role in the Labour Party changed little, their position in society was transformed, mainly for the worse. Total membership of trade unions, which peaked at 13.3 million in 1979, fell by 1992 to 9 million; trade union density – the proportion of workers belonging to unions – dropped in the same period from 55 per cent to 31 per cent. With a handful of exceptions, only unions that swallowed others in mergers grew in size.[15] The proportion of workers in large enterprises whose wages were determined in part by collective bargaining fell from more than three-quarters to around a half.[16]

There were several reasons for the decline in union strength. The most obvious was the disappearance of jobs in many industrial sectors where the unions were strong as a consequence of recession and changes in government industrial policy and technology. The collapse of much heavy industry, construction and traditional manufacturing in the early 1980s hit all the blue-collar trade unions hard, but particularly the construction workers', engineers' and transport workers' unions. Membership of the NUM fell because of pit closures. The printing unions lost members as a result of changes in printing technology.[17]

Equally significant, however, was the fact that most of the jobs that replaced those that were lost were not full-time and permanent, in large workplaces where unions were recognized by management. The jobs created from the early 1980s onwards were overwhelmingly in small workplaces in the service sector, often with managements hostile to unions, and many of them were part-time and temporary. Whereas most of the jobs lost in the 1980s had been done by men, most of the new ones were taken by women. The unions recognized that all this was a challenge to their traditional approach to recruitment – but few had any credible ideas about how to deal with it.

Changing patterns of employment and the unions' difficulties in adapting to them were still only part of the story. The unions' weakness in the early 1990s was also the result of the battering they had received at the hands of the Tory government. The Tories had come to power in 1979 in the wake of the 'Winter of Discontent' promising 'a fairer balance between the rights and duties of the trade union movement', and in their first term made a start on constraining the unions' freedom of action. The 1980 Employment Act limited picketing by strikers to their place of work, outlawed secondary industrial action except in certain tightly defined circumstances, restricted the closed shop and repealed Labour's 1975 provisions for statutory recognition of unions. Another Employment Act in 1982 narrowed the definition of a legitimate trade dispute to outlaw sympathy strikes, added further restrictions on the closed shop and, most important, removed unions' immunity from liability in actions of tort. This meant that for the first time since 1906, it was made possible for employers to apply for injunctions against unions and sue them for damages of up to £250,000 – with no limit on fines for contempt of court if the union ignored an injunction, and the ultimate sanction of sequestration.

The unions responded by talking tough about uniting to defy the new legislation, but their resolve had not had a chance to be tested before Labour, promising repeal of the Tory laws, crashed to defeat in the 1983 general election. The party won just 28 per cent of the vote: among skilled manual workers, its share was less than a third and among unskilled manual workers less than a half. As the government set about preparing the legislation that became the 1984 Trade Union Act – introducing compulsory pre-strike ballots four weeks before a stoppage, mandatory direct elections every five years for union executives, and compulsory ballots to approve unions' political funds – the trade union right, led by TUC general secretary Len Murray, drew back from the fray. At the 1983 TUC congress he made a passionate plea for 'responsible and realistic leadership', the most important element of which was staying within the law. His approach was dubbed 'new realism' by the press.

But the trade union left had different ideas, and no one more so than Arthur Scargill, elected President of the National Union of Mineworkers in 1982 on a platform of uncompromising opposition to pit closures. In March 1984, after the National Coal Board announced the closure of Cortonwood colliery in South Yorkshire and a massive cut in the capacity of the industry as a whole, Scargill got the NUM executive to declare a national strike.

The strike lasted a year and ended in a humiliating defeat, with the NUM's assets sequestered by the courts and its industrial power broken. Precisely why it failed was a cause of bitter controversy in trade union and Labour circles that still has not died away. For many, particularly on the left, the strike was a heroic attempt to prevent pit closures and preserve working-class communities. It was defeated only by military-style policing and because other trade unions and the Labour leadership offered the NUM lukewarm support. For others, including Neil Kinnock and most of the rest of the Labour leadership, the culprits were the leaders of the NUM, especially Arthur Scargill, who refused to legitimize the strike with a national ballot, lost public support by condoning picket-line violence and then rejected all possibilities of compromise. A few critics even argued, *sotto voce*, that the strike was doomed to failure from the start because the National

Coal Board and the government were so well prepared for a confrontation with the NUM.[18]

Whatever the reasons for the miners' defeat, however, there
can be no doubting that its effect on the union movement – reinforced by the subsequent crushing of the printing unions at
Wapping by Rupert Murdoch – was to strengthen the hand of the
'new realists', now led by Murray's successor as TUC general secretary, Norman Willis. This in turn was reflected in a toning down
of Labour's stance on employment legislation. By the time of the
1987 election the unions had been persuaded that, instead of
promising a simple repeal of the Tory legislation, the party should
back retention of its two most popular elements – compulsory ballots for union executive elections and before strikes.

Labour's 1987 election defeat made the unions even more
willing to compromise: as Lewis Minkin notes, there was soon
'virtually complete agreement among TUC officials, and among a
growing number of union leaders (albeit more on the right than
on the left) that the Conservative government legislation on union
industrial action had built upon and consolidated a more or less
permanent body of opinion among union members and in the
centre ground of the electorate. Thus the Labour Party could no
longer be saddled with a blanket commitment to repeal the entire
legislation.'[19] When employment law was considered, like everything else, in Labour's policy review, the TUC submitted a paper,
drafted by Willis's deputy, John Monks, arguing that a Labour
government should give priority to changing the most unfair
aspects of the law. The implicit assumption was that a grand repeal
of all Tory legislation was off the agenda.

Michael Meacher, appointed employment spokesman by
Kinnock in 1987 and the chair of the policy review group on
'people at work', thought differently. To Kinnock's annoyance, he
set about producing what was in essence a detailed elaboration of
policy as it had been before the 1987 election – and, despite
Kinnock's strenuous efforts, he at first got his way. In spring 1989,
the proposals on trade union law contained in *Meet the Challenge,
Make the Change*, the first report of the policy review, included an
extension of the definition of lawful industrial action to include
sympathy strikes where workers had a 'genuine interest in the

outcome of a dispute'. After the 1989 TUC congress passed a TGWU resolution calling for a return to union immunities as they had been in 1979, Meacher indicated that Labour policy was compatible with it.

But Kinnock soon got his revenge. Charles Clarke, his chief aide, fixed a deal with the union leaders over Meacher's head to reach an agreement that preserved the possibility of unions being sued for unlawful industrial action. Days before the 1989 Labour conference, the TGWU accepted a form of words concocted for Clarke by Lord Irvine, according to which the unions' liabilities would remain but industrial relations would be handled by special courts which would not have the power to sequester a union's entire assets. The party conference backed the new line, and within a month Kinnock had removed Meacher from his brief and replaced him with Tony Blair.[20]

The new employment spokesman continued the process of shifting Labour policy away from the promise of a simple repeal – most notably on the closed shop, where all the unions, apart from the National Graphical Association, acquiesced as he embraced the individual's right not to join a union. (An important factor here was the inclusion of the right not to join in the European Commission's social charter, which the unions had endorsed wholeheartedly after Jacques Delors' TUC speech in 1988.) Blair also tightened up the definition of sympathy action that a Labour government would tolerate and made it clear that there would be strict rules on picketing. Labour went into the 1992 election promising a 'fair framework of law for both employers and unions'. According to the manifesto: 'There will be no return to the trade union legislation of the 1970s. Ballots before strikes and for union elections will stay. There will be no mass or flying pickets.'

Meanwhile, the government pressed on with its assault on the power of organized labour. The 1988 Employment Act had introduced further restrictions on the closed shop, a ban on disciplinary measures by unions against strike-breaking members, and compulsory postal voting for union elections and pre-strike ballots; the 1990 Employment Act made the pre-entry closed shop and secondary industrial action wholly illegal and obliged union officials to repudiate or take responsibility for unofficial strikes. The government's last initiative before the 1992 election was a Green Paper proposing, *inter alia*, abolition of the Wages Councils (which set minimum wages in several industries), introduction of the right to join the union of one's choice (which undermined TUC's Bridlington Agreement to prevent unions from poaching other unions' members), and a ban on automatic deduction of union dues by employers, known as 'check-off', except where trade unionists gave written authorization. All these measures found their way into law as the 1993 Trade Union Reform and Employment Rights Act.

What put the unions right at the top of Labour's agenda after the 1992 general election had nothing to do with any of this, however. The weekend after the general election – and before Kinnock had said that he was resigning – first John Edmonds of the GMB, then Bill Jordan and Gavin Laird of the AEU, then the general secretaries of just about every other large trade union except NUPE, declared publicly in favour of John Smith becoming Labour leader or let it be known that this was their view.

The result, unsurprisingly, was outrage throughout the party at the union barons bouncing Labour into accepting Smith. Labour's arrangements for leadership elections, before 1992 less of a hot potato than parliamentary selections, immediately became a key issue in the contest to succeed Kinnock, with first Bryan Gould and then John Smith declaring in favour of OMOV (although Gould subsequently qualified his position). It was at this point that various 'modernizers' were quoted in the press as arguing that Labour's links with the unions had cost it the election. By May, when Kinnock managed to push a resolution through the NEC for OMOV in parliamentary selections, Labour seemed set for an interminable wrangle over the union link.

In June, in an attempt to dampen down the controversy, the NEC decided to set up a 'Review Group on Links between Trade Unions and the Labour Party' to look into the whole question of the party–union relationship.[21] It agreed readily enough to implement the reduction of the union block vote at party conference from 90 per cent to 70 per cent, with an option of reducing it to 50 per cent once individual membership reached 300,000. After a few meetings, the review group also seemed likely to come up with a scheme acceptable to all its members – and, they believed, to Smith – that gave union members who paid the political levy a role as 'registered supporters' in the party's leadership elections and candidate selections. Only one member of the committee as originally constituted, Nigel Harris of the AEU, wanted straight OMOV all round.

After Bryan Gould lost his place on the NEC, Smith decided to give Tony Blair his place on the review group. Blair was implacably opposed to anything other than OMOV for parliamentary selections and wanted an electoral college for leadership elections in which MPs and MEPs had half the votes and individual party members the other half, with no role for the unions – and he was prepared to fight hard to get his way. After the review group produced a draft final report advocating a 'registered supporters' scheme for levy-payers, Blair stonewalled.

When the draft was leaked selectively to the press in early December, Clare Short, who backed the scheme, was in no doubt that Blair was responsible. 'Malevolent forces are at work,' she wrote in *Tribune*. 'There have been two spates of misleading leaks from the working party, apparently motivated by those who wish for a divorce. The leakers' efforts seem calculated to antagonize trade unions and thus make necessary reform more difficult. There is also a clear attempt to bounce our new leader into "taking on" the unions. I am not a conspiracy theorist, but it is now clear to me that there are well-placed people in our midst who want to model the British Labour Party on the American Democratic Party. They feel strengthened by Bill Clinton's victory and our defeat. Just as history is turning in our direction, these forces wish to complete the New Right agenda. They wish to push organized labour out of any legitimate political role . . . If they succeed they would recreate the Social Democratic Party but this time it would be within rather than outside the Labour Party.'[22]

Blair stood his ground. 'I believe it should be one member, one vote. There should not be two classes of membership,' he told a television interviewer. 'We have block votes determining everything.

That's got to go.' He was insistent, however, that he was not arguing for a divorce between Labour and the unions. 'I don't believe that the Labour Party will ever sever its link with the trade unions, and I don't think it should do so. What I do think is necessary, however, is that the Labour Party is able and confident when it addresses people at the next election to say: "We are a party that is addressing the entire country and we will form our policies and govern on the basis of the interests of the entire country."'[23] (He subsequently told *Tribune* that he did not envisage the unions losing their position on constituency party general committees: 'Of course unions will maintain a role there and on the NEC.')[24]

Largely because of Blair's obstruction of 'registered supporters', the review group eventually produced an interim report in February 1993 merely setting out options, which was then sent out to parties and unions for consultation.[25] To the disappointment of Blair and Gordon Brown, John Smith compromised with the unions on leadership elections, agreeing to a reform of the electoral college that gave a third of the votes to unions, a third to MPs and MEPs and a third to individual members, with each section working on an OMOV basis. This was passed by the Labour conference in Brighton that autumn by a massive majority.

On parliamentary selections, though, nothing seemed to break the stalemate. Smith threw his support behind a compromise scheme developed by John Prescott and Tom Sawyer (and supported by Blair and Brown) for allowing trade unionists who paid the political levy to become full members for a nominal membership fee, known as 'levy-plus'. But the TGWU, the GMB, MSF and several smaller unions refused to budge – even after Smith went out of his way to get them on board, declaring at the TUC congress that 'full employment remains at the heart of Labour strategy' and making it known that he would resign if he did not get his way. Even at the beginning of the Labour conference, it looked likely that OMOV for parliamentary selections would be defeated. It won the day only after the MSF delegation at the conference decided at the last minute on a 19–17 vote to abstain rather than oppose and John Prescott delivered an emotional and famously ungrammatical speech arguing for Smith's favoured option.

It was great political theatre – and the changes pushed through by Smith undoubtedly made a difference to Labour. The new system for leadership elections made it impossible for the party's enemies to question the democratic legitimacy of its most important internal elections. Never again could trade union leaders bounce the party into accepting their choice for Labour's top two jobs. OMOV in parliamentary selections meant that unions, or indeed any other organized group, would find it much more difficult to control certain seats through their political machines. The reduction of the block vote at Labour conference to 70 per cent, with an option of a further reduction to not less than 50 per cent once individual membership reached 300,000, was a long-overdue diminution of the union delegations' dominance.

But it would be wrong to exaggerate the implications of the constitutional reforms that were passed at the 1993 Labour conference. Blair would almost certainly have won the leadership election in 1994 under the old rules, simply because most unions would have opted for the candidate most likely to win the next election. More important in the longer term, even though the new system for leadership elections cannot so easily be attacked for being undemocratic, it shares the old system's other major weaknesses. Because the franchise is wider than the Parliamentary Labour Party, it is still possible that Labour could end up with a leader who is backed by the party in the country but not by the PLP; and the procedure is far too unwieldy to be used to change leader in a hurry. Dropping a leader who has become an electoral liability, as the Tories ditched Edward Heath and Margaret Thatcher, is no easier than it was between 1981 and 1993. That is not a problem now – but it might be four years or eight years hence.

As for OMOV in parliamentary selections, its practical effect so far is arguable. Partly because Labour Party members have not generally wanted to replace sitting MPs, partly because of the obstacles to deselection imposed by Kinnock, only one sitting MP – David Young in Bolton South East – lost a selection contest in a seat unaffected by boundary changes in the pre-1997 round of selections. What was most noticeable about the candidates selected to replace retiring MPs, and in Labour's 1997 target seats generally, was the preponderance of people with strong local links, particularly council leaders – which was precisely the same common feature in the equivalent group before 1992. Of the 178 Labour MPs first elected in 1997, 120 are former councillors. On the other hand, OMOV has reduced the ability of unions to get their people selected, which is one reason that the 1997 intake contains so few manual workers. Politically, the Labour MPs elected for the first time in 1997 are overwhelmingly leadership loyalists, but that cannot be put down to the system used to select them as candidates except where they were imposed.

The reduction of the block vote at the party conference has similarly made less of an impression than the party leadership claims – even though it was cut to 50 per cent, on Blair's insistence, in 1995, as soon as individual party membership reached 300,000 and not gradually as the unions had wanted.[26] The big four unions, the TGWU, Unison, the GMB and the AEEU, still commanded nearly a third of the total vote at the 1996 conference.

How long Labour's 1993 internal settlement will last is a moot point. Since Blair became leader in 1994, he has consistently hinted that a divorce between unions and party is just a matter of time. 'Trade unions will have no special or privileged place within the Labour Party,' he declared just before being elected.[27] 'It is in the unions' best interests not to be associated merely with one party. The influence of the trade unions will come from being a broad voice of working people, not a direct party political voice or one that is concerned for the narrow interest of individual unions,' he wrote in the *New Statesman* a few months later.[28] 'Nobody believes in this day and age that the business of the Labour Party is to be the political arm of the trade union movement,' he told the *Observer* in autumn 1995.[29]

Blair did little that actually changed the party's constitutional relationship with the unions before the 1997 election. He discontinued the practice of unions sponsoring individual MPs, replacing it with a system for union funding of parties in target seats, and he caused a stir by bouncing the unions into accepting a plebiscite of the membership on the draft manifesto in 1996.[30]

But there were all sorts of hints that Blair would move to ditch the party–union link. Elimination of the block vote was one of the proposals in the memorandum by Blair's adviser Philip Gould that the *Guardian* splashed on its front page during TUC congress week in 1995; and the idea of changing the membership of the NEC was discussed by the 'Party into Power' exercise set up by Tom Sawyer as general secretary in 1995. Sawyer made it clear that he envisaged a radical dilution of trade union representation on the party's ruling body, which itself would have a much smaller policy role.[31] The clearest indication of what might be in store came during the week of the TUC congress in September 1996 from one of the Labour leader's closest political allies, Stephen Byers, the MP for Wallsend and a junior employment spokesman. Over Dover sole and Muscadet at the Seafood restaurant in Blackpool, he told four journalists that Blair might hold a plebiscite of Labour members on whether they wanted to retain the union link, possibly within weeks of winning a general election. If the vote went Blair's way, he said, he would force a divorce through the party conference on the back of it. As Byers had intended, the story duly appeared in the papers without any reference to him – the conversation was on lobby terms – but a Blair aide blew his cover, forcing him to issue a wholly unconvincing denial.[32]

Meanwhile, Blair went out of his way as leader of the opposition to distance himself from the unions on policy. The unions, he told Jimmy Young on the day of his election as leader, could expect 'fairness not favours' from a Labour government. As he explained in an interview with the *New Statesman*: 'The old relationship didn't do either of us much good. The new relationship should be one in which the unions take their place as part of a healthy, democratic society and are treated fairly in terms of legislation at the workplace . . . It's quite absurd that the unions have been cast out as if they were an alien part of British society. But it's also important for the Labour Party to make clear it represents the governing interests of the whole country.'[33]

Thus he repeatedly rejected union calls for a return to the tripartite negotiating bodies of the 1970s and successfully faced down every attempt to get Labour to agree to a figure for its promised minimum wage before the election. He pushed through his new Clause Four against the opposition of several unions that felt – rightly as it turned out – that it would presage abandonment of Labour's promises of renationalization of the water companies and the railways. The spring 1996 policy document that formed the basis for the employment policies in the 1997 manifesto, *Building Prosperity*, largely drawn up by Stephen Byers, committed Labour to a 'flexible' labour market, drawing back from the party's previous promise of full protection from unfair dismissal from an employee's first day at work and ruling out any change in the law governing strike ballots.[34] During the 1996 tube drivers' dispute, Blair got David Blunkett to float the idea of binding arbitration to prevent public sector strikes – a proposal firmed up a couple of months later and supplemented with a suggestion of compulsory re-balloting of striking union members if their employer makes a significant new offer.[35]

For its statutory recognition procedure, Labour eventually adopted a version of the cumbersome and employer-friendly American system, whereby more than half the 'relevant' workers in a workplace would have to sign a declaration that they wanted a union to represent them and then would have to go through a complex arbitration and voting procedure if an employer refused their demand before the union won recognition.[36] As for the Social Chapter of the Maastricht Treaty, which introduced qualified majority voting in the Council of Ministers on certain aspects of employment law, Blair made it clear from late 1995 onwards that Labour would not necessarily accept everything agreed through it. 'We will not impose the so-called German or European model of social and employment costs,' he said at the start of the election campaign. 'If there is any attempt to impose costs through the European Social Chapter, we will resist it, if necessary by veto, though there is no evidence that any such move is contemplated.'[36]

Labour's 1997 manifesto was lighter on commitments to union rights than any previous one. Blair summed it up perfectly in an article in the *Daily Mail* five weeks before polling day: 'Even after the changes the Labour Party is proposing in this area, Britain will remain with the most restrictive trade union laws anywhere in the western world.'[38]

Of the union leaders, John Monks, who succeeded Norman Willis as TUC general secretary in 1993 and immediately set about transforming the TUC's creaking bureaucracy into a media-friendly machine, was generally supportive of Blair. He made it clear that he could live with – and see the advantages for both sides of – an end to the union–Labour link. He backed Blair's line on 'fairness and favours' and acted as a behind-the-scenes power-broker to minimize union–party conflict.[39] In February 1997, the TUC produced a document on future relations with a Labour government which called for an increase in 'conciliation, mediation and arbitration to ensure that industrial disputes and the risk to the public are minimised' and was welcomed warmly by Blair.[40]

But the general secretaries of the three biggest unions, John Edmonds of the GMB, Bill Morris of the TGWU and Rodney Bickerstaffe of Unison, were hostile to Blair's whole 'project' – except when it came to electing a Labour government – and they clashed time and again both in private in the Contact Group and in public. Blair responded in kind. Soon after Clause Four was changed, the Labour leader was reported as remarking: 'If Labour loses the next election, it will be the fault of Bill Morris, John Edmonds and Rodney Bickerstaffe.'[41] It was an open secret that Blair supported the challenge by Jack Dromey, the husband of Harriet Harman, for Morris's job in spring 1995.

What now? There are plenty of problems ahead for the unions' relations with the Blair government, most obviously public sector pay and the minimum wage, although there is also likely to be friction at some point over Labour's promised employment rights legislation and the impact of the Social Chapter.

The difficulty with public sector pay is simple. Public sector workers, who are still overwhelmingly unionized (70 per cent of them are in unions, compared with less than 30 per cent in the private sector), have fallen behind their counterparts in the private sector and many have not had an increase for some time as a result of constraints on public spending. They think Labour should do something about it, but Labour came to power com-mitted to spending plans inherited from the Tories – which means no big increases. Unison, the TGWU and the GMB have negotiated a long-term pay and conditions deal with the local authorities, and the hope is that it will lead to industrial peace. But there can be no guarantee that it will stick, and if it doesn't there could be trouble for the Labour government. Equally important, it doesn't cover education or the health service, where dissatisfaction over pay and conditions is rife.

As for the minimum wage, the plan is that the independent Low Pay Commission led by George Bain will set it 'sensibly' and 'according to the economic circumstances of the time'. The lower the minimum wage, the less happy the union leaders will be and the more likely industrial action will be. Nor will the unions be pleased if the employment rights legislation is weak or if Labour refuses to sign up to measures they want under the Social Chapter.

Yet it would be foolish to exaggerate the dangers to Labour from industrial militancy. Despite the fall in unemployment since 1992, there were still more than 1.6 million people out of work in May 1997 and employees of all kinds feel insecure. (It is also likely that unemployment will rise again sooner rather than later as the Tories' pre-election boom peters out.) The unions are weaker than at any time in fifty years. They still face most of the restrictions on strikes inherited from the Tories, and they are still losing members – total union membership was down to eight million in 1996. Many are in dire straits financially. In small enterprises and in sunrise industries their position is more precarious than ever. And however unhappy they become with the Labour government, few union leaders will want a return to Tory rule, if only because of Labour's promised statutory recognition procedure. All in all, there is little prospect of what Blair calls 'a return to the 1970s'.[42]

As for the formal link between the unions and the party, all the unions suspect that Blair would like a divorce. This could be mutually beneficial. If accompanied by an overhaul of Labour's decision-making procedures to involve members in more than occasionial plebiscites, it could make the party a much more democratic organization. For the unions, it would liberate a large amount of money for other purposes, and would free them from the constraints imposed by the need to appear loyal to Labour.

The idea that it would necessarily make Labour more right-wing or less responsive to working-class interests is nonsense: Labour today is no more left-wing or sensitive to the working class than any of its sister parties in continental Europe that have long since shed formal ties to the unions (if indeed they ever had them).

But there are also problems with a divorce. For a start, the unions themselves would have to agree to it (because of their dominance of the party conference) which they might not do – despite a growing sense that they would be better off outside Labour[43] – even if an overwhelming majority of Labour's individual members voted for it in a plebiscite. In the longer term, Labour without the unions would be deprived of the force for stabilization that prevented the collapse of the party in the 1930s and again in the 1980s. If at some point in the future Labour were to suffer another catastrophic defeat like 1931 or 1983 – a strange idea today, perhaps, but few would have predicted the Tories' 1997 collapse just after the 1983 election – it would find it much more difficult to pick itself up again without the financial and political resources of the trade unions behind it.

The biggest difficulty with party and unions going their separate ways, however, is that Labour remains dependent on the unions for money despite increased revenue from membership subscriptions and donations after Blair became leader. In 1995, union affiliation fees accounted for 54 per cent of the party's £12.5 million income, and that does not include various hidden subsidies.[44] Of course, the unions could still give money if they had no constitutional link with Labour, but it is unlikely that they would hand over as much.

Labour could plug the gap by introducing state funding of political parties. But that is politically difficult for the simple reason that it would involve taxation. The alternative is raising more money from individual and corporate donors, particularly the latter. It might just work. Labour is better placed than ever before to get its snout in the corporate trough. It has dropped any remaining vestiges of unfriendliness to business, and now has suitors queuing up for favours in every commercial sector. It also has a network of former apparatchiks who have taken to selling their services in the lobbying world.

But the dangers of going down this path are obvious. Money is a powerful agent of influence – and no one has yet invented a way of making wholly transparent the relationship between political donor and political party. This applies, of course, to union funding as well as to any other sort. But at least union cash exerts its influence on Labour mainly in the interests of the have-nots rather than the haves, and it does so in ways that are easy to track and to counter if necessary. Even with the most rigorous regulatory framework, corporate and individual donations are by their nature much murkier. If the choice is between being in the pockets of the trade unions or in those of, say, Rupert Murdoch, the Israel lobby and British Aerospace, the former is infinitely preferable. Labour is a long way from becoming a corrupt creature of business interests like the US Democrats or the Italian Socialist Party under Bettino Craxi – and it should resist the temptation to become one.

10

DETERRENCE FOREVER?
NEW LABOUR AND DEFENCE

It is a measure of Labour's enduring touchiness on defence policy that the launch of the government's 'strategic defence review' – less than a month after Tony Blair won his massive landslide – had the air of a damage-limitation exercise.

The defence secretary, George Robertson, chose to announce his plans on the day after Boris Yeltsin, Bill Clinton, Blair and the other leaders of European North Atlantic Treaty Organization (NATO) countries met in Paris to sign the agreement between Russia and NATO that will allow the Atlantic alliance to expand eastwards. The next day, Clinton was due in London to address the cabinet at Number Ten Downing Street. The timing could not have been better. The seemingly spectacular breakthrough in East–West relations lent credibility to Labour's case for re-examining Britain's defence needs and the role of the armed forces. And with the Anglo-American 'special relationship' so obviously flowering, who could claim that Labour's plans would threaten the Atlantic alliance?

Yet Robertson was strangely subdued when he appeared at his press conference at the Ministry of Defence with the chief of general staff, General Sir Charles Guthrie. His message was one of reassurance to anyone who might still think that the review would run down Britain's defences. 'Since the end of the Cold War, the security risks to the United Kingdom have changed fundamentally,' he said. 'We no longer face a threat of general war in Europe. But new security challenges confront us, including the proliferation of weapons of mass destruction, aggressive nationalism and international terrorism. We must ensure that Britain is ready to face those challenges.'

He promised that the review would not bring into question British membership of NATO or the continued existence of Britain's 'independent deterrent'. Nor would it be 'driven by the Treasury'. 'I don't think it is realistic to say that, in the present strategic circumstances, defence spending is going to increase,' he said, but went on, 'What we have to do is to work out how best to spend what it is we are spending at the moment.' Moreover, there would be no moratorium on military procurement decisions; and Britain would retain a capability for 'high intensity' warfare. 'It is sometimes only if you have got a capability of fighting a high-intensity war that you are able then to deal with the peacekeeping tasks we get involved with . . . I was in Bosnia last week and it's some of the heavy armour we deployed in Bosnia that stopped the fighting from going on in that country.' To reinforce the point that Labour was really not planning to do anything rash, Robertson suggested that the review provided 'a unique opportunity to produce a non-partisan approach to Britain's defence in the next century'.

Nicholas Soames, formerly armed forces minister in John Major's Tory government, was quick to denounce the review as a smokescreen for spending cuts, and the Campaign for Nuclear Disarmament (CND) issued a statement decrying the failure of the review to deal with nuclear weapons policy – but otherwise the response was muted. Even the *Daily Telegraph* could not bring itself to condemn Robertson's announcement, confining its grumbling to his remark that military spending was unlikely to increase.

To understand Labour's sensitivity on defence, it is necessary to revisit the mess Labour made of the breakdown of East–West *détente* in the late 1970s and early 1980s. From the late 1940s until then, defence and security policy had been fairly simple for Labour. The party's leaders were committed Atlanticists, seeing NATO, underwritten by the American promise to use nuclear weapons against a Soviet attack on Western Europe, as the cornerstone of Britain's defence policy; and they were in favour of Britain remaining a substantial military power itself with its own nuclear weapons. NATO was the brainchild of the Labour foreign secretary between 1945 and 1951, Ernest Bevin, and it was the Attlee government that made the decision, in secret, to proceed with the British bomb. The 1964–70 Wilson government went ahead with the Polaris submarine-launched ballistic missile programme that it inherited from the Tories (although it built four rather than five boats to carry the American missiles with their British warheads).[1] While both 1945–51 and 1966–70 governments oversaw substantial reductions in Britain's overseas military commitments (the former by withdrawing from India, the latter by closing UK bases 'East of Suez'), both resisted cuts in military spending any larger than were strictly necessary on economic grounds.

In all this, the party leadership had the unswerving loyalty of the overwhelming majority of Labour MPs and (until the early 1970s) the party's National Executive Committee. The party's ordinary members were less enthusiastic about Atlanticism, nuclear weapons and defence spending, and on occasion their views prevailed at the party conference, most famously in 1960, when it voted narrowly against Hugh Gaitskell and the leadership for unilateral nuclear disarmament.[2] There were also intermittent back-bench rebellions on defence and security questions, notably on military spending, which remained much higher in Britain as a proportion of GDP than in most continental European countries even after the withdrawal 'East of Suez'. But even the 1960 conference vote, at the height of CND's first wave, was easily overturned the next year, and none of the back-bench rebellions caused a government defeat in the Commons.

From 1970, however, the NEC swung sharply to the left, and from 1974 there were growing tensions between its thinking on defence – broadly speaking, that in a period of *détente*, military spending should be cut and the nuclear arms race stopped – and the actions of the Wilson and Callaghan governments. Both Labour's 1974 election manifestos promised a reduction of British defence spending to the European NATO average; and the October 1974 manifesto pledged not to replace Polaris. In the next couple of years, a defence study group set up by the NEC developed detailed plans for radical reductions in defence spending, published in 1977 as *Sense About Defence*.[3] The government took no notice. In 1974, without any publicity, let alone public discussion, it approved a programme for upgrading Polaris to Chevaline, a decision that was only made public in 1980. In 1976, it decided to let the US deploy nuclear-armed F-111 bombers in the UK; in 1977 it announced an increase in defence spending from 1979; and in 1978, it agreed in principle (again in secret) to NATO's plans to modernize American long-range theatre nuclear weapons in Europe. Early in 1979, prime minister Jim Callaghan discussed with US president Jimmy Carter – secretly, of course – the possibility of replacing Polaris with a new American submarine-launched missile system.[4]

It was not until some months after Labour lost the 1979 general election that the party's differences over defence really caught fire. The immediate cause was NATO's announcement on 12 December 1979 of the decision to station new American intermediate-range nuclear force (INF) missiles – cruise and Pershing 2 – in Europe. The publicly stated reason was to balance Soviet deployments of SS20 missiles; in fact, the decision was essentially a matter of the US reassuring jittery West European governments that it was serious about maintaining its nuclear guarantee to Europe. Of the 516 missiles scheduled for deployment, 160 cruise were to be deployed in Britain. Within a fortnight of the announcement, the Soviet Union had invaded Afghanistan; and a few weeks after that a television programme revealed that the government was planning to publish a pamphlet giving advice on what to do in the event of a nuclear attack, *Protect and Survive*. The spectre of nuclear war had returned to haunt Europe.

Protest groups sprang up throughout Britain, and CND, which in the mid-1970s had dwindled to some 4,000 members, enjoyed a burst of growth. Many of the recruits to the new movement were persuaded by the historian Edward Thompson's pamphlet *Protest and Survive*, an excoriating polemic against NATO's INF 'modernization' and for a nuclear-weapons-free Europe, published in spring 1980 and an instant bestseller.[5] Thompson was also the main author of the *Appeal for European Nuclear Disarmament*, published around the same time, which became a rallying point for movements against nuclear weapons throughout western Europe as well as the basis for the European Nuclear Disarmament organization in Britain.[6] The left majority on the Labour NEC responded to the upsurge in protest by getting the party to call a demonstration against the new missiles in London in June: more than 20,000 people turned out. The protest movement was given further momentum by events during the summer. At home, the government announced that it would buy the American Trident submarine-launched nuclear missile system to replace Polaris: abroad, it became clear that Ronald Reagan, an inveterate cold warrior, would be the next US president. In October, the Labour conference voted for a non-nuclear defence policy. A few weeks later, CND's London rally, its first national demonstration for years, attracted some 80,000 people.

The rapid growth of opposition to cruise and Trident inside the Labour Party played a major role in prompting the defection of the 'Gang of Four' – Roy Jenkins, David Owen, Shirley Williams and William Rodgers – to form the Social Democratic Party in early 1981. The founders of the SDP were united by hatred of Labour's left-wing activists and enthusiasm for the European Community, but their strongest mutual link was their unstinting Atlanticist pro-nuclear stance on defence.[7] It was not that they were particularly keen on cruise and Trident: in fact, they were divided over the new NATO INF deployments (Rodgers, the Labour defence spokesman in 1979–80, backed the 1979 decision, but Owen was initially against it) and unconvinced by the case for Trident.[8] But they were keen supporters of the American nuclear guarantee to Europe, and were not prepared to put the unity of NATO in jeopardy. They were also implacably opposed to unilateral nuclear disarmament by Britain. Their case against Trident was simply that it was too expensive a way of retaining Britain's status as a nuclear power: opposing

Trident did not mean backing the unilateral decommissioning of Polaris.

Denis Healey argues in his autobiography that such sentiments were perfectly consistent with Labour policy until after the 1983 general election – and in a way they were. Labour did not officially back unilateral abandonment of Polaris until late 1983. But to the Gang of Four, as to many Labour Atlanticists, it seemed, by the time of the 1980 party conference, that Labour's drift towards the unspeakable heresies of unilateralism and neutralism had become unstoppable. The final straw was the Parliamentary Labour Party's election of Michael Foot as leader in preference to Healey in early November 1980. Foot was a veteran critic of Atlanticism and of nuclear arms: back in 1947, before the creation of NATO, he had been one of the authors of a seminal Labour left pamphlet arguing against an alliance with America,[9] and in the 1950s he had been CND's most outspoken advocate in Labour's ranks. Less than a fortnight before being elected leader, he had been one of the main speakers at CND's giant rally in London.[10] The plan to form the SDP was finalized within weeks of his taking office.

Atlanticists remained in a majority in the shadow cabinet even after the creation of the SDP, and Healey, the most senior of them, was appointed shadow foreign secretary by Foot. (His deputy from 1982 was George Robertson, then the thrusting young star of the Labour right in Scotland, who had made a name for himself as an outspoken opponent of unilateralism.[11]) But Atlanticist influence was substantially reduced by defections to the SDP,[12] and Healey was in no position to impose his authority. No sooner had the Gang of Four finally gone in spring 1981 than Tony Benn announced that he would challenge Healey for the deputy leadership – an election that would take place under new rules, agreed in early 1981, which for the first time gave the trade unions and constituency Labour parties a role in electing Labour's leader. During the spring and summer of 1981, Labour was torn apart by a bloody contest that Healey eventually won by the narrowest of margins. Remarkably, Foot and Healey found time in September to visit Moscow, where they were told by Leonid Brezhnev that the Soviet Union would be prepared to reduce its own INF missiles in Europe – the SS20s – if the US agreed not to deploy cruise and Pershing.[13] With superpower arms control talks by now in deadlock, it might have been an avenue worth exploring, but when they got home they were simply lampooned for *naiveté* by the press and the Tories.

There was a lull in Labour's civil war after the deputy leadership contest, but it lasted only a few months – and defence and foreign policy again played a part once combat resumed. This time the cause for dispute was not nuclear arms and East–West relations (by now in a dire state after the declaration of martial law in Poland in December 1981) but an event in one of the few remaining British colonies: the Argentinian invasion of the Falklands in April 1982. Foot saw the invasion as 'an act of naked, unqualified aggression, carried out in the most shameful and disreputable circumstances',[14] and immediately endorsed the Thatcher Government's decision to send a task force to recover the islands, while supporting diplomatic efforts to secure an Argentinian withdrawal. Many on the left disagreed, arguing that the government was spending vast sums of money and risking massive casualties for the sake of a handful of sheep farmers. Foot's old newspaper *Tribune*, where Chris Mullin, a member of Benn's inner circle, took over as editor the week after the sinking of the Argentine cruiser *Belgrano*, turned on the Labour leader with a vengeance. In a Commons debate on 20 May, thirty-three Labour MPs defied the whips' instructions to abstain and voted against the government.

Labour's Falklands controversy died down after the comprehensive British victory, but it was followed by further internal rows, the cumulative effect of which was to divert the party leadership from preparations for fighting the next election, while the 'Falklands factor' and the first signs of economic recovery turned the Tories' fortunes around in the opinion polls. Defence policy was one of the major casualties. It was left largely to the defence study group of the National Executive Committee, and because it couldn't agree on whether Polaris should be negotiated away or abandoned altogether, it failed to complete its deliberations before Thatcher called an election for 9 June 1983. Labour's manifesto tried to have it both ways, arguing on one hand that Polaris should 'be included in the nuclear disarmament negotiations in which Britain must take part' and on the other that Labour would 'after consultation, carry through in the lifetime of the next parliament our non-nuclear defence policy.'[15] Unsurprisingly, the policy fell apart almost as soon as Foot and Healey were asked to expand upon what would happen to Polaris if negotiations were unsuccessful, with Foot saying that it would be scrapped and Healey saying that it would be kept. To make matters worse, Jim Callaghan made a speech in his constituency just a fortnight before polling day denouncing his party's disarmament policy. For Labour's already tottering campaign, it was the last straw. On election day, the party took just 27.6 per cent of the popular vote, its lowest share since 1918.

The Labour right was convinced that unilateralism was a major reason for the débâcle. According to Roy Hattersley, the right's candidate in the leadership contest that followed Foot's post-election resignation, 'Unilateral nuclear disarmament, getting rid of our nuclear weapons when other countries did not get rid of theirs, was the most unpopular policy on which the Labour Party has ever fought a general election.'[16] But it was the left's argument, that the problem was simply sheer confused thinking on defence, that prevailed. With the imminent arrival of cruise and relations between the superpowers in apparently ever-deepening crisis, the movement against nuclear weapons was now at the peak of its strength. Its leaders – Edward Thompson, Bruce Kent, Joan Ruddock – had become national political figures. Inside Labour, the mood was even more strongly unilateralist than before the election. Hattersley was easily defeated in the leadership election by Neil Kinnock, like Foot a long-time supporter of CND, who was determined to develop a clear and unambiguously non-nuclear defence policy. One of Kinnock's first acts as Labour leader was to speak at CND's 400,000-strong rally in Hyde Park on 24 October 1983, just days before the arrival of the first cruise missiles in Britain.

What eventually emerged from the NEC study group was the document *Defence and Security for Britain*, which was passed by Labour's 1984 conference. It promised that a Labour government would remove all US nuclear bases from British soil, decommission Polaris and cancel Trident. Britain under Labour would remain in NATO but work to change it from within, arguing for greater autonomy for the European 'pillar' of the alliance, a European nuclear-weapons-free zone and an end to NATO's strategy of 'flexible response', whereby a conventional Soviet attack on Western Europe would be met with the use of nuclear weapons. The ultimate goal was dissolution of both superpower-dominated blocs (at some unspecified time). On Britain's overall defence spending, the document recommended a reduction, particularly on the forces' 'out-of-area' (non-European) roles.

Defence and Security was without a doubt a vast improvement on the muddle that had preceded it. But it was by no means the last word on defence and foreign policy. It was short on detail in several areas, notably the level of military spending that a Labour government would sustain, and its foreign policy framework was underdeveloped. It skated over the fact that other members of NATO, particularly the US, would not take kindly to a Labour government trying to implement its non-nuclear policy. Worse, it did little to elaborate how Labour wanted NATO to change in pursuit of the goal of a bloc-free Europe, and said almost nothing about Labour's assessment of Soviet intentions.

This might not have mattered too much if the party had followed up the *Defence and Security* document by using its ideas as a springboard and making a concerted effort to persuade the public of the virtues of a radical new defence and foreign policy. Instead, Labour drifted listlessly. A document on military spending and the defence industry, *Defence Conversion and Costs*, was eventually produced by a policy committee in summer 1986 – and another committee beavered away on a new foreign policy framework that emphasized the role of disarmament in securing *détente*. But there was no attempt to mount any sort of campaign on defence, even after the 1985 party conference voted for one, and the work on making defence policy an element in a coherent strategy for ending the Cold War never saw the light of day. In both cases, a key factor was the influence of Peter Mandelson,

Labour's director of communications from late 1985. Mandelson was an orthodox Atlanticist right-winger who saw the non-nuclear defence policy as a liability: he even complained about Labour Party staff members wearing CND badges to work. If Labour was stuck with this policy, he believed the best thing to do was to give it as little publicity as possible. Failing that, the only way to sell it was to push the message that Labour was keen on strong conventional defence, a staunch supporter of NATO and a loyal ally of the US. Talk of dissolving the blocs would simply frighten the voters.

This approach would have been of dubious merit under any circumstances. The idea that Labour could get away with not mentioning defence was, as Robin Cook said at the time, almost breathtakingly short-sighted. So too was the notion that the non-nuclear policy could be made credible if Labour refused to question the assumption that the Soviet Union was bent on attacking Western Europe. What made Mandelson's tactics especially risible was that they placed a high priority on emphasizing Labour's loyalty to the Atlantic alliance just when the Tories were at their most vulnerable over Thatcher's fawning support for America in general and Ronald Reagan in particular. The cabinet spent much of 1985 arguing about the US president's pet Star Wars programme for a ballistic missile defence system – which Thatcher backed enthusiastically, to the horror of her foreign secretary, Geoffrey Howe, and most of the governments of NATO Europe.[17] In January 1986, Michael Heseltine walked out of the cabinet after Thatcher sabotaged his attempts to get a European consortium to take over the near-bankrupt helicopter company Westland rather than the US company Sikorski. And in April 1986, Thatcher allowed Reagan to launch a bombing raid on Libya using US F-111s based in Britain – a decision that was opposed by two-thirds of the British population.[18] Had Labour seized on all this to press home the case for a radical recasting of Britain's 'special relationship' with the US, at the very least it might have put the Tories on the defensive. Instead, it fluffed its chances, muting its attacks on the government for fear of appearing 'anti-American'.

In December 1986, jolted into action by grumbling by

activists and MPs, Labour finally launched a defence campaign, 'Modern Britain in a Modern World: The Power to Defend Our Country'. Largely formulated by Mandelson, it had nothing to say about changing the balance of power in NATO, nothing about the future of Europe or about the reasons for believing that the Soviet Union was not about to invade Western Europe. Instead, it faithfully followed the advice of the Shadow Communications Agency, Mandelson's advisory group of advertising executives, that Labour should become 'the party that puts the defence of Britain first: that believes in strong, stable, effective defence; that believes in spending more on the Royal Navy, the air force and the army; that is a staunch and committed member of NATO'.[19] According to one of the defence campaign leaflets, 'Cancelling the £10 billion Trident – half of it spent in America – will enable Labour to order more British defence equipment.' All of the publicity material for the campaign was liberally decorated with Union Jacks.

Unsurprisingly, this pitch proved completely unconvincing, and the campaign was rapidly abandoned.[20] Just about all that could be said in its favour was that it was not as embarrassing as Labour's next major defence policy set-piece, the visit by Kinnock and Healey to Reagan in March 1987. By now, in the wake of the October 1986 Reykjavik summit between Reagan and Gorbachev, the superpowers were negotiating seriously on what became the 1987 Intermediate Nuclear Forces treaty – the agreement that marked the beginning of the end of the Cold War – and Labour was prepared to soften its line on cruise as long as talks were in progress. But Reagan was not interested. The Labour pair were given a cursory meeting at which the president mistook Healey for the British ambassador.

Less than three months later, Labour was humiliated again – this time by the British electorate. On 11 June 1987, the party took 31.7 per cent of the vote, just four percentage points more than in 1983. Once again, the campaign was dominated by defence. The centrepiece of the Tories' last-week offensive was a poster bearing the slogan 'LABOUR'S DEFENCE POLICY' above a picture of a soldier with his hands up as if in surrender – a reminder of Kinnock's extraordinary statement in a television interview earlier in the campaign that his party's response to a Soviet invasion of Britain would be to 'make any occupation totally untenable'.

The non-nuclear policy was immediately blamed for the 1987 election defeat by many Labour-sympathetic journalists,[21] and several of its supporters, among them Joan Ruddock (newly elected as a Labour MP), were worried enough about the party leadership's intentions to spring to its defence. But there were few signs over the summer that there were any plans to ditch it. The Labour conference in Brighton in October voted overwhelmingly in favour of retaining the policy, and defence spokesman Denzil Davies appeared quite happy with that. 'There is no possibility that the Labour Party will go into the next election with a policy other than a non-nuclear defence policy,' he declared.[22]

The new shadow foreign secretary, Gerald Kaufman, who was appointed chair of the policy review group dealing with defence and foreign affairs, had different ideas – as indeed did Davies' deputy, Martin O'Neill. They saw the success of the super-power negotiations on INF, which concluded in December 1987 with an agreement to eliminate not just cruise, Pershing and the SS20s but all land-based nuclear missiles with a range of between 500 and 5,500 km, as giving Labour an excuse to drop the unilateral non-nuclear policy. In the new international climate, Labour could credibly say that Polaris and Trident, along with the US nuclear bases in Britain that would remain after the INF treaty took effect, would be bargained away. As Kaufman put it just before the treaty was signed: 'The unilateralist nature of our non-nuclear defence policy has been overtaken by other countries doing what in the past we would do alone if necessary.'[23]

Kinnock, to the surprise of many of his colleagues, was increasingly coming round to the same opinion, and from early 1988 set about getting Labour's policy changed. Unfortunately, his first attempts to get the ball rolling were singularly inept, not least because he didn't tell Davies what was going on. In May, after Kinnock was reported by the *Independent* as having told its senior editorial staff over lunch that he thought unilateralism was finished,[24] Davies responded by describing the report as 'a piece of

Tory journalistic fiction'. 'The policy remains the same as it was laid down by conference. We'll cancel Trident,' he told *Tribune*.[25] Kinnock pressed on regardless, telling a television interviewer a few weeks later: 'There is no need now for something-for-nothing unilateralism . . . The log-jam is broken.' Ten days later, Davies resigned by making a telephone call to the Press Association at dead of night complaining that he was being excluded from decision-making by the leader. Faced with uproar from unilateralists in the Parliamentary Labour Party, Kinnock backtracked, telling the *Independent* in an interview that, on Polaris and Trident, 'decommissioning is still our position'.[26] But the next month, Martin O'Neill, promoted to take Davies's place, caused further consternation by hinting that a change in the Labour policy on US bases was in the offing: 'The American bases would have to go eventually,' he told *Tribune*, 'but the methods by which they would be removed would vary from case to case.' A Labour government would have to 'negotiate a change in NATO strategy' so that the nuclear-armed F-111s based in Britain – the main US nuclear force that would remain in Britain after the INF Treaty took effect and at the time due to be fitted with new tactical air-to-surface nuclear missiles – were not simply moved to continental Europe.[27]

After this somewhat farcical mix-up, it was no surprise that Kinnock's attempt to get a motion through the party conference that year proposing multilateral and bilateral steps towards nuclear disarmament as well as unilateral ones was thrown out after a successful mobilization by the unilateralists. But it was clear that the days of the non-nuclear defence policy were numbered. In January 1989, at a Fabian Society weekend school in Oxford, O'Neill made it even clearer, heaping praise on a new Fabian pamphlet that opposed unilateral removal of the F-111s from Britain (arguing instead for a multilaterally negotiated withdrawal of battlefield nuclear weapons from Europe and revision of NATO's doctrine of 'flexible response') and raised the possibility of putting Polaris and Trident into negotiations.[28] 'The withdrawal of American nuclear facilities from Britain will not add to the safety of Europe or these islands if withdrawal simply means a transfer to Belgium or the Netherlands,' he proclaimed. As for Polaris, withdrawal of 'a relatively small number of ageing missiles . . . would not greatly enamour the British public'. The independent deterrent, he said, should be negotiated away, possibly in return for Soviet naval cuts or else in the second stage of the Strategic Arms Reduction Talks.

Two months later, after a trip to Moscow during which the Soviet authorities made it clear that they had no interest in a bilateral deal on British nuclear arms, Kaufman and O'Neill sat down to write the policy paper on defence for inclusion in the report of the policy review. What they came up with contained few surprises for anyone who had been following their pronouncements in the previous six months, but it was nevertheless a comprehensive revision of Labour's stance. Instead of decommissioning Polaris and cancelling Trident, a Labour government would build three rather than four Trident submarines and put British nuclear weapons into international negotiations. And it would back talks on NATO strategy and on short-range tactical nuclear weapons, opposing NATO's moves to 'modernize' them as compensation for the INF reductions.[29]

Kaufman and O'Neill did their best to keep the document under wraps – and they managed to prevent any substantial leak. But the Labour grapevine was soon buzzing with rumours of its contents, and substantial minorities of the shadow cabinet and of the NEC were furious at what they saw as an underhand attempt to bounce Labour into changing policy without adequate discussion. *Tribune* collected signatures for a 'Disarmament Appeal' in support of a non-nuclear defence policy, which it published in its issue of 31 March: the signatories included Margaret Beckett, David Blunkett, Jo Richardson, Joan Ruddock, Clare Short and Chris Smith. Six weeks later, however, the revolt had passed. After an emotional intervention from Kinnock repudiating unilateralism, the NEC voted by a large majority to endorse the document, rejecting Blunkett's attempt to amend it to include the option of unilateral disarmament measures if multilateralism failed to get results. 'There was not a gesture to the rest of us,' Blunkett told *Tribune* after the meeting, although Robin Cook, with Kinnock's agreement, successfully introduced an amendment to allow bilateral measures in the same circumstances.[30] Any unilateralist hopes that the party conference would overturn the NEC on the policy were dashed during the summer by the decision at the public-sector union NUPE's conference to abandon its own commitment to a non-nuclear defence policy. And at the beginning of October, the party conference duly backed Kinnock, rejecting unilateralism by 3.6 million votes to 2.4 million.

Even as Kinnock and Kaufman manoeuvred the change through the party, the 'new' policy – in fact a reversion to old-fashioned nuclear Atlanticism – looked remarkably inappropriate because of the extraordinary pace of events in Eastern Europe as Communist rule unwound. In June 1989 Poland held semi-democratic elections. A fortnight later, the funeral of Imre Nagy, the Hungarian reform-Communist leader who defied Moscow in 1956, was held in Budapest thirty-one years after his execution; 200,000 people turned up. In August, Tadeusz Mazowiecki became the first non-Communist Polish prime minister since the war. In September, Hungary opened its borders to allow East Europeans to travel to the West. Within six weeks, after Gorbachev had told the East German regime that he would not use Soviet troops to put down dissent in East Germany, a massive peaceful protest movement had toppled Erich Honecker and brought down the Berlin Wall. By mid-November, the revolution had spread to Czechoslovakia. By the end of the year, Communist Eastern Europe – and the Cold War – were things of the past.

So too was Labour's ability to think innovatively about defence and foreign policy. The party welcomed the democratic revolutions in the East of course, but the battle against the non-nuclear policy had stiffened the leadership's resolve to do nothing whatsoever that could be interpreted as being 'soft' on defence, regardless of its merits. That meant toeing the government line and not asking awkward questions. When the 1989 Labour conference voted for a reduction in British defence spending to the West European NATO average, Kaufman and Kinnock simply said that they would ignore the vote; and when NATO persisted with plans to modernize its short-range tactical nuclear weapons in Europe by introducing new air-to-surface missiles, O'Neill qualified Labour's hitherto unambiguous opposition.[31] The party had little of consequence to say about German unification or the future security structure of Europe except to insist that NATO should remain in place.[32]

The Labour leadership's determination to follow the government on defence had its first and only real test during the long armed stand-off and short war that followed Saddam Hussein's invasion of Kuwait in August 1990. Throughout, Kinnock and Kaufman gave unqualified support both to the government (first under Margaret Thatcher and then under John Major) and to the US-led anti-Saddam alliance, and in the end they felt their stance was vindicated by the success of the allied forces in liberating Kuwait. Which in a superficial way it was – although within weeks the allies' victory seemed rather less important than their failure to support the Shi'ia and Kurdish rebellions against Saddam by pushing on to Baghdad. Today, more than six years on, the failure to overthrow Saddam's murderous regime appears little short of criminally negligent.

From the start of the crisis right through to the final allied ground offensive, however, the problem in the eyes of many on the left was not that Kinnock and Kaufman were insufficiently critical of the limits of the allies' war aims: it was that their enthusiasm for appearing tough had blinded them to the dangers of war with Saddam. Until the ground fighting started, Iraq appeared a far more daunting military power than it actually turned out to be, and there was widespread concern that any attempt to retake Kuwait by force would result in unacceptably high casualties among civilians and troops on both sides, particularly if Saddam used his chemical weapons. For a smaller group on the hard left, the Labour leadership seemed to be sanctioning an imperialist adventure in defence of the interests of American oil companies.

Within a fortnight of the Iraqi invasion of Kuwait, CND, the Green Party, the Communist Party, various Trotskyist groups and the Campaign Group of Labour MPs set up a campaign against the war – the Committee to Stop War in the Gulf – and although it found few supporters in the PLP outside the hard left, it picked up significant backing from Labour's activists before foundering in sectarian bickering.[33] At the 1990 Labour conference, four-fifths of constituency Labour Party delegations voted for an anti-war resolution, which was defeated by the block votes of most of the big trade unions. As the autumn wore on and Saddam refused to back down despite the deployment of a massive multinational force in Saudi Arabia, the PLP became increasingly restive. A growing number of soft-left back-benchers joined the hard left in defying the leadership in Commons votes, while soft-left front-benchers – several of whom, including some shadow cabinet members, had for some time been meeting privately as the 'Supper Club' in a Whitehall pub room, with Clare Short as the main co-ordinator – tried to exert pressure on Kinnock behind the scenes, urging a more positive attitude towards various proposals for peaceful resolution of the crisis.[34]

The biggest parliamentary rebellion came on 15 January 1991, as the US ultimatum for Saddam to withdraw from Kuwait ran out. After a Commons debate on the Gulf, fifty-five Labour MPs voted against the government (including two junior front-benchers, John McFall and Maria Fyfe, who resigned their posts the next day) and thirty-one did not vote (including Tony Banks, David Blunkett, John Fraser, Joan Lestor, Joan Ruddock and Clare Short from the front bench). There were fewer rebels in the lobbies once 'Operation Desert Storm' began a couple of days later with the aerial bombardment of Iraq, but the soft left grew more and more uncomfortable as the assault continued. John Prescott in particular made it clear that he was prepared to back only limited allied war aims. By the beginning of the next month, Kinnock's attempts to hold the line were looking increasingly desperate. Then someone leaked the minutes of a Supper Club meeting to the press, and the appearance of a burgeoning anti-leadership conspiracy gave him the opportunity he needed to carpet his front-bench critics one by one. Clare Short resigned from her junior front-bench post in order to be able to speak her mind, and the rest agreed to keep quiet. The danger of a revolt finally melted away after the allied rout of Saddam's army between 24 and 28 February.

Kinnock was lucky: backing the government on the Gulf was a gamble that paid off, and the ease of the allied victory exposed many of the left's worries about military intervention as unfounded. But it was a gamble motivated by electoral considerations rather than a clear-headed assessment of the crisis and its implications. The Labour leadership had not carefully weighed up the risks of war against those of sticking to sanctions; nor had it thought long and hard about what it would mean for the main military powers of the West to continue to act as 'global policemen' in the 'New World Order'. It had simply clung to the government's coat-tails for fear of what might happen in the opinion polls if it did not.

Labour continued to toe the government line in the next major international crisis in which Britain became embroiled – the dis-integration of Yugoslavia and the subsequent war in Bosnia. This time, however, the line was very different. Instead of intervening to punish Serbian aggression – against Croatia in 1991–2 and against Bosnia between 1992 and 1995 – the government did everything in its power to avoid any military action.

By early 1991, it was clear that Slovenia and Croatia saw no place for themselves in a federal Yugoslavia dominated by Serbia (which was the aim of Serbian president Slobodan Milosevic) and were preparing to secede. Out of touch with what was happening, the British government failed to recognize Slovenia and Croatia when they declared independence in June 1991, and instead put its faith in increasingly desperate diplomatic efforts by the EC to hold Yugoslavia together, from late summer 1991 co-ordinated by Lord Carrington, the former British foreign secretary.[35]

These efforts came to nothing, largely because by October Milosevic had launched the Yugoslav People's Army (JNA) and local Serb paramilitaries in a full-scale war on Croatia to grab as much territory as possible for a rump federation run from Belgrade. In January 1992, on German insistence, the EC changed tack, belatedly recognizing Slovenia and Croatia. Milosevic then turned his attentions from Croatia to Bosnia-Herzegovina, moving columns of tanks and artillery into position ready for a takeover. The British government continued to insist that the problem was 'premature recognition'. On 1 March, those parts of Bosnia not under the control of local Serb paramilitaries voted almost unanimously for independence in a referendum; a little more than

a month later the JNA and the paramilitaries unleashed a co-
ordinated seizure of Bosnian territory, killing or expelling the
non-Serb population and beginning an artillery bombardment of
Sarajevo that soon turned into a full-blown siege.

The response of the British government, facing an imminent election, was to do nothing, despite the appeals of the
Bosnian government for help. As the Serbian forces continued
their ruthless programme of 'ethnic cleansing', ministers in
London talked of the conflict as a 'civil war' in which all sides were
guilty. It followed that the right course of action for the international community was not to aid Bosnian resistance to the Serb
aggression – whether with arms or through direct military intervention – but to get the 'warring factions' to stop fighting and
negotiate some mutually agreed division of territorial spoils.
While pursuing these diplomatic aims, Britain provided a handful
of troops to escort UN humanitarian aid convoys to the beleaguered Bosnians: their numbers were later increased to provide
human shields in besieged Bosnian enclaves – the so-called 'safe
areas' set up in 1993.

This remained the stance of the Major government throughout the war. Britain resisted every call to lift the UN arms embargo
on Bosnia, part of a 1991 blanket ban on arms sales to all the
republics of Yugoslavia that had little effect on Serbia because it
controlled the JNA's substantial armoury but which crippled the
Bosnian war effort. Almost as bad, Britain consistently opposed
NATO air strikes against Serbian military installations, agreeing to
them only under massive US pressure in 1994–5. And, perhaps
worst of all, it repeatedly supported plans to dismember Bosnia as
a means of securing peace. In 1992–3, the government gave its
blessing to the disastrous plan for 'cantonization' of Bosnia on
ethnic grounds, put together by Lord (David) Owen (who
replaced Carrington as EC negotiator in late 1992) and Cyrus
Vance (appointed as UN negotiator at the same time), the main
result of which was to encourage Bosnia's Croats to rise against the
Bosnian government to grab as much land for themselves as they
could. After the Vance–Owen plan was rejected by the Bosnian
Serbs, London backed Owen's equally hopeless plan for a three-
way partition of Bosnia, rewarding the Serbs with nearly all their

conquests, which he drew up with Thorvald Stoltenberg, the former Norwegian foreign minister who succeeded Vance in spring 1993. And after that it lent its support to a succession of other partitionist 'peace plans', culminating in the deal forced on the combatants by the US in late 1995, just as the Bosnian army, in alliance with Croatia, appeared to be on the verge of inflicting defeat on the Serbs.

And how did Labour position itself through all this? Jack Cunningham, appointed shadow foreign secretary in 1992, just as the Serbs' 'ethnic cleansing' crimes hit the headlines, distinguished himself in his two years in the post by his indolence, ignorance and slavish adherence to the British government line on Bosnia. David Clark, the shadow defence secretary throughout the Bosnia war, was no better.[36] As Sarajevo was slowly strangled, both were content to parrot platitudes about the immense complexity of the Bosnian crisis, the guilt of 'all sides' in the conflict, the dangers of allowing Bosnia to defend itself by lifting the arms embargo and the impossibility of any meaningful NATO military intervention. In the first critical year of the war, the only member of the shadow cabinet who took the case for military intervention in support of Bosnia at all seriously was Michael Meacher, who was then punished by being moved from his post as overseas development spokesman in the autumn 1993 shadow cabinet reshuffle. Two back-benchers, Calum MacDonald and Malcolm Wicks, were tireless in their efforts to change the party line, and they were supported by a small group of their colleagues[37] as well as by *Tribune* and the *New Statesman*. By far the most effective dissident from Labour's pro-government line, however, was Michael Foot, who at the age of eighty-two produced a remarkable pro-Bosnia film with his wife Jill Craigie.

If the Gulf and Bosnia were the most visible defence and foreign policy questions of the early 1990s, they were not the only ones. Despite Labour's abandonment of its non-nuclear stance in 1989, the Tories still believed that Labour was vulnerable on nuclear arms because it had not promised to keep them as long as anyone else had them, and from spring 1991, confident after the victory in the Gulf war, they went back on the offensive, accusing Kinnock and Kaufman of supporting nuclear disarmament by the back door.

True to form, Kinnock's first attempt to clarify the position confused the issue. 'We have at no stage . . . made a commitment to get rid of all nuclear weapons for as long as others have them,' he told a press conference in April 1991. In July, Kaufman had another try, writing in the *Guardian* that, under Labour, 'Britain would remain a participant' in nuclear arms reduction talks 'until they are successfully and finally concluded with an agreement by all thermo-nuclear powers completely to eliminate these weapons'. Journalists were briefed that this implied that a Labour government would indeed keep nuclear weapons as long as anyone else had them, and the next day Kinnock let it be known that he had allowed his CND membership to lapse. Bruce Kent described Kaufman's article as 'a final surrender to David Owen, Peter Jenkins, Robert Maxwell, Alf Garnett and all'; John Prescott and Clare Short publicly distanced themselves from Kaufman's remarks.[38] Any ambiguity about Labour's position was finally dispelled by Kinnock in early September, within days of the failed coup against Gorbachev that brought on the end of Communist rule in the Soviet Union, when he declared on television that 'we would retain the nuclear weapons right through the process of negotiation. So in other words there will be retention until the extermination of nuclear weapons.'[39]

Labour has stuck to this line on British nuclear arms ever since. The 1992 manifesto promised: 'Labour will retain Britain's nuclear capability, with the number of warheads no greater than the present total.' According to the party's most recent document on defence and foreign policy, *A Fresh Start for Britain: Labour's Strategy for Britain in the Modern World*, published in summer 1996, 'We will retain the British nuclear deterrent, Trident. When satisfied with verified progress towards our goal of the global elimination of nuclear weapons, we will ensure British nuclear weapons are included in such negotiations.'[40] The 1997 manifesto, *New Labour: Because Britain Deserves Better*, used an almost identical form of words.

Labour still has problems with nuclear arms. No one in the

party is at all clear why Trident is there except as a vague all-purpose warning to the world that Britain is not be messed about: the justifications for retaining it put forward by Labour defence and foreign affairs spokesmen are that most of the money has already been spent on building it and that it might come in useful in the Middle East. There is also still considerable resistance among party members to the pro-nuclear position: both the 1993 and 1994 Labour conferences voted to cancel Trident (although those in 1995 and 1996 backed the leadership).

Most important, perhaps, is that Tony Blair and his foreign secretary Robin Cook have rather different ideas as to what party policy will mean in practice. While Blair as leader of the opposition emphasized Labour's commitment to Britain remaining a nuclear weapons power – even declaring, when asked at the launch of the 1996 document whether he would 'press the button', that 'you have to envisage circumstances in which your nuclear deterrent can be used', Cook as shadow foreign secretary from 1994 developed an ambitious set of goals for international nuclear disarmament agreements. (They include a comprehensive test ban treaty; a rigorous and intrusive new regime for verifying stocks of nuclear weapons and the materials required to build them; a no-first-use treaty signed by all nuclear powers; and, ultimately, a world-wide ban on production and possession of nuclear weapons.) It is possible to imagine circumstances in which Cook's vigorous pursuit of disarmament agreements, particularly on nuclear testing and production of fissile materials, would create friction with the armed services and fierce arguments in the cabinet.

Nevertheless, nuclear arms should not cause the Labour government too much trouble in its first term. It is extremely unlikely that Blair will have to make a decision on whether or not to press the button; and it is equally improbable that international nuclear disarmament negotiations will reach the point at which a world-wide nuclear weapons ban is on the agenda. Few expect a revival of unilateralism either in the Labour Party or outside it. The main targets of the 1980s movement against nuclear arms, the US cruise bases, have been dismantled, and most other American nuclear weapons have been withdrawn from Britain.[41] CND is a shadow of its former self in numbers and influence, and it is difficult to imagine this changing unless there is a dramatic deterioration in international relations or an appalling accident involving Trident.

If Labour wins a second term in 2002, however, the nuclear issue could return to haunt it. Trident will be worn out some time in the early 2020s. Because of the time it takes to develop new weapons systems, a decision on whether to go ahead with a successor will have to be made – if there is no international agreement to ban nuclear weapons – between 2005 and 2010. It is impossible to predict what the world will be like then, but it is hard to believe that Labour's leaders will sanction a 'follow-on-to-Trident', let alone that they will get the backing of the party if they do.

In the meantime, however, just about everything else in British foreign and defence policy will need to be clarified by Labour in its first term, right down to the structure, function and size of Britain's armed forces. Since the end of the Cold War, the defence budget has been reduced substantially: it currently stands at around £22 billion a year – about 3 per cent of GDP, compared with an average of 4.5 per cent between 1985 and 1989 and a current European NATO average of 2.3 per cent. Since 1990, the number of regular non-civilian armed forces personnel has fallen from more than 300,000 to 220,000. But, as Labour has argued, the cuts have been haphazard and arbitrary: neither of the Tory government's studies on which they were based – 'Options for Change' in 1990 and 'Front Line First' in 1994 – explicitly addressed the crucial question of what Britain's armed forces are there for in the post-Cold War world.

Insofar as Britain's defence policy stance makes sense, it is on the assumption that Britain faces two potential threats – from a resurgent Russia and from maverick regimes in the Middle East. Without these twin dangers, there would be no justification for NATO, at least as it currently exists as a means of locking the United States into Europe's security structure; no justification for levels of military spending anywhere near those Britain now sustains; and little reason for maintaining the British intelligence bureaucracy. The threat of an attack from Russia is the only conceivable military rationale for retaining the British Army of the Rhine and an RAF presence in Germany (albeit both much reduced in size and with new roles), for going ahead with the European Fighter Aircraft or for backing the extension of NATO into East-Central Europe while excluding Russia. In a similar vein, there is no military justification for retaining the Royal Navy at its current size or for turning the British Army of the Rhine into the core of a NATO Rapid Reaction Force if there is unlikely to be any need for Britain to engage in 'power projection' in defence of western interests in the Middle East. The potential threat to such interests also provides a convenient pretext for Britain's arms sales to several of the region's more unsavoury regimes.

But do Britain or Western Europe as a whole *really* face these potential dangers – and if they do is the current defence policy stance the best way to deal with them? There are good reasons for scepticism. The case for believing that Russia could become a real threat to European security in the foreseeable future is extremely weak. Of course, despite Boris Yeltsin's promise at the signing of the Founding Act on Mutual Relations, Co-operation and Security in May 1997 that Russia would no longer target its nuclear missiles on NATO countries, Russia retains substantial nuclear and conventional arsenals, which it has been rather less willing to dismantle of late than in the early 1990s; and it is anything but politically stable. In the next few years, it could certainly find itself with an authoritarian government, possibly with strong backing from the military, that plays relentlessly on anti-western themes. But it is implausible to suggest that its armed forces will be in any state to threaten Europe for some time to come: the once mighty Red Army cannot even keep down a rebellious province these days: witness Chechnya. Equally important, there is a strong argument that the best way of ensuring that Russia does not turn nasty is not to treat it as an enemy but to engage in trust-building diplomacy – by negotiating verifiable disarmament agreements and by offering it help to become more democratic, perhaps even by inviting it to join NATO.

The argument for a major potential danger to Western Europe from the Middle East is only a little stronger. There are of course several regimes that thrive on anti-western rhetoric, but none is currently in a position to threaten the supply of oil on which Western Europe, and to a lesser extent the US, rely, let alone to pose a direct military threat (except possibly through terrorism). This might change at some point in the future, particularly if currently pro-western regimes are toppled by radical Islamist revolutions or if existing 'rogue' regimes – Libya, Iran, Iraq – develop or acquire long-range ballistic missiles and nuclear weapons.

But such an outcome is by no means as inevitable as western doom-mongers believe it to be. Nuclear weapons technology cannot be uninvented, but the capacity to build a bomb is not as easily acquired as fashionable opinion suggests. Iraq failed to do it despite fifteen years' effort and massive expenditure on a programme that in 1990 employed more than 20,000 – and today the international controls on the export of technology and materials necessary to build a bomb are much tougher than they were when Saddam's spending spree was at its height.[42] Strengthening the international testing and proliferation regimes could further reduce the likelihood of 'rogue' states acquiring nuclear arms. Similarly, ballistic missiles are not the easiest things to manufacture, let alone to import undetected, and their proliferation, too, could be limited by enforcing and strengthening existing international agreements. In other words, there's a strong case for arguing that the best way for the West to counter any putative threat from the Middle East is not preparing for military intervention but engaging in energetic arms-control diplomacy, particularly if it is reinforced by a move away from propping up corrupt pro-western oligarchies in much of the Arab world.

If indeed the threats to Western Europe from Russia and the Middle East are best prevented diplomatically rather than prepared for militarily, it obviously makes sense for Britain to pare down its defence budget further and reallocate what remains – for example, to provide emergency peace-keeping forces for the United Nations. It also makes sense for the US to reduce its commitment to NATO even more, which in turn means Europe taking more responsibility for its own security.

At the very least, this suggests that Labour's defence review has some fundamental questions that it ought to address. But recent history suggests that it is unlikely to do so. From 1992 to 1997, Labour had little to say about the future of NATO except to urge caution in enlargement eastwards until it became clear that Bill Clinton was insistent upon it. It embraced wholeheartedly the idea that there is a real threat to western interests in the Middle East – according to David Clark, the party's defence spokesman, 'from dictators who can actually cause damage on our civilized west'[43] – and backed NATO's every move to develop mobile 'rapid reaction' capabilities in the region. It also gave unstinting support to Britain's main arms procurement programmes, notably the European Fighter Aircraft, and made it clear to Britain's services chiefs that further cuts in defence spending were not on the agenda. Tony Blair summed up Labour's approach perfectly in an article in the *Daily Telegraph* in February 1997 in which he declared: 'My pledge to our armed forces is that we will offer a period of stability . . . We will keep to the spending plans already laid down for the next two years, which should provide the framework to allow sound planning.'[44]

In line with this conservatism, the idea that, at some time in the not too distant future, the United States might decide that the Europeans should look after their own security fills Labour with fear. Although the 1996 policy document backed greater European defence collaboration, including development of the West European Union as the European 'pillar' of NATO, it explicitly ruled out 'establishment of a European army or proposals to give the European Union a greater competence': the basis of the policy was wholly Atlanticist. Blair himself recognizes that 'the nature of our relationship with the US has changed' and has argued for the strengthening of the London–Paris–Bonn axis so that the US is able to deal with a more united European entity than at present.[45] But he yearns for the 'special relationship' with the US that Britain is supposed to have enjoyed in the days of Churchill and Roosevelt or Thatcher and Reagan. As he put it in a speech in New York: 'I see Britain's role today as an absolutely crucial one in helping further to strengthen and consolidate the relationship between the US and Europe . . . whatever new security arrangements are envisaged will need to be set firmly within the context of NATO . . . It is absurd to imagine that, for Britain, there is a choice to be made between the relationship with Europe and that with the US. On the contrary, the real value to the US of the British role in Europe lies in the influence we can and will exert to help keep Europe firmly linked to the US in defence, outward-looking, open to trade and investment.'[46]

Blair's inner circle is dominated by Atlanticist true believers, among them Jonathan Powell, Peter Mandelson, Roger Liddle and Philip Gould – Powell, a former diplomat in the British embassy in Washington, is especially fervent. All the new government's ministers at the MoD are notable for their pro-Americanism. 'If they weren't all bought up by the bloody CIA, they might as well have been,' as a not particularly left-wing cabinet cynic put it.

George Robertson, given the job of defence secretary after a lacklustre spell as shadow Scottish secretary, was in the early 1980s one of the most vigorous opponents of Labour's anti-nuclear defence policy as a junior spokesman on defence and then foreign affairs. He is a veteran of the British Atlantic Committee, a Foreign Office-funded pro-American pressure group, and he has a reputation for 'brown-nosing to the State Department', as a colleague put it. At least, though, Robertson has a record as a pro-European. John Gilbert, now with a peerage and the job of armed forces minister, is a relic of the old Labour anti-European Atlanticist right of the 1960s.[47] A junior defence minister in the 1974–9 Labour government – in which role he was a champion of NATO, increased military spending and upgrading Britain's nuclear forces – in the 1980s he was Labour's most consistent, and most consistently unpleasant, back-bench propagandist for NATO and nuclear arms, somehow hanging on to his position on the Commons defence select committee until 1987 despite his vocal repudiations of party policy. His appointment is a calculated snub to what remains of Labour's unilateralist lobby. Another member of the MoD ministerial team, John Spellar, for years the chief fixer for the right-wing electricians' union, was almost as vocal an opponent of unilateralism in the early 1980s.[48]

The problem that Blair, his inner circle and the ministers at the MoD do not appear to have recognized is that the special relationship is over, except in the field of intelligence. The Americans are leaving Europe, and they want a new set of arrangements with the continent as a whole – and that means, inevitably, that Britain's future dealings with the United States will be increasingly mediated through the European Union. If Britain can help along the process of European integration and make sure that the new Atlantic relationship is friendly and constructive, the Americans will of course be pleased. But the US political class is less susceptible than ever before this century to British charms. It believes on the whole that Germany is a far more important European partner than Britain – and that the Europeans should be paying for their own security. Even though Clinton is undoubtedly pleased to have seen the back of John Major and was quite happy to bask in the warm glow of Blair's electoral triumph when he visited London four weeks after the new government took office, he is not interested in giving Blair privileged treatment.

In the long run, a further gradual loosening of US–UK ties and the development of a far more European orientation to British security policy are inevitable. Eventually, a British government will have to develop a post-Atlanticist security policy along with its continental allies. Although foreign secretary Robin Cook has recognized this, the chances of Labour doing it in its first term appear slim indeed. Even Cook will not sanction the idea of the EU taking charge of European security policy.

The same difficulties with breaking with the *status quo* underlie Labour's approach to defence industrial policy. Again, it is not hard to see why: the British defence industry is a major export-earner and employer. Britain is currently the world's second-largest exporter of arms, selling some £5 billion-worth of kit last year, about 25 per cent of the world arms export market in cash terms. According to the most recent government statistics, 360,000 people in Britain are directly reliant on the defence industry for employment, about 2 per cent of the total number of people in work: according to the industry, the figure is much higher.

But these jobs come at a price. The 1979–97 Tory government's encouragement of arms exports left considerations of

morality behind. No one should need reminding of the scandal of
British sales of military equipment to Iraq, of the sleaze surrounding the massive (£15–20 billion) al-Yamamah arms-for-oil
deal with Saudi Arabia, or of the government's procrastination in
the face of evidence that Hawk aircraft supplied to Indonesia were
being used against the civilian population of East Timor. The
chances are, moreover, that the defence industry bonanza will not
last. Forty per cent of its £5 billion export earnings last year came
from the al-Yamamah deal with Saudi Arabia, which is now cutting back on its arms imports, and it is difficult to see where else
Britain can flog its wares. The world market for arms is declining
in the wake of the Cold War, and it is fiercely competitive. Much
of the equipment that British companies have on sale is more
expensive or technically inferior to its competitors – particularly
that on offer from the giant defence conglomerates in the US.

For the defence manufacturers, there is a simple remedy:
getting the government, or West European governments acting
together, to spend money on the development of new products
that can compete with the best available elsewhere. But even massive expenditure cannot guarantee success. Britain's biggest single
procurement project, the European Fighter Aircraft, currently
being developed with Germany, Italy and Spain, is set to cost a
total of £40 billion, at least £14 billion of which will come from
the British tax-payer. The programme, designed at the height of
the Cold War to produce a plane capable of matching the best
Soviet aircraft, is now nearly ten years behind schedule. American
fighters of equivalent performance are already in service and available to would-be purchasers at two-thirds of the likely price of the
EFA. On any rational assessment, the Eurofighter looks an extraordinary waste of money – even if it keeps 14,000 or so British
workers in jobs at British Aerospace, GEC and various smaller
subcontractors.

In opposition, Labour promised more stringent controls on
the arms trade. The 1997 manifesto included promises of bans on
'the import, export, transfer and manufacture of all forms of anti-
personnel landmines' and on exports of arms to countries that
might use them 'for internal repression or international aggression'. Yet the party was notably evasive on the sale of Hawks to

Indonesia and never objected to selling arms to the Saudis. Just three months before the 1997 general election Blair was quoted by a British Aerospace magazine as saying: 'Winning export orders is vital to the long-term success of Britain's defence industry. A Labour government will work with the industry to win export orders.'[49] As for the massive subsidies that the tax-payer has to fork out to sustain the arms manufacturers, Labour simply kept quiet, backing the European Fighter Aircraft without serious question. As Blair put it: 'Eurofighter will form the cornerstone of the RAF's capability as we enter the next century . . . we are committed to supporting the programme.'[50]

There is a powerful case for greater daring in government. Robin Cook started well, announcing a ban on the manufacture and export of landmines and promising in his Foreign Office mission statement to 'put human rights at the heart of our foreign policy'. 'We are going to press for a European Union code of conduct to make sure that if we say "No, this export is wrong", no other European company then takes up the contract,' he said.[51] But within a fortnight, junior defence minister John Reid was saying that there were 'exceptional circumstances' in which the landmines ban would not apply, while George Robertson was pleading with the German government not to pull out of the Eurofighter programme as it attempted to cut public spending to meet the convergence criteria for European economic and monetary union. When Cook announced the government's new criteria for allowing arms exports in late July 1997, he disappointed campaigners against the arms trade by refusing to backdate the measures to put a stop to sales of Hawks to Indonesia agreed by the Tories. The power over government exercised by the military industrial complex is not quite yet a thing of the past.

11

SPEAKING WITH ONE VOICE
PETER MANDELSON AND PARTY DISCIPLINE

On the face of it, members of Tony Blair's new cabinet should have had nothing but gratitude for Peter Mandelson after Labour's 1997 election victory. He had, after all, run an immensely professional campaign in which everything had gone better than the wildest optimist could have predicted.

Yet if there was one thing that dampened their euphoric mood the weekend after polling day it was Mandelson's announcement on the Sunday morning, before he was officially appointed as a minister, that he was getting a key role in the government. 'I am there to assist in the strategic implementation of our policies and to make sure that our programme is kept on track and moving forward and to ensure that these policies are effectively presented to the public and the party,' he told a television interviewer. Tony Blair wanted to 'create a strong centre in government, so that all its various arms and departments have a very clear direction, how they are going to form part of the overall picture, so that we can very rapidly start implementing and delivering what we stood for and what we pledged to the British people'.[1]

Mandelson's official rank was modest: minister without portfolio attached to the Cabinet Office, number two to the Chancellor of the Duchy of Lancaster, David Clark. But it soon became clear that his influence as minister co-ordinating 'the

strategic implementation of government policies and their effective presentation to the public' would be immense. Not only was
he given the job of chairing the daily meetings of a committee
responsible for dealing with government's overall public relations
efforts, he was appointed to more ministerial committees than
any of his colleagues apart from John Prescott, covering constitutional reform, London, home and social affairs, the environment,
local government, economic affairs, Europe, legislation, welfare to
work and food safety.

He had apparently landed exactly the role in government
that he had enjoyed in opposition – Blair's enforcer, supreme spin-
doctor and meddler-in-chief – with a job description he had partly
written himself. *The Blair Revolution*, the book he co-authored
with Roger Liddle in 1996, argued for a drastic centralisation of
power in the government, with the Cabinet Office playing the
key part both in co-ordination and in 'providing policy innovation
and actively promoting ideas to the various departments'.[2]

The majority of cabinet members, who had hoped that
Mandelson would be rewarded for his role in Labour's election
campaign with a departmental brief that kept him out of the way –
perhaps minister for the arts, which he had indicated he would be
happy to do – resigned themselves to having their lives made miserable again. Such was the resentment at his position that
ministerial colleagues could barely conceal their glee when he
was given responsibility for co-ordinating the millennium celebrations, a job they believed might just prove to be his downfall.

Mandelson first became a hate figure for many of Labour's senior
figures as the party's director of campaigns and communications
between 1985 and 1990. By the time he arrived in the Commons
as MP for Hartlepool in 1992, he had already built up a host of
enemies in the Parliamentary Labour Party and shadow cabinet.
They consoled themselves with the knowledge that, regardless of
the influence Mandelson had enjoyed in his former life at party
headquarters, as a new boy at Westminster he had to start afresh
on the bottom rung of the ladder. He did not languish there for
long, however. Barely two years later he had not only become the

highest flyer of the 1992 intake, but was credited with wielding more power and influence in the Labour Party than anyone bar Tony Blair himself.

Peter Benjamin Mandelson was born in London in 1953, into a comfortably off family: his father was advertising manager of the *Jewish Chronicle*, his mother a secretary. Home was in middle-class Hampstead Garden Suburb. It was also a Labour Party family, in more ways than one: Mandelson's parents were long-time active members, and his maternal grandfather was Herbert Morrison, former leader of the London County Council, home secretary in the wartime coalition government under Winston Churchill, then deputy prime minister and foreign secretary in Clement Attlee's government. Harold and Mary Wilson lived round the corner from the Mandelsons and were family friends – Peter and his older brother grew up with the Wilson children. Once Wilson became prime minister, he got to visit them in Downing Street.

While at Hendon County Grammar School, where he won the disapproval of his headmaster for helping to organize campaigns against the school's prefect system and plans for turning it into a comprehensive, Mandelson himself joined the party at the age of sixteen. He became active in the Labour Party Young Socialists, and after finishing his A-levels joined the Young Communist League. He did not stay long, but while he did he was sufficiently dedicated to sell the *Morning Star* outside Kilburn underground station and be an official steward of the YCL's 1971 congress.[3] He took a year out before university to do community work in Tanzania (teaching and working in a hospital) before returning to study philosophy, politics and economics at St Catherine's College, Oxford.

He was back in the Labour Party fold by this time and threw himself into university life, becoming president of its United Nations Association and a member of the executive of the Labour Club – two positions that allowed him to pursue his greatest interests, foreign affairs and Labour politics. On leaving Oxford he went to work for the British Youth Council – the British wing of the International Youth Council, which was headed by Charles Clarke, who Mandelson had already got to know while he was at university and Clarke was president of the National Union of Students. In 1978 he was elected to Lambeth council, where the Labour group was led by 'Red' Ted Knight. It was here that he acquired a lasting hatred of the far left and met Roger Liddle, a fellow councillor who led the SDP group in Lambeth. Meanwhile, following a spell as a researcher at the TUC, he landed a job as researcher to Albert Booth, Labour's transport spokesman after the defeat of Jim Callaghan's government in 1979. The man who interviewed him for the post was John Prescott, then a junior spokesman under Booth. Mandelson spent the next two years working for both of them.

In 1982 he left to work for LWT's *Weekend World*, first as a researcher and then as a producer. Here he made some of his most valuable contacts: John Birt, now director-general of the BBC; Samir Shah, now head of BBC news and current affairs; Greg Dyke, who became head of Pearson's television operations; and Barry Cox, still at LWT and one of Blair's wealthy backers. When Mandelson left LWT they remained good friends and went on to form part of a powerful network of media executives.

John Prescott used to joke privately that he owed the Labour Party an apology for introducing Mandelson to politics, for it was the future deputy Labour leader who in autumn 1985 secured his former charge the position of the party's director of campaigns and communications. Mandelson, about to turn thirty-two, was one of the shortlisted applicants for the newly created post. He had impressed members of the NEC with his influential contacts and his eagerness to improve the party's image and media operations. He was undoubtedly committed and energetic. Yet despite universal agreement that a turnaround in Labour's public presentation was sorely required, the new-fangled approach Mandelson appeared to promise was regarded with some suspicion. Prescott reassured hesitant NEC members that his ex-employee was a hard worker, dedicated, and the right man for the job. His advice tipped the balance in Mandelson's favour.

Even Mandelson's detractors acknowledge that, at the time, he was just what the party needed. Labour's communications, internal and external, were abysmal. The new director arrived at Walworth Road in the middle of the extensive shake-up of party headquarters that followed Labour's disastrous performance in the 1983 election. He immediately set about moulding his department along the lines he wanted. His old friend Charles Clarke was now Neil Kinnock's chief of staff (it was Clarke who had encouraged him to apply for the director's job), and it was not long before Mandelson had become one of the tight band of confidantes around the Labour leader. None of them, however, envisaged that he would soon be a key player in his own right. As a fellow-member of Kinnock's inner circle put it: 'I don't think anyone thought he would somehow come to great prominence. We thought, and so it proved, that he would be an effective professional in what was a moribund organization. Peter was the archetypal modernizer, and rightly so. He contributed a tremendous amount to the modernization of the public relations of the Labour Party.'[4]

But Mandelson himself made clear from the start that he saw his remit as extending beyond public relations. As he told the *Guardian* in a rare early interview following his appointment: 'Communications means throwing your net much wider than publicity. It means deciding what we say, how we say it, and which spokesmen and women we choose to say it.'[5]

One of his own first recruits into the 'charmed circle' around Kinnock was advertising executive Philip Gould. Commissioned by Mandelson, he produced a report on Labour's public relations proposing the creation of an outside body of floating professionals, volunteers sympathetic to the Labour cause, in the advertising and marketing field. The Shadow Communications Agency was soon up and running (see chapter 1). Volunteers in other fields were also recruited to discuss ways of improving the party's image. Mandelson set up a 'shadow press group', which acted as a small sub-group of the SCA. It consisted of Mandelson, Patricia Hewitt (the Labour leader's press secretary), and half-a-dozen journalists considered loyal to Kinnock – including Alastair Campbell (then with the *Daily Mirror*), John Lloyd (at the time editor of the *New Statesman*, a position Lloyd freely admitted Kinnock helped him to get), and Philip Whitehead (a television journalist who had been MP for Derby North between 1970 and 1983).

As would soon become characteristic of the group's way of

working, it met in secret and even senior colleagues in other departments did not know of its existence. Formal party processes and the NEC – Mandelson's ostensible employer – were obstacles to the group's effectiveness. They were, however, easily bypassed because of his good relations with Clarke and Kinnock, and it was soon apparent that he saw his role as working for the leader as opposed to the party. While senior elected politicians played some part in the SCA, their presence was relatively transient whereas Mandelson, Gould, Clarke and Hewitt were constantly present and so formed its core. This soon led to resentment and accusations that marketing men, PR razzmatazz and packaging Neil Kinnock were being given a higher priority than popularizing the party's policies.

Particularly after the 1987 election, soft left figures in the shadow cabinet – notably Prescott, Bryan Gould, Robin Cook and Michael Meacher – found themselves increasingly marginalized as Mandelson and his friends promoted their own political allies (most prominently Gordon Brown and Tony Blair) as Labour's key television performers. In addition, unattributed stories by Westminster correspondents that rubbished those same soft-left figures began to appear in the newspapers. Inevitably, it filtered back from journalists in the Lobby to the politicians concerned that the 'briefings' were coming from sources close to Mandelson, and faithfully reflected Kinnock's views. As Mandelson himself would later acknowledge, he was fulfilling 'my . . . role as Neil Kinnock's mouthpiece'.[6]

At first, few people realized what Mandelson was up to. Another member of the small group of individuals at the top of the party who were trusted by Kinnock gives a revealing account of how even those who worked closely with Mandelson became aware of his aggressive 'spin-doctoring' activities only once they were well underway: 'What wasn't obvious to all of us, even Neil, was the relationship Peter was developing with the press. Certainly for the first year he was there, we had no inkling. But by 1987 it was pretty clear that he'd got a way with reporters. They were either eating out of his hand or were terrified of him, and he had a clique of them who were prepared to take almost everything he said and use it. One of the dangerous aspects of it was that some of them shared his political project. More dangerously, he seemed to have developed a way of stringing along, threatening and flattering journalists. It was an unhealthy relationship – some were in, some were out. This gave him a line to the press that no one, not Tory Central Office, not us in the Labour Party, had ever managed before. Journalists at that time loved him or hated him. But it wasn't all that obvious to the politicians that he was doing it or how he was doing it. The end result, which only eventually became clear to us, was that the way individual members of the shadow cabinet came to be seen by the press and public was deeply coloured by Peter's views, and those views accorded with Neil's.'[7]

Though Mandelson has often been painted as simply being a brilliant salesman who would, in the words of another former party director, 'believe in nationalizing the top 200 monopolies if he thought it would win votes',[8] he has in fact always been a political operator. 'Some people say that Peter is simply Machiavellian because he likes being like that,' according to a former colleague. 'Not true. Doing what he does is only part of the means to a political end, and to understand him you need to understand that he's a very, very right-wing member of the Labour Party. That's what he fights for, and with great vigour.'[9]

This view accords with that of Peter Lennon, a journalist who remembers Mandelson from LWT and later recalled: 'Colleagues were astonished that such a brilliant mind should show not the slightest interest in film-making. His reasons for enjoying the work on *Weekend World* are transparently those of a trainee politician.'[10] To those who worked closely with him at Walworth Road, it quickly became clear that Mandelson had a political as well as technical agenda, particularly on defence policy (see chapter 10).

Labour's 1987 defeat was the first campaign in which the party 'won the campaign but lost the election' – a silver-lining soundbite coined by Mandelson at the time and soon adopted by political analysts. Yet regardless of such bullish pronouncements Mandelson was, according to an associate, 'very depressed, and was near as dammit looking to get out'.[11] He applied for at least one other job – a senior post with the BBC which he didn't get – before eventually informing Kinnock and Charles Clarke that he intended to seek nomination as a parliamentary candidate.

Clarke in particular regarded the move to break up the 'dream team' based around Kinnock, himself and Mandelson as an absolute betrayal. Kinnock felt greatly let down, not simply because 'one of the few people I trust', as he privately described Mandelson, was removing himself from the leader's side at a point when the team required greatest stability (the post-1987 policy review was not yet complete, and the long haul of selling it to the voters in time for the next election was soon to begin), but also because he believed Mendelson's decision showed he had concluded that Labour simply could not win power under its present leader.

Whether this was the case or not, Mandelson was in a better position to make such a judgement than many others. The extensive private polling and focus group analysis that was now being carried out continually by Philip Gould revealed consistently disastrous personal ratings for Kinnock, regardless of the popularity of the party itself. Gould reported directly to Mandelson, who then decided what to pass on to Kinnock and others. Much of the polling data on Kinnock was held back from the NEC and shadow cabinet, some of it even from Kinnock himself. Mandelson, however, had full access.

After winning selection for the safe Labour seat of Hartlepool in 1990, he intended to stay in his job up to the election. Kinnock and Clarke, but most especially the NEC, refused to allow him to do so, citing party procedure. Many on the NEC had by now come to fear and loathe Mandelson, and seized the chance to force him to forfeit what they saw as his illegitimate influence. Reluctantly, he resigned. Before leaving, he insisted that his role throughout the comprehensive policy review process had been merely that of 'providing the "glitznost" to go with [Labour's] *perestroika*', and the party's revival in the polls was 'the result of political hard graft, not communications magic'.[12]

Mandelson's friends make much of the fact that since his departure, none of his successors as director of communications has managed to stay the course. His continued 'interference', however, is cited by others as the major factor in the acrimonious resignations of both John Underwood (his immediate replacement) and then Joy Johnson, after each had served just a year in the job. But as befits the activities of a master spin doctor, the Mandelson version of events following his decision to become an MP involves much rewriting of history. By his own account, he played little part in the run-up to the 1992 election campaign – indeed, he publicly criticized it after Labour's defeat, and his closest allies insist it was 'incredibly badly-managed compared to 1987' as a result of his absence.[13] In reality, Mandelson played a key part in the campaign that even today he has never publicly acknowledged (though if Labour had won, perhaps he would have done so). The rift with Kinnock and Clarke, though never fully repaired, soon healed enough for him to be allotted an informal role. Throughout 1990 and 1991 he was a member of the private Campaign Advisory Team, the central body that mapped out the party's strategy up to and including the election campaign itself. It met in secret, usually on Thursdays, in the offices of Clive (now Lord) Hollick. Other members were Jack Cunningham (the shadow cabinet campaigns co-ordinator), David Hill (an ex-aide to Roy Hattersley, called in to replace John Underwood), general secretary Larry Whitty, Charles Clarke, Neil Stewart (another Kinnock aide), Hollick (one of Labour's wealthy business backers), Philip Gould, and in its later stages Patricia Hewitt.

The secrecy was necessary for two important reasons: Kinnock's increasing paranoia and mistrust of those outside his own tiny inner circle, and the intense personal animosity towards Mandelson among senior Labour figures who had been at the receiving end of his unattributable briefings to the press. The fact that the existence of the group was confidential was a considerable obstacle to effective implementation of its decisions by party head-quarters, but the antagonism towards Mandelson was a bigger one. According to one of those who attended the select gatherings, 'We simply could not have got a coherent decision-making team operating at all unless we did it secretly.' Mandelson dropped out of the meetings as the election drew closer, but 'right up to polling day his influence was there, either directly through Kinnock or indirectly through Philip Gould'.[14]

The election of John Smith as leader following Labour's defeat in 1992 began a hiatus in Mandelson's career. Smith had no personal or political affection for Mandelson, and neither did his aides. They did not like his methods, and saw no benefit in having on board someone so hated, as he now was, by other members of the shadow cabinet and the NEC. Smith also favoured a more tolerant approach to those who disagreed with him, rather than Kinnock's 'for me or against me' attitude. That Mandelson had certain talents was nevertheless recognized, and he was put in charge of the Newbury by-election campaign in mid-1993.[15] Other than this, however, he found his offer of services to Smith rebuffed. Although two of his allies, Gordon Brown and Tony Blair, won key roles in determining strategy, the newly elected MP for Hartlepool was no longer a major player.

He was forced to content himself with providing advice to Brown and Blair, often acting as their spin doctor in the process, most notably on how to shift Smith towards pushing OMOV through more forcefully than he was originally inclined.[16] Otherwise, during his brief period as a humble back-bencher he proved himself a committed pro-European, coming out in strong favour of a single European currency during the rancorous Commons debates on the Maastricht treaty in 1993. As a result he was offered, and accepted, a vice-chairmanship of the cross-party European Movement (Edward Heath was its president, Edwina Currie another vice-chair).

It wasn't until Blair's decision to run for the top job after Smith's death that Mandelson came in from the cold – at first covertly (again, due to the deep hostility towards him from all sides of the parliamentary party), and after Blair's formal accession openly. He has been at his side ever since, though Gordon Brown has never forgiven him for backing Blair for the leadership.

Blair appointed Mandelson to the whip's office in autumn 1994, and a year later promoted him to junior front-bench civil service spokesman. But it was on the additional, and far more influential, job of chairing Labour's general election planning group that he concentrated his activities, spending more time at the party's new high-tech Millbank Tower campaign centre (he often referred to it as 'my Millbank') than anywhere else. The role was specially created for Mandelson following his own suggestion at the beginning of 1995, but took until the end of the year to put into effect because of objections from Brown.[17] In the meantime, Mandelson played a central part in Blair's informal advisory groups on policy and strategy (see chapter 1).

He also set to work with Roger Liddle on the book that became *The Blair Revolution*. The initial proposal, submitted to various publishing houses at the beginning of 1995, was a blueprint for the thoroughly modernized party he wished Labour to become: among other things, it argued for Labour to adopt the constitution of the old SDP, a coalition with the Liberal Democrats whatever the size of a Labour government's majority, no-strike deals in the public sector, abolition of universal child benefit, and an end to the 'over-representation of Scotland and Wales at Westminster' following devolution. Expectation mounted when news of the book and what it might contain reached the press: how would a front-bencher, even one as close to Blair as Mandelson, carry off advocating a string of policy proposals that ran so counter to official Labour policy?[18] The final product turned out to be the publishing non-event of the year. When *The Blair Revolution* was launched in February 1996, the controversial sections outlined in the original proposal had been filleted out.

Pre-publicity and Mandelson's reputation as an 'evil genius' ensured the book sold well. But from Mandelson's perspective it was a failure. He wanted it to prove his credentials as an intellectual politician of stature rather than as the mere beneficiary of the patronage of first Kinnock and now Blair. In making sure that *The Blair Revolution* contained nothing that would conflict with the party line – with the exception of a bizarre plan to lend young couples a £5,000 'dowry' as a deposit for a mortgage if they got married – he guaranteed that it merely confirmed his reputation as a propagandist.

Nevertheless, the book did contain ideas for reforming the machinery of central government that proved prescient in many respects. After singing the praises of Margaret Thatcher's 'leadership in government' and her 'early demonstration of her strength of will' in taking on an obstructive civil service to privatize the

British National Oil Corporation, Mandelson and Liddle made the case for a 'formalized strengthening of the centre of government' to 'provide the means of formulating and driving forward strategy for the government as a whole', focused on the role of Number Ten Downing Street and the Cabinet Office.

At Number Ten, they argued, 'there is need for a stronger political presence . . . providing political advice and contacts which neither the private office nor the Cabinet Office can do because they are not supposed to get involved in politics and cannot meet the prime minister's central need: to focus on and manage the government's political strategy and programme'. 'The political office at Number Ten, the policy unit and the press office all have political roles to play, and, in the case of the political and policy functions at least, there is a need for a strong figure to bind them and their work together and to act as the prime minister's principal political adviser.'

As for the Cabinet Office, despite some welcome additions to its functions under deputy prime minister Michael Heseltine, 'it currently sees its job chiefly as knocking heads together in Whitehall – getting agreement between departments on behalf of the prime minister – and the cabinet secretary acts as the principal manager of the process of government. This is essential, but it is a reactive role . . . A more proactive approach will be particularly important if a Blair-led government wants to create areas of cross-departmental administration which are not covered by existing Whitehall structures . . . The Cabinet Office should be more akin to a Department of the Prime Minister and Cabinet, charged with actively carrying forward the cross-departmental policies agreed by the cabinet.'[19]

Not all the reforms to the machinery of government suggested by Mandelson and Liddle in The Blair Revolution came to pass in the first weeks of the Blair government – and they nowhere suggested the appointment of a minister without portfolio attached to the Cabinet Office. But the beefed-up Number Ten and Cabinet Office at the centre of their plan for centralizing power within government are essentially what Blair put into practice, and their idea that the prime minister needed 'a senior colleague who can help smooth over frictions and disagreements in the cabinet (a role that Willie Whitelaw fulfilled for Mrs Thatcher, acting as deputy premier, though not formally designated as such)' is a fair summary of Mandelson's own view of himself.

How Mandelson's role will work out in practice will be closely watched. The idea of co-ordinating policy and presentation makes perfect sense: governments that do not present a united front to the world are not credible. It is easy, moreover, to understand why Blair decided to appoint Mandelson to the key co-ordinating role. Mandelson is feared by much of the cabinet and the media, is utterly ruthless and, most important, is a loyal and trusted ally who will do what he is told. As long as he retains Blair's confidence and Blair retains the confidence of the cabinet, he will be one of the most powerful figures in the government.

Nevertheless, he is not a conciliator, as Whitelaw undoubtedly was, and he is not trusted by most of the cabinet, including, crucially, Gordon Brown, John Prescott and Robin Cook, none of whom have any intention of ceding influence to him. It is not inconceivable that rather than 'help smooth over frictions and disagreements in the cabinet' Mandelson will actually turn them into major crises.

By comparison with the potential problems that Blair and Mandelson have in dealing with disagreements at the highest level of government, the difficulties they and the whips are likely to face from the Parliamentary Labour Party are small, at least in the short term. Of the 418 Labour MPs elected in May 1997, nearly one quarter are ministers, whips or parliamentary private secretaries, and most of the rest are keen to make their way up the greasy pole. Because Labour has a giant overall majority, in the normal course of events the chances of the government suffering a defeat in the Commons are minimal – to the extent that fifty MPs at a time are being given a week's leave of absence from the Commons on a rota basis to nurture their constituencies. Even so, Blair made it clear to the PLP at the start of the parliamentary session that he will not put up with rebellious behaviour, and the whips reinforced the message. All Labour MPs were given personal electronic pagers so that they know at all times what is expected of them – a particularly effective ploy with many of the 178 MPs elected for the first time in 1997.

Nevertheless, there are at least a few putative rebels on Labour's back benches. Between 1992 and 1997, thirty-eight of Labour's 270-odd MPs voted more than twenty times against the instructions of the whips in the House of Commons: twelve of them rebelled more than forty times.[20] Only five of the thirty-eight are not now MPs. The most persistent rebels came from the hard left Campaign Group, which currently claims thirty-four members, six of them from the 1997 intake; most of the rest were Labour's hardcore Eurosceptics. Most of the rebellions between 1992 and 1997 were over various aspects of the Maastricht Treaty, the biggest in 1993 when no fewer than sixty-eight Labour MPs, a quarter of the PLP, defied the whip to vote against the government rather than abstain. Again, the vast majority are still MPs. Maastricht apart, there were small but significant rebellions over defence spending, Tory tax cuts and the Prevention of Terrorism Act.

Of course, for this rebel core to be more than a minor occasional nuisance it would need to be much bigger – which brings up the hardy perennial question of what happens to the parliamentary left. At present its prospects are difficult to judge, not least because it is in flux. The Campaign Group – set up in 1982 after the Tribune Group split over Tony Benn's challenge to Denis Healey for Labour's deputy leadership and Michael Foot's first moves to expel Militant from the party – has been marginal from the start but particularly since 1988, when it backed Benn's quixotic challenge to Neil Kinnock for the party leadership (with Eric Heffer taking on his deputy Roy Hattersley). Some of its members had however been secretly hoping for a small Labour majority in the 1997 election, which would have given them some real leverage. The giant Labour majority left it at odds over what to do, with its old-guard leaders, Benn and Dennis Skinner, arguing for no change in the group's refusal to co-operate with anyone else on the parliamentary left, while others, among them Alan Simpson, the group's chair, made the case for greater flexibility.

The parliamentary soft left is in an even more transitory state. The Tribune Group, from its inception in 1966 until 1982 the sole left-wing caucus in the Parliamentary Labour Party and the source of many of the parliamentary rebellions against the Labour government of the 1970s, over the economy, civil liberties, defence and Europe, still exists in name but is effectively moribund.[21] Fought over for years by left-wing and leadership-loyalist factions, it ceased to exist as a coherent caucus in the mid-1980s and finally expired even as a viable forum for discussion in 1994–5 when Peter Hain and most of its left wing resigned from it after being voted out of its key positions by Gordon Brown, Tony Blair and others who objected to Hain's criticisms of Brown's economic policy (see chapter 2). The rump leadership-loyalist Tribune Group did not meet between summer 1996 and the 1997 election, and its treasurer at the time, Margaret Hodge, was so firmly convinced it was dead that she did not bother to collect any subscriptions. When the editor of the *Tribune* newspaper, Mark Seddon, wrote to the group's chairman, Jim Cunningham, shortly after the election to suggest that the group relinquished the paper's name, Cunningham promised a relaunch of the group, but the likelihood of this is slim.

The main forum for the soft left is now What's Left, an invitation-only discussion network set up by Hain and others not long after resigning from the Tribune Group. There is no formal membership, but between forty-five and fifty MPs, including some front-benchers and some members of the Campaign Group, take part in its regular private meetings. Attenders have included Hain, overseas development spokeswoman Clare Short, environment minister Michael Meacher, foreign office minister Derek Fatchett, regional affairs minister Dick Caborn, PLP chairman Clive Soley, his deputy Jean Corston, and back-benchers Chris Mullin, Roger Berry and Richard Burden; deputy prime minister John Prescott and foreign secretary Robin Cook have kept up friendly relations and a dozen members of the new intake have joined the group. What's Left is emphatically not in the business of 'oppositionism', say its supporters: it plans to remain low key and exercise influence on the government. But if it manages to avoid being wrecked by leadership loyalists muscling in and if the Campaign Group drops its policy of splendid isolation, they believe that it is possible that a viable left caucus of between seventy-five and a hundred

MPs will eventually emerge in the PLP, including up to thirty of the 1997 intake.

The parliamentary left's organizational weakness is not, however, its only problem or its biggest one. For some years, it has lacked anything like the confidence, drive or sense of direction of the Labour modernizers. The disagreements over tactics that were the original cause of the Tribune-Campaign split have been overlaid by deeper differences as the parliamentary left has grappled with – or failed to grapple with – the myriad economic, political and social changes since the early 1980s: globalization and the decline of the economic powers of the state, the Tories' privatizations and their assault on organized labour, the declining salience of class identity in British politics, the increasing economic and political integration of Western Europe, the collapse of communism and the end of the Cold War, climate change and the rise of the environmentalist movement, the outcry at the inadequacy of Britain's democratic institutions. There is no agreed left position in the PLP today on the economy, Europe, constitutional reform (particularly the electoral system), the future of the welfare state, and much else besides. Insofar as the parliamentary left has found unity of purpose in recent years, it has been in fighting unsuccessful rearguard actions against changes initiated by the party leadership – on public ownership, on defence, on the closed shop, on OMOV, on Clause Four. The main exception came when Ken Livingstone and others managed to salvage some credibility for the hard left in the wake of the Benn-Heffer leadership fiasco by pushing for radical cuts in defence spending to fund increased investment in production and infrastructure.

During the 1992–7 parliament, Peter Hain came closer than anyone else on the Labour back benches to defining a left 'project': his book *Ayes to the Left*, published in summer 1995, made a cogent case for a 'libertarian socialism' that was Keynesian in its economics, environmentalist, anti-Maastricht but pro-European, and in favour of radical constitutional change, including electoral reform but not proportional representation.[22] But even Hain fell a long way short of articulating a new left consensus. The book was criticized by some on the left, with some justification, for hanging on to Keynesianism in one country long after it had ceased to be possible; others attacked it for its criticisms of 'statist' socialism. Hain's refusal to embrace PR disappointed the growing band of his colleagues who rightly believe it an essential prerequisite of a genuinely pluralist politics, but it was far too radical for the many left-wing defenders of the first-past-the-post *status quo*. In any case, Hain was appointed as a whip soon after *Ayes to the Left* was published. After the election, he was made a junior minister in the Welsh Office, with no option but to toe the government line.

There are plenty of MPs with the ability and independence of mind to help set the political agenda from the left – Roger Berry, Richard Burden, Ken Livingstone, Chris Mullin and Alan Simpson, for example. But apart from Livingstone, who is not popular among his fellow MPs, there is no one who is an obvious candidate for leadership of the back-bench left in parliament, and it remains to be seen how far anyone is ready to risk the isolation and opprobrium that will inevitably go with developing, and then consistently advancing, a coherent alternative to the government line.

The upshot of all this is that in the short term, unless Blair makes a move to ditch Labour's link with the trade unions or dismantle the welfare state, dissent among Labour MPs is less likely to be expressed through caucus groups of the left or centre-left – there is no formal right-wing group these days even on paper – than by single-issue and special interest coalitions in the PLP. As between 1992 and 1997, anti-Europeanism is the obvious cause to ignite rebellion, although it is difficult to see how anything apart from a decision to enter a single European currency would stir more than the usual forty to fifty suspects. Otherwise, it is worth keeping an eye on Labour's proportional representation lobby (which suspects that the promised referendum on the electoral system for the House of Commons will not take place or will be somehow sabotaged), its Scottish and Welsh MPs, its enthusiasts for English regional assemblies (particularly in the north-east), its civil libertarians and its defence policy radicals. Still, the mathematical facts of Labour's commanding majority are all-important: eighty-nine Labour MPs would have to combine with every single non-Labour MP in parliament to force a defeat on the government.

In the medium term, everything depends on the overall performance of the government – which is where the crystal ball mists over.

Much the same prognosis applies to Blair's relations with the rest of the Labour Party, with the partial exception of its representatives in the European Parliament (see chapter 3). It is basking in the warm glow of victory – and, as with the Parliamentary Labour Party, the people in it have changed. Of the 410,000 members Labour claimed in 1997, no fewer than 220,000 have joined since Blair became leader in 1994. Common sense suggests that most of them are well-disposed towards him.

What's more, the left in the party at large is a shadow of what it was in the early 1980s, and indeed it has been for years. The overwhelming majority of the early-1980s local government left was persuaded of the error of its ways by the failure of the confrontational tactics adopted by left-wing councils in the mid-1980s. Many of its veterans have now spent more than a decade trying to run councils as well as possible within the tight budgetary constraints imposed by central government – and most have become converts to the idea that the primary tasks of councils are providing 'value-for-money' services and attracting investment to their areas. Most of the Trotskyists who once played a crucial role in many local parties and on several councils are no longer part of the Labour Party, largely because of the purge undertaken by Neil Kinnock between 1983 and 1992.[23] Arthur Scargill, a key figure in the hard left as president of the National Union of Mineworkers, left Labour with a group of his core supporters after Clause Four was changed to set up the Socialist Labour Party. Many other one-time left activists have either left the Labour Party in disillusionment at its rightwards drift or are no longer active.

The Labour Co-ordinating Committee, in the early 1980s the key activist group straddling soft left and hard left and later the main soft left rank-and-file grouping, had by the early 1990s become little more than a circle of young would-be career politicians, all advocates of 'modernization', working as researchers for front-bench Labour MPs. By the 1997 general election it was moribund, although it lives on as a network of friends working as lobbyists, government special advisers and party apparatchiks and as the publisher of the journal *Renewal*.[24] There is now no effective soft left organisation among activists, although the MPs in What's Left are trying to create one.

Tribune still acts as a forum for left activists and has been consistently critical of Blair, and there are several groups and networks still operating on the hard left, the most important of them the Campaign for Labour Party Democracy and other pressure groups in the Labour Left Liaison umbrella group and the Campaign Group Supporters Network.[25] But they are more marginal than at any time since the early 1980s – and, like the left in the PLP, Labour's activist left has found it difficult to cope with the way the world has changed since the early 1980s. As a result it has generally found itself divided except in resisting (or grumbling about) the party leadership's 'modernization' drive. Like the PLP left, it is particularly at odds over the economy, Europe and electoral reform.

Almost as important, the institutional balance of power in the party has shifted radically since the early 1980s, partly but not only through constitutional reforms, so that the influence of the National Executive Committee and the party conference (and thereby party activists and the trade unions) has declined, while that of the party leadership has increased. Blair's intention is to continue this process, initially by reducing the policy-making role of the NEC, restructuring its membership, tying it into supporting the government and diluting the powers of the conference. His critics suspect that his goal is a party in which the unions and activists have little or no role beyond providing money and personnel for campaigning, with a largely passive party membership that is given the opportunity from time to time to endorse the leadership's plans through plebiscites. Obviously, the further that Labour moves in this direction, the less likely are the sort of conflicts between party and government that dogged it in the 1970s.

Nevertheless, it is difficult to imagine a constitutional settlement that would guarantee harmony in all circumstances. The party constitution is important in mediating the relationship of party and government, but what matters most is what the members think of the government's performance. Although the left is weaker than it has been for years, it has not disappeared. If, against all odds, it manages to develop a political stance that is more than reactive and backward-looking, it just might experience a revival if Blair is a disappointment.

As for the intellectual left – such as it is after eighteen years of Conservative rule and the wreckage of Keynesianism, social democratic corporatism, 'actually existing socialism', the '57 varieties' of Trotskyism and neo-Leninism and all but the most supple 1968-vintage libertarian leftism – what is most remarkable is how tentative its embrace of New Labour has been.

There is of course a great sense of relief among left-leaning serious journalists and political thinkers that the Tories have gone, and there is a small core of out-and-out enthusiasts for the government with key positions in the quality press. Most important is a group of high-brow commentators who are personally close to Blair, notably Ian Hargreaves and John Lloyd at the *New Statesman* (owned since spring 1996 by Geoffrey Robinson, now paymaster general in Gordon Brown's Treasury), Martin Kettle at the *Guardian*, Andrew Adonis at the *Observer* and Donald MacIntyre at the *Independent*. Among the think-tankers, Geoff Mulgan of Demos is now an adviser to Number Ten, and a host of policy wonks with connections to the Institute of Public Policy Research and the Fabian Society are now installed in Whitehall or in other positions to influence the government. The Labour Co-ordinating Committee quarterly *Renewal* provides a broadly New Labour intellectual forum, as does *Renewal*'s 'ideas network', Nexus. Several prominent centre-left intellectuals who put reform of the constitution at the centre of their politics, among them Anthony Barnett, have enthused at length about the prospects with Labour in power.

But it is more noticeable who is out of the loop or not quite in it, even among sympathisers with the Blair government. Of the broadsheet papers, the *Observer* made the most of Labour's 1997 election victory, posting the slogan 'the paper for the new era' above its masthead – but in truth under the editorship of Will Hutton its political centre of gravity is well to the left of the government. The *Guardian* under Alan Rusbridger has kept its distance from Labour in power just as it did from Labour in opposition, and the *Independent* under Andrew Marr has done much the same. *The Economist*, where David Lipsey, an aide to the last Labour government, is political editor, has been sympathetic but critical; the *Financial Times* is only as enthusiastic as its position as a journal of record will allow. The government has plenty of friends in the upper echelons of broadcasting, but broadcast journalists are mainly tepid about it – not least because they have borne the brunt of Labour's spin-doctoring – and are in any case constrained by strict rules governing impartiality.

Among public intellectuals of the left, the reservations have been more marked. Stuart Hall, the most influential proponent during the 1980s of the idea that Labour's class-based political culture had lost touch with the real world and needed to be radically modernized, delivered a series of withering assaults on the Blair 'project' before the election, the last of them co-written with Martin Jacques, editor of *Marxism Today* in the 1980s and one of Blair's biggest fans when he was elected in 1994.[26] The intellectuals around *New Left Review* have been equally critical.[27] So too have feminists suspicious of New Labour's rhetoric of family values and hostility to single mothers, civil libertarians wary of its proposals for young offenders and a host of others. David Marquand has warned of the tensions between New Labour's conservative economic vision – that 'Britain should seek competitive advantage in the global market-place through low non-wage labour costs, correspondingly low levels of social protection and deregulated labour markets' – and its belief in citizen empowerment through constitutional reform. Even Anthony Giddens, director of the London School of Economics and broadly supportive of New Labour, expressed his doubts about the party's inadequate thinking on the environment and its authoritarian moralism within days of its election victory.[28]

It is significant that, with the exception of a collection of essays edited by Giles Radice and two slim volumes published just before the 1997 election by the economist Richard Layard and the

Labour MP Tony Wright, no book-length statement of the New Labour case has appeared since *The Blair Revolution* in early 1996.[29] Mandelson and Liddle's lifeless tome remains the nearest thing the contemporary Labour Party has to Anthony Crosland's *The Future of Socialism* or Roy Hattersley's *Choose Freedom*.

The guardedness of the left intelligentsia does not of course mean that it will be in revolt against the government within months, still less that a significant part of it – or any individual – will develop a coherent popular critique of New Labour. The intellectual left in Britain has always been fragmented, but it has never been more dissipated than it is today. It is also lacking in confidence after at least two decades in which the foundations of many left-wing views of the world have been profoundly shaken. There is no magazine, web site, think tank or discussion group network that yet looks set to become influential in pushing a credible all-embracing left alternative to the policies of the Labour government.

This could change very quickly, however. Thanks to the efforts of Charter 88, there is now a consensus among a broad swathe of left-leaning opinion behind a democratic, pluralist, civil libertarian overhaul of the British state far more radical than that proposed by New Labour. Most of the thinking left is also much more pro-European than New Labour, keener on redistributive taxation and increased public spending, and more committed to feminism and environmentalism. The undesirability of Leninist forms of political organization, the stupidity of insurrectionism and the impracticality of a command economy are all but taken for granted except by a small minority. Although there is no agreement on the intellectual left about what constitutes a viable macroeconomic strategy in the face of globalization, there is at least a worthwhile argument going on. In other words, there is real potential for establishing a left alternative to New Labour in the realm of ideas – which would at least give a focus to the beleaguered Labour left and might just, in the best of all possible worlds, provide the basis on which a credible libertarian green left party could be created after introduction of proportional representation.

The Labour leadership feigns lack of interest in what the left intelligentsia thinks about it – but in reality it is worried about the fragility of its base of intellectual support. In February 1996, Blair made the bizarre decision to call a secret meeting of what the *Guardian* called '80 intellectuals and businessmen' to give them a pep talk about New Labour's 'openness to new ideas', and he has subsequently spared no effort to get the intelligentsia on board: his office even played a role in making sure that Geoffrey Robinson ended up as owner of the *New Statesman* and that Ian Hargreaves became its editor.[30]

It is possible that New Labour will make its approach as much the common sense of the coming decade as Margaret Thatcher made her mix of what Andrew Gamble called 'the free economy and the strong state' the common sense of the 1980s. But it is more likely that its main means of dominating the political agenda will remain tight news management. It is as spin doctor rather than as man of ideas that Peter Mandelson really matters today.

CONCLUSION

There can be no doubt that Labour has changed dramatically since the early 1980s. The chaotically disorganized party that lost the 1983 general election has been transformed into the ruthless New Labour machine that swept all before it in 1997 – and in programmatic terms, the differences are even starker.

Whereas in 1983 the Labour manifesto backed widespread nationalization, a big increase in public borrowing to boost the economy, a hike in spending on social security, health and education, a shift in 'the tax balance towards those who can best afford to pay' and a key role for the trade unions in economic management, the party today has forsaken nationalization, is no longer Keynesian in its approach to macroeconomic policy, has ditched its explicit commitment to a redistributive tax and benefits system and has abandoned even the vaguest hint of openness to corporatism.

Indeed, it now backs unequivocally the idea that the only way for a country to prosper in the modern globalized economy is to guarantee monetary and fiscal stability and to ensure that its infrastructure and 'flexible labour markets' – in other words, low wages, low social costs, weak trade unions and lack of legal constraints on firing surplus workers – are attractive to investors. It has embraced business wholeheartedly and distanced itself from the trade unions (although formally they retain massive influence in Labour's organization and still provide something like half of the party's income). The 1997 manifesto promised to 'provide stable economic growth with low inflation, and promote dynamic and competitive business at home and abroad', with 'no increase in the basic or top rates of income tax'. Instead of proposals to increase pensions and other social security benefits, it put forward a 'welfare-to-work' scheme to get the young unemployed, the long-term jobless and single parents off the dole and outlined a vague 'new framework' for provision of second pensions.

The party has also discarded the social liberalism that was once its hallmark, taking instead a populist stance in favour of tough law and order measures, 'strong families' and 'responsibilities as well as rights' for everyone (but especially, it seems, social security claimants). Whereas in 1983 the Labour manifesto promised 'withdrawal from the European Economic Community', the 1997 manifesto promised 'leadership in Europe'. In 1983, Labour had a non-nuclear defence policy and was highly critical of NATO; in 1997, it was in favour of keeping Britain's nuclear weapons and was uncompromisingly Atlanticist. The 1997 manifesto included a swathe of environmentalist promises where in 1983 there were none, and put forward a radically different set of proposals for constitutional reform. Whereas in 1983, Labour wanted to abolish the House of Lords and introduce devolution to Scotland, in 1997 the Blair government was elected on promises of referendums on devolution to Scotland and Wales, removal of the voting rights of hereditary peers, incorporation of the European Convention on Human Rights into British law and a referendum on reform of the electoral system.

But if Labour has been transformed since the early 1980s, many of the biggest changes are not recent. The party's policies changed more under Neil Kinnock between 1983 and 1992, in particular during the policy review that followed Labour's 1987 defeat, than from 1992 to 1997; and most of the crucial changes between 1992 and 1997 were well underway before Tony Blair became leader in 1994.

Kinnock replaced the promise of withdrawal from the EEC with a commitment to constructive engagement in Europe almost as soon as he became leader, and he took the first steps towards ditching nationalization, Keynesianism and corporatism before 1987. By 1992 all had been excised from Labour's programme in favour of an economic policy that emphasized improving the skills of the workforce as the key to reducing unemployment. Also abandoned during the policy review were unilateral nuclear disarmament, support for the closed shop and all but the most modest proposals for redistribution through the tax and benefits systems. It was in this period that Labour first tentatively embraced environmentalism and Kinnock set the ball rolling on electoral reform and backed a Bill of Rights.

Between 1992 and 1994, under the leadership of John Smith, Labour firmed up its commitments on the constitution, most notably by supporting a referendum on electoral reform, and made the decisive moves towards populism on law and order, the family and 'responsibilities as well as rights', largely as a result of Blair's efforts as shadow home secretary. It also laid the groundwork for the 'welfare-to-work' approach to reform of the welfare state in place of redistributive tax and benefits measures through the Commission on Social Justice, although its report was not published until after Smith's death. As for Labour's organizational and presentational changes, the most important, the introduction of modern marketing techniques, took place before 1987, and the second most important, the introduction of one member, one vote party elections, was passed by the 1993 party conference.

Blair is undoubtedly a master of the sweeping political gesture, and he made plenty of them as leader of the opposition – notably the change to Clause Four and the 1996 plebiscite on the draft manifesto. Under his leadership, Labour became ever more populist on crime and morality, dramatically more pro-business, even keener on flexible labour markets and more resigned than ever before to the powerlessness of the state in the face of market forces. But if political leadership is to be judged in terms of policy rather than tone, Blair must be seen as a beneficiary of his predecessors' efforts. He added little to what they had already done, and on the constitution and the environment gave every indication that he would much rather some of their innovations had never happened.

In many ways, moreover, Labour's policy shifts since the early 1980s have been reversions to positions it held before 1979. Gordon Brown's monetary and fiscal conservatism recalls that of Denis Healey as chancellor after he imposed austerity in 1975 (and even further back, the ideas of Ramsay MacDonald and Philip Snowden in the 1920s). The populist line on Europe taken by Blair and Robin Cook is very similar to the attitude of most of the Labour leadership in the late 1960s and 1970s, although in very different circumstances. In defence policy, there has been a return to the nuclear Atlanticism dominant in the party from the 1940s until 1980, although again the context is not the same. In adopting removal of the political powers of hereditary peers in place of abolition of the House of Lords (or immediate introduction of an elected second chamber, the position Labour took under Kinnock), Blair has retreated to where Labour was in the 1960s; devolution for Scotland and Wales is unfinished business from the 1970s. Populism on law and order was every bit as characteristic of Jim Callaghan as home secretary in the late 1960s as it is today of Jack Straw.

In short, the making of New Labour has been going on a long time – and New Labour owes a lot more than it cares to admit to the old Labour right of the 1960s and 1970s, even though it rejects the egalitarian Keynesianism and civil libertarianism of Anthony Crosland and the corporatism of the Social Contract.

But what motivated Labour to reinvent itself in this way? One reason is undoubtedly electoral opportunism. Since the mid-1980s, Labour has defined its politics less in terms of what it believes ought to be done (and what it should persuade the public to support) than by what market research says is popular. Everything the party has done has been tested relentlessly on focus groups of target voters, and many of its policy shifts are explicable in terms of their impact on public opinion. The renunciation of unilateral nuclear disarmament, the adoption of tough rhetoric on crime and the 'work-shy', the repudiation of nationalization, the abandonment of Keynesianism, the ditching of redistributionism on tax and benefits, the marginalization of the left and the unions – all were to a large extent the products of shameless calculations of potential electoral gains.

Equally important, much that Labour did between 1983 and 1997, but particularly after Blair became leader, was aimed at reassuring people in positions of power – in the media, industry, the City, the military, the police, the US government and so on – that Labour was no longer a threat. Although there were few votes to be had directly here, the idea was that if the powerful did not kick up a fuss about the prospect of a Labour government, or perhaps even welcomed it, Labour's trustworthiness in the eyes of the voters would soar.

Yet the making of New Labour was not just a matter, as the traditional left would have it, of pandering to voters and to powerful vested interests. In terms of party reform, expelling Militant produced approving headlines but also removed an anti-democratic virus from the party. One member, one vote internal party elections were a long-overdue democratization as well as a useful symbolic victory for John Smith over the unions and the left.

More important, Labour's change of heart on Europe was not only popular but also a principled rejection of isolationism and xenophobia; and its embrace of environmentalism and adoption of a programme of comprehensive constitutional reform both became much more than the pragmatist gestures that they were at first. The new government has an unrepeatable chance to help make the European Union more directly accountable to its citizens, to institute a genuinely green tax regime and transport policy, and to start a thoroughgoing democratization of the British state. It will need to be pressed on all this – but there are grounds for at least cautious optimism.

Most important of all, Labour's abandonment of Keynesianism was not simply a means of proving to target voters and the City that Labour took a responsible attitude to economic management: contrary to what most of the traditional left believes, it was also a rational response to the failure of the French socialists' expansionist experiment in 1981–3 and the implosion of the Lawson boom. There is a still a strong case for believing that the European Union post-EMU will have the economic weight to pursue Keynesian demand management at a supranational level – and again Labour will need to be pressed on this, at the very least to work with the new French government and other continental

social democrats on developing the role of the European
Investment Bank and on pushing for Europe-wide infrastructural
projects.

In the meantime, Labour is right to emphasize the importance of globalization in defining the context in which it has to
operate. Globalization has substantially reduced the scope for
independent action of any medium-sized nation state in economic
policy, has made the crucial factor in determining economic success the ability to attract footloose investment, and has led to a
permanent increase in insecurity of employment for a large section of the workforce.

Here, however, the problem is that Labour's eagerness to
please on tax and its closeness to business have led it astray even
though it has correctly identified the problem. If globalization
puts a premium on competing internationally on the basis of
labour costs, skills and infrastructure, and if it means that insecurity of employment has become the norm for many workers,
there are obviously implications for policies on education,
employment, social security, transport and a whole lot more
besides. But it does not follow that the goal of all policy should be
to spread employment insecurity, as the more extreme advocates
of 'flexible labour markets' in the business world would like, or
that the unemployed should be hounded into 'workfare' schemes.
What is more, it is difficult to see how many of the changes necessary to equip Britain with a skilled workforce, a modern
infrastructure and the means of compensating for employment
insecurity can be made without the state raising a lot more money
to spend through taxes on income and consumption.

This is particularly apparent in education and transport,
even with the best possible results from the government's blitz on
standards and its attempts to invigorate partnerships with the private sector. But the same argument applies at the interface of
employment and social security policy.

Most obviously, it remains to be seen whether enough will be
spent on 'welfare-to-work' to make it worthwhile for participants.
More fundamentally, there are the problems of how to secure over
their lifetimes the living standards of those working on low wages,
in low-income self-employment and in temporary and part-time

jobs. There are serious problems in many industries with introducing a minimum wage because of its likely effects on employment – and insecurity of employment means that there are many people who are not going to be able to contribute to funded social insurance schemes, particularly for pensions. On the assumption that people should not be left to starve on poverty wages or inadequate pensions, there is a strong case here for the state to become more rather than less actively redistributive, providing more generous in-work benefits rather than opting for a minimum wage and taking an enhanced role in pension provision. If means-testing is to be avoided, this points towards citizen's income as the best possible solution. Yet this would mean tax increases – and so has been ruled out by Labour. Indeed, so desperate is Labour not to be seen as a high-tax party that it is now desperately trying to find a way of off-loading pensions on to some form of funded social insurance system, the least appropriate model of provision for an insecure society.

As we write this in summer 1997, the euphoria that swept the country in the early hours of 2 May has begun to dissipate – but it still seems rather churlish for anyone on the left to raise doubts about New Labour. Much of what the government did in its first hundred days was admirable: its immediate indication to the European Union that the years of Tory obstructionism were over; Robin Cook's ban on production of landmines and his Foreign Office mission statement with its emphasis on human rights and environmentalism; the lifting of the ban on trade unions at GCHQ. The promises in the Queen's Speech of legislation to reduce class sizes, incorporate the European Convention on Human Rights into British law and introduce devolution to Scotland and Wales were no less welcome for being familiar. Where the new government's actions jarred, the effects were not serious.

But most of the government's measures simply need time to take effect before they can be judged. It is too early to tell whether Gordon Brown's decision to make the Bank of England independent will prove inspired or foolish, whether his first budget will have the effect he hoped for or whether 'welfare-to-work' will prove coercive or empowering. The same goes for whether David Blunkett's drive on school standards does more than upset teachers, whether Jack Straw sticks to the crass populism he adopted in opposition or whether John Prescott's conversion to environmentalism is more than skin-deep.

Labour's recent history in opposition and the careers of its leading figures give us plenty of clues about what to expect – but the only near-certainty is that the government's honeymoon will not last forever. Blair's fate rests on what Harold Macmillan described as 'events, dear boy, events'.

NOTES

1 DOWN TO BUSINESS: TONY BLAIR AND THE NEW LABOUR 'PROJECT'

1 For more detail see John Rentoul, *Tony Blair*, (Little Brown, 1995) and Jon Sopel, *Tony Blair: The Moderniser* (Michael Joseph, 1995).

2 Rentoul, *Tony Blair*, chapter one.

3 Peter Thomson, quoted in Rentoul, *Tony Blair*.

4 *Evening Standard*, 16 November 1993.

5 Martin Jacques, interview with Tony Blair, *Sunday Times*, 17 July 1994.

6 Rentoul, *Tony Blair*, chapter one.

7 *Sunday Telegraph*, 18 March 1990, quoted in Rentoul, *Tony Blair*.

8 Robert Crampton, 'Labour exchange', *The Times*, 30 September 1995. Blair claimed Macmurray as a pioneer of the communitarian anti-liberalism epitomized by his 'tough on crime, tough on the causes of crime' stance, but there is a strong case for arguing that he was essentially liberal. See Samuel Brittan, 'Blair's real guru', *New Statesman*, 7 February 1997.

9 Martin Jacques, interview with Tony Blair, *Sunday Times*, 17 July 1994.

10 There is a vast literature on the Labour Party in the 1980s. For Foot and Kinnock, see Mervyn Jones, *Michael Foot* (Gollancz, 1993), Robert Harris, *The Making of Neil Kinnock* (Faber, 1984) and Michael Leapman, *Kinnock* (Unwin Hyman, 1987). Foot's account of the 1983 election is in *Another Heart and Other Pulses* (Collins, 1984); his *Loyalists and Loners* (Collins, 1986) contains an acerbic portrait of Tony Benn that is unmissable. Benn's diaries on this period (*The End of an Era: Diaries 1980–1990*, Hutchinson, 1992) are disappointing by comparison with their predecessor volumes but still essential. Healey's memoirs, *The Time of My Life* (Michael Joseph, 1989), are less frank than they could be but entertaining and full of insights. On Bennism, see David and Maurice Kogan, *The Battle for the Labour Party* (Fontana, 1982) and Patrick Seyd, *The Rise and Fall of the Labour Left* (Macmillan, 1987). On the local government left, see Stewart Lansley, Sue Goss and Christian Wolmar, *Councils in Conflict: The Rise and Fall of the Municipal Left* (Macmillan, 1989), John Carvel, *Citizen Ken* (Chatto, 1984) and Hilary

Wainwright, *Labour: A Tale of Two Parties* (Chatto, 1987). The best overviews are Eric Shaw's two surveys, *The Labour Party Since 1979* (Routledge, 1994) and *The Labour Party Since 1945* (Blackwell, 1996).

11 The Blairs' friends in the Hackney Labour Party included Maggie Rae, a solicitor friend of Cherie and much later chair of the Fabian Society; her partner Alan Haworth, now secretary of the Parliamentary Labour Party; the *Financial Times* journalist John Lloyd, editor of the *New Statesman* in 1986–7 and now back at the magazine as associate editor; John Carr, then a big player in the Greater London Council, who became project manager for the 'rapid rebuttal' unit at the heart of Labour's 1997 election campaign; his wife Glenys Thornton, subsequently chair of the Greater London Labour Party and one of the leading figures in the Fabian Society; Charles Clarke, then Neil Kinnock's chief of staff, now MP for Norwich South; and Barry Cox, Blair's next-door neighbour, then head of corporate affairs at London Weekend Television, who was chief fundraiser for Blair's 1994 leadership campaign.

12 Anthony Blair, 'The illogic of three men in wigs', *New Statesman*, 1 February 1980, 'Thatcherism, logic and the law', *New Statesman*, 22 February 1980, and 'Codes today', *New Statesman*, 29 August 1980.

13 Quoted in Rentoul, *Tony Blair*, p. 87.

14 See for example Eric Hobsbawm, 'The forward march of Labour halted?', in Francis Mulhearn and Martin Jacques (eds), *The Forward March of Labour Halted?* (Verso, 1981), and Anthony Heath, Roger Jowell and John Curtice, *How Britain Votes* (Pergamon, 1985).

15 Quoted in Colin Hughes and Patrick Wintour, *Labour Rebuilt: The New Model Labour Party* (Fourth Estate, 1990), p. 23.

16 For a hard left view of Kinnock's assault, see Richard Heffernan and Mike Marqusee, *Defeat From the Jaws of Victory: Inside Kinnock's Labour Party* (Verso, 1992).

17 Hughes and Wintour, *Labour Rebuilt*, p. 50.

18 The membership of the SCA changed over time, but its core members initially, according to Hughes and Wintour, were Mandelson, Patricia Hewitt from Neil Kinnock's office (see below), Philip Gould and his business partner Deborah Mattinson, Chris Powell (managing director of the advertising agency Boase Massimi Pollitt) and his BMP colleagues Peter Herd, Alan Tilly and Paul Leeves, Leslie Butterfield of the agency Abbott Mead David Vickers, Bob Worcester and Brian Gosschalk of the polling organization MORI, and Richard Faulkner of Westminster Communications. Hewitt, Gould, Mattinson, Powell and his BMP colleagues remained at the core of the operation in 1992, with Mandelson taking a less direct role after being selected as Labour candidate for Hartlepool in 1990 and leaving his post as director of communications. Other SCA members in 1992 included Richard Glendenning of the polling organisation NOP, the pollster Richard Jowell and Mandelson's eventual successor as director of communications, David Hill.

19 BBC2, *Newsnight*, 22 June 1983.

20 *New Statesman*, 4 September 1987.

21 Blair had joined the Tribune Group on the advice of Brown in 1985. The group, named after the weekly of the same name but with no formal connection to it, was from its inception in 1966 until 1982 the single left caucus in the Parliamentary Labour Party. It divided over Tony Benn's failed deputy leadership bid of 1981, when several of its members did not back him, and the split was formalized over Michael Foot's subsequent proposals to introduce a register of party groups as a means of getting rid of Militant. The anti-register hard left formed the Campaign Group, leaving the Tribune Group as the PLP's soft left caucus. There was an

attempt after the 1987 election, which saw an influx of left MPs, to get a joint Campaign–Tribune slate for the shadow cabinet elections – but the right of the Tribune Group, including Blair, Brown and Jack Straw, was strongly opposed to the idea, and in the end each group ran its own list. See chapter 11.

22 See Hughes and Wintour, *Labour Rebuilt*, chapter four; Shaw, *The Labour Party Since 1979*, chapter four. The SCA's arguments were reinforced by the analysis of the 1987 result put forward by the writers associated with the Communist Party magazine *Marxism Today*, then at the height of its influence under the editorship of Martin Jacques. See, for example, Charles Leadbeater, *The Politics of Prosperity* (Fabian Society, 1987).

23 See subsequent chapters.

24 The broadcast known as 'Jennifer's Ear' was a fictional account, loosely based on an amalgam of several true stories, of a small child who had been forced by Tory cuts in health spending to wait for a simple ear operation. It was extremely effective – until a Labour press officer claimed erroneously that the story it told was an account of the actual case of a girl named Jennifer, who was soon traced and found to have a slightly different story to the one told in the broadcast, a fact ruthlessly exploited by the Tories.

25 *Fabian Review*, 9 May 1992.

26 Tony Blair, 'Drawing on an inner strength', *Guardian*, 30 June 1992.

27 Tony Blair, interview on BBC Radio 4, 18 March 1993, quoted in Blair, *New Britain: My Vision of a Young Country* (Fourth Estate, 1996). Blair subsequently said that he had come to the same conclusion as Clinton about 'rainbow coalition' politics much earlier. 'I'll never forget a Republican convention in 1984 just before the presidential election. Someone took the platform and said: "When did you ever hear the Democrats say 'No' to anyone?" It was an absolutely defining criticism of the Democrats. They were surrounded by self-interest groups that they never said "No" to. In the end you had the Republicans representing the country with the Democrats representing this rainbow coalition of interests. Whether Clinton succeeds or fails, his strength was to break free of that.' *Evening Standard*, 18 July 1994, quoted in Rentoul, *Tony Blair*, p. 275.

28 Tony Blair, lecture to Charities Aid Foundation, 8 July 1993.

29 See Nicholas Jones, 'Blair's debt to Bobby', *Guardian*, 25 July 1994.

30 Tony Blair, *Change and National Renewal* (1994). The manifesto was written by Andrew Smith MP and David Miliband, then secretary of the Commission on Social Justice and subsequently Blair's chief policy adviser. It was edited by the *Guardian* journalist Martin Kettle.

31 Tony Blair, speech to Fabian Society 'Whatever next?' conference in London, 18 June 1994, published in pamphlet form as *Socialism* (Fabian Society, 1994).

32 Nearly 1 million people voted in the election, 170,000 of them individual members (69 per cent of those eligible to vote) and 780,000 trade unionists (20 per cent of those eligible).

33 *Guardian*, 19 June 1991.

34 Tony Blair, speech to Labour conference, 4 October 1994.

35 Quoted in Stephen Brooke, *Labour's War: The Labour Party During the Second World War* (Oxford University Press, 1992), p. 108.

36 See Alec Cairncross, *Years of Recovery: British Economic Policy 1945–51* (Methuen, 1985).

37 See Ken Coates, *Common Ownership and the Labour Party: The Debate About Clause Four* (Spokesman, 1995).

38 For a good summary, see Eric Shaw, *The Labour Party Since 1945* (Blackwell, 1996), chapter five.

39 On the 1974–9 government's industrial policy, see Malcolm Sawyer, 'Industrial policy', in Michael Artis and David Cobham (eds), *Labour's Economic Policies 1974–79* (Manchester University Press, 1991).

40 For the most comprehensive left response, see Coventry, Liverpool, Newcastle and North Tyneside Trades Councils, *State Intervention in Industry: A Worker's Inquiry* (Spokesman, 1980).

41 Labour Party, *New Hope for Britain* (1983).

42 Labour Party, *Britain Will Win* (1987).

43 Labour Party, *It's Time to Get Britain Working Again* (1992).

44 See Giles Radice, *Southern Discomfort* (Fabian Society, 1992) and Jack Straw, *Policy and Ideology* (Blackburn Labour Party, 1993). Kinnock declared against Clause Four in a television programme broadcast in early 1994.

45 Patrick Seyd and Paul Whiteley, 'Red in tooth and Clause', *New Statesman & Society*, 9 December 1994.

46 Tony Blair, speech to Clause Four conference; 29 April 1995.

47 Tony Blair, speech to British American Chamber of Commerce, New York, 11 April 1996.

48 *Sunday Times*, 1 September 1996.

49 *Observer*, 2 October 1994.

50 The pressure group, the Labour Initiative on Co-operation (LINC), ended up with an impressive list of sponsors among the centre-left intelligentsia and published several pamphlets to put its case. See in particular Pete Ruhemann, *What's the Beef: Labour and Liberal Democrat Policies Compared* (1995).

51 *Guardian*, 27 May 1995.

52 Roy Jenkins, speech to Nexus conference at the London School of Economics, 1 March 1997.

53 Will Hutton, *The State We're In* (Jonathan Cape, 1995).

54 See Andrew Gamble and Gavin Kelly, 'Stakeholder capitalism and one nation socialism', *Renewal*, January 1996. For a radical critique of Hutton's idea of stakeholder capitalism and argument for employee share ownership schemes as an alternative, see Charles Leadbeater and Geoff Mulgan, *Mistakeholding* (Demos, 1996).

55 The members of the commission were Bob Bauman (chairman of British Aerospace), Bob Bischoff (chairman of Boss Group), James Hall (managing partner of Andersen Consulting), Jan Hall (European chief executive of GGT Group), Sir Christopher Harding (chairman of Legal and General), Lucy Heller (chairwoman of Verso, the small left-wing publisher), Lord Hollick, Gerald Holtham (director of the IPPR), Alan Hughes (director of the ESRC centre for business research in Cambridge), John Kay (chair in economics at the London Business School), Richard Layard (director of the Centre for Economic Performance at the London School of Economics), John Monks (general secretary of the TUC), David Sainsbury (chairman of Sainsbury's) and George Simpson (managing director of GEC).

56 Commission on Public Policy and British Business, *Promoting Prosperity: A Business Agenda For Britain* (Vintage, 1997).

57 Tony Blair, speech at launch of report of Commission on Public Policy and British Business, 21 January 1997.

58 *Daily Mirror*, 22 November 1996.

59 On the *Sun*, see Peter Chippendale and Chris Horrie, *Stick It Up Your Punter!* (Heinemann, 1990). For its role in the 1992 general election campaign, see Martin Linton, *Was it the Sun Wot Won It?* (Nuffield College, 1996).

60 Tony Blair, speech to NewsCorp Leadership Conference, Hayman Island, Australia, 17 July 1995.

61 Tony Blair, 'Left with no option', *Guardian*, 24 July 1995.

62 English wrote of Blair that he 'surprised us instantly by saying that not everything the Thatcher government was doing was wrong or stupid and in his view a sensible Labour government should not necessarily change too many things. It was a pretty refreshing start to a relationship with a Labour politician. But we all liked it and him. And so Tony became a regular visitor, at that time our only link to the paranoid and neurotic Labour Party of Neil Kinnock . . . When we talked about trade unions and what they had done to kill the British newspaper industry, Blair acknowledged what we had gone through. And he indicated quite clearly that, if in power, the position would not be restored to the point where we would have to face that again. Naturally, we wanted to believe him. At one lunch, the *Daily Mail*'s editor, Paul Dacre, mentioned one of his paper's justified current obsessions – the social and welfare costs of single mothers and what that was doing to society. This was something that had been raised with both John Major and John Smith and had brought an almost identical response – a knee-jerk politically correct dismissal of the subject. But, to Paul's surprise, Blair made it clear that he shared his concerns.'

63 Blair's attitude to the left-of-centre press was in remarkable contrast to his wooing of the right-wing press and its owners. The Mirror Group, run since the demise of Robert Maxwell by David Montgomery, was friendly to the point of sponsoring Labour recruitment campaigns, but Blair and his office moaned time and again when the up-market titles it partly owned, the *Independent* and the *Independent on Sunday*, failed to give him the support that they felt he deserved: just before the 1997 election, his aides even suggested to Montgomery that he fire Andrew Marr as editor of the daily paper for being insufficiently keen on New Labour. Blair's dislike of the *Guardian*, Labour's most consistent champion in the quality press, and its editor Alan Rusbridger, was famous throughout the world of journalism – and the Labour leader so hated being criticized by the *New Statesman* that his allies made sure that it was bought by a Labour MP in early 1996 and turned into a Blair-loyalist magazine. The leader's office even at one point discussed the idea of taking over and neutralizing *Tribune*, selling fewer than 10,000 copies a week, after it became a forum for complaints about the New Labour 'project'. Blair summed up his gripes in an interview with *The Times* in autumn 1995. 'As each change is made, some who form that perfectly valid but fairly narrow culture of the *Guardian*, *New Statesman*, *Tribune* and all the rest, have described each one of those changes as a shift to the right. When I first started talking about crime, it was said this was right-wing. If you go on a council estate, Labour voters say their number one problem is law and order. If you are not addressing those problems, you are not addressing their lives. If you go to the *Mirror* and *Sun* readers that vote Labour, they understand entirely well why modernizing is sensible.' (*The Times* 18 September 1995).

64 The National Policy Forum, with 75 members drawn from the Parliamentary Labour Party, the NEC, the European Parliamentary Labour Party, local government, regional Labour parties, the unions and Labour's women's, ethnic minority and youth organizations, came out of a 1990 Labour conference decision. The big idea behind it was that Labour needed a 'rolling programme' like its west European social democratic sister parties. The policy forum, by providing a way of involving a representative cross-section of party members and working by consensus, would be able to provide it rather better than the combination of NEC and annual conference. It started meeting in 1993 and played a big role in Labour's policy-making under the chairmanship of Robin Cook in 1995–7. It was liked by the party leadership because it was a good way of testing out ideas and modifying

them so that the party conference would be unlikely to oppose them, but was widely criticized for the opacity of its procedures and its lack of accountability.

65 Labour Party, *New Labour, New Life for Britain* (1996).

66 Martin Jacques, interview with Tony Blair, *Sunday Times*, 17 July 1994.

67 David Miliband, born in 1964, is the son of Ralph Miliband, the Marxist political theorist and activist. Educated at a north London comprehensive school, Oxford University and the Massachusetts Institute of Technology, he began life in Labour politics helping out in Tony Benn's basement archive as a teenager, then worked for Ken Livingstone at the Greater London Council during his student vacations. He joined IPPR as a research fellow after MIT, specialized in education, and rose to prominence as secretary of the Commission on Social Justice in 1992–4. For his ideas, see Andrew Glyn and David Miliband, *Paying for Inequality* (IPPR, 1994) and his introduction to David Miliband (ed.), *Reinventing the Left* (Polity, 1994), a series of papers written for an IPPR seminar in 1993. His younger brother Ed is a special adviser to Gordon Brown. Miliband is now director of policy in the Downing Street policy unit.

Alastair Campbell, born in 1956 into a middle-class family in Keighley, was educated at a comprehensive school in Leicester and Cambridge University. He started his journalistic career writing soft porn articles for *Forum* magazine and graduated to the *Daily Mirror* in 1983 as a reporter. He became a close friend of Neil Kinnock, Peter Mandelson, Gordon Brown and Tony Blair, and in 1989 became the *Mirror's* political editor – in which role he famously assaulted Michael White of the *Guardian* after he made a joke about the death of Robert Maxwell, the *Mirror's* proprietor. After the *Mirror* was taken over by David Montgomery in 1993, Campbell was squeezed out and joined *Today*, Rupert Murdoch's mid-market tabloid. Shortly before being head-hunted by Tony Blair as his press secretary, he made a blistering attack on John Smith's caution as Labour leader in an article in the *Spectator* that makes amusing reading today: 'There are few if any circumstances I could envisage that would lead me not to vote Labour, but if I thought Labour wouldn't spend more on health and schools, or that they wouldn't adopt a more interventionist approach to the economy, or that they wouldn't raise my taxes, then I'd have to think a bit. This is not an "irresponsible shopping list". It is the absolute minimum, surely, that the public will accept of Labour.' (Alastair Campbell, 'Here's one Labour supporter who's not so happy', *Spectator*, 30 April 1994.) His partner Fiona Millar, another journalist much favoured by the Labour establishment since the late 1980s, is now media minder for Cherie Blair. Campbell was appointed chief press secretary by Blair in May 1997.

68 Jonathan Powell, born in 1946, is the brother of Sir Charles Powell (Margaret Thatcher's foreign affairs adviser) and Chris Powell (chief executive of BMP, Labour's advertising agency). Educated at Oxford and Pennsylvania universities, he joined the diplomatic service and rose to become first secretary of the British embassy in Washington. He followed Bill Clinton on the campaign trail in 1992 and met Tony Blair when the future Labour leader went on his fact-finding mission to the US in 1993. Powell remained Blair's chief of staff after May 1997.

Derek Scott, born in 1947 and educated at Liverpool University and the London School of Economics, was a special adviser to chancellor Denis Healey in the 1970s and subsequently an adviser to Jim Callaghan when he was leader of the opposition. He stood as SDP candidate for Swindon in 1983 and 1987, returning to Labour in 1991. He is married to Elinor Goodman, the Channel Four News journalist. He was made chief economic adviser in the Number Ten policy unit in May 1997.

69 Tim Allan, a Cambridge graduate who joined Blair's team from television while he was shadow home secretary, is now a Number Ten press officer, as is Hilary Coffman, who has worked for every Labour leader since the early 1980s. Geoff Norris, a former chair of Scottish Labour students, joined Blair after working as an adviser to Robin Cook when trade and industry spokesman, and is now responsible for transport and trade and industry issues in the Number Ten policy unit. Sally Morgan, a party apparatchik at Labour's Walworth Road headquarters, was taken on by Blair because of her trade union connections and is now political secretary of the Number Ten political unit, which has responsibility for liaison between government and the Labour Party. Pat McFadden, another former chair of Scottish Labour students, came to Blair after working for Donald Dewar and is now responsible for constitutional issues in the Number Ten policy unit.

Other current members of the Number Ten policy unit who worked for Blair in opposition are Liz Lloyd (responsible for environment, agriculture and home affairs) and Peter Hyman (in charge of press liaison). James Purnell, who worked for Blair when shadow home secretary then moved to the IPPR and the BBC as a consultant, is in charge of heritage, housing, training and information technology.

70 Roger Liddle was special adviser to Bill Rodgers when he was transport secretary in the 1970s Labour government. A fellow Lambeth councillor with Mandelson, he was a founder member of the SDP in 1981 and served on its national committee from 1981 to 1986. He contested the parliamentary seat of Vauxhall for the SDP in 1983 and Fulham in the 1986 by-election, joined the Social and Liberal Democrats after the 1988 merger between the Liberals and all but the Owenite rump of the SDP and fought Hertfordshire North for the Liberal Democrats in the 1992 general election. He was a member of the Liberal Democrats' federal policy committee for most of the period between 1988 and 1995 and was author of their 1994 European manifesto. For his reasons for defecting back to Labour, see Roger Liddle, 'A new deal in hand', *Guardian*, 17 July 1995; for *The Blair Revolution* (Faber, 1996), see chapter 11. Liddle was a *New Statesman* columnist in 1996–7, writing a series of (very dull) memorandums to senior Labour front-benchers on what they should do. Now he can do it for real and get paid much more for it. Liddle is responsible for Europe and defence policy in the Downing Street policy unit.

71 Geoff Mulgan is by far the most interesting of Blair's key advisers. Educated at Oxford University, where he was briefly a member of the Trotskyist Militant Tendency, and the Massachusetts Institute of Technology, he made his name in Labour politics while working for the Greater London Enterprise Board, the body set up by the Greater London Council under Ken Livingstone to develop an interventionist economic policy for the capital. (Livingstone remains an admirer of his intellectual abilities.) In the mid-1980s he became a regular contributor to the Communist Party monthly *Marxism Today*, edited by Martin Jacques, to whom he was introduced by Charles Leadbeater, a friend from Oxford. He was hired as an adviser by Gordon Brown in 1991, and in 1992, after *Marxism Today* folded, left to set up Demos with Jacques to promote an eclectic 'post-ideological' politics. Mulgan is above all an enthusiast for small-scale experimentation, and has been influenced by a wide range of disparate thinkers and movements: management theorists, the American communitarians (Demos was responsible for introducing Amitai Etzioni to the British public by publishing the pamphlet *The Parenting Deficit* in 1994), even the decentralist libertarian left (the veteran anarchist Colin Ward is a hero). For Mulgan's ideas on the GLC, see Geoff Mulgan and Ken Worpole, *Saturday Night or Sunday Morning: From Arts to Industry – New Forms of*

Cultural Policy (Comedia, 1986). His main *Marxism Today* essays are collected in his book *Politics in an Anti-Political Age* (Polity, 1994). More recently, see Geoff Mulgan and Robin Murray, *Reconnecting Taxation* (Demos, 1993), which argues for a radical reform of the tax system to give it popular legitimacy, and Geoff Mulgan, *Connexity* (Chatto and Windus, 1997) for his synthetic overview of contemporary capitalism. The easiest way to sample Demos' output is the reader, edited by Mulgan, *Life After Politics: New Thinking for the Twenty-First Century* (Fontana, 1997). Mulgan is responsible for 'special projects' in the Downing Street policy unit.

72 Patricia Hewitt was born in Australia in 1948, the daughter of a high-ranking Australian civil servant who subsequently became a businessman. Educated at the Australian National University and Newnham College, Cambridge, she began her political career in the early 1970s as women's rights officer of the National Council for Civil Liberties. She was general secretary of the NCCL from 1974 to 1983 and rapidly made a name for herself as an outspoken socialist feminist. She was a prominent Bennite in the early 1980s Labour Party, joined Kinnock as press secretary in 1983 and was his policy co-ordinator in 1988–9. She played a key role in the Shadow Communications Agency between 1985 and 1992, and was one of the founders of the IPPR, serving as its deputy director between 1989 and 1994. For her civil libertarian phase, see her *Rights for Women* (NCCL, 1975) and the NCCL guide *Civil Liberties* which she co-edited in 1975. More recently, see her *About Time: The Revolution in Work and Family Life* (IPPR, 1993).

73 *Guardian*, 12 September 1995.

74 Blair's reliance on his inner circle was also the main reason that Roland Wales, hired by John Smith as director of policy, and Joy Johnson, taken on as director of communications in early 1995, quit the party soon after the Gould memorandum leak. Wales, a high-powered economist at the Bank of England who had taken a massive pay cut to join the party, found himself taking minutes of meetings rather than contributing anything substantial to policy discussions and left in early autumn. Johnson, a senior BBC journalist who was close to Gordon Brown, found that her job was made impossible by the interventions of Mandelson and Campbell.

2   UNLIMITED SUPPLY:
GORDON BROWN AND THE ECONOMY

1 See Edinburgh *Student*, 9 December 1970.

2 Gordon Brown, 'The gut of UCS', Edinburgh *Student*, 1971.

3 See Tim Dawson, 'Brown's cool days', *Sunday Times Scotland*, 26 November 1995.

4 Judy Goodkin, 'A Childhood: Gordon Brown', *The Times*, 15 May 1993.

5 Gordon Brown (ed.), *The Red Paper on Scotland* (Edinburgh University Student Publications Board, 1975).

6 In 1975, Gramsci (1891–1937), who died after eleven years of fascist imprisonment, was something of a cult figure among younger intellectuals on the British left, and his significance was much contested. For the revolutionary left, Leninist and libertarian, Gramsci was a hero of the workers' councils movement in Turin in 1919–20; for those of a more reformist disposition, particularly in the Communist Party but also on the Labour centre-left, his *Prison Notebooks* (a substantial selection from which had been published for the first time in English in 1971) appeared to provide the rationale for a politics that was non-insurrectionist, more radically democratic than Labour's tepid parliamentarism and more broadly based than the emphasis on militant class struggle of the CP old guard and the Trotskyists.

In Scotland, the revival of the 'national question' (the Scottish National Party had taken 30 per cent of the vote in the October 1974 general election and Labour was tearing itself apart over devolution) had made Gramsci's ideas about the necessarily national character of successful revolutions the height of intellectual fashion, particularly at Edinburgh University. In June 1974 the university hosted the First National Day Conference on Gramsci, the papers from which were published in three consecutive issues of *New Edinburgh Review*, the quarterly journal published by the Edinburgh University Student Publications Board, along with translations by Hamish Henderson of Gramsci's letters from prison. Two of the intellectuals who played a crucial role in popularizing Gramsci's ideas in Scotland in the early 1970s, Tom Nairn and Ray Burnett, were contributors to *The Red Paper*.

For Gramsci himself, see the various selections from Gramsci's work published by Lawrence and Wishart since 1971 and also Henderson's translations of Gramsci's letters, along with an introduction, in Antonio Gramsci, *Letters From Prison* (Zwan, 1988). The most incisive approaches to Gramsci in English are Gwyn A. Williams, *Proletarian Order* (Pluto, 1974) and Paul Piccone, *Italian Marxism* (University of California, 1983), but the most influential on the British left are Giuseppe Fiori, *Antonio Gramsci* (New Left Books, 1970, translated by Tom Nairn), Perry Anderson's article 'The antinomies of Antonio Gramsci' in *New Left Review* 100 (November 1976) and various books and articles by Ernesto Laclau, Chantal Mouffe and Anne Showstack Sassoon, published in the late 1970s and early 1980s. Far and away the best overview of the Scottish intellectual scene in the mid-1970s is Christopher Harvie, *Scotland and Nationalism*, 2nd edition (Routledge, 1994). For the classic application of Gramscian Marxism to nationalism in Britain, see Tom Nairn, *The Break-up of Britain* (New Left Books, 1977).

7   Only one MP joined Sillars, John Robertson, but the 'magic party' was backed by several dissident Labour officials and intellectuals. Tom Nairn and Neal Ascherson were briefly members, as was Brown's brother, Andrew.

8   Christopher Harvie, *Scotland and Nationalism*, 2nd edition (Routledge, 1994), p. 230.

9   Gordon Brown, *Maxton* (Mainstream, 1986).

10   Andy McSmith, *John Smith* (Verso, 1993), p. 121.

11   The group was chaired by Andrew Graham (economics fellow at Balliol College, Oxford, and a former economic adviser to Harold Wilson) and its most influential members apart from Eatwell were Meghnad Desai (professor of economics at the London School of Economics and a Labour peer from 1991) and Gavyn Davies (chief UK economist at the City analyst Goldman Sachs and a onetime adviser to the 1974–9 government). Other participants included Neil Mackinnon (another City analyst), John Hills (also from the LSE), Dan Corry (the Labour Party's economic policy adviser, who became chief economist at the Institute for Public Policy Research in 1992 and is now a special adviser at the Department of Trade and Industry) and Gerald Holtham (a former OECD economist then working in the City, who went on to become director of the IPPR in 1994).

12   Gould had not changed his mind about the European Community since taking against it while working as a junior diplomat in Brussels in the mid-1960s. As a young MP, after working for the 'no' campaign in the 1975 referendum on membership of what was then called the Common Market, he had become a protégé of Peter Shore, the leading anti-European of the Labour right throughout the late 1970s and early 1980s. Shore, as trade and industry secretary, made Gould his parliamentary private secretary in 1976 and, as shadow trade and industry secretary, gave him his first front-bench post as a City spokesman in 1983. See Gould's

autobiography, *Goodbye to All That* (Macmillan, 1995). Gould's fullest statement of his ideas is in *Socialism and Freedom* (Macmillan, 1986). Jack Straw, Robin Cook and John Prescott were also Shore protégés.

13 Labour Party, *Meet the Challenge, Make the Change* (1989).

14 McSmith, *John Smith*, p. 154.

15 Eric Shaw, *The Labour Party Since 1945* (Manchester University Press, 1996).

16 Labour Party, *Looking to the Future* (1990). By a cruel irony, the only comprehensive account of what Gould's industrial policy would have looked like (complete with an introduction by Gould) appeared after this document had ditched his whole approach. See Keith Cowling and Roger Sugden (eds), *A New Economic Policy for Britain* (Manchester University Press, 1990).

17 Labour Party, *It's Time to Get Britain Working Again* (1992).

18 John Eatwell, 'The Development of Labour Policy 1979–92', in Jonathan Michie (ed.) *The Economic Legacy 1979–92* (Academic Press, 1992).

19 John Maynard Keynes, *Essays in Persuasion* (1931), quoted in Robert Skidelsky, *John Maynard Keynes: Volume Two – The Economist as Saviour* (Macmillan, 1992), p. 233.

20 John Maynard Keynes, 'Liberalism and Industry', in H.L. Nathan and H.H. Williams, *Liberal Points of View* (1927), quoted in Geoffrey Foote, *The Labour Party's Political Thought* (Croom Helm, 1985), p. 140.

21 On the growing influence of the Soviet model of socialism, see John Callaghan, *Socialism in Britain* (Blackwell, 1987) and for an overview of the influence of the Soviet Union on the British left, Paul Anderson and Kevin Davey, 'Moscow gold? The true story of the Kremlin, British communism and the left', *New Statesman & Society*, 7 April 1995.

22 See John Campbell, *Nye Bevan and the Mirage of British Socialism* (Weidenfeld and Nicolson, 1987), chapter three. Bevan himself was, however, scornful of Keynes' Liberalism.

23 See Elizabeth Durbin, *New Jerusalems: The Labour Party and Democratic Socialism* (Routledge, 1985), Foote, *The Labour Party's Political Thought* and Noel Thompson, *Political Economy and the Labour Party* (UCL Press, 1996).

24 It is a mistake, however, to see the 1944 White Paper as Keynesian: it is essentially a compromise between supporters and opponents of Keynes.

25 See Robert Skidelsky, *Keynes* (OUP, 1996), chapter 6.

26 Anthony Crosland, *The Future of Socialism* (Jonathan Cape, 1956), p. 30; Aneurin Bevan, *In Place of Fear* (MacGibbon and Kee, 1952), p. 31.

27 From the left, see Andrew Glyn and Bob Sutcliffe, *British Capitalism, Workers and the Profit Squeeze* (Penguin, 1970); and from the right, Keith Middlemas, *Politics in Industrial Society* (André Deutsch, 1979).

28 Thompson, *Political Economy and the Labour Party*, chapter 16. The fullest 1970s case for the AES is in Stuart Holland, *The Socialist Challenge* (Quartet, 1975).

29 Edmund Dell, *A Hard Pounding* (Oxford, 1991).

30 Denis Healey, *The Time of My Life* (Michael Joseph, 1989) p. 378. According to Healey, Keynes' theories 'ignored the economic impact of social institutions, particularly the trade unions; in fact Keynesian policies were unlikely to work in Britain without strict control of incomes, a point of which the Treasury was already aware . . . Keynes was right in saying that adequate demand is a necessary condition for full employment; but, given the inadequacy of the information available and the uncertainty about how people will use their money, fine tuning of demand is not possible . . . I became an eclectic pragmatist.'

31 Given that former members of the Communist Party are often given these days to congratulating themselves on their political prescience during the Thatcher years,

it is worth noting that much of the intellectual momentum behind the revival of the AES in the early 1980s (and thus for the 'longest suicide note') came from CP economists. See, for example, Sam Aaronovitch, *The Road From Thatcherism: The Alternative Economic Strategy* (Lawrence and Wishart, 1981).

32 There is, however, a complicating factor. France (unlike Britain) was a member of the ERM at this time and was committed to maintaining the parity of its currency against the Deutschmark. Instead of abandoning its expansionism, the Mitterrand government could have responded to its balance of payments problems by floating the franc out of the ERM and imposing import controls – a course of action that was very much in line with the British AES and was advocated by the nationalist left of the French Socialist Party. It is possible that such drastic measures would have worked – but more likely that they would have led to a collapse of the franc and hyper-inflation.

33 For Healey's views on economic policy in the mid-1980s, see *The Time of My Life*, part four.

34 *New Statesman*, 28 December 1984, quoted in McSmith, *John Smith*, p. 105.

35 Roy Hattersley, 'Labour's plan for rebuilding Britain', *Tribune*, 24 February 1984.

36 *Tribune*, 10 May 1985.

37 Roy Hattersley, *Choose Freedom* (Michael Joseph, 1987), *Economic Priorities for a Labour Government* (Macmillan, 1987).

38 Gould, *Goodbye to All That*, p. 183.

39 Gordon Brown, *Where There is Greed . . .* (Mainstream, 1989), chapter 1. Although this is the fullest account by a Labour politician before 1992 of what 'supply-side socialism' is all about, it has a strangely unfinished feel to it. Brown at no point engages directly with Labour's Keynesians, and there is no concluding chapter.

40 Brown was also by this point seen internationally as a likely senior member of a British Labour government – to the extent that, among his many foreign trips, he could count attendance (in June 1991, along with Smith) of a meeting of the Bilderberg Group, the secretive Atlanticist elite network, in Germany. Others present included Bill Clinton, Henry Kissinger and Jacques Santer.

41 Will Hutton, 'An agenda for the 1990s', in Jonathan Michie (ed.) *The Economic Legacy 1979–92* (Academic Press, 1992).

42 See *European Labour Forum*, the quarterly magazine edited by the left-wing pro-European Labour MEP Ken Coates, summer 1992.

43 Paul Anderson, interview with John Smith, *Tribune*, 19 June 1992. Smith mentioned the possibility of realignment again in a speech to Labour MEPs in June, then again in the Commons in early July. See McSmith, *John Smith*, p. 210.

44 *Tribune*, 18 September 1992.

45 McSmith, *John Smith*, p. 231.

46 Gordon Brown, 'Europe still the answer', *Tribune*, 25 September 1992.

47 Conversation with authors. A coded account of what Labour would have done is in Meghnad Desai, 'And then I woke up . . .', *Tribune*, 13 November 1992. Three months after Black Wednesday, Brown grudgingly admitted – more or less – that Labour would have gone for realignment if it had won. He told *Tribune*: 'It is now quite clear that the government could have asked the German authorities in particular to consider a realignment. All the information that has now become available shows that there was a far more comprehensive realignment possible and that the government ruled it out without discussing it in detail. Faced with the choice between realignment within the ERM and leaving the ERM in order to devalue, many of the difficulties could have been avoided with a realignment.' (Paul Anderson, interview with Gordon Brown, *Tribune*, 1 January 1993).

More recently, it has emerged that the CBI would have urged an immediate devaluation if Labour had won (although it kept quiet after the return of the Tories), see Graham Ingham, 'Is there fudge at ten to three?', *Guardian*, 11 November 1996.

48 Gordon Brown, 'Europe still the answer', *Tribune*, 25 September 1992.

49 *Tribune*, 2 October 1992. Gould claims in his autobiography that Brown had gone so far as to say that 'if the Germans had revalued the mark as a means of stabilizing the ERM or at least relieving some of our difficulties for a time, he would want to see the pound revalued in line with the mark'. Gould, *Goodbye to All That*, p. 265.

50 The others included John Prescott, Frank Dobson, David Blunkett, Michael Meacher and, to a lesser extent, Jack Straw.

51 Roger Berry, Derek Fatchett, Peter Hain and George Howarth, *The Left in Europe* (Tribune Group of MPs, November 1992). For the Tribune MEPs' response, see Wayne David, *Building on Maastricht* (Tribune Group of MEPs, March 1993).

52 Precisely how far 'globalization' has affected the economic powers of the nation state is much disputed. For the argument that globalization has had a massive effect, see Anthony Giddens, *Beyond Left and Right: The Future of Radical Politics* (Polity, 1994) and John Gray, *After Social Democracy* (Demos, 1996). For a much more sceptical view, see Paul Hirst and Graeme Thompson, *Globalisation in Question: The International Economy and the Possibilities of Governance* (Polity, 1996).

53 Gordon Brown, speech to launch Labour's 'Campaign for Recovery', November 1992.

54 See, for example, Gordon Brown, 'First principles', *Tribune*, 26 February 1993.

55 Labour Party, *Labour's Economic Approach* (1993).

56 Will Hutton, 'Brown's economic policy caught in political crossfire', *Guardian* 1 May 1993.

57 See, for example, Gordon Brown, 'There are no quick fixes', *Tribune*, 7 May 1993.

58 John Smith, speech to TUC Congress, 7 September 1993.

59 Gordon Brown, *How We Can Conquer Unemployment* (Labour Finance and Industry Group, September 1993).

60 Will Hutton, 'Brown discovers Labour's identity with Keynes' help', *Guardian*, 28 September 1993.

61 The pamphlet, *What's Left?*, was published under the imprint of the *Tribune* newspaper, from which the group took its name but which had no formal connection with it. On the eve of publication, the group's chair, George Howarth, produced a press statement denouncing the pamphlet as 'mischievous', for release by the party press office. Much to the amusement of everyone but Brown and Howarth, it was mistakenly faxed not to the press office but to Hain's own fax machine.

62 For an accessible account of the development of the European Community budget, see John Pinder, *European Community: The Building of a Union* (OUP, 1995).

63 For Holland's early 1980s ideas, see Stuart Holland (ed.), *Out of Crisis: A Project for European Recovery* (Spokesman, 1983) and Michael Barratt Brown, 'Europe: saying no is not enough', *Tribune*, 23 September 1983.

64 Ken Coates, 'A European recovery programme', paper to the European Parliamentary Labour Party, 25 September 1992; Stuart Holland, 'Towards a people's Europe', *New Statesman & Society*, 2 October 1992; Ken Coates and Michael Barratt Brown (eds), *A European Recovery Programme* (Spokesman, 1993).

65 Balls, *Euro-Monetarism*, p. 14.

66 Labour Party, *Labour's Budget for Jobs*, *Labour Party News* supplement, January 1993.

67 Labour Party, *Labour's Economic Approach* (1993).

68 Labour Party, *Economic Renewal in the European Community* (1993).
69 In a speech in Brussels in January 1995, during a visit in which he castigated Labour MEPs for their hostility to changing Clause Four, Blair said: 'The agenda set by Jacques Delors on economic development must be pursued' (Tony Blair, speech in Brussels, 11 January 1995). Four months later in Bonn he elaborated: 'We should ensure that every citizen and region of the European Union is able to share in prosperity. That is why we need a well-resourced and effective policy of structural funds for our regions, an active European Investment Bank and a much more active policy for developing trans-European infrastructure networks.' (Tony Blair, speech in Bonn, 30 May 1995).
70 Labour Party, *A New Economic Future for Britain* (June 1995).
71 Paul Anderson, interview with Robin Cook, *New Statesman & Society*, 9 February 1996.
72 Ken Coates, who had clashed with Tony Blair over Clause Four in early 1995, felt personally let down by Labour's abandonment of the Delors plan. In a book published on the eve of Labour conference in 1996, he complained, 'New Labour's leaders, reversing the policy of John Smith, gave no support to their own party members and others in the European Parliament who were pressing upon the Commission to act.' Michael Barratt-Brown and Ken Coates, *The Blair Revelation* (Spokesman, 1996), p. 168.
73 Gordon Brown, speech to Labour Finance and Industry Group, 17 August 1993.
74 Brown says that there was no such deal. 'There was never any discussion of jobs in that way,' he told the *New Statesman* (Kirsty Milne, interview with Gordon Brown, *New Statesman & Society*, 5 August 1994).
75 Prescott's campaign for the leadership and deputy leadership had the demand for full employment at its core. He declared on 10 June 1994: 'Full employment is a major issue and the people in this country do believe that everybody should have a chance to make a contribution . . . I believe we can find work for all who want it.' But he refused to suggest a timetable for achieving it, which rather weakened the power of his argument.
76 Gordon Brown, speech to 'New policies for the global economy' conference, 27 September 1994. Apart from this infamous passage – which in fact describes clumsily but accurately where Brown was getting his ideas ('neo-classical endogenous growth theory' is about introducing various factors not normally considered in models of economic growth, in particular the impact of technical knowledge and skills, into mainstream thinking about economics) – this speech was one of Brown's better attempts to summarize his approach to economic management. 'Countries which attempt to run national go-it-alone macroeconomic policies based on tax, spend and borrow policies to boost demand, without looking at the supply-side of the economy, are bound these days to be punished by the markets in the form of stiflingly high interest rates and collapsing currencies. The only way in which recovery can be sustained without inflation accelerating is if internationally co-ordinated macroeconomic policies are combined with supply-side policies to boost investment in industry, skills and infrastructure . . . Past Labour governments tried to counter the injustice and failings of free market forces by substituting government for market, and often saw tax, spend and borrow policies as the isolationist quick fix for national decline. The fact is that these policies cannot work in the highly integrated environment in which we live.'
77 Gordon Brown, speech to Labour Finance and Industry Group, 17 May 1995.
78 Tony Blair, Mais Lecture, 22 May 1995, published as 'The British experiment – an analysis and an alternative' in Tony Blair, *New Britain: My Vision of a Young Country* (Fourth Estate, 1996).

79 Hutton told the *New Statesman* in late 1996: 'Balls was the person at the *FT* closest to my thinking. We had a fine time at City dinners siding with each other against the orthodoxies of the day . . . Scott is a routine economic thinker, perfectly competent but an ordinary economist. Everyone agrees that Balls has a more considerable economic mind.' Caroline Daniel, 'The Apparat: 6. Ed Balls', *New Statesman*, 1 November 1996.

80 Will Hutton, 'By George, this is not what Labour needs', *Guardian*, 29 May 1995.

81 The idea of a reduced starting rate for income tax was not as new as it seemed to most commentators: back in 1989, *Meet the Challenge, Make the Change* had included a proposal for a 15p starting rate.

82 *The Economist*, 4 November 1995.

83 Andrew Dilnot, 'Brown's 10p plan fails to aid those in poverty trap', *Daily Telegraph*, 20 November 1995.

84 Andy McSmith, *Faces of Labour* (Verso, 1996), p. 358.

85 Meacher's research assistant, Ian Willmore, covered for him by saying that he had written the piece without showing it to his boss.

86 Gordon Brown, 'Responsibility in public finance', 20 January 1997.

87 Brown had indeed been toying with the idea of such a tax for some time, but he finally ruled it out in early 1997 after Blair persuaded him that it was incompatible with Labour's determination to shed its 'tax and spend' image. See Nicholas Jones, *Campaign 1997* (Indigo, 1997).

88 Paul Anderson, 'Brussels doubts', *New Statesman & Society*, 13 January 1995.

89 Robin Cook, interview on LWT *Jonathan Dimbleby* programme, 2 February 1997.

90 *The Times*, 21 February 1997.

91 Alistair Darling, born in 1953, has been MP for Edinburgh Central since 1987. Educated at Aberdeen university, a former lawyer and regional councillor for Lothian, he joined the front bench as a junior home affairs spokesman in 1988 and was made a spokesman on Treasury and economic affairs in 1992. A one-time unilateral nuclear disarmer and Eurosceptic, he has been a leadership-loyalist since becoming an MP.

Geoffrey Robinson, born in 1938, has been MP for Coventry North West since winning a 1976 by-election. Educated at Cambridge and Yale Universities, he worked as a Labour Party researcher in the mid-1960s and then as an executive in the car industry before becoming an MP in 1976. He subsequently acted as chief executive for the co-operative that attempted to revive the motorcycle company Triumph at its Meriden works and set up his own engineering company, Transfer Technology, which made him a millionaire. Business took precedence over his political career for most of the 1980s. Although he served on the front bench in junior positions dealing with science (1982–3) and trade and industry (1983–6), he stepped down from the front bench in 1986 citing 'personal reasons', never specified, and adopted a low profile – in the 1988–9 session of parliament, for example, he failed to make a single speech in the Commons – until, with Blair's backing, he emerged to buy the *New Statesman* in 1996 in order to make it 'more supportive of the Labour Party'. He owns several homes at home and abroad, which he has often put at the disposal of high-placed Labour politicians.

Dawn Primarolo, born in 1954, became MP for Bristol South in 1987 following the deselection of the sitting Labour MP chief whip Michael Cocks. A former law centre adviser, legal secretary, academic and Avon county councillor, she joined the front bench as a junior health spokeswoman in 1992, and in 1994 was promoted to spokeswoman in the Treasury team.

Helen Liddell, born in 1950, won John Smith's former Monklands East seat (since renamed Airdrie and Shotts) in a June 1994 by-election. Educated at

Strathclyde University, she worked for the Scottish TUC from 1971 to 1976, becoming head of the economics department and later assistant secretary, then spent a year as a BBC economics correspondent, before becoming secretary of the Scottish Labour Party in 1977, a job she kept until 1988. She then became director of corporate affairs of the Robert Maxwell-owned *Daily Record* and *Sunday Mail* – in which role she earned a reputation as Maxwell's hatchet-woman north of the border. While there she also wrote and had published *Elite*, an Edwina Currie-style political bonkbuster. In 1993 she became chief executive of the Business Venture Programme. She joined the front bench as a junior spokeswoman on Scotland in 1995.

92 Margaret Beckett, born in 1943, worked as a metallurgist before becoming a Labour Party researcher. She first entered parliament as MP for Lincoln in 1974. She served as PPS to Judith Hart for a year, then joined the whips office, and in 1976 became a junior minister for education, making her one of the few in Tony Blair's cabinet with previous experience of government. At the 1979 election she failed to hold her seat, and returned to the Commons after a four-year gap as MP for Derby South. A member of the Campaign Group at this time, she was on and off the NEC during the early 1980s, becoming a permanent fixture from 1988. She joined the front bench as assistant spokeswoman on social security in 1984, and was promoted to shadow chief secretary to the Treasury in 1989 after winning a place in the shadow cabinet. After becoming deputy leader in 1992, she took on the brief of shadow leader of the House, and shadow cabinet campaigns co-ordinator. Following John Smith's death she served as Labour's acting leader during the leadership contest, in which she ran for both leader and deputy leader. When Tony Blair took over he appointed her shadow health secretary – widely seen as a demotion from her pre-leadership position – but in 1995 she was promoted to shadow trade and industry secretary. She has a reputation as a hard-leftist turned steely pragmatist. Though no modernizer, Beckett is one of Labour's big hitters, trusted by Gordon Brown and considered supremely competent and able, particularly under fire: during the 1997 election campaign, she was wheeled out on to *Newsnight* whenever the going got rough for Labour.

93 *Financial Times*, 7 May 1997.

94 *Financial Times*, 13 January 1997.

95 *Guardian*, 7 May 1997.

96 William Keegan, 'Help! Labour's lost its monetary marbles', *Observer*, 11 May 1997.

97 Kenneth Clarke, 'Death of a tried and tested strategy', *Financial Times*, 7 May 1997.

3 CONTINENT ISOLATED:
ROBIN COOK AND EUROPE

1 Cook's ministerial team at the FCO consists of Henderson, Derek Fatchett, Tony Lloyd and Baroness (Liz) Symons. Both Fatchett and Lloyd are close political allies of Cook from the Labour soft left. Fatchett, MP for Leeds Central since 1983, is responsible for the Middle East and North Africa. A former university lecturer, on becoming an MP he at first joined the hard left Campaign Group but left it in 1985. He was made a junior front-bench spokesman on education in 1987, moving to employment and training (1988–92) then trade and industry (1992–4) and defence (1994–5) before becoming a foreign affairs spokesman. A former member of CND, his one big political difference with Cook is electoral reform: he is a leading figure in Labour's First Past the Post campaign.

Tony Lloyd, MP for Stretford since 1983, is responsible for the Commonwealth, the United Nations, security policy and human rights. Another former university lecturer and one-time CND member, he joined the front bench as a junior transport spokesman in 1987, moving to employment (1989–94) then environment (1994–5) before becoming a foreign affairs spokesman. In 1992, he supported Bryan Gould for both the Labour leadership and deputy leadership; in 1994 he supported John Prescott for both positions.

The other two members of the FCO team are not noted as soft leftists. Doug Henderson, MP for Newcastle-upon-Tyne since 1987, was a GMB union official and regional organizer before entering parliament and was on the executive of the Scottish Labour Party from 1979 to 1987, spending two years as its chairman. He was successively a junior front-bench spokesman on trade and industry (1989–92), local government (1992–4), Citizen's Charter (1994–5) and home affairs (1995–7). When Henderson was appointed as minister for Europe after Cook had vetoed Blair's suggestion of Sir David Simon, the chairman of BP (who eventually got a post as minister for trade and competitiveness in Europe at the Department of Trade and Industry), nothing was known about his views on any European issue: he had never expressed any.

Liz Symons, who has responsibility for North America and the Caribbean, was until she received a peerage in 1996 the general secretary of the First Division Association, the elite civil service trade union. She has a reputation as an Atlanticist Blair loyalist.

2   *Scotsman*, 24 May 1997.
3   Tony Blair, speech to PES congress in Malmö, Sweden, 5 June 1997.
4   Robin Cook, note to Andrew Roth of Parliamentary Profiles, 1982.
5   This was an important role because of the Heath government's 1972 Housing Finance Act, the most contentious effect of which was to force councils to increase rents. Edinburgh was 'one of the councils that defied the Edward Heath Housing Finance Act,' as Cook put it proudly in an interview with the *Guardian* in 1988 ('Rough rider on the campaign trail', *Guardian*, 26 January 1988), although it did not go as far as the councillors of Clay Cross in Derbyshire who were surcharged for their defiance.
6   Robin Cook, 'Scotland's housing', in Gordon Brown (ed.) *The Red Paper on Scotland* (EUSPB, 1975).
7   Robin Cook and Dan Smith, *What Future in Nato?* (Fabian Society, 1978).
8   Robin Cook, 'Taming the secret services', *Tribune*, 2 December 1977.
9   Quoted in *Scotsman*, 16 January 1977.
10 *Guardian*, 12 December 1983.
11 Robin Cook, 'No room for separatism in Europe', *Scotsman*, 17 June 1975.
12 *Tribune*, 24 June 1977. Other signatories who subsequently played key roles in Labour politics included Neil Kinnock and Bryan Gould.
13 *Tribune*, 30 April 1982.
14 Like Jack Straw, he voted for John Silkin in the first round of the deputy leadership contest and switched to Benn in the second round. He attacked the Trotskyist Militant Tendency in a *Tribune* article in 1982.
15 See chapter 4.
16 Labour Party, *Campaigning for a Fairer Britain* (1983).
17 Robin Cook, speech to Socialist Group of the European Parliament, 15 November 1983; *Financial Times*, 16 November 1983.
18 Robin Cook, press release 9 January 1984; Robin Cook, 'When the banker should say Non', *The Times*, 20 March 1984.
19 Robin Cook, 'Why Europe needs a new Messina', *The Times*, 28 February 1984.

20 *The Times*, 14 May 1984.

21 *New Socialist*, 1 March 1984.

22 George Orwell, 'Toward European unity', *Partisan Review* July–August 1947, in Sonia Orwell and Ian Angus (eds), *Collected Essays, Journalism and Letters of George Orwell, Volume Four* (Penguin, 1970). The reason for Orwell's pessimism was simple: there were 'active malignant forces working against European unity' – the hostility of Russia, America and the Catholic church.

23 Richard Crossman, Michael Foot and Ian Mikardo, *Keep Left* (New Statesman, 1947).

24 R.W.G. Mackay, *Federal Europe* (Michael Joseph, 1940). Mackay (1906–1960) is a fascinating forgotten figure, one of the few Labour left-wingers of the 1940s whose concerns remain pertinent today. He threw himself into the European federalist cause in the early years of the war, rescuing the Federal Union, the main British European federalist pressure group, from bankruptcy; after that, he became organizing secretary of the left-wing party Common Wealth, founded by Richard Acland and J.B. Priestley in 1941 to fight wartime by-elections in Tory-held seats. At this time he wrote a book putting the left case for proportional representation, *Coupon or Free?* (Secker and Warburg, 1943). (Labour had agreed an electoral truce, whereby it would not fight the Tories in by-elections in 'their' seats, and vice versa – for the duration of the wartime coalition; Common Wealth won three famous by-elections between 1943 and 1945, at Eddisbury, Skipton and Chelmsford, on a radical left-wing platform, but of its 23 candidates in the 1945 general election, only one, E.R. Millington in Chelmsford, was successful, and he and Acland soon joined Labour. Acland won the Gravesend by-election for Labour in 1948 and served as MP until 1955.) Mackay moved from Hull to Reading North at the 1950 election and was defeated in 1951. On Mackay, see Richard Mayne and John Pinder, *Federal Union: The Pioneers* (Macmillan, 1990). On Common Wealth, see Angus Calder, *The People's War* (Panther, 1971).

25 Gaitskell recorded in his diary for 4 December 1947: 'Most of the evening was spent discussing Kim Mackay's proposals for integrating western Europe politically and economically. This was, in the main, severely and deservedly criticized on the ground that it was economically irrelevant in the short period and offered no particular advantages in the long period.' See Philip Williams (ed.), *The Diary of Hugh Gaitskell* (Jonathan Cape, 1983).

26 Kenneth O. Morgan, *Labour in Power* (Oxford, 1984) chapter nine; R.W.G. Mackay, *Britain in Wonderland* (Gollancz, 1948), second (US) edition *You Can't Turn the Clock Back* (Ziff-Davies, 1948).

27 Mackay, *You Can't Turn the Clock Back*, chapter three.

28 In 1929, the Ramsay MacDonald Labour government responded to the proposal of Briand, then French prime minister, for a European union by belatedly despatching a communiqué that declared: 'Exclusive and independent European union of the kind proposed might emphasize or create tendencies to inter-continental rivalries.' See Kevin Featherstone, *Socialist Parties and European Integration* (Manchester, 1988). On the federalist cause in the late 1930s, see Richard Mayne and John Pinder, *Federal Union: The Pioneers* (Macmillan, 1990).

29 Clement Attlee, *Labour's Peace Aims* (Labour Party, 1939).

30 Hugh Dalton, *Hitler's War: Before and After* (Penguin 1940).

31 Harold Wilson, 'The economic aspects of federation', in Federal Union Research Institute, *First Annual Report* (1940). This paper, along with many others of interest, is excerpted in Walter Lipgens (ed.), *Documents on the History of European Integration* (Walter de Gruyter/European University Institute, 1988).

32 Aneurin Bevan, 'Labour's European policy', *Tribune*, 7 April 1944.

33 Altiero Spinelli (1907–86) was later a member of the European Commission and subsequently an MEP, in which role he was the principal author of the Draft Treaty on European Union passed by the European Parliament in 1984, which paved the way for Maastricht.

34 Quoted in Ben Pimlott, *Hugh Dalton* (Jonathan Cape, 1985), p. 566.

35 Healey's pamphlet, *Feet on the Ground* (Labour Party, 1948), was wholly pragmatist in tone. 'Europe's history of separate national existence has produced clearly defined interest groups. Where such groups exist no written constitution can by itself compel them to act against their perceived interests. More than most federal governments, a European federation would require forcible sanctions against secession. The prolonged and bloody American Civil War is not an encouraging precedent.' An excerpt is published in Denis Healey, *When Shrimps Learn to Whistle* (Michael Joseph, 1990).

36 Jean Monnet (1888–1979) is rightly considered the father of the European Community. He was co-author of the proposal for an Anglo-French Union in 1940, and after the war was made head of the French Planning Commission.

37 Labour Party, *European Unity* (1950). Herbert Morrison, the foreign secretary who succeeded Bevin, said of the Schuman plan: 'It's no good. The Durham miners won't wear it.'

38 Quoted in Pimlott *Hugh Dalton*, p. 581. Pimlott also recounts several stories of Dalton's calculated rudeness to the French and German delegations at Council of Europe meetings in Strasbourg.

39 Quoted by John Campbell, *Nye Bevan and the Mirage of British Socialism* (Weidenfeld and Nicolson, 1984).

40 *Tribune*, 30 August 1957. Denis Healey makes much the same point from the right in his memoirs: 'I felt . . . that if we could not solve our problems on our own, we could scarcely hope to survive in the jungle of competition with European economies far more efficient than our own.'

41 Hugh Gaitskell, speech to Labour conference, 3 October 1963. After the speech, the conference passed a policy document, *Labour and the Common Market*, drafted by Peter Shore, then Labour's head of research, arguing that 'our connections and interests, both political and economic, lie as much outside Europe as within it . . . Britain should not enter and the present negotiations should be brought to an end.' Shore says that his briefings were what persuaded Gaitskell to come out against the Common Market. See Peter Shore, *Leading the Left* (Weidenfeld and Nicolson, 1993).

42 Ben Pimlott, *Harold Wilson* (HarperCollins, 1992), p. 434.

43 Pimlott, *Harold Wilson*, chapter 20.

44 See Tom Nairn's polemic, *The Left Against Europe?* (Penguin, 1973), for a stunning and still pertinent demolition of the anti-Market left.

45 Labour's anti-Europeans have always argued that the 'treachery' of the 69 gave the government victory, but this neglects the fact that the rebels decided to rebel only because Heath made the vote a free one for Tory MPs. If the Tories had imposed a whip to make their anti-Europeans toe the line, the government would have won easily even if the 69 had voted against with the rest of their Labour colleagues. See Pimlott, *Harold Wilson*, chapter 25.

46 Labour Party, *Let us Work Together* (1974).

47 Labour Party, *Britain Will Win With Labour* (1974).

48 The cabinet voted 16–7 in favour of the renegotiated terms on 18 March 1975; those who voted against were Tony Benn, Barbara Castle, Michael Foot, Peter Shore, John Silkin, Willy Ross and Eric Varley. On 9 April, 145 Labour MPs voted against the government on the terms, with 137 for and 33 abstentions. Junior ministers were evenly split among pros and antis. See Pimlott, *Harold Wilson*, chapter 28.

49 Until 1979, members of the European Parliament had been appointed. De Gaulle had blocked the idea of direct elections while he was French president, and after his demise the Community had been more concerned with expansion than with improving its democratic accountability. For a dissident Labour argument for an elected European Parliament, see David Marquand, *Parliament for Europe* (Jonathan Cape, 1979). Marquand, the Labour MP for Ashfield from 1966 to 1977, left parliament to join Jenkins in Brussels, where he was responsible for relations between the European Parliament and the Commission. He subsequently joined Jenkins again in the SDP.

50 Conversation with authors.

51 Labour Party, *New Hope for Britain* (1983).

52 *New Socialist*, a monthly, enjoyed formal editorial independence from the party leadership – but Weir found out precisely what that meant after he decided to come out for tactical voting against the Tories in 1987: he was summarily fired by Kinnock.

53 Labour Party, *Britain Will Win* (1987).

54 See, for example, Christine Crawley, Glyn Ford, David Martin and David Morris, 'Kamikaze politics', *Tribune*, 12 December 1986, which reports, 'The current epithet for the British Labour members, which originated among the Spanish socialists, is *Los Japoneses* (The Japanese), deriving from the occasional discovery in remote island jungles of Japanese soldiers who didn't know the war was over.'

55 Margaret Thatcher, speech in Bruges, 20 September 1988.

56 Labour Party, *Meet the Challenge, Make the Change* (1989).

57 Labour Party, *Looking to the Future* (1990).

58 Labour Party, *Opportunity Britain* (1991).

59 Paul Anderson, 'Fudge and mudge?', *Tribune*, 29 November 1991.

60 Labour Party, *Prosperity Through Co-operation* (1993).

61 See David Butler and Martin Westlake, *British Politics and European Elections 1994* (St Martin's Press, 1995).

62 See Barbara Castle, *Fighting All the Way* (Macmillan, 1983).

63 Butler and Westlake, *British Politics and European Elections 1994*, p. 28.

64 For what might be called the mainstream EPLP view on the development of Europe, see Glyn Ford, Glenys Kinnock and Arlene McCarthy (eds), *Changing States: A Labour Agenda for Europe* (Mandarin, 1996). A coded indication of the EPLP's dissatisfaction with the Labour leadership on European policy was Ford's article 'Labour must get ready for Europe' (*New Statesman*, 10 January 1997), which argued that the party was largely unprepared for dealing with any aspect of the EU in government. The regional list system for European Parliament elections is discussed in chapter 8.

65 Cook decided not to run 'reluctantly and with a heavy heart', according to a circular letter explaining his decision he sent to supporters who had urged him to contest the leadership election. 'It has not been an easy decision, and I have kept an open mind about whether to run for as long as possible. It is clear from the many approaches I have received that I have a considerable basis of support among the active members of the Labour Party. However, it is equally clear from the soundings my colleagues and others have taken that there is not sufficient support among the wider membership of the party and the trade unions for my candidacy.' Robin Cook, letter to supporters, June 1994.

66 Ewan MacAskill, 'Shadow boxers threaten Blair KO', *Scotsman*, 24 November 1995.

67 Paul Anderson, interview with Robin Cook, *New Statesman & Society*, 9 February 1996.

68 See, for example, Tony Blair 'I'm a British patriot', *Sun*, 17 March 1997, in which he wrote on EMU: 'If the issue does arise in the next parliament – and we say if – there is a triple lock in place: first the Cabinet must agree; second parliament must give its backing; most of all, the people must have the final say in a referendum.'

69 Labour Party, *New Labour: Because Britain Deserves Better* (1997).

70 *Financial Times*, 7 April 1997.

4 GET A MOVE ON:
JOHN PRESCOTT'S SUPER-MINISTRY

1 *Sunday Times*, 23 February 1997.

2 John Prescott press release, 2 May 1997.

3 Graham Turner, interview with John Prescott, *Sunday Telegraph*, 15 May 1994.

4 Colin Brown, *Fighting Talk: The Biography of John Prescott* (Simon and Schuster, 1997).

5 Raphael Samuel, 'Labour's rough diamond', *Guardian*, 2 June 1992.

6 *Not Wanted on Voyage* condemned 'the unholy alliance of Labour government, Tory opposition, press, shipowners and international capital' against the seamen, and argued for the replacement of the government's wage controls with a 'socialist incomes policy' and demanded nationalization of the shipping industry.

7 Prescott's earlier role in the seamen's strike proved no obstacle. The man who called him to the front bench was Roy (now Lord) Mason, one of those Prescott had singled out in *Not Wanted On Voyage*. In it Prescott criticized Mason, as shipping minister in 1966, for being too close to the ship-owners. Mason later recalled that Prescott was appointed in spite of this 'because he was good. He came in with all his experience in shipping, the merchant navy and safety at sea. He knew his subject.' Quoted in Brown, *Fighting Talk*, p. 115.

8 He flew to Reykjavik with his 'peace plan', but his efforts were disowned by the British government. The message sent to British embassies by foreign secretary Jim Callaghan declaring that 'there is no truth in the story that Prescott is acting on my behalf' is printed in full in Brown, *Fighting Talk*, p. 122.

9 Quoted in Brown, *Fighting Talk*, p. 118. In line with this, whereas in the early 1970s, Prescott had argued against an elected European parliament, which would grant democratic legitimacy to the EEC, by 1977 he had accepted that such a parliament was inevitable, and argued instead that its powers should be strictly limited.

10 David Marquand, *Parliament for Europe* (Jonathan Cape, 1979), p. 76.

11 *Sunday Telegraph*, 24 April 1988.

12 Jim Callaghan was also impressed by Prescott's performance in Europe. In 1979 he offered Prescott the job of becoming the party's nominated European Commissioner, to succeed Roy Jenkins (who would step down in 1981). Prescott, set on staying at Westminster, turned down the offer.

13 Prescott's promotion caused some raised eyebrows because he had opposed Kinnock's attempt at Labour's 1984 party conference to introduce one member, one vote for the selection of parliamentary candidates.

14 Address by John Prescott to National Union of Mine-workers rally, Sheffield City Hall, 8 November 1984. Quoted in Brown, *Fighting Talk*.

15 Paul Morley, 'Labour Party animal', *Esquire*, June 1994.

16 John Prescott, *Planning for Full Employment: Options for a Modern Employment Strategy* (1985). See *Observer*, 29 September 1985.

17 John Prescott, *Real Needs – Local Jobs* (1987), quoted in Colin Brown, *Fighting Talk*, p. 158.

18 Prescott later received an added insult when the jobs package put together by Gould was finally launched to the public, and it was made clear that the shadow employment secretary's presence was not required on the press conference platform. Prescott insisted on being there, and was allowed on condition he said nothing.

19 Prescott knew Mandelson from the time when the latter worked briefly as a researcher to Albert Booth. Prescott's reference for him was decisive in securing him the job of director of communications.

20 Phil Kelly, interview with John Prescott, *Tribune*, 4 December 1987.

21 Labour Party, *Moving Britain into the 1990s* (1989).

22 Phil Kelly, interview with John Prescott, *Tribune*, 30 September 1988.

23 Paul Anderson, interview with John Prescott, *Tribune*, 27 March 1992.

24 *Observer*, 10 February 1991.

25 Prescott's only prime-time appearance was on satellite television. Kept off Labour's A-list of campaign stars, he decided to run his own campaign from Hull. He managed to circumvent Labour's press officers and book himself on to Sky TV's *Election Call* on 18 March 1992, where he proceeded to drop a clanger by admitting that 'there may be some shake-out in some of the jobs in certain areas' as a result of the party's introduction of a minimum wage. Just the day before, on BBC1's *Election Call*, employment spokesman Tony Blair had insisted that the minimum wage would have no such effect.

26 John Prescott, interview on TV-am *Frost* programme, 14 June 1992.

27 *Guardian*, 18 June 1992.

28 John Prescott, 'Second's thoughts', *New Statesman & Society*, 5 June 1992.

29 *Daily Telegraph*, 5 June 1992.

30 John Prescott, interview on BBC1 *Breakfast with Frost* programme, 15 May 1994, quoted in John Rentoul, *Tony Blair* (Little, Brown, 1995).

31 Paul Morley, 'Labour Party animal', *Esquire*, June 1994.

32 *The Times*, 4 June 1994.

33 *The Times*, 25 February 1993.

34 Labour's Ian Pearson won Dudley West from the Tories on a swing of 29 per cent to Labour. In Littleborough and Saddleworth, the Liberal Democrats' Chris Davies won the previously Tory seat, with Labour's Phil Woolas in second place, after a bitter campaign noteworthy for Labour's accusation that Davies was 'soft on drugs'. Many Labour MPs were dismayed by the campaign run by Prescott and Peter Mandelson, and Richard Burden caused a storm when he expressed his reservations about Labour's tactics in the *New Statesman* after Davies' victory. (See Richard Burden, 'Time to renew New Labour', *New Statesman & Society*, 11 August 1995).

35 Worse than not being invited, however, he had been misled by Blair in advance of the gathering, the members of which included Gordon Brown, Peter Mandelson, Jonathan Powell, Alastair Campbell, David Miliband, Tom Sawyer and Joy Johnson. Prescott had requested a meeting with Blair, who replied that he had no time free over the weekend because of family commitments.

36 The row led to a bitter falling out between Prescott and Short that spilled over after the latter was removed from her post in July 1996 and moved to overseas development. Soon after being demoted, Short gave a widely reported interview to the *New Statesman* in which she talked of 'some people who are meant to be on my side, one of whom I thought was a really good friend of mine, being dishonest and trying to hurt and damage me'. It did not take much guessing to whom she was referring. See *New Statesman*, 2 August 1996. By coincidence, Blair was on holiday at Robinson's villa in Tuscany when his magazine published the Short interview.

37 Gordon Brown, speech 1 May 1996.

38 *Guardian*, 15 May 1996.

39 Although he made a point of acknowledging the 'legitimate concern about health risks to workers and communities around nuclear plants' and was in favour of combined heat and power schemes and developing renewable sources of energy, he was essentially a pragmatist. 'We have to recognize that nuclear power will be playing a part, contributing towards British energy requirements, certainly to the end of this century,' he told *Tribune*. See Phil Kelly, interview with John Prescott, *Tribune*, 4 December 1987.

40 Anthony Crosland, *A Social Democratic Britain* (Fabian Society, 1971).

41 Donella H. Meadows *et al*, *The Limits to Growth* (Earth Island, 1972).

42 The distinction between environmentalists, who believe in ameliorative changes to improve the environment, and political ecologists, who hold to a radical critique of industrialism and believe in a transformation of society and its relations with the natural world, is well explained in Andrew Dobson, *Green Political Thought* (second edition, Routledge, 1995).

43 For the story of the Lucas plan, see Hilary Wainwright and Dave Elliot, *The Lucas Plan: A New Trade Unionism in the Making* (Allison and Busby, 1982). For the best teasing out of its implications for the use of technology, see Mike Cooley, *Architect or Bee?* (Chatto and Windus, 1987).

44 On Sizewell B, see John Valentine, *Atomic Crossroads: Before and After Sizewell* (Merlin, 1984) and Tony Hall, *Nuclear Politics: The History of Nuclear Power in Britain* (Penguin, 1986).

45 Robin Cook, 'Towards an alternative ecological strategy', *New Ground*, issue 2, spring 1984. It is amusing to note which colleague Cook singled out for particular criticism in this piece. 'Consider for instance one contribution to the debate, *How to Win*, published by Spokesman, for which Michael Meacher has provided a lucid exposition of the AES which can serve as our exemplar. Meacher argues unequivocally in favour of exponential growth: "The key premise for this objective [full employment] was that it could be brought about if, and only if, a steady and sustained expansion of the economy could be realized . . ." The next question is: how can such a sustained economic expansion be achieved? Meacher eventually settles for a target of 3 per cent annual growth in GNP.

'Such a target begs more questions than whether it can be achieved, which is the one to which Meacher addresses himself. What would be the diseconomies of such "steady and sustained" growth? How much more pollution? How much faster the depletion of natural resources that cannot be replaced? How much further dehumanization of the labour process in the relentless search for greater output? We ought at least to ask what quality of growth is desirable as often as we ask what quantity of growth is necessary . . . Might we not rewrite Meacher's premise so that it reads: "The key premise for full employment is that it can be brought about if, and only if, we shed the obsession with growth through high technology mass production that got us here in the first place"?'

46 Labour Party, *Charter for the Environment* (1986).

47 For a critical view of the 'greening' of Labour in the 1980s, see Martin Ryle, *Ecology and Socialism* (Radius, 1988). For a more sympathetic account, see Mike Robinson, *The Greening of British Party Politics* (Manchester University Press, 1992).

48 World Commission on Environment and Development (chaired by Gro Harlem Brundtland), *Our Common Future* (Oxford University Press, 1987).

49 Labour Party, *Meet the Challenge, Make the Change* (1989).

50 Chris Smith, 'Only socialists can be really green', *Tribune*, 21 July 1989.

51 See David Pearce, Anil Markandya and Edward Barbier, *Blueprint for a Green Economy* (Earthscan, 1989), usually known as the 'Pearce report'.

52 Labour Party, *An Earthly Chance* (1990).

53 Ben Webb, 'A green recovery', *Tribune*, 26 March 1993.

54 With a couple of exceptions, the parliamentary membership of the environment policy commission read like the attendance list of a secret caucus meeting of the soft left. Apart from Chris Smith, the MPs on it were Robin Cook (then trade and industry spokesman); John Prescott (transport and subsequently employment); Michael Meacher (overseas development until October 1993); Mo Mowlam (national heritage from October 1993); Frank Dobson (transport from October 1993); Clare Short (environment team until October 1993); Gavin Strang (agriculture from October 1993); George Howarth (environment team from October 1993); Andrew Smith (Treasury team); Joyce Quin (employment team until October 1993); Dawn Primarolo (health team); Jim Cousins (trade and industry team) and Joan Walley (transport team). The trade union members were Diana Jeuda of the shopworkers' union USDAW (with Smith, the co-convenor); Judith Church of MSF and Vernon Hince and Dave Ward of the Rail, Maritime and Transport union. Other members included Ken Collins MEP, chair of the European Parliament's influential environment committee, John Harman, leader of Kirklees council, and Peter Soulsby, leader of Leicester city council. The secretary of the commission was Stephen Tindale and its advisers Michael Jacobs, Susan Owens, Hugh Raven and Nick Robins – as high-powered a group as is imaginable.

55 Labour Party, *In Trust for Tomorrow* (1994).

56 Martin O'Neill, interview on BBC1 *On the Record* programme, 1 January 1995.

57 Stephen Tindale, 'A green unpleasant stand', *New Statesman & Society*, 20 January 1995. Tindale was by this point working at the think-tank IPPR on green taxes. See Gerald Holtham and Stephen Tindale, *Green Tax Reform: Pollution Payments and Tax Cuts* (IPPR, 1996).

58 Charles Secrett, 'Neither red nor green', *Red Pepper*, February 1997.

59 *Independent*, 3 March 1997.

60 Clive Ponting, *Breach of Promise: Labour in Power 1964–70* (Hamish Hamilton, 1989) p. 112.

61 Gavin Strang is one of the few members of the current government with previous governmental experience. First elected in 1970, he was briefly a junior energy minister and then a junior agriculture minister in the 1974–9 Labour government. He was a stalwart of the Parliamentary Labour CND group in the 1980s, serving as its secretary between 1982 and 1984 and then as its chairman from 1984 to 1987, and was for several years a member of the Campaign Group of Labour MPs.

62 Michael Meacher, like Strang, has previous governmental experience. First elected in 1970, he was a junior industry minister under Tony Benn in 1974–5, then a junior health and social security minister under Barbara Castle in 1975–6, then a junior trade minister under Edmund Dell and then John Smith until 1979. In opposition from 1979, he played a major role in the left-wing revolt that culminated in Tony Benn's bid for Labour's deputy leadership in 1981, and in 1983 he stood himself for the deputy leader's job as the hard left candidate. He was elected to both the National Executive Committee and the shadow cabinet for the first time the same year. Under the leadership of Neil Kinnock, for whom he was a crucial left-wing supporter in the mid-1980s, he was successively health and social security spokesman (1983–7), employment spokesman (1987–9, a post he lost after falling out with Kinnock on the union closed shop) and social security spokesman (1989–92). He lost his NEC seat in 1988. After 1992, he remained on the shadow cabinet as overseas development spokesman (1992–3), national heritage spokesman (1993–4), transport spokesman (1994–5) and

employment spokesman (1995–6) before getting the environmental protection portfolio.

63 Hilary Armstrong, first elected in 1987, is a former polytechnic lecturer and local councillor who inherited her father's safe Durham North West seat. A junior education spokeswoman under Jack Straw from 1988 to 1992, she became Smith's PPS when he was elected leader and has been a member of the NEC women's section since 1993. She returned to the front bench as a junior member of the Treasury team in 1994 and was made local government spokeswoman in 1995.

64 First elected in 1983 in place of the deselected right-winger Fred Mulley, Dick Caborn was Prescott's campaign manager for his 1988, 1992 and 1994 deputy leadership bids and was a member of his office when he was deputy leader between 1994 and 1997.

65 On policy, the party's main effort between 1994 and 1997, a document produced by Short just before she was relieved of her post, added little to what had gone before. See Labour Party, *Consensus for Change* (1996).

66 Jack Cunningham's consultancies, declared in the register of members' interests, caused Friends of the Earth to demand his removal from his post at MAFF less than a week after his appointment.

67 Meacher toyed with environmentalist ideas in the early 1980s, warning in his 1982 book *Socialism With a Human Face* against 'reckless and relentless pressure to maximize economic growth at all costs' and putting forward the possibility of a 'steady state economy' in which 'the total population and the total stock of physical wealth are maintained roughly constant at some desired levels'. But he remained very much on the orthodox left in his backing for the Alternative Economic Strategy: it was not until the late 1980s, after global warming hit the headlines, that he really embraced environmentalism. His 1992 book *Diffusing Power* puts turning back 'the rising tide of pollution-generating growth before it swamps the delicate ecological balance of the planet' at the centre of its argument. See Michael Meacher, *Socialism With a Human Face: The Political Economy of Britain in the 1980s* (Allen and Unwin, 1982); *Diffusing Power: The Key to Socialist Revival* (Pluto, 1992).

68 John Prescott press release, 2 May 1997.

5 CLASS STRUGGLE:
DAVID BLUNKETT AND EDUCATION

1 Quoted in *The Times*, 21 May 1997.

2 David Blunkett, 'Time's up for schools that fail', *The Times*, 20 May 1997.

3 George Varnava, 'Named and shamed in passion for punishment', *Times Educational Supplement*, 30 May 1997.

4 Susan Crosland, *Tony Crosland* (Jonathan Cape, 1982), p. 148. She continues: '"Why not Scotland?" I asked out of pure curiosity. "Because their schools come under the secretary of state for Scotland." He began to laugh at his inability to destroy their grammar schools.'

5 Labour's argument about private education has been a constant since the 1945–51 government decided not to bring private schools into the state system. The 1964–70 government set up a Public Schools Commission to examine ways of phasing out private education, but to the disappointment of the left it concluded that nothing much could be done. Labour was elected in 1974 promising to abolish direct grant schools (the small number of fee-paying schools that were partially funded by the state) and to end the private schools' tax privileges, but only the former made it on to the statute book: its main effect was to increase the number

of independent fee-paying schools. The 1983 Labour manifesto stated: 'Private schools are a major obstacle to a free and fair education system . . . We shall . . . withdraw charitable status from private schools and all their other public subsidies and tax privileges. We will also charge VAT on the fees paid to such schools; phase out fee charging; and integrate private schools within the local authority sector where necessary.' By 1987, the threat to take over private schools had been dropped.

6 Anthony Crosland, *The Future of Socialism* (Jonathan Cape, 1956), p. 188. On the development of Labour policy on comprehensive schools, see Michael Sullivan, *The Development of the British Welfare State* (Harvester Wheatsheaf, 1996); Howard Glennerster, *British Social Policy Since 1945* (Blackwell, 1995).

7 Quoted in Robert Harris, *The Making of Neil Kinnock* (Faber, 1984).

8 Jack Straw, 'Paradise postponed', *Guardian*, 7 July 1992.

9 See Melanie Phillips, 'Educashun still isn't working', *Guardian*, 28 September 1990. Straw was in no doubt that he deserved the admiration. After the 1992 election defeat he congratulated himself in an article in the *Guardian* on his effectiveness as education spokesman. 'I have confronted four secretaries of state, visited 250 schools and colleges, and issued 316 press notices, innumerable speeches and policy launches. I have seen and smelled more decaying classrooms and school lavatories than any civilized nation should tolerate,' he boasted. 'Education was a significant strength for Labour right up to and through polling day . . . MORI, in a post-election survey, asked voters whether education standards would have gone up or down if Labour had won the election. The response was that 72 per cent said that they would have gone up.' (Jack Straw, 'Paradise postponed', *Guardian*, 7 July 1992).

10 Labour Party, *Time to Get Britain Working Again* (1992).

11 Labour Party, *Opening Doors to a Learning Society* (1994).

12 Tony Blair, interview on BBC1 *On the Record* programme, 28 June 1994.

13 As Blunkett – twelve years old at this time – put it in his autobiography, the family was 'desperately poor. I do not use the term lightly. Those who have never experienced real poverty are all too often very sentimental about it and about poor people in general. I have to smile at this and think: if only you knew what it was like, you would have known all about aspirations and expectations, and why it was that, in the community in which I grew up, escaping the poverty trap and achieving success were the key aims. That is why I am so keen to give people ladders out of poverty, to give them a hand up rather than a hand-out. My mother, at one stage, had only bread and dripping in the house for us to eat.' David Blunkett with Alex MacCormick, *On a Clear Day* (Michael O'Mara, 1995), p. 50.

14 Blunkett, *On a Clear Day*, p. 64.

15 Blunkett, *On a Clear Day*, p. 65.

16 Blunkett, *On a Clear Day*, p. 100.

17 For more on Blunkett's early political career, see Andy McSmith's chapter on him in his *Faces of Labour* (Verso, 1996).

18 McSmith, *Faces of Labour*, p. 157.

19 Through a new employment department at city hall, the council established training centres, offered incentives to the private sector to come to Sheffield, expanded the city's direct labour force and encouraged creation of worker co-operatives. It was the epitome of a 'tax and spend' programme, paid for by high rates, and was reliant on union involvement – but Blunkett still defends it. 'It gave the feeling that there was an effort being made to protect people from what was a calamity for the whole community,' he told McSmith (*Faces of Labour*, p. 156). There are sympathetic accounts of the Sheffield experiment in Hilary Wainwright, *Labour A Tale of*

Two Parties (Chatto and Windus, 1987) and Patrick Seyd, *The Rise and Fall of the Labour Left* (Macmillan, 1987). Blunkett himself outlined what he saw as the aims of the council in 1983 in a Fabian pamphlet he wrote with Geoff Green, *Building from the Bottom: The Sheffield Experience.*

20 *Tribune*, 5 December 1986.

21 *Hansard*, 20 June 1990. Blunkett said: 'People have an absolute right to be themselves, to reject contact with men or to shun any physical contact with them. That is their choice, but that is not the same as accepting that there is some automatic or inalienable right to child-bearing. Child-bearing is not a right. It is part of the unfathomable life force. That is why man and woman must take responsibility for the well-being and love of the child.'

22 Blunkett, *On a Clear Day*, p. 60.

23 *Tribune*, 1 August 1986.

24 *Tribune*, 22 November 1985.

25 See Stewart Lansley, Sue Goss and Christian Wolmar, *Councils in Conflict: The Rise and Fall of the Municipal Left* (Macmillan, 1989).

26 Blunkett strongly resisted abandonment of unilateral nuclear disarmament in 1987–9. In summer 1988, just months before rising to the front bench but following a television interview in which the Labour leader distanced himself from the party's policy, he issued a public statement declaring: 'If an unnecessary and devastating split in the party is to be avoided, the leader needs to make clear that his words were not an abandonment of his long-standing commitment to which so many of his allies have placed their trust.' After some behind-the-scenes skirmishing, Kinnock drew back from pushing the point any further, but the next spring Gerald Kaufman and Martin O'Neill produced a document that ditched Labour's commitment to a non-nuclear defence policy. At the NEC meeting that discussed the document, Blunkett proposed an amendment stating that a Labour government would take 'independent steps to remove nuclear weapons and bases from our soil' if after five years negotiations had failed to bring about a nuclear-free Europe. It was rejected, and Blunkett complained to the press about Kinnock's unwillingness to compromise. He subsequently backed the left's call for a reduction of British defence spending to the west European average (see chapter 12).

   Blunkett made less of a public fuss over Europe. Nevertheless, he publicly opposed sterling joining the exchange rate mechanism of the European Monetary System in 1990, and in November 1991, just before the Maastricht summit that agreed the terms of European union, wrote to *The Times* declaring that he had 'long been a sceptic about the enthusiasm for greater economic integration'. After the 1992 general election defeat, he acted as manager for Bryan Gould's Eurosceptical leadership campaign and argued strongly for a pro-devaluation position during the summer 1992 currency crisis. He subsequently complained that Britain was being rushed into making a decision on Maastricht and in November 1992 came out against what he called a 'bankers' Europe'. Just before Labour's 1994 European conference, he issued a statement deploring the '*tafelwein* culture' promoted by advocates of a federal Europe.

27 Blunkett was a strong supporter of the expansion of decentralized forms of 'social ownership', and his views were reflected in the 1986 policy document he co-authored with John Smith, *Social Ownership*.

28 Blunkett was co-convener of a policy review group dealing with measures for making public services more efficient and accountable. Its report reflected Blunkett's favourite theme of empowering citizens by participation in community organizations and emphasized that service quality was paramount. It proposed fines on local authorities if their 'consumers' (local residents) suffered services

below a certain standard, and suggested performance-related pay and fixed-term contracts for chief officers. On Blunkett's support for Kinnock against Benn, see David Blunkett, 'How to divide your friends and unite your opponents', *Tribune*, 22 April 1988.

29 Tony Blair, interview on BBC1 *Good Morning With Anne and Nick* programme, 1 December 1994.

30 David Blunkett, letter to members of the Parliamentary Labour Party, 2 December 1994.

31 David Blunkett, interview on BBC Radio 4 *The World This Weekend* programme 1 January 1995.

32 Labour Party, *Diversity and Excellence: A New Partnership for Schools* (1995).

33 Roy Hattersley, 'Back to the blackboard', *Guardian*, 4 August 1995.

34 David Blunkett, 'Big balancing act', *Guardian*, 9 August 1995.

35 Blunkett's words were to cause him some embarrassment during the Wirral South by-election campaign in early 1997, when Labour told voters that it would not abolish grammar schools unless parents at those schools wanted them abolished.

36 Although still in his early forties, Michael Barber has had an extraordinary range of experience in education. Starting out as a teacher, he chaired Hackney's education committee and was head of the National Union of Teachers' education department before entering academia, first as professor of education at Keele University and then as dean of new initiatives at the Institute of Education, London University. He was an adviser to the DfEE even under the Tories, and was appointed to the trouble-shooting group sent in to sort out the failing Hackney Downs school in east London in 1995. He was appointed chair of Labour's Literacy Task Force by Blunkett in summer 1996. The most easily accessible account of his approach is his book *The Learning Game: Arguments for an Education Revolution* (Gollancz, 1996).

Tim Brighouse sprang to national fame when he was described by education secretary John Patten as a 'nutter' in 1993 – a joke that turned sour after Brighouse successfully sued him for libel. Brighouse was chief of education in Oxfordshire for most of the 1980s before becoming professor of education at Keele, where he was succeeded by Barber (with whom he had collaborated on a pamphlet for the Institute for Public Policy Research) on taking up the job in Birmingham. His appointment as vice-chair with Woodhead of the Labour government's standards task force in May 1997 caused some raised eyebrows: the pair spent much of 1995 and 1996 involved in a public row over the testing criteria used by Woodhead's Office for Standards in Education.

Other key advisers to Blair and Blunkett before the election included Leisha Fullick, chief executive of Islington council and a former director of education in the south London borough of Lewisham; Kathryn Riley of the Roehampton Institute in London, who advised on the changing role of local authorities; and David Reynolds of Newcastle University, an authority on international educational comparisons and an enthusiast for basic literacy and numeracy teaching in Taiwan. Reynolds was appointed chair of Labour's Numeracy Task Force in spring 1997. Tony Blair's head of policy, David Miliband, formerly secretary of the Commission on Social Justice, took a particular interest in developing education policy. A former colleague of his at the IPPR, Josh Hillman, was largely responsible for Labour's plans for a University for Industry to provide access to training. See Geraldine Hackett, 'Blunkett revises with help of professors', *Times Educational Supplement*, 6 October 1996.

37 Labour Party, *Excellence for Everyone: Labour's Crusade to Raise Standards* (December 1995).

38 Melanie Phillips, 'Labour's new class consciousness', *Observer*, 10 December 1995.

39 Labour Party, *Aiming Higher: Labour's Plans for Reform of the 14 to 19–plus Curriculum* (March 1996); *Target 2000* (May 1996); *Lifelong Learning: Labour's Plans for Improving Access to Further and Higher Education, Adult and Continuing Education* (May 1996); *Learn As You Earn: Labour's Plans for a Skills Revolution* (April 1996).

40 In fact, according to a study by Caroline Benn and Clyde Chitty published the previous month, Blair had set up an Aunt Sally to attack. They found that mixed-ability teaching was used by fewer than a fifth of schools even for eleven- and twelve-year-olds; classes for thirteen- and fourteen-year-olds were not mixed ability in 97 per cent of schools. See Clare Dean, 'Labour preaches to convert', *Times Educational Supplement*, 14 June 1996.

41 Labour Party, *Early Excellence: A Head Start for Every Child* (November 1996).

42 Labour Party, *New Labour: Because Britain Deserves Better* (1997).

43 Stephen Byers, the MP for Wallsend from 1992 to 1997 and for Tyneside North since 1997, is one of the high-flyers of the Blair Labour Party. Born in 1953 and single, he was educated at a grammar school, a further education college and Liverpool Polytechnic, later becoming a law lecturer there. His political career began when he was elected to North Tyneside council in 1980: he rose to become deputy leader between 1986 and 1992. He was chairman of the Association of Metropolitan Authorities education committee between 1990 and 1992, in which position he led negotiations on pay and conditions with teachers and lecturers from the employers' side. Tony Blair made him a whip in 1994, and the next year he was promoted to become a junior employment spokesman. In this role, he earned the enmity of the trade unions for his dogged refusal to commit Labour on the level of the minimum wage and his lack of enthusiasm for workers' rights. He made the headlines after telling a group of journalists over dinner at a Blackpool restaurant in TUC congress week in 1996 that Blair planned to ditch Labour's formal link with the unions (see chapter 9).

44 Estelle Morris, the MP for Birmingham Yardley, is another high-flyer from the 1992 intake. Born in 1952 and single, she was educated in state schools and at Coventry College of Education and taught in an inner-city comprehensive school. She was a member of Warwick council from 1979 to 1991, serving as leader of the Labour group for seven years. She became a whip in 1994 and was made a junior education spokeswoman the following year.

Kim Howells, the MP for Pontypridd since a 1989 by-election, has a colourful political history. Born in 1946 and grammar school-educated, he went to Hornsey College of Art where he was one of the organizers of a famous student occupation in 1968 that inspired a generation of campus radicals. He subsequently worked briefly as a steelworker and as a miner before resuming his studies and landing a job as a lecturer in 1975. He joined the National Union of Mineworkers as a researcher in 1979, becoming the NUM South Wales Area research officer and journal editor in 1982, in which role he was one of the union's most vocal critics of Arthur Scargill's handling of the 1984–5 miners' strike. He joined the front bench as a junior overseas development spokesman in 1993 and held a string of junior positions from then on, ending up as a junior trade and industry spokesman between 1995 and the 1997 general election. He is an ultra-modernizer with an endearing habit of speaking his mind, particularly on the subject of Welsh parochialism and his distrust of Celtic nationalism. He caused a small storm in 1996 by arguing that Labour should stop using the word 'socialist' on the grounds that it no longer meant anything.

Tessa Blackstone has a long record as an academic educationalist and right-wing Labour policy wonk. Born in 1942, she was educated at a grammar school and the London School of Economics. She was a lecturer at the LSE from 1966 to 1975, then joined the Central Policy Review Staff – the cabinet think tank – as an adviser, leaving to become a professor at the Institute of Education, London University, a post she held until 1983. She then worked as director of education at the Inner London Education Authority until 1987, when she became master of Birkbeck College, London University, and was given a peerage by Neil Kinnock. She was an opposition spokeswoman in the Lords on education and science from 1988 to 1992 and on foreign affairs from 1992 to 1997. She was chair of the Institute for Public Policy Research from its foundation in 1988, and has adorned innumerable committees, among them the general advisory council of the BBC, the planning board of the Arts Council and the boards of Thames Television and the Royal Opera House.

45 The Third International Maths and Science Study, quoted in *The Economist*, 29 March 1997.

46 It is not universally agreed that levels of educational attainment and economic success go together. For example, Peter Robinson of the London School of Economics Centre for Economic Performance argues that the link between the two is weak: the US is the world's most dynamic economy yet does poorly in the international league tables of maths and science performance. Taking this view, what is far more important for economic dynamism is not general educational attainment but the amount of encouragement given to research and innovation by an education system.

6 THE PARTY'S OVER:
NEW LABOUR AND WELFARE

1 Tony Blair, speech at Cadcam, Aylesbury estate, Southwark, 2 June 1997.

2 *Guardian*, 3 June 1997.

3 The other main elements of the Beveridge system were child allowances, introduced before Labour's 1945 election victory, and death and maternity grants. On the Beveridge report and the 1945–51 Labour government, see Paul Addison, *The Road to 1945* (Macmillan, 1982); Kenneth O. Morgan, *Labour in Power 1945–51* (Oxford 1985); Nicholas Timmins, *The Five Giants: A Biography of the Welfare State* (HarperCollins, 1995); Howard Glennerster, *British Social Policy Since 1945* (Blackwell, 1995); Michael Sullivan, *The Development of the British Welfare State* (Prentice Hall, 1996).

4 Glennerster, *British Social Policy Since 1945*, p. 41.

5 Richard Titmuss (1907–73) was an extraordinarily influential figure. During the Second World War, he had been the official historian of wartime social policy, working in the Cabinet Office – his account of social policy during the war, *Problems of Social Policy*, published in 1950, is still definitive – and his experience in this role had converted him from Liberalism to ethical socialism. At the LSE, where he occupied the chair from 1950 until his death in 1973, he was largely responsible for defining social administration as an academic subject. His empirical research and theoretical writing covered just about every aspect of the welfare state.

6 In the early 1950s, for example, Titmuss and Abel-Smith did the empirical research that dished Tory claims that NHS costs were spiralling out of control – which not only forced the government to abandon the idea of going back to an insurance-based health system but also persuaded the Labour right that there was no problem in returning to a 'free at the point of use' NHS. The research was fed into the Guillebaud Committee on NHS costs and financing, set up by the Tory government in 1952, and appeared in book form as *The Cost of the National Health Service* (Cambridge, 1959).

7 Brian Abel-Smith and Peter Townsend, *New Pensions for Old* (Fabian Society, 1955).

8 For Titmuss's theories of the welfare state see Richard Titmuss, *Essays on the Welfare State* (Allen and Unwin, 1958); *The Irresponsible Society* (Fabian Society, 1960); *Commitment to Welfare* (Allen and Unwin, 1968); and *The Gift Relationship* (Penguin, 1970).

9 See Richard Titmuss, *Income Distribution and Social Change* (Allen and Unwin, 1962); Brian Abel-Smith and Peter Townsend, *The Poor and the Poorest* (LSE, 1965).

10 Glennerster, *Social Policy in Britain*, p. 109.

11 Timmins, *The Five Giants*, p. 277.

12 Frank Field, *Freedom and Wealth in a Socialist Future* (Constable, 1987), p. 259. This book, complete with an introduction from Neil Kinnock, is probably the most coherent case for the sort of policies Labour advocated in the mid-1980s. Its central idea was for a massive increase in child benefit as the flagship innovation of a Labour government. There is very little in it that suggests its author's current enthusiasm for compulsory private pensions.

13 See Department of Social Security, *Households Below Average Income* (1996).

14 The policy review group most concerned with social security was that on economic equality, chaired by John Smith and Diana Jeuda (of the shopworkers' union USDAW). Members throughout its life included Margaret Beckett, Rodney Bickerstaffe, Robin Cook, Bill Morris and Chris Smith; Michael Meacher and Clare Short joined in 1989. Sub-groups of the economic equality group involved several outside experts, among them Chris Pond of the Low Pay Unit, Ruth Lister of the Child Poverty Action Group and John Hills of the London School of Economics.

15 Bryan Gould, speech in Basildon, 20 June 1992.

16 Bill Morris, 'Get to the point', *New Statesman & Society*, 17 July 1992. He went on: 'If there is a continuing need to satisfy the principle of universality, we could have a universal minimum floor for child benefit, for instance. It could be set at a much lower level than at present, with additional payments for those who actually need it while giving nothing extra to the well-off who currently receive the same as those in poverty.'

17 John Smith, speech to launch leadership campaign, 30 April 1992.

18 Apart from Gordon Borrie and Patricia Hewitt, the members of the Commission were: Tony Atkinson (professor of political economy at Cambridge University, formerly of the LSE and a long-standing Fabian), Anita Bhalla (an Asian journalist from Birmingham), John Gennard (professor of industrial relations at the University of Strathclyde), The Very Rev. John Gladwyn (provost of Sheffield cathedral and an architect of the Archbishop of Canterbury's inner-city initiative 'Faith in the City'), Christopher Haskins (chairman of Northern Foods, the only business representative on the panel), Penelope Leach (the popular child psychologist), Ruth Lister (former director of the Child Poverty Action Group), Ethnie McLaughlin (a social administration academic at Queen's University Belfast), Emma MacLennan (vice-chair of the Low Pay Unit pressure group, a former Labour Party employee and wife of John Smith's adviser David Ward), David Marquand (Labour MP for Ashfield between 1966 and 1977, a founder member of the SDP in 1981 and a Liberal Democrat adviser from 1988 to 1994, when he rejoined Labour), Bert Massie (director of the Royal Association for Disability and Rehabilitation), Steven Webb (an economist at the Institute for Fiscal Studies and an adviser to the Lib Dems), Margaret Wheeler (an officer of the Confederation of Health Service Employees), and Bernard Williams (the Oxford

philosopher and former husband of Shirley Williams). There are good thumbnail biographies in Stephen Overell, 'Great and good?', *Tribune*, 22 January 1993.

19 The two 'interim reports' were *The Justice Gap* and *Social Justice in a Changing World* (IPPR, 1993). The final report was published as Commission on Social Justice, *Social Justice: Strategies for National Renewal* (Vintage, 1994).

20 *Social Justice*, p. 94.

21 The members of the Dahrendorf Commission, set up by Paddy Ashdown in late 1993, were Lord Dahrendorf, Frank Field, Carolyn Hayman (the joint managing director of Korda), Ian Hutcheson (the head of a large food processing firm), Will Hutton, David Marquand, Dr Andrew Sentance of the London Business School (a former director of economic affairs at the CBI) and Ian Wrigglesworth (a former president of the Liberal Democrats and a former Labour MP who defected to the SDP). The Rowntree Inquiry Group was chaired by Patrick Barclay (former chairman of the Social Security Advisory Committee), with John Hills of the LSE (a Labour adviser) as its secretary. Its other members were Tessa Baring (chair of Barnados), Michael Bett (deputy chairman of British Telecom and chairman of the Social Security Advisory Committee), Vivienne Coombe (of NCH Action for Children), Howard Davies, Kathleen Kiernan (a population expert at the LSE), Ruth Lea (the ITN economics editor), Pamela Meadows (director of the Policy Studies Institute think-tank), John Monks, Robin Wendt (chief executive of the Association of County Councils), John Willman (features editor of the *Financial Times*, former general secretary of the Fabian Society and former joint-editor of the Labour Party magazine *New Socialist*) and Tricia Zipfel (director of the Priority Estates Project). For a comparison of the three reports' findings, see James McCormick and Carey Oppenheim, 'Options for change', *New Statesman & Society*, 26 January 1996.

22 Peter Townsend, speech to TGWU 'In place of fear' conference, 31 October 1994.

23 He developed his argument most fully in Peter Townsend and Alan Walker, *The Future of Pensions: Revitalising National Insurance* (Fabian Society, 1995).

24 Frank Field, *An Agenda for Britain* (Harper Collins, 1993).

25 Frank Field quoted in the *Guardian*, 25 October 1994. His position on pensions is most fully stated in Frank Field and Matthew Owen, *Private Pensions For All* (Fabian Society, 1993).

26 Frank Field, *Making Welfare Work* (Institute of Community Studies, 1995).

27 Frank Field, letter to the *Guardian*, 30 May 1995.

28 Meghnad Desai, *Citizen's Income Bulletin*, February 1995.

29 Labour Party, *Labour's New Deal for Britain's Under-25s* (1995).

30 Labour Party, *Getting Welfare to Work: A New Vision for Social Security* (1996).

31 Chris Smith, 'Tiger feats?' *New Statesman & Society*, 26 January 1996.

32 Labour Party, *Security in Retirement* (1996).

33 Frank Field, 'How to open the benefit trap', *Independent*, 1 July 1996.

34 Barbara Castle and Peter Townsend, *We Can Afford The Welfare State* (Security in Retirement for Everyone, 1996).

35 Harriet Harman, born in 1950, comes from an affluent middle-class family. Her father was a distinguished consultant physician, her mother a lawyer, and she was educated privately at St Paul's Girls School before studying politics at York University. After York she qualified as a solicitor and got her first job at Brent Law Centre in north London, where she met her future husband, Jack Dromey, and Patricia Hewitt, then general secretary of the National Council for Civil Liberties (since renamed Liberty). Harman joined the NCCL in 1978, shooting to national prominence when in 1980 she was prosecuted by the government for contempt of court after giving copies of documents obtained for a defence case and already read

out in open court to a journalist from the *Guardian*. She was found guilty but ten years later was cleared by the European Commission of Human Rights, forcing the law to be amended as a result.

She was elected MP for the safe Labour seat of Peckham in a 1982 by-election and rapidly acquired a reputation as a 'soft left' feminist leadership loyalist. She joined the front bench as a junior social services spokeswoman in 1984 and was promoted to deputy health spokeswoman in 1987. After the 1992 general election she was elected to the shadow cabinet for the first time and John Smith appointed her shadow chief secretary to the Treasury. She did not fare well in her new role, however – and was voted off the shadow cabinet in 1993. Smith kept her in her post regardless. In 1994, Tony Blair made her employment spokeswoman in his first reshuffle, and in 1995 he shifted her to health.

36 Tony Blair, speech to social policy conference in Amsterdam, 24 January 1997.

37 Labour Party, *New Labour: Because Britain Deserves Better* (1997).

38 Alan Howarth, born in 1944 and educated at Rugby and King's College, Cambridge, was an assistant master at Westminster, the public school, between 1968 and 1974. He left teaching to become personal assistant to the chairman of the Conservative Party, Willie Whitelaw, and did the same job for his successor, Lord Thorneycroft, before becoming director of the Conservative Research Department in 1979. He was a vice-chairman of the Tory Party in 1980–1 and was elected Tory MP for Stratford upon Avon in 1983. He quickly established a reputation as an ultra-dry right-winger with a particular bent for the sort of education reforms advocated by Rhodes Boyson and his allies: student loans, replacement of the teacher unions with a professional body, letting schools opt out of local education authority control. He was appointed Boyson's parliamentary private secretary in 1985, became an assistant whip in 1987 and a whip in 1988, and between 1989 and 1992 was a junior education minister. He defected to Labour in 1995 and was selected for the safe Labour seat of Newport East in early 1997.

Another minister with responsibilities for welfare-to-work is the paymaster general, Geoffrey Robinson, at the Treasury.

39 Martin Taylor, an Old Etonian and former *Financial Times* journalist, has a team of four civil servants. He told the *New Statesman* that he planned to work on his report two days a month and deliver it in spring 1998.

7 LOCK UP YOUR DAUGHTERS: JACK STRAW AND HOME AFFAIRS

1 *Hansard*, 19 May 1997.

2 Kenneth O. Morgan, *Labour in Power 1945–51* (OUP, 1984).

3 George Orwell, then the vice-chairman of the Freedom Defence Campaign, set up to support anarchists imprisoned for publishing anti-militarist propaganda in 1945 and then kept going as a libertarian alternative to the then Communist-dominated National Council for Civil Liberties, wrote to his friend George Woodcock: 'It's not easy to have a clear position, because, if one admits the rights of governments to govern, one must admit their right to choose suitable agents, and I think any organization, e.g. a political party, has the right to protect itself against infiltration. But at the same time, the way in which the government seems to be going to work is vaguely disquieting, and the whole phenomenon seems to me part of the general breakdown of the democratic outlook. Only a week or two ago the Communists themselves were shouting for unconstitutional methods to be used against the Fascists, now the same methods are to be used against themselves, and in another year or two a pro-Communist government might be using them against

us. Meanwhile, the general apathy about freedom of speech etc. constantly grows, and that matters much more than what may be on the statute book.' Quoted in George Woodcock, *The Crystal Spirit* (Cape, 1967).

4 Anthony Crosland, *The Future of Socialism* (Jonathan Cape, 1956).

5 Roy Jenkins, *The Labour Case* (Penguin, 1959).

6 Stephen Dorrill and Robin Ramsay, *Smear!* (Fourth Estate, 1991).

7 James Callaghan, *Time and Chance* (Collins, 1987), p. 231.

8 Quoted in Christopher Hitchens and Peter Kellner, *Callaghan: The Road to Number Ten* (Cassell, 1976).

9 Quoted in Hitchens and Kellner, *Callaghan.*

10 Callaghan, *Time and Chance*, p. 267.

11 Callaghan, *Time and Chance*, p. 260.

12 See Lewis Minkin, *The Contentious Alliance: Trade Unions and the Labour Party* (Edinburgh, 1991) chapter seven.

13 Jenkins, *A Life at the Centre*, chapter 21.

14 A particular influence on Thatcher's thinking was the Institute for the Study of Conflict, a right-wing think-tank set up in 1970 by Brian Crozier, a veteran anti-Communist propagandist whose activities were at various times funded by the US Central Intelligence Agency. Crozier and his ISC colleague Robert Moss, director of the Economist Intelligence Unit and author of apocalyptically gloomy *The Collapse of Democracy* (Temple Smith, 1975), provided Thatcher with regular briefings on subversion in Britain that she appears to have taken entirely seriously. See Richard Cockitt, *Thinking the Unthinkable: Think-tanks and the Economic Counter-revolution 1931–1983* (HarperCollins, 1994); Robin Ramsay, *The Clandestine Caucus: Anti-Socialist Campaigns and Operations in the British Labour Movement Since the War*, a special 1996 edition of *Lobster* magazine.

15 See Peter Hain, *Political Trials in Britain* (Penguin, 1984); James Michael, *The Politics of Secrecy* (Penguin, 1982).

16 E.P. Thompson, 'The state of the nation', in *Writing by Candlelight* (Merlin, 1980).

17 See Roy Hattersley, 'The Framework for a Labour Britain' in Gerald Kaufman (ed.), *Renewal: Labour's Britain in the 1980s* (Penguin, 1983).

18 See, for example, his speech in the Commons on 12 March 1985.

19 Roy Hattersley, *Choose Freedom* (Michael Joseph, 1987).

20 Labour Party, *A Statement of Democratic Socialist Aims and Values* (1988).

21 Labour took an ambiguous and opportunist position on the Rushdie affair, trying to balance civil libertarian concerns with pandering to Muslim voters. Hattersley, whose Birmingham constituents included many Muslims, condemned the death sentence on Rushdie but argued that the paperback edition of *The Satanic Verses* should not be published. The most vocal Labour defender of Rushdie was Michael Foot.

22 Labour Party, *Time to Get Britain Working Again* (1992).

23 Tony Blair, interview on BBC Radio 4 *The World this Weekend* programme, 10 January 1993.

24 Tony Blair, 'Why crime is a socialist issue', *New Statesman & Society*, 29 January 1993.

25 Tony Blair, speech to Labour Party activists in Wellingborough, 19 February 1993.

26 ICM poll in the *Guardian*, 11 March 1993.

27 Tony Blair, speech to criminology conference in Alloa, 25 June 1993.

28 Amitai Etzioni, *The Spirit of Community* (Simon and Schuster, 1993).

29 Paul Anderson and Kevin Davey, 'Import duties', *New Statesman & Society*, 3 March 1995.

30 *Guardian*, 8 October 1994.

31 Tony Blair, letter to the *Observer*, 30 January 1994.

32 The worth of these assurances was revealed by Jack Straw after he succeeded Blair as shadow home secretary. He told a Liberty-Charter 88 fringe meeting at the 1996 party conference that Labour had no plans to tamper with any of the measures in the Criminal Justice Act once it won office: 'We didn't vote against the second reading of the bill, so it would be inconsistent of us to repeal it.' Even on those important matters of principle that Labour had, in Blair's words, 'vigorously opposed' – such as the erosion of the right to silence – the party would only 'see how it works out'. Jack Straw, speech to Liberty-Charter 88 Labour Party conference fringe meeting, 2 October 1996.

33 The shadow home affairs team was, however, well aware of the unpopularity of its stance with the young. In autumn 1994, after a summer marked by mass protest against the bill, Straw admitted to a meeting of the Parliamentary Labour Party civil liberties group that his children had been asking him: 'What did you do against the Criminal Justice Bill, daddy?' Alun Michael, the number two in the home affairs team under Blair and Straw, knew too. His own daughter was a committed environmental activist – and she made a point of never using her surname to ensure that she would not be associated with her father's parliamentary activities.

34 *Daily Mail*, 31 January 1997.

35 Jack Straw, 'Profile', *House* magazine, 1 July 1988.

36 At the same time, she took on Brian Abel-Smith, professor of social administration at the London School of Economics. His job was to provide the thinking behind policy and to come up with the ideas; Straw's was to work the machine. 'I employ Brian for his brains and Jack for his low cunning,' she once remarked. (Quoted in profile of Jack Straw, *Observer*, 26 July 1987).

37 See, for example, Jack Straw, 'European Monetary System: the final act in locking Britain into the Common Market', *Tribune*, 13 October 1978.

38 Labour Party, *Report of the Annual Conference and Special Conference of the Labour Party 1980*, p. 170.

39 Barbara Castle, *Fighting All the Way* (Macmillan, 1993), p. 529.

40 *Financial Times*, 21 November 1994.

41 Labour Party, *A Quiet Life: Tough Action on Criminal Neighbours* (June 1995).

42 Criticism by the Magistrates Association and Penal Affairs Consortium, the *Guardian*, 20 June 1995.

43 *Guardian*, 5 September 1995.

44 Jack Straw, speech to the launch of the Lewisham Community Safety Strategy, Lewisham Town Hall, 4 September 1995.

45 Jack Straw, letter to the *Guardian*, 6 September 1995.

46 *Observer*, 2 June 1996.

47 Donald Dewar, interview with BBC1 *On the Record* programme, June 1996.

48 *Guardian*, 3 June 1996.

49 See the *Sunday Times* and the *Observer*, 2 June 1996.

50 Tony Blair, speech to Commonwealth Press Union conference, South Africa, 14 October 1996.

51 Jack Straw, speech to the University of Salford, 18 September 1996.

52 Towards the end of his first year in the post, he had a private meeting with the director and other senior members of Liberty. The organization had traditionally provided Labour home affairs spokespersons with advice and information, and often acted as an initial sounding board for policy proposals. But it was now increasingly finding itself in the position of expressing public doubts about the party's emerging new policies. 'He completely blew his top,' according to one of

those present at the meeting. 'He let us know in no uncertain terms that as far as he was concerned, we were a bunch of middle-class whingers being "unhelpful" while he was tackling the concerns of ordinary people. He was not the slightest bit interested in the concerns we were raising.'

53 John Major, speech to the Conservative Central Council, 2 April 1995; see also *The Times*, 3 April 1995.

54 *Hansard*, 10 March 1993.

55 See, for example, Martin Kettle, 'Cowardice in the face of the ruling class', *Guardian*, 3 April 1996, which hit home particularly hard with Straw.

56 *Observer*, 7 April 1996.

57 Hurd condemned the 'race for votes' that the bill represented, and warned against pressure on judges from the public and politicians to pass long sentences. Baker questioned the effectiveness of minimum sentences and demanded that more attention be paid to rehabilitating prisoners. See *Hansard*, 4 November 1996.

58 The bill proposed the appointment of a new Commissioner – a senior serving or retired judge – to handle complaints, which could only be made after the fact. He would have the ability only to overturn an authorization retrospectively, and any evidence found would still be admissible in court even if the search by which it was uncovered was subsequently declared improper. In addition, the Commissioner's decision on any complaint could not be 'appealed or questioned in any court'. Meanwhile, since the police would be authorizing themselves as they went along anyway, such searches would automatically be within the law as they were carried out.

59 Jack Straw, letter to the *Guardian*, 30 November 1996. Labour voted with the government against a House of Lords amendment which proposed that a judge, rather than a police officer, be appointed the authorizer for each use of the new powers.

60 A further reason he gave for Labour's non-opposition was that the bill also brought the police into line with the security services. MI5's remit had already been extended to include ordinary police work, and it had been granted similar statutory powers with the Security Services Act. In fact, the Police Bill simply introduced a new inconsistency by giving the police greater licence to snoop on individuals than that enjoyed by MI5; the security services require authorization from the home secretary to undertake specific acts of invasive surveillance involving phone-taps, bugs and trespass. The illogicality of Straw's case for tacitly supporting the bill was further compounded by a legal angle presented by three barristers for Liberty. It held that the powers which the chief police officers would gain from the bill violated the European Convention on Human Rights – which Labour was firmly pledged to incorporate into British law. Article 8 of the ECHR states that 'Everyone has the right to respect for his private and family life, his home and his correspondence'. Within weeks of setting out his defence of Labour's position on the Police Bill, Straw happily restated the party's pledge to incorporate the ECHR into British law when he enjoyed top billing at an Institute for Public Policy Research conference on the constitution.

61 Jack Straw, interview on BBC Radio 4 *Today* programme, 17 January 1997.

62 Tony Blair, interview on ITV *Walden* programme, 24 July 1994.

63 Sheila Rowbotham, 'An open letter to Tony Blair', *New Statesman & Society*, 29 July 1994.

64 Christopher Hitchens, interview with Tony Blair, *Vanity Fair*, March 1995.

65 Tony Blair, speech to Labour Party conference, 1 October 1996. One effect of the Labour leader's demonstrations of his religious beliefs was to prompt the leaders of the other main parties to declare their Christianity; both John Major and Paddy

Ashdown let it be known that they too got down on their knees and prayed, 'in all circumstances' and 'every night' respectively. See Roy McLoughry, *Belief in Politics* (Hodder and Stoughton, 1996). Another effect was to make Christian socialism suddenly highly fashionable in the Labour Party. Membership of the Christian Socialist Movement, Labour's Christian society, trebled to 5,000 between 1994 and 1996 – and at least a few of the new recruits saw, like Blair, no contradiction between talking at length to newspapers about their deeply held religious beliefs and insisting that they were an entirely private matter.

66 Tony Blair, speech to the Commonwealth Press Union conference, Cape Town, South Africa, 14 October 1996.

67 Tony Blair, interview on BBC Radio 4 *The World this Weekend* programme, 15 October 1996.

68 Labour Party, *Tackling the Causes of Crime: Labour's Proposals to Prevent Crime and Criminality* (October 1996), and Labour Party, *Parenting* (November 1996). *Early Excellence: a head start for every child*, a document produced by Labour's education spokesman, David Blunkett, also contained proposals for improving parenting.

69 Frances Lawrence, 'My manifesto for the nation', *The Times*, 21 October 1996.

70 After first insisting that the difficulty of defining these weapons made effective legislation virtually impossible, Howard later gave way to Labour's campaign and the government supported Labour's proposals for restrictions on the sale and advertising of such knives.

71 See David Rose, *In The Name of the Law* (Vintage, 1996) for a comprehensive account of the tremendous pressures on the criminal justice system.

72 *Hansard*, 9 June 1997.

73 Jack Straw, interview on BBC Radio 4 *Today* programme, 3 January 1997.

8 VOTE EARLY, VOTE OFTEN:
NEW LABOUR AND THE CONSTITUTION

1 *Scotsman*, 16 May 1997.

2 Of the other appointments at the Scottish Office, the most significant was that of Brian Wilson, the minister responsible for education and industry, MP for Cunninghame North since 1987. Born in 1948, he has a long political history, contesting his first parliamentary seat for Labour unsuccessfully as long ago as 1974. The founder of the *West Highland Free Press* – just about the only one of the many alternative local magazines set up in the 1960s and 1970s to flourish into a successful business – he was a radical left-winger and opponent of devolution in the 1970s but changed his mind on devolution in the early 1980s and since being elected has been a consistent soft left leadership loyalist. He was a junior frontbench spokesman from 1988, on Scotland (1988–92), citizen's rights and open government (1992), transport (1992–4 and again 1995–6) and trade and industry (1994–5). He was Labour's election planning co-ordinator in 1996–7.

Wilson apart, the ministers at the Scottish Office are Henry Mcleish, MP for Fife Central since 1987 and a long-standing soft left leadership loyalist, Sam Galbraith, MP for Strathkelvin and Bearsden since 1987, and Malcolm Chisholm, MP for Leith from 1992 to 1997 and now for Edinburgh North and Leith, one of a handful of Campaign Group members of the government.

3 Fiona Millar, interview with Donald Dewar, *House* magazine, 22 January 1996.

4 Collette Douglas-Home, interview with Donald Dewar, *Scotsman*, 21 May 1990.

5 Fiona Millar, interview with Donald Dewar, *House* magazine, 22 January 1996.

6 Fiona Millar, interview with Donald Dewar, *House* magazine, 22 January 1996.

7 Donald Dewar, press release, 9 November 1969.

8   *Scotsman*, 18 March 1978.
9   *Sunday Telegraph*, 8 April 1978; see also *Guardian*, 7 April 1978.
10 After Labour's 1979 election defeat, Dewar was one of the Atlanticist Labour right's most articulate spokesmen, writing regularly in *Labour Weekly*. He was a co-founder of the right-wing group Solidarity in 1981, a member of its steering committee and its Scottish co-ordinator. He backed Roy Hattersley for leader and deputy leader in 1983.
11 For the origins of the Scottish National Party and the history of Scottish nationalism in the twentieth century, see Christopher Harvie, *Scotland and Nationalism* (Routledge, 1994).
12 Tam Dalyell, *Devolution: The End of Britain?* (Jonathan Cape, 1977).
13 For Labour and Scottish devolution since the 1970s, see Andrew Marr, *The Battle for Scotland* (Penguin, 1992).
14 Leo Abse, who retired as an MP in 1987, is the author of a bizarre psycho-biography of Tony Blair, *The Man Behind the Smile: Tony Blair and the Politics of Perversion* (1996).
15 Tony Blair, speech in Cardiff, 15 July 1994.
16 *Scotsman*, 19 November 1994.
17 Opinion polls in the early and mid-1990s consistently showed that 50 per cent of Scots preferred devolution to all other options, with 30 per cent backing independence and 30 per cent supporting the *status quo*.
18 Gordon Brown, speech to meeting in Westminster, 12 January 1995.
19 John Prescott, interview on BBC1 *Breakfast With Frost* programme, 5 March 1995.
20 *Scotsman*, 8 March 1995.
21 Labour Party, *A Choice for England* (1995). To keep Prescott on board after putting off elected English regional assemblies, Blair agreed to set up a regional policy commission, chaired by Bruce Millan, to look into prospects for regional industrial policies. It reported in June 1996, recommending regional development agencies for every English region and a shift in emphasis in regional economic policy from attracting inward investment to fostering local enterprises.
22 *Glasgow Herald*, 20 February 1996; *Scotsman*, 20 May 1996.
23 Ron Davies was duly appointed secretary of state for Wales after the 1997 Labour election victory – although how long he survives is a moot point. The MP for Caerphilly since 1983, he is a Tribunite left-winger of the old school and not close to Tony Blair. Born in 1946, he began his political career as a local councillor. He was a whip from 1984 to 1987, joined the front bench as agriculture spokesman in 1987 and was made shadow Welsh secretary in 1992 after being elected to the shadow cabinet to fill the vacancy left by the resignation of Bryan Gould. He was a critic of the Labour leadership's line on the 1990–1 crisis and war in the Gulf and caused a stir in 1996 when he declared that he was a republican and that the Prince of Wales was unfit to become King.

The progress of Peter Hain, the MP for Neath since a 1991 by-election and now an under-secretary in the Welsh Office, will also be an indication of how far Blair runs an inclusive regime. He has a long career as a radical left-winger, going back to his youth in South Africa. He first made a name for himself in Britain as an anti-apartheid campaigner and chairman of the Young Liberals (1971–3) and was press officer of the Anti-Nazi League between 1977 and 1980. He joined Labour in 1977 and played a major part in various left-wing caucuses throughout the 1980s. Towards the end of the decade he attempted repeatedly to secure a reunification of the party's hard and soft left groupings. He contested Putney unsuccessfully in the 1983 and 1987 general elections. After 1992, as secretary of the Tribune Group, he was the most prominent critic of Labour's support of the

Maastricht Treaty (see chapters 2 and 3). Blair made him a whip in 1995 and a junior spokesman on employment in 1996. Davies' other under-secretary is Win Griffiths, the MP for Bridgend since 1987, a soft left leadership loyalist and long-standing pro-devolutionist. The MEP for South Wales from 1979 to 1989, he was a junior front-bench spokesman on the environment (1990–2), education (1992–4) and Wales (1994–7).

24 The Liberal Democrat reaction came close to wrecking the Labour–Lib Dem joint consultative committee on constitutional reform set up by Blair and Paddy Ashdown in October 1996 and convened by Robin Cook and Robert Maclennan. Eventually the parties agreed to disagree about the referendums, with the Lib Dems declaring that they would do nothing to stand in the way of Labour's legislation on devolution referendums. See the report of the Labour-Lib Dem joint consultative committee on constitutional reform published on 5 March 1997.

25 *Guardian*, 29 June 1996.

26 Neal Ascherson, *Independent on Sunday*, 8 September 1996.

27 Crossman's bill involved removing the voting powers of the hereditary peers but allowing them to sit and speak in the chamber. Salaried members of the Lords would be appointed by the leaders of the various parties in the Commons in numbers that reflected their Commons voting strengths. A similar plan for getting rid of hereditary peers was put forward by a Conservative committee chaired by the late Lord Home in the late 1970s, but was abandoned and forgotten once Margaret Thatcher won the 1979 election.

28 Labour Party, *It's Time to Get Britain Working Again* (1992).

29 Labour's 1983 manifesto, *New Hope for Britain*, promised to 'take action to abolish the undemocratic House of Lords as quickly as possible and, as an interim measure, introduce a bill in the first session of parliament to remove its legislative powers'. The policy dated back to a 1977 party conference decision to abolish the Lords that Jim Callaghan had refused to incorporate in the 1979 Labour election manifesto. Tony Benn even hatched a grand plan to swamp the Lords with 1,000 life peers sent there with the sole purpose of outvoting its in-built Tory majority to ensure its demise.

30 Labour Party, *New Labour: Because Britain Deserves Better* (1997).

31 Labour Party, *A New Agenda for Democracy: Labour's Proposals for Constitutional Reform* (1993).

32 Tony Blair, John Smith memorial lecture, 7 February 1996.

33 Quoted in Mervyn Jones, *Michael Foot* (Gollancz, 1993), p. 313.

34 Peter Mandelson and Roger Liddle, *The Blair Revolution* (Faber, 1996), p. 205.

35 See, for example, his John Smith memorial lecture in February 1996.

36 Lord Desai and Lord Kilmarnock, *Destiny Not Defeat: Reforming the Lords* (Fabian Society, 1997).

37 STV is the system, currently favoured by the Liberal Democrats, in which electors in multi-member constituencies would mark their ballot papers '1, 2, 3' and so on in order of preference. Candidates reaching a certain proportion of the vote on first preferences are declared elected, then the second preferences of the candidate with least first preferences are redistributed. The process continues until all seats are filled.

38 AV is a system that retains single-member constituencies from FPTP but changes the marking of ballots to '1, 2, 3' and so on in order of preference. If no candidate gets 50 per cent of first preferences, the second preferences of the candidate with the fewest votes are added to the other candidates' totals. This process continues until one candidate has more than 50 per cent of the vote. There are several variants, one of which, the supplementary vote, designed by Labour MP Dale

Campbell-Savours, was recommended for the Commons by Labour's working party on electoral systems in 1993. Labour's most consistent advocate of AV has been Peter Hain, who was propounding its merits long before he became an MP. See his *Proportional Misrepresentation* (Wildwood House, 1986).

39 On Labour and electoral reform from 1900 to 1931, see Martin Linton, *Labour's Road to Electoral Reform* (Labour Campaign for Electoral Reform, 1993).

40 The Ullswater conference is a model of how not to discuss changing the electoral system. Its initial considerations were no more than a string of statements of what divided the parties on their desired electoral systems. AV was put forward not for any intrinsic merits but as the lowest common denominator that the Liberals and Labour could agree if nothing else were possible.

41 Barry Jones and Michael Keating, *Labour and the British State* (OUP, 1985) p. 56.

42 Proportional representation is a recurrent theme among the small parties of the British left – and among those who would like to set them up. The Communist Party argued for it almost from its first days as an electoral party; Common Wealth, the 1940s left party set up by Richard Acland, J.B. Priestley and others to fight by-elections against the Tories that Labour would not contest during the wartime big party truce, made much the same point. Labour's electoral reformers in the 1930s and 1940s tended to be sympathizers with the efforts of these parties – although often they were motivated by nothing more than a commitment to fairness. The CP remained in favour of PR until its demise in 1989, and its successor, Democratic Left, has taken a strong stance in favour of it. The radical libertarian left in the Socialist Society from the early 1980s (John Palmer, Hilary Wainwright, Richard Kuper) has taken a similar position in anticipation of setting up a new left-green party, as indeed has the Green Party and Arthur Scargill's Socialist Labour Party.

43 See Linton, *Labour's Road to Electoral Reform*, chapter two.

44 Neil Kinnock described Charter 88 as a group of 'whiners, whingers and wankers' when it was launched, but he became a member in 1992.

45 See for example Richard Kuper, *Electing for Democracy: Proportional Representation and the Left* (Socialist Society, 1990); Helena Catt, *The Intelligent Person's Guide to Electoral Reform* (*New Statesman & Society* supplement, June 1990).

46 AMS is the system currently backed by most of Labour's proportional representation lobby, including Robin Cook. The single-member constituency element in an AMS system can be either FPTP or AV, and in most existing versions there is a threshold of a certain number of constituency seats or percentage of the vote (in Germany three seats or 5 per cent) before a party wins seats from regional lists. There are several variants, among them the mixed member system, a minimalist version that Labour MP Jeff Rooker recommended strongly to Labour's working party on electoral systems in 1993.

47 Labour Party, *Democracy, Representation and Elections: First Report of the Working Party on Electoral Systems* (1991).The Plant working party initially consisted of two academics (Raymond Plant, the chair, and Ben Pimlott); six MPs (Margaret Beckett, Alistair Darling, John Evans, Bryan Gould, Jo Richardson and Jeff Rooker), two trade unionists (Tom Burlison of the GMB and Richard Rosser of TSSA), two members of the House of Lords (Patricia Hollis and Reg Underhill), an MEP (Geoff Hoon), a representative each for the Scottish and Welsh parties (Murray Elder and Ken Hopkins respectively) and three representatives of head-quarters in London (Geoff Bish, Joyce Gould and Tim Lamport). After the 1992 election, the line-up changed marginally. MPs Graham Allen and Hilary Armstrong, MEP Gary Titley, Labour general secretary Larry Whitty, Judith Church of MSF and Scottish Labour general secretary Jack McConnell joined the

committee; Richardson and Hopkins left it. Underhill died before the final report was published.

48 Neil Kinnock, interview on BBC Radio 4 *The World this Weekend* programme, 5 January 1992.

49 Labour Party, *Second Interim Report of the Working Party on Electoral Systems* (1992), *Report of the Working Party on Electoral Systems* (1993).

50 The regional list system is used in Scandinavia and by most continental European countries for European elections. Like STV, it involves multi-member constituencies, but unlike under STV voters vote not for individual candidates but for a party list of candidates. Seats are allocated proportionately among parties, with the individuals elected according to their position on the list. There are several variations under which voters can split lists or reorder candidates' positions on a list.

51 Steve Platt, interview with Tony Blair, *New Statesman & Society*, 15 July 1994.

52 Labour Party/Liberal Democrats, *Report of the Joint Consultative Committee on Constitutional Reform*, 5 March 1997. The Labour representatives on this committee were Robin Cook, Donald Dewar, Jack Straw, Ann Taylor, George Robertson, Ron Davies, Liz Symons and Raymond Plant. The Lib Dems were Robert Maclennan, Jim Wallace, Nick Harvey, Tom McNally, John Macdonald QC, Dawn Oliver, Michael Steed and Anthony Lester.

53 *New Statesman*, 21 March 1997.

9 IN PLACE OF BEER AND SANDWICHES: NEW LABOUR AND THE UNIONS

1 Ian McCartney has been MP for the Lancashire seat of Makerfield since 1987. Born in Scotland in 1951, he is a long-time ally of John Prescott: he was a young merchant seaman when Prescott was a major player in the 1966 seamen's strike (see chapter 4). After that, he worked as a local government manual worker and a chef. In 1971 he became unemployed and spent the next two years on the dole, before becoming a Labour Party organizer. He served on Wigan Borough Council from 1982 to 1987. He has been a consistent supporter of a statutory minimum wage: in 1988 he co-sponsored a Commons bill to introduce one. He was made a health spokesman in 1992; in 1994 he joined the front-bench employment team. In the leadership campaign that followed the death of John Smith, in which McCartney campaigned for Prescott, he played a key behind-the-scenes role liaising between the Prescott and Blair camps. Like Prescott, he is a firm supporter of Labour's link with the trade unions and is an effective, energetic prosecutor of any brief given him. His *Who's Who* entry includes the fact that he 'led [a] paper boy strike' in 1965, and that he is 'head of the McCartney family, a family of proud working-class stock'.

Andrew Smith, MP for Oxford East since 1987, is an able, if unflamboyant, soft-leftist. Born in 1951, he was a sociology tutor for the Open University before entering parliament, and an Oxford city councillor from 1976 to 1987. He was a junior front-bench spokesman on higher education from 1988 to 1992, joined the Treasury team in 1992 and became shadow chief secretary to the Treasury in 1994. In 1996 he was made shadow transport secretary in place of Clare Short (who was demoted to shadow overseas development secretary), in which position he was mostly noted for his low public profile. He has no particular record of being friendly towards the unions, but unlike Byers he is not (yet) considered hostile by them. The junior employment minister in the DfEE, Alan Howarth, is another matter: in his previous life as a junior Tory education minister he was an arch-enemy of the teacher unions (see note 38, chapter 6).

2 John Edmonds, speech to GMB conference, 2 June 1997.
3 The historical parts of this chapter inevitably draw on Lewis Minkin's two monumental studies, *The Labour Party Conference* (Manchester, 1978) and *The Contentious Alliance: Trade Unions and the Labour Party* (Edinburgh, 1991).
4 Richard Crossman summed up the point of the 1918 constitution cynically but accurately: 'Since it could not afford, like its opponents, to maintain a large army of paid party workers, the Labour Party required militants – politically conscious socialists to do the work of organizing the constituencies. But since these militants tended to be "extremists", a constitution was needed which maintained their enthusiasm by apparently creating a full party democracy while excluding them from effective power. Hence the concession in principle of sovereign power to the delegates at the annual conference, and the removal in practice of most of this sovereignty through the union block vote on the one hand and the complete independence of the Parliamentary Labour Party on the other.' Quoted in Barry Jones and Michael Keating, *Labour and the British State* (Oxford, 1985).
5 See Minkin, *The Contentious Alliance*, chapter 1.
6 The PLP had previously elected a chairman rather than a 'chairman and leader' – a titular difference, but an important one in helping to establish the predominance of the PLP position (then held by Ramsay MacDonald) over the chairmanship of the party in the country (held by Arthur Henderson). The latter position later became that of general secretary. The PLP executive committee was renamed the parliamentary committee in 1951 to avoid confusion with the NEC: it is more commonly known as the shadow cabinet.
7 Ramsay MacDonald, speech to Labour conference 1928, quoted in Minkin, *The Labour Party Conference*, p. 14.
8 Clement Attlee, *The Labour Party in Perspective* (Left Book Club, 1937), p. 136.
9 The 1937 constitutional changes created an NEC of twenty-five members plus party leader and treasurer, divided into a twelve-member union section elected by union delegations at party conference, a seven-member constituency section elected by constituency delegations, a five-member women's section elected by the whole conference and a single socialist society representative elected by socialist society delegations. With the addition of the deputy leader (in 1953) and a youth representative elected by the party's youth conference (in 1972), this is the make-up of the NEC to this day, although there is provision for a member from the party's Black and Asian Socialist Society when its membership reaches 5,000.
10 Hugh Gaitskell, speech to TUC congress 1959, quoted in Minkin, *The Contentious Alliance*, p. 96.
11 The TGWU and AEU were at this time the two biggest unions at Labour conference. The other big unions to move left in the late 1960s were the Union of Shop Distributive and Allied Workers (which elected Richard Seabrook general secretary in 1968) and the National Union of Mineworkers (which elected Lawrence Daly general secretary the same year). This meant that of the 'big six' unions at Labour conference in 1969, four, commanding 40 per cent of the vote at conference, were left-led. The trade union left, particularly Jones, forged a close alliance from the late 1960s with the Tribunite left of the PLP, particularly Michael Foot, and with *Tribune* newspaper. See Minkin, *The Contentious Alliance*, p. 116.
12 On the constitutional battle of 1979–81, see Minkin, *The Contentious Alliance*; Patrick Seyd, *The Rise and Fall of the Labour Left* (Macmillan, 1987); David and Maurice Kogan, *The Battle for the Labour Party* (Kogan Page, 1983).
13 See *Tribune*, 4 October 1991.
14 Labour Party, *NEC Report 1993*.
15 Between 1979 and 1992, the number of unions affiliated to the TUC fell from 109

to 74 as a result of mergers. The most important were: the TGWU's swallowing of the agricultural workers; the GMWU's acquisition of the boilermakers, textile workers, garment workers and the white-collar union APEX to become the GMB; the creation of the GPMU from four print unions; the amalgamation of ASTMS and TASS to create MSF; the merger of the seafarers' and railworkers' unions into RMT; and the creation of the AEEU from the engineers' and electricians' unions. The process has continued since. The public sector unions COHSE, NUPE and NALGO became Unison; the two postal and telecommunications workers unions formed the Communications Workers Union in 1995; and two civil service unions, the IRSF and NUCPS, became PTC in 1996.

16 See Robert Taylor, *The Future of the Trade Unions* (Deutsch, 1994).

17 The engineers' union, with 1.5 million members in 1979, had fewer than 1 million in 1985 and fewer than 700,000 in 1992. The TGWU dropped from 2.1 million in 1979 to 1.4 million in 1985 and just over 1 million in 1992. The NUM, more than 250,000-strong in 1979, had 135,000 members in 1985 and just 40,000 in 1992. These three unions account for more than half the decline in union membership between 1979 and 1992.

18 For a left perspective on the miners' strike, see Huw Benyon (ed.), *Digging Deeper* (Verso, 1985); and for a position close to Kinnock's, Martin Adeney and John Lloyd, *The Miners' Strike* (Routledge, 1986).

19 Minkin, *The Contentious Alliance*, p. 470.

20 For different interpretations of the Kinnock–Meacher battle over industrial relations policy, see Minkin, *The Contentious Alliance*, appendix to chapter 14, and Colin Hughes and Patrick Wintour, *Labour Rebuilt*, chapter 10.

21 The members of the review group who were MPs, although they sat on it as members of the NEC, were Margaret Beckett, Tony Blair (from October 1992), Robin Cook, John Evans, Bryan Gould (until October 1992), John Prescott and Clare Short. The union members were Tom Burlison (GMB), Gordon Colling (GPMU), Tony Clarke (UCW), Nigel Harris (AEU), Diana Jeuda (USDAW), Margaret Prosser (TGWU), Richard Rosser (TSSA) and Tom Sawyer (NUPE). Labour's general secretary Larry Whitty and the party's director of organization (Joyce Gould until March 1993 and Peter Coleman thereafter) represented the party apparatus. Lewis Minkin, the historian, was a co-opted member.

22 Clare Short, 'Unions: time for reform not divorce', *Tribune*, 18 December 1992.

23 Tony Blair, interview on BBC1 *On the Record* programme, 17 January 1993, quoted in John Rentoul, *Tony Blair* (Little, Brown, 1995), chapter 15.

24 Paul Anderson, interview with Tony Blair, *Tribune*, 29 January 1993.

25 See *Tribune*, 26 February 1993 for a summary of the options.

26 Quite the most absurd claim that the party has made in recent years is that it has abolished the block vote. It has, however, disguised it: first, since 1993, by expressing conference votes as percentages; and, secondly, since 1994, by publishing voting strengths not by union but by delegate and declaring that it is up to individual delegates how they vote.

27 *Financial Times*, 23 July 1994.

28 Tony Blair, 'No favours', *New Statesman & Society*, 18 November 1994.

29 Sarah Baxter and Andrew Jaspan, interview with Tony Blair, *Observer*, 10 September 1995. The 1997 manifesto proudly proclaimed: 'New Labour is the political arm of the British people.'

30 See Paul Anderson, 'Blair's plebiscite', *New Statesman & Society*, 5 April 1996.

31 Steve Richards, interview with Tom Sawyer, *New Statesman & Society*, 12 July 1996.

32 *The Times*, 13 September 1996. Nicholas Jones gives an entertaining account of the incident in *Campaign 1997* (Indigo, 1997).

33 Steve Platt, interview with Tony Blair, *New Statesman & Society*, 15 July 1994.

34 Labour Party, *Building Prosperity: Efficiency and Fairness at Work* (1996). One shadow cabinet member described this document at the time as 'the feeblest employment policy document I have ever seen from the party. It is an utter abdication of the left's intellectual ground to Thatcher's view of the labour market, where any attempt to provide more than a bare minimum of protection for employees is an unacceptable burden on business.'

35 On the tube drivers' strike, see *Evening Standard*, 16 July 1996. For the firming up of the position and re-balloting, see David Blunkett, 'Why Labour won't go back to the bad old days', *Evening Standard*, 10 September 1996. The latter article, published in the middle of the week of TUC congress, caused a furore among the unions. Eventually Blunkett was forced to declare that Labour had no plans for new legislation to make arbitration compulsory or to make re-balloting compulsory.

36 *The Times*, 28 March 1997. There was some confusion about who should be responsible for arbitration in disputes over union recognition during the election campaign: Gordon Brown said 'a judge' but Robin Cook said later the same day that it should be the Central Arbitration Committee, an obscure body that is not headed by a judge. Party sources later clarified the position by saying that any dispute would go first of all to the Arbitration and Conciliation Service, ACAS, and then if that did not work to the Central Arbitration Committee, which might in future be headed by a judge.

37 *Independent*, 11 March 1997.

38 Tony Blair, 'No return to the strike-bound 70s', *Daily Mail*, 26 March 1997.

39 Even Monks was not wholly pro-Blair. In spring 1995, for example, he came out publicly against David Blunkett's policy of closing failing schools.

40 TUC, *Partners for Progress* (1997).

41 *Observer*, 7 May 1995.

42 Tony Blair, 'We won't look back to the 1970s', *The Times*, 31 March 1997.

43 The big union leaders are less keen than is usually assumed on maintaining the link. Bill Morris, general secretary of the TGWU, told the *New Statesman* in 1995: 'We've invested a lot supporting Her Majesty's Opposition. With some big bucks. Mega. I have to ask myself as a manager of scarce resources where we would be today if we had used some part of that in backing T&G members.' Senior figures in Unison, the GMB and MSF have relayed similar feelings to the authors. See Ben Webb, 'What unions want', *New Statesman & Society*, 8 September 1995.

44 Labour Party, NEC Report 1996.

10   DETERRENCE FOREVER?
NEW LABOUR AND DEFENCE

1 A comprehensive account of Britain's nuclear weapons programme is in Robert S. Norris, Andrew S. Burrows and Richard W. Fieldhouse, *Nuclear Weapons Databook Volume Five: British, French and Chinese Nuclear Weapons* (Westview Press, 1994).

2 The 1966 conference also voted against the leadership – then in government – on military spending, and the 1973 conference voted against the leadership for removal of US Polaris bases from the UK.

3 Its authors included two researchers who were to become leading intellectual lights of the 1980s peace movement, Mary Kaldor and Dan Smith.

4 See Dan Keohane, *Labour Party Policy on Defence Since 1945* (Leicester University Press, 1993), chapter two.

5 E.P. Thompson, *Protest and Survive* (CND/Bertrand Russell Peace Foundation, 1980).

6 The other key people involved in drawing up the *END Appeal* included Dorothy Thompson, Ken Coates of the Bertrand Russell Peace Foundation (now a Labour MEP), Mary Kaldor, Dan Smith and Bruce Kent. END in Britain was never a large organization (indeed, it did not even have a membership structure at all until the late 1980s) and it effectively divided into two groups after disagreements between Coates and Thompson in 1982–3. But it played a crucial role in the 1980s peace movement, both by pushing a less parochial political agenda than CND and by ensuring that CND was critical of both sides in the Cold War. In the Labour Party, END was highly influential. More than sixty Labour MPs signed the appeal in 1980. Of current Labour politicians (apart from Coates), the most active in END were Robin Cook, Mo Mowlam, Mike Gapes, Glyn Ford and Peter Crampton.

7 This went back a long way. David Owen, the foreign secretary between 1977 and 1979, had been a junior defence minister between 1968 and 1970, and the other three were veterans of Hugh Gaitskell's battle against nuclear unilateralism in the early 1960s. Rodgers played a particularly crucial role as secretary of the Campaign for Democratic Socialism, the ginger group that successfully led the attempt to overturn the 1960 Labour conference's vote for unilateral nuclear disarmament: both Jenkins and Williams had been supporters. Other CDS supporters that found their way into the SDP included Austen Albu, John Diamond, Stephen Haseler, Bryan Magee and Dick Taverne. Many observers believe that the organization was covertly funded by money from the US government. For an account of the CDS and its Cold War context, see Robin Ramsay, *The Clandestine Caucus: Anti-Socialist Campaigns and Operations in the British Labour Movement Since the War*, a special 1996 edition of *Lobster* magazine.

8 William Rodgers told the Commons: 'It was the view of the previous government that theatre nuclear modernization was essential, and that is our view today.' (*Hansard*, 24 January 1980). According to Denis Healey, 'Owen, like me, had opposed the concept of a Eurostrategic balance, which was the justification for putting cruise missiles into Britain; he had opposed modernizing Polaris, and continued to oppose replacing Polaris with Trident as militarily unnecessary, accelerating the arms race, and too expensive.' Denis Healey, *The Time of My Life* (Michael Joseph, 1989) p. 480.

9 The pamphlet, *Keep Left*, co-written with Richard Crossman and Ian Mikardo, is discussed in chapter 3. On non-alignment as the basis for a Labour security policy, its opposition to Bevin was stark: 'By accepting the American lead in a world alliance against Russia, we shall merely ensure that every small country has to choose between the bleak alternatives of anti-communism and communism. We shall sharpen the conflict instead of healing it; and, the sharper the conflict, the less time both right and left will have for democracy and socialism . . . The task of British socialism must be, wherever possible, to save the smaller nations from this futile ideological warfare and to heal the breach between the USA and the USSR. But we cannot do this if we ourselves have taken sides either in a Communist bloc or in an anti-Bolshevik axis.' As an alternative to a US-dominated anti-Soviet bloc, the pamphlet proposed a European security pact 'voluntarily renouncing the most deadly offensive weapon of modern warfare'. Richard Crossman, Michael Foot and Ian Mikardo, *Keep Left* (New Statesman, 1947). The party's official response, the pamphlet *Cards on the Table* (Labour Party, 1947), was written by its young international officer, Denis Healey.

   It would be wrong, however, to claim that there was a simple continuity in

Foot's position over thirty-five years. Along with most of the rest of the Labour left, he dropped the idea of a 'third way' foreign policy in 1948, after the Communist seizure of power in Czechoslovakia and Moscow's rejection of Marshall Aid, and backed an alliance with the US. When NATO was formed in 1949, only a handful of Labour MPs, most of them Communist fellow travellers, were opposed. It was only the Korean war and NATO's early-1950s programme for German rearmament that reawakened Labour left dissent on defence and foreign policy. See Mark Jenkins, *Bevanism: Labour's High Tide* (Spokesman, 1979), Paul Anderson and Kevin Davey, 'Moscow gold? The true story of the Kremlin, British communism and the left', *New Statesman & Society*, 7 April 1995.

10 It would be a mistake to claim that Foot was elected *because* of his support for CND, however. That was undoubtedly part of his appeal to the PLP left, but his narrow victory (ten votes in the second round) relied on the support he got from some sections of the PLP right. Most right-wingers who backed him did so because they shared his antipathy to the European Community, although a few – perhaps enough to have tipped the balance – were future defectors to the SDP who decided to back Foot because it would make the creation of a new party that much easier. See Ivor Crewe and Anthony King, *SDP: The Birth, Life and Death of the Social Democratic Party* (Oxford, 1995), part 1.

11 George Robertson, a Labour right-winger even when a student at Dundee University between 1964 and 1968, first made a reputation for himself as a pro-devolutionist on the executive of the Labour Party in Scotland in the 1970s (he was its chair in 1977–8). First elected to parliament at the age of thirty-one in the May 1978 Hamilton by-election, after the 1979 general election defeat he joined the front bench as a junior Scottish spokesman and became secretary of the right-wing Manifesto Group of Labour MPs. He was made a junior defence spokesman in 1980 – in which position he joined the pro-American British Atlantic Committee, partly financed by the Foreign Office – and a junior foreign affairs spokesman the following year. Throughout the early 1980s, he was a consistent and outspoken opponent of Labour's non-nuclear defence policy, although unlike some of his colleagues he kept his reservations to himself in the 1983 election campaign. He was put in charge of Europe policy in 1985 and became shadow Scottish secretary in 1993, but retained a keen interest in defence and security policy even when he had no responsibility for it.

12 The list of key Labour Atlanticists who joined the SDP is impressive. It included: John Cartwright (MP for Woolwich 1974–92, chair of the PLP defence committee 1979–81 and a member of the Commons defence select committee); Lord Kennett (who as Wayland Young had been one of Labour's main advisers on defence and foreign affairs in the 1960s); Evan Luard (MP for Oxford 1966–70 and 1974–9 and a junior foreign office minister 1969–70 and 1976–9); John Roper (Labour MP for Farnworth 1970–83, long active in various Atlanticist organizations and a junior defence spokesman 1979–81); James Wellbeloved (MP for Erith and Crayford 1965–83 and a junior defence minister 1976–9); and Alan Lee Williams (Labour MP for Hornchurch 1966–70 and 1974–9, director of the British Atlantic Committee 1972–4 and chair of the PLP defence committee 1976–9). Unfortunately, this aspect of the SDP is barely mentioned by Crewe and King.

13 See Mervyn Jones, *Michael Foot* (Gollancz, 1994) chapter 13.

14 *Hansard*, 3 April 1982.

15 Labour Party, *New Hope for Britain* (1983).

16 Chris Mullin, interview with Roy Hattersley, *Tribune*, 19 July 1983.

17 Reagan first brought up the idea of Star Wars, the Strategic Defence Initiative, in

March 1983. At first, few European NATO politicians realized he was serious. When they did, most decided that they didn't like it: a ballistic missile defence shield for the US, they believed, would encourage it to withdraw from its commitment to defend Western Europe, and European participation in the project would mean that the US military would get the sole benefit of a vast amount of European high technology. They also worried about the effects on East–West *détente* of what amounted to a unilateral US abrogation of the 1972 Anti-Ballistic Missile treaty. The main exception was Margaret Thatcher, who in December 1984 endorsed SDI, then set the government on to negotiating terms for British participation. See *European Nuclear Disarmament Journal*, summer 1986.

18   See Paul Anderson and Mary Kaldor (eds), *Mad Dogs: The US Raids on Libya* (Pluto, 1986); Geoffrey Smith, *Reagan and Thatcher* (Bodley Head, 1990), chapter 16.

19   'Defence strategy', SCA paper, October 1986, quoted in Dan Keohane, *Labour Party Defence Policy*, p. 70. There were plenty of objections to this line of thinking. Mary Kaldor, a member of the policy committee working on a new foreign policy framework, argued that emphasizing conventional strength was entirely counterproductive because it simply reinforced the popular idea that there really was a Soviet threat. Instead, Labour should be arguing for 'political changes that indicated Soviet willingness to reduce its role in Eastern Europe' (such as removal of all nuclear weapons from East Germany, Czechoslovakia and Poland or legalization of Solidarnosc) as the counterpart to British nuclear disarmament. See 'Labour and the East', *European Nuclear Disarmament Journal*, October–November 1986.

20   Virtually its only defender after the event was Mike Gapes, Labour's international officer, now the MP for Ilford South. See his 'The evolution of Labour's defence and security policy', in Gordon Burt (ed.), *Alternative Defence Policy* (Croom Helm, 1988).

21   See, for example, John Lloyd, 'How to win in 1991', *New Statesman*, 19 June 1987; Peter Kellner, 'Labour's future: decline or democratic revolution', *New Statesman*, 19 June 1987; Ian Aitken, 'The double fudge on disarmament', *Guardian*, 22 June 1987; Hugh MacPherson, *Tribune*, 26 June 1987.

22   *Guardian*, 2 October 1987.

23   *Guardian*, 28 November 1987.

24   *Independent*, 10 May 1988.

25   *Tribune*, 13 May 1988.

26   *Independent*, 20 May 1988.

27   *Tribune*, 22 July 1988.

28   Nick Butler, Len Scott, David Ward and Jonathon Worthington, *Working for Common Security* (Fabian Society, 1989). The authors were, respectively, the treasurer of the Fabian Society, a former adviser to Denis Healey, an adviser to John Smith and a former adviser to Labour's front-bench defence team.

29   Colin Hughes and Patrick Wintour, *Labour Rebuilt: The New Model Party* (Fourth Estate, 1990), pp. 114–20.

30   *Tribune*, 12 May 1989.

31   Martin O'Neill told *Tribune* in December 1989 that 'if, in the early 1990s, with a Labour government in power, the United States were to seek to locate a new generation of air-launched systems in Europe, we'd oppose it in NATO on the grounds that such deployments were compensation for ground-launched cruise' but continued: 'If the Americans won the argument in NATO, we'd accept the new systems if we weren't the only country to accept them.' (*Tribune*, 22 December 1989).

32 See Mike Gapes, *After the Cold War: Building on the Alliances* (Fabian Society, 1990). Here, Labour's international officer warned against development of a West European security structure based on the European Community.

33 For a critical account of the Committee to Stop War in the Gulf, see Henry Worthington, 'Ruthless cuckoos in the dovecote' in the now-defunct libertarian socialist journal *Solidarity*, autumn 1991. A more sympathetic picture of the anti-war movement's efforts is in Richard Heffernan and Mike Marqusee, *Defeat From the Jaws of Victory* (Verso, 1992).

34 The shadow cabinet members of the 'Supper Club' were Margaret Beckett, Ann Clwyd, Michael Meacher, John Prescott and Jo Richardson. Other members included Dick Caborn, Jim Cousins, Mark Fisher, Paul Flynn, Joan Lestor, Joan Ruddock, Chris Smith, Keith Vaz and Mike Watson. The club did not include the two biggest figures on the soft left, Robin Cook and Bryan Gould.

35 See Branka Magas, *The Destruction of Yugoslavia* (Verso, 1993); Noel Malcolm, *Bosnia: A Short History* (Macmillan, 1996); Mark Thompson, *A Paper House* (Hutchinson, 1992); David Rieff, *Slaughterhouse: Bosnia and the Failure of the West* (Vintage, 1995); Laura Silber and Alan Little, *The Death of Yugoslavia* (Penguin, 1995).

36 Off the record to *Tribune* journalist Ben Webb, David Clark even gave credence to the story – put about by the Serbs and swallowed by General Lewis MacKenzie, the Canadian commander of the UN forces in Sarajevo – that the notorious May 1992 Sarajevo 'bread-queue massacre', when twenty-two people died after a Serb mortar bomb attack, had been the responsibility of the Bosnian government (the idea being that it was trying to attract sympathy to itself and force NATO to intervene). In late June 1997, it was revealed by the *Sunday Times* that hotel bills incurred by Clark and junior front-bench defence spokesman John Reid during a trip to Switzerland in 1993 to meet the Bosnian Serb leader Radovan Karadzic had been paid by a lobbyist close to Karadzic – and that Clark and Reid had not declared the payment. See *Sunday Times*, 29 June 1997. The revelation followed the suspension of the back-bench MP Bob Wareing for failing to declare a consultancy contract with a company run by a Serbian-born businessman.

37 In April 1993, at the height of the public outcry over Serbian atrocities in Bosnia, seventeen MPs signed a statement circulated by MacDonald and Wicks arguing for military intervention, including if necessary the use of ground troops, to protect Bosnian civilians from attack. They made strange bedfellows: among them were figures from the hard left (Chris Mullin, Max Madden, John Austin-Walker), the soft left (Peter Hain, Angela Eagle, Mike Watson, Michael Connarty), the centre (Hugh Bayley, Nick Raynsford) and the right (Peter Mandelson, Frank Field). See *Tribune*, 23 April 1993. At various other times, another fifty or so Labour MPs backed tougher action on Bosnia than the party leadership was prepared to consider.

38 *Tribune*, 19 July 1991.

39 Neil Kinnock, interview on TV-am *Frost* programme, 8 September 1991.

40 Labour Party, *A Fresh Start for Britain: Labour's Strategy for Britain in the Modern World* (1996).

41 *Independent*, 15 December 1996.

42 See Donald MacKenzie, 'Wasting assets', *London Review of Books*, 23 January 1997.

43 John Pilger, 'Death for sale', *Guardian*, 12 November 1994.

44 Tony Blair, 'Labour's order of battle', *Daily Telegraph*, 3 February 1997.

45 Tony Blair, speech at *Time* magazine dinner, 30 November 1995, reprinted as 'New Nation State' in Tony Blair, *New Britain: My Vision of a Young Country* (Fourth Estate, 1996).

46 Tony Blair, speech to British–American Chamber of Commerce, New York, 11 April 1996.

47 John Gilbert, the MP for Dudley from 1970 to 1974 and Dudley East from February 1974 until his retirement from the Commons in 1997. Born in 1927, he was educated at Oxford and in the United States and lived in North America for most of the 1950s and early 1960s. A vehement opponent of British membership of the Common Market in the early 1970s, he was a strong supporter of Peter Shore's doomed bid for the Labour leadership in 1983. As well as opposing Labour's non-nuclear defence policy throughout the 1980s, he was alone on the Labour benches in backing British participation in US president Ronald Reagan's Star Wars project. He used his position on the Commons defence select committee to pursue his own agenda, although he distinguished himself (and probably saved himself from deselection) with his probing of ministers over the Westland affair in 1986. He was, and remains, a hate figure on the Labour left.

48 John Spellar, the MP for Warley West since 1992, was briefly MP for Birmingham Northfield in 1982–3, but he came to prominence in Labour politics because of his role in the Electrical, Electronic, Telecommunication and Plumbing Trades Union. After acting as personal assistant to the notoriously right-wing EETPU general secretary Frank Chapple (who was made a life peer by Margaret Thatcher in 1985), he became the union's head of research and a speech-writer to Chapple's equally right-wing successor, Eric Hammond. The EETPU was an opponent of Labour's non-nuclear defence policy throughout the 1980s, and Spellar distanced himself from it explicitly before losing his seat in 1983. He was a junior front-bench defence spokesman before the 1997 election. The other minister at the MoD, John Reid, used to be a member of the Communist Party, but has long since been an loyal nuclear Atlanticist.

49 *Financial Times*, 7 February 1997.

50 *Financial Times*, 7 February 1997. It is interesting to note that the chairman of British Aerospace, Bob Bauman, and the managing director of GEC, George Simpson, were on the Institute for Public Policy Research Commission on Public Policy and British Business whose Labour-sympathetic report was published in January 1997. See chapter 1.

51 *Guardian*, 13 May 1997.

11   SPEAKING WITH ONE VOICE:
PETER MANDELSON AND PARTY DISCIPLINE

1 *Sky News*, 5 May 1997.

2 Peter Mandelson and Roger Liddle, *The Blair Revolution: Can New Labour Deliver?* (Faber, 1996).

3 Seumas Milne, 'The leader's little helper', *Guardian*, 11 February 1995.

4 Conversation with the authors. See also Nyta Mann, 'Top Spinner: notes towards an unauthorised biography of Peter Mandelson', *New Statesman & Society*, 8 March 1996.

5 Kathy Myers, interview with Peter Mandelson, *Guardian*, 25 November 1985.

6 Peter Mandelson, 'Out of the darkness', *Guardian*, 28 September 1996.

7 Conversation with the authors.

8 Conversation with the authors.

9 Nyta Mann, 'Top spinner', *New Statesman & Society*, 8 March 1996.

10 *Guardian*, 2 October 1989.

11 Conversation with the authors.

12 *Guardian*, 16 February 1990.

13 Colin Byrne, Mandelson's deputy when the former was communications director, then as now one of his most loyal supporters, quoted in Nyta Mann, op cit.

14 Mandelson's post-1992 defeat criticisms of the campaign focused on mistakes during the three-week campaign itself, for which he had the useful alibi of having been occupied in Hartlepool.

15 Labour lost, scoring its lowest percentage of the poll in any by-election since 1945.

16 Mandelson's true opinion of John Smith's leadership is glimpsed in an article he wrote for *Fabian Review* just after the 1997 election: 'We're doing so well because we got our act together as a would-be government three years ago. We are enjoying the harvest of the hard work undertaken in opposition. There was a clarity of leadership and objectives, knowing what needed to be done to create a genuine New Labour Party, not simply a re-glossed, spray-on, re-shaped Labour Party.' 'Three years ago' was of course when Tony Blair became Labour leader: everything that happened before belongs in the Mandelson view of history to Labour's 'unelectable' era.

17 This dispute between Mandelson and Brown is set out in previously unpublished private memorandums submitted to the Labour leader. In a memo to Tony Blair dated 31 January 1995, Mandelson sets out the case for formally being appointed head of election planning in order to legitimize his advisory role to the leader. This was necessary not only to protect Mandelson to some extent from complaints at his unauthorised status from other Labour politicians, but also because Gordon Brown – whose relationship with Mandelson had been bitter ever since the leadership election – was formally chair of the shadow cabinet campaigns committee, which met each day to plan campaigning strategy. This was a role Brown jealously guarded. In order to ensure a role for himself, Mandelson wrote to Blair: 'I suggest that a separate election-planning group is given responsibility for preparing technical papers on the election itself for consideration by the leader's committee. This group would comprise around half a dozen individuals with expertise from your office and Walworth Road and outsiders whom it would otherwise be difficult to use. If I were to chair this group it would help to legitimize my role and membership of the strategy committee and presentation to the leader's committee.' Brown deeply disagreed with the idea that a separate strategy committee chaired by Mandelson was needed. In a memo (dated 1 February 1995) to Blair, in response to Mandelson's suggestion, he wrote: 'I remain strongly of the view that the committee must be an NEC-based committee rather than a committee emanating from the leader's committee. With the NEC campaigns and elections committee still in place, a parallel committee evolving from the leader's committee would institutionalize parallel structures, blurring lines of authority and hampering the decision-making process . . . I envisage a two-tier committee structure. The NEC election strategy committee would meet once a month and would formulate and oversee the implementation of the campaign strategy and long-term planning for the election campaign. It would be chaired by me and would be composed of a number of members of the NEC and relevant staff. The second tier of the proposed structure would be an executive committee, reporting to the NEC election strategy committee . . . It would be composed of politicians and relevant advisers – head of polling, head of opposition facts, heads of advertising, head of campaigns organization and the general secretary when he wishes to attend.' Behind this complicated exchange of counter-proposals over committees was Brown's desire to keep Mandelson's influence to a minimum: Brown could not stop Blair taking Mandelson's advice informally, but he hoped to restrict his official power. In the end, however, it was Mandelson's view that won the day.

18 This original synopsis was leaked to the press. See the *Guardian*, 18 July 1995, and for a more detailed leak, the *Observer*, 24 December 1995. See also the chapter on Mandelson in Andy McSmith, *Faces of Labour* (Verso, 1996).

19 Mandelson and Liddle, *The Blair Revolution*, chapter ten.

20 See the survey (*Blair's Bastards*) by two academics at the University of Hull, Philip Cowley and Philip Norton, reported in the *Independent on Sunday*, 29 September 1996. The twelve who rebelled more than forty times were: Dennis Skinner (95 rebellions), Harry Barnes (75), Jeremy Corbyn (64), Alice Mahon (52), the late Bob Cryer (51), Eddie Loyden (49), Terry Lewis (48), Max Madden (46), Ken Livingstone (44), Dennis Canavan (42), Alan Simpson (41) and Audrey Wise (40).

21 The Tribune Group in the late 1970s constituted just over a quarter of the PLP. More than half its members voted against the government forty or more times between 1974 and 1979; of the twenty-seven Labour MPs that rebelled 70 or more times, all were Tribunites. See Patrick Seyd, *The Rise and Fall of the Labour Left* (Macmillan, 1987).

22 Peter Hain, *Ayes to the Left: A Future for Socialism* (Lawrence and Wishart, 1995).

23 Militant, which dominated Liverpool Labour politics in the 1980s and had three supporters as MPs in the mid-1980s, finally lost its foothold in the party after standing its own candidate against Labour in the 1991 Liverpool Walton by-election: both its MPs at that point, Dave Nellist and Terry Fields, were banned from the 1991 Labour conference and replaced as Labour candidates before the 1992 election. It now exists as the Socialist Party in England and Wales and Scottish Militant Labour in Scotland, with its support concentrated in Liverpool and in Glasgow, where as Militant it played a leading role in organizing the anti-poll tax campaign of the late 1980s. Tommy Sheridan, its charismatic young Scottish leader, won 11 per cent of the vote in the 1997 election standing for the Scottish Socialist Alliance in Glasgow Pollok. On Militant, see Michael Crick, *The March of Militant* (Faber, 1986). The other Trotskyist entryist group that acquired a reputation as a serious threat inside Labour, Socialist Organiser, in fact a tiny sect composed mainly of students, was purged almost as ruthlessly as Militant before the 1992 election. In 1995, mere co-operation between Socialist Organiser and *Labour Briefing*, the monthly hard-left magazine, was enough for Labour's National Executive Committee to refuse to endorse Liz Davies, a member of the *Briefing* editorial board, as candidate in Leeds North East – even though she had been against working with Socialist Organiser.

24 The Labour Co-ordinating Committee was set up in 1978 on the initiative of Michael Meacher and Frances Morrell (then an adviser to Tony Benn and in the 1980s the leader of the Inner London Education Authority) as a left-wing research and propaganda group. Among its first members were the MPs Bob Cryer, Bryan Gould, Stuart Holland, Jeff Rooker, Brian Sedgemore and Audrey Wise, the journalists Chris Mullin (later editor of *Tribune* and now an MP) and Stuart Weir (later editor of *New Socialist* and then the *New Statesman*) and several trade unionists, among them Tony Banks. The LCC played a major role in arguing for the Alternative Economic Strategy (see chapter 2) and then became a key part of the coalition pushing for reforms to the Labour constitution in 1979–81, backing Tony Benn's bid for the deputy leadership in 1981. But the group broke with the Bennite left in support of Michael Foot's plans to expel Militant in 1982 – in part because of an influx of anti-Trotskyist student activists – and in 1985 was one of the main movers in the 'realignment of the left', as *Tribune* editor Nigel Williamson dubbed it, whereby a large section of the Bennite left came out explicitly in support of Neil Kinnock as Labour leader. Within a couple of years, the left (most

prominently Peter Hain and Ken Livingstone) had been marginalized in the group; in 1988, the LCC opposed the attempt by Benn and Eric Heffer to oust Kinnock and Roy Hattersley as leader and deputy leader, although it was split over John Prescott's challenge to Hattersley.

The LCC in the mid-1980s was important in mobilizing support not only for Kinnock but also for the emergent soft left around him. Tony Blair (who joined the LCC in 1982), Gordon Brown and Robin Cook were all LCC favourites. Innumerable LCC activists of the 1980s have played important roles in Labour politics in recent years, usually as unseen members of the apparatus: the best known now are Charles Clarke and Patricia Hewitt. For an acerbic hard left account, see Richard Heffernan and Mike Marqusee, *Defeat From the Jaws of Victory: Inside Kinnock's Labour Party* (Verso, 1992), chapter six.

During the 1990s, the LCC's activists concentrated their efforts on fighting the hard left in the constituencies and lobbying for one member, one vote for Labour Party elections; the group's intellectuals concentrated on producing a quarterly journal, *Renewal*, launched in 1993 under the editorship of Paul Thompson. With an editorial board including Blair, Cook, Hewitt, David Miliband, Margaret Hodge, Jack Dromey, Clare Short and Tony Wright as well as a sprinkling of left academics (among them Paul Hirst, Geoff Hodgson, David Marquand, Anne Phillips, Mike Rustin, Martin Shaw), *Renewal* is the nearest thing there is to an intellectual house organ of Blairism apart from the *New Statesman*. In 1996 it set up an 'ideas network', Nexus, based on e-mail and the Internet.

25 The Campaign for Labour Party Democracy, set up in 1973, was the main activist group that organised for the changes to the Labour constitution introduced in 1979–81, mandatory selection of parliamentary candidates and the electoral college for leadership elections (see chapter 9). It reached the height of its strength in 1982, with more than 1,200 members and more than 150 constituency parties affiliated, but subsequently declined, enjoying a revival of sorts during the battle on one member, one vote and most recently during the controversy over the leadership's plans to change the role of the National Executive Committee and the annual conference. On the CLPD in its pomp, see David and Maurice Kogan, *The Battle for the Labour Party* (Fontana, 1983) and Seyd, *The Rise and Fall of the Labour Left*.

In 1986, the CLPD and the Campaign Group came together with various other hard left organizations (among them the Labour Women's Action Committee, Labour CND, Labour Party Black Sections and the small Trotskyist group Socialist Action) to form Labour Left Liaison, which remains one of two main networks on the Labour hard left. The other one is the Campaign Group Supporters Network (CGSN), which has its origins in disputes between LLL and the MPs in the Campaign Group in the early 1990s. To cut a long story short, the CGSN now involves many of the activists from what used to be a major rival to LLL, Labour Party Socialists (the Labour Party part of the Socialist Movement set up in the wake of the Socialist Conference held in Tony Benn's constituency of Chesterfield in 1987), and many of the supporters of *Briefing* magazine.

The constantly shifting divisions and alliances on the activist hard left are incomprehensible even to most active Labour Party members. But these days most of the arguments boil down to disputes over whom the Labour hard left should be friendly towards outside the party (currently, the choice appears to be among Arthur Scargill, the anti-roads protest movement, the *Morning Star* and what used to be Militant) and whether it should be thinking about setting up a new left party (with the antis tending to oppose proportional representation and the pros backing it).

26 Stuart Hall and Martin Jacques, 'Blair: is he the greatest Tory since Thatcher?', *Observer*, 13 April 1997.

27 See, for example, Robin Blackburn, 'Reflections on Blair's velvet revolution', *New Left Review* issue 223, May–June 1997.

28 David Marquand, 'Blair's split personality', *Guardian*, 16 July 1997; Anthony Giddens, 'Centre left at centre stage', *New Statesman*, May 1997 special edition.

29 Giles Radice (ed.), *What Needs to Change* (HarperCollins, 1996); Richard Layard, *What Labour Can Do* (Walker, 1997); Tony Wright, *Why Vote Labour?* (Penguin, 1997).

30 See the satirical magazine *Casablanca*, summer 1996, for an account of the *New Statesman* saga.

INDEX